The Philippines
in
Bible Prophecy

Know the TRUTH, Know Your ROOT, Know Your DESTINY

Volume 1

OBED HAVILAH

The Philippines in Bible Prophecy

ISBN Paperback Vol. 1: 979-8-9884659-2-8
ISBN Hardback Vol. 1: 979-8-9884659-0-4
ISBN eBook Vol. 1: 979-8-984659-1-1

Published by Ophireum Foundation

The moral rights of the author have been asserted.

Disclaimer: The author and publisher have made every effort to ensure the accuracy of the information herein; however, the author and publisher do not assume any responsibility for errors, inaccuracies, or omissions. The author and publisher shall have neither liability nor responsibility to any person or entity with respect to any loss or damage caused or alleged to be caused directly or indirectly by the information contained in this book.

Scriptures in this publication are quoted from New King James Version, unless otherwise noted.

DEDICATION

This work is dedicated for the glory of our Almighty Father and His Son Yeshua (Jesus Christ) - our Creator, King, and Savior, for the salvation of mankind and the beginning of the works commissioned to the peoples of the isles.

"Grace to you and peace from God our Father and the Lord Jesus Christ."

TABLE OF CONTENTS

CONTENTS

FOREWORD

Warning: This book is highly offensive to those who do not want to seek the truth. But this is the guiding light to those who want to begin their journey in seeking the truth.

What will hinder us from knowing the truth?

The number one culprit in knowing the truth is our pride and arrogance. We think that all that we have been told are true and correct. So, we mock those who are correcting history and conspiracy theorist as if those who wrote the history are infallible authority that can never get wrong or be influenced by those who are shaping the history according to their agenda. We forgot to consider that all things we have been told can be just an illusion. We just accept what have been told and never question it. And once there is someone questioning the illusion, we immediately shut down our brain so that it will not disturb our belief system. Even if we really do not know the truth about our belief. We immediately go into a defensive mode or otherwise known as cognitive dissonance.

What is a cognitive dissonance?

According to the online Britannica, "cognitive dissonance, the mental conflict that occurs when beliefs or assumptions are contradicted by new information. The unease or tension that the conflict arouses in people is relieved by one of several defensive maneuvers: they reject, explain away, or avoid the new information; persuade themselves that no conflict really exists; reconcile the differences; or resort to any other defensive means of preserving stability or order in their conceptions of the world and of themselves."

So, we easily defend ourselves, pretending that we know everything and that nobody can tell us otherwise. We immediately reject the facts or evidence being presented. Our brain shutdown the senses that we rather become dumb, blind, deaf and ignorant rather than looking the alternate reality. This is the very reason why we cannot see and hear the truth, because we do not know and believe in the true living God of the Bible who said in Revelation 12: 9;

"⁹So the great dragon was cast out, that serpent of old, called the <u>Devil and Satan, who deceives the whole world</u>; he was cast to the earth, and his angels were cast out with him."

Satan is real and he deceives and divide (divide et impera) the whole world that is why God said through Paul in Romans 3: 10 (NLT);

"¹⁰As the Scriptures say, "No one is righteous—not even one.""

If we believe in the God of the Bible, then why we believe what we believe in this world? The lies, division, and deceptions are so much obvious today than in any other time. But we refuse to recognize the evilness of this world. Even if it is so obvious as the many religions and governments of this world, we still dwell in the illusions of believing that it is good.

It is very clear in the above verse that Satan deceives the whole world. Not just a few, but the whole world. All of us. Why not consider what God have said that we are all deceived and find out what is the truth according to His words?

By the way, when religions are mentioned in this book, it pertains to the prison houses of Satan as mentioned in the Bible. Although this truth is very hard to swallow because I thought being a born-again Christian is the ultimate truth. It is hard to accept the fact that Satan can deceive me (denial/cognitive dissonance), yet that is exactly what happened. And that is the truth.

If we honestly dig deeper, <u>professing Christians</u> are no other than pagan religions because our <u>doctrines and traditions are all pagan beliefs</u> and unbiblical like many other religions. We are called professing Christians because we proclaim that we believe in the God of the Bible and yet we do not obey what the God of the Bible have commanded us to do. Instead, we follow the commandments and traditions of man (paganism) rather than the God we profess to believe. Just as Jesus Christ said in Matthew 15: 3, 8-9;

"³He answered and said to them, "Why do you also transgress

the commandment of God because of your tradition?

[8]"These people draw near to Me with their mouth, and honor Me with their lips, but their heart is far from Me.

[9]And in vain they worship Me, teaching as doctrines the commandments of men.' """

Fully well, we profess to believe in Christ, but we deny believing and obeying His laws. We rather believe in man who said that His commandments have been done away rather than the God who said in John 14: 15, saying;

"[15]"If you love Me, keep My commandments.""

Why does this book specifically address prophesying Christians? Is it just an attempt to criticize and discredit our religion?

The reason for mentioning prophesying Christians in this book is twofold. Firstly, it is to expose us to the light and truth so that we may be stirred emotionally and spiritually by the word of God. This process of being offended and be brokenhearted can lead us to be awakened from our spiritual slumber and embrace the illuminating power of the Lord, thus experiencing His transformative healing.

Secondly, it is crucial to note that this exposure is not meant to attack or discredit anyone's religion. On the contrary, it is an expression of God's love, intending to reveal His truth and provide divine correction. This guidance is motivated by love, aiming to help believers transition from darkness to light. Prophesying Christians are particularly addressed because they are seen as being closer to God, sincerely believing in Him. Nonetheless, despite our genuine belief and sincerity, we are sincerely deceived prompting the need for guidance and correction.

I do not blame my ministers or pastors because we are all deceived. We sincerely seek and believed in God, but we are sincerely deceived. But now, the light of the truth has come, and we need to decide whether to move out of the darkness of the prison houses of Satan's deceptions or not.

Our land is ravaged with many of these prison houses of Satan. In fact, God identified the peoples of the isles in Isaiah 42 that are in prison houses in verse 22, saying;

"²²But this is a people robbed and plundered;
All of them are snared in holes,
And they are <u>hidden in prison houses</u>;
They are for prey, and no one delivers;
For plunder, and no one says, "Restore!""

But the light will come and has come in verse 7;
"⁷To open blind eyes, <u>to bring out prisoners from the prison</u>,
Those who sit in darkness from the prison house."

God intends to free us from our prison houses by giving us the light so that we may see beyond the illusion of our religions and to open the door of the prison houses. God will make the way, but we need to do the work to move out of prison towards the light. God will not drag us out of prison. We need to walk towards Him willingly and with joy like a kid shouting "freedom!" as one come running out of the house to the playground.

We cannot see the prison house if we are in it. Just like we cannot see the whole coin if it is too close to our eyes. Just give the light a chance in our lives. And if the light is not good for you then the door of the prison houses is always open. You have a choice to make. But know this well that religions have ravage and divided us as a people.

Are you offended and ready to fight back for your religion? Consider that <u>the truth</u> of the word of God is highly offensive just as Jeremiah 6: 10 said;

"¹⁰To whom shall I speak and give warning, that they may hear?
Indeed their ear is uncircumcised, and they cannot give heed.
Behold, the word of the Lord is a reproach (offense) to them;
They have no delight in it."

The light and the truth are highly offensive to those who are sons of disobedience and do not want to be corrected that it become to them as 1 Peter 2: 8 said;

"⁸"A stone of <u>stumbling and a rock of offense</u>.""

But God said in Romans 9: 33;

"³³"Behold, I lay in Zion a <u>stumbling stone and rock of offense</u>, and whoever believes on Him will not be put to shame.""""

Jesus Christ is the Rock of offense to those who do evil and love to dwell in darkness. But His word is for correction to those who wants the truth as mentioned in 2 Timothy 3: 16;

> ""¹⁶All Scripture is given by inspiration of God, and is profitable <u>for doctrine</u>, <u>for reproof</u>, <u>for correction</u>, <u>for instruction</u> in righteousness, ..."

We all need correction because Satan is the god and ruler of this world. We all have been deceived and divided. That is why "no one is righteous, not even one".

But the good news is God will call the people of the isles (v4) into righteousness as He said in Isaiah 42: 6;

> """⁶"I, the Lord, have called You in righteousness, ...""""

And while Satan is dividing humanity with his many prison houses away from the Father, Yeshua (Jesus Christ) is trying to unite those who believe in Him to the Father just as he said in John 17: 20-23;

> ""²⁰"I do not pray for these (His disciples) alone, but also for <u>those who will believe in Me</u> through their (disciples) word; ²¹that <u>they all may be one</u>, as You, Father, are in Me, and I in You; that <u>they also may be one in Us</u>, that <u>the world may believe that You sent Me</u>. ²²And the glory which You gave Me I have given them, that <u>they may be one just as We are one</u>: ²³I in them, and You in Me; that they <u>may be made perfect in one</u>, and that <u>the world may know that You have sent Me</u>, and have loved them as You have loved Me."

And Jesus Christ declared the Father as the only true God in John 17: 1-3, saying;

> "¹..."Father, the hour has come. Glorify Your Son, that Your Son also may glorify You, ²as You have <u>given Him authority over all flesh</u>, that He should <u>give eternal life</u> to as many as You have given Him. ³And <u>this is eternal life</u>, that <u>they may know You, the only true God</u>, and <u>Jesus Christ whom You have sent</u>."

***

When government is mentioned in this book, it pertains to those politicians (from president to barangay captains) and business establishments (the cabal) who rule and manipulate the people into their agenda. We were deceived into believing that the government is "we, the people". We were made to believe that we have power over them. But that is obviously far from the truth, they have the power over us. Remember pandemic?

One of the proofs of these lies is the illusion of election. We were made to believe that one become powerful to elect a leader according to their freedom to choose during election. We feel we have the power over them because we are the one going to elect or dictate who will lead us. We go to voting precincts as if we are gods who will anoint somebody under us to become our servant leader (another deceptions). We feel proud voting. But then we fail to realize that time after time, we become the servants of those we though we elected. They are not serving the people who purportedly elected them, they are serving their master (the cabal) who groomed them from the very beginning and anoint them to their positions at an appointed time.

Elections are just one of their businesses. It is a win-win situation for them. They make people like fools going to the voting precincts even under the rain or under the sun, while they run to the bank laughing with their election earnings. This too have divided us.

But why we are so easily deceived?

Because we do not know the real living God. And so, we are blind and living in darkness. In fact, Jesus said in John 3: 19, that people love darkness rather than light;

> "[19]And the judgment is based on this fact: God's light came into the world, but <u>people loved the darkness more than the light</u>, for their actions were evil."

So, when truth or light is presented, we tend to retreat into darkness of our cognitive dissonance. We become defensive and retreat into our comfort zone. We do not want to be disturb from the comfort of darkness, otherwise our evil ways will be exposed to the light of the truth.

How then should we counter this cognitive dissonance in our life? God's answer is very succinct, **humility**.

Consider the following words of God on how we will benefit if we humble ourselves before the Lord;

"²When pride comes, then comes shame;

But with the humble is wisdom." (Proverbs 11: 2)

"⁶But He gives more grace. Therefore He says:

"God resists the proud,

But gives grace to the humble."" (James 4: 6)

"⁹The humble He guides in justice,

And the humble He teaches His way." (Psalms 25: 9)

"²⁸You will save the humble people;

But Your eyes are on the haughty,

that You may bring them down." (2 Samuel 22: 28)

There are many benefits if we humble ourselves before the Lord than Satan's doctrine of pride and arrogance. In fact, Proverbs 16: 18, said;

"¹⁸Pride goes before destruction,

And a haughty spirit before a fall."

This verse cannot be further from the truth during this scamdemic. Many proud educated people pretend they know science and health far better than anybody else. They put their trust in their government and the health industry as their gods of science. So, whatever they say, they believe as truth without question. And when the proud people were told to roll up their sleeves, they did it without hesitation. And they are even proud to be part of it not knowing that they made them fools. They proudly believe that the injection is safe and effective, and "science-base" as they have been told. And they easily believe in it as if they really know the science behind the deadly injection. Or are they just proud to pretend? Or perhaps, they forgot or are blind to consider that science can be all about power than seeking the truth.

Many parents are also so proud and excited to line up their

children to be injected. Only to find out later how deadly if not damaging this injection to their children. If 40% excess mortality rate is already catastrophic to adults, how much more a 1000 + % to the children in Europe.

But we never heard these from governments and mainstream media who perpetrated the covid scam and flashing daily deaths and infections in their screen. As if nothing is happening although real deaths are occurring on a daily basis in both children and adults. The data of these vaccine injury and deaths are also coming from the government website that monitor adverse events in developed countries. The very authority responsible for implementing this monitoring system is also the entity that manipulates and alters the data according to their own agenda.

What about poor countries such as the Philippines? Nothing. No monitoring. But social media will tell us the difference how deaths are so frequent after the vaccination compared to before and during the scam.

But people will reason out it is all but natural death. It is not cause by the injection. Even though that is the only variable that might have triggered the sudden deaths (SADS) of their love one's. They could not admit to themselves they have been deceived (fooled). They are too proud to accept error. How much more to think that they have been fooled by the very government and the medical industry they loved and trust to protect them. People are dying like flies. And social media platforms are full of condolences.

And just what God have said, "pride comes, before destruction".

***

There are so many Bible translations around. Some translations went too far that it has change the original meaning and some translate the Bible according to their personal opinion and agenda. There is no perfect translation so far that have been known other the 1611 King James Version (KJV) which is believed to be the most accurate among the many versions. But the problem is, it is using old English language that is hard to understand by those who are none native speaker of that language like us – the peoples of the isles.

In this book, KJV is used to study sensitive or in-depth topics that requires accuracy as word for word meaning or translation from the original. The New King James Version (NKJV) is the most Bible quotations used here for ease of understanding, unless otherwise noted in parenthesis the version used.

Other translations used are New Living Translation (NLT), Good News Translation (GNT), and Berean Study Bible (BSB) versions. The reason for using these translations other than the KJV is for understanding or clarity of the message being conveyed by the word of God according to what a common or majority of the people can understand. Otherwise, we should be using 1611 King James Version or the Masoretic Text for accuracy.

The Bible is a mysterious coded word of God. It can be understood in a multi-dimensional way if we have the Spirit of God to understand His words. It is a compact presentation of His messages to humanity, presenting Himself and the works that the Son and the Father have done and will be doing.

The Bible can be understood on a personal dimension as God is talking to us personally and guiding us how we live our lives. Just like a user's manual that anybody can use to their benefits. It can also be understood in the spiritual dimension by which God have called you to perform important tasks according to His purpose and calling. The historical dimension revealing to us what He has done and what we are today. The prophetic dimension of what He is about to do to His creations in the future. And many other dimensions that are beyond our imagination because the word of God is a puzzle and a mystery deeply coded that it is hard to understand by those whom He did not intend to understand.

But the Bible interprets itself like a matrix as stated in Isaiah 28: 13;
"[13]But the word of the Lord was to them,
"Precept upon precept, precept upon precept,
Line upon line, line upon line,
Here a little, there a little,…""

That is why many Bible verses will be repeated in discussing different subjects or topics like connecting the dots. Even one word or one line in a verse connects the dots to multiple topics. Hence, the reason for underlining the words to give emphasis to its connection to the subject being discussed.

The Bible is full of mystery that this book is no way complete as to what God wants us to do or to be. This is just the tip of the iceberg as they say. Perhaps God will reveal to us wisdom, instructions, guidance, etc., etc. in a need-to-know basis. Many things will be revealed to us as we get closer to Him.

***

Who am I, you may ask that you may believe. What are my credentials or authority or great accomplishments so that you may believe in what I say?

I, a nobody. I have not accomplished anything great in my life. My education is irrelevant in the matters of Godly pursuit. And even if I have several layers of PhD's in my pocket, that will not be the key to understanding the word of God. In fact, as one goes into the higher educational system, one drifted farther away from God. Why? Because of pride and arrogance of what one has accomplished through the false educational system. They become the center rather than God.

So, who am I is not of importance for you to believe in what is written in this book. In fact, with all honesty and humility, what is written in this book is beyond my mental capacity to think, to connect the dots of the matrix, and to solve mysteries or puzzles. Nor should I say that God talked to me or revealed these things to me as if I am special to Him. No, I am just ordinary person like everybody else who is tasked to deliver His message to You (the peoples of the isles). I am just a scribe and a messenger. A lowly servant.

In that case, do not believe in me, but rather believe in God who sent this message to You (the isles) for the time have become so evil once again in the hearts of men. Even so, do not just believe, prove all things (1 Thess. 5: 21). Prove even God if He is real or not so that our faith may be full.

This book is composed of two volumes and four sections.

Volume One contain the Section One will tell us who and what is God and what are the proofs of His existence. It answers the question, "can we prove God? Section Two explain about the identities of God's enemy and our enemy. It will enlighten us how the enemy operates and influences us physically and spiritually. And Section Three gives us a glimpse of who we are as a people, the prophetic evidence, where we are mentioned in the Bible symbolically and geographically. How the enemy control the world and us as a people and the real identity and location of our enemy. Furthermore, this section discusses who is the Creator.

Volume Two contain Section Four about our missions and works as the servants of God. It discusses how we can know and grow in the knowledge of God to discover our calling and the works appointed unto us.

My fellow islanders: brothers and sisters, I urge you to pray hard directly to our Father in heaven in the name of His Son Jesus Christ (Yeshua) that He may grant us wisdom and understanding to His words and message presented in this book for our time. So that we may glorify Him in obedience and serve Him according to His purpose and calling us into righteousness.

If you hear His voice, do not harden your heart.

Please read and reread this book at least 3X. Try to decipher the underline words like decoding a puzzle or a riddle. Or let individual word float to make sense when connecting the dots.

Do not judge this book but judge yourself according to this truth.

Arise and let His light shine upon us!

INTRODUCTION

The world has descended into darkness full of lies, deceptions, and lawlessness. The wickedness of human civilization has once again reign in the hearts of men. There is no resolve insight. Only trouble ahead is clear. But we still have hope in the light. The light that will guide us through darkest hours. That light is our Lord Jesus Christ.

If we seek and allow Christ to reign in our lives and walk according to His ways and obey His laws and commandments, we shall become light also. Light that will shine through us, into the world in the darkness of the hour.

Where can we find the light? The light is in the word of God. The word of God is the Holy Bible. It is God's way to talk to humanity if one is eager and willing to listen. Jesus Christ (Yeshua in Hebrew) is the Word in John 1: 1;

"¹In the beginning was the Word, and the Word was with God, and the Word was God. ²He was in the beginning with God."

And the Light in John 8: 12;

"¹²Then Jesus spoke to them again, saying, "I am the light of the world. He who follows Me shall not walk in darkness, but have the light of life.""'

Why the Bible?

Why should we believe in the Bible?

Of the many gods of this world, only the God of the Bible have claimed that He created the Heaven, the heavens and the earth and all the things that are in it, including mankind as He said in Isaiah 45: 12;

"[12] "I have made the earth, and created man on it.

I—My hands—stretched out the heavens, and all their host I have commanded.""'

Then in Acts 4: 24, Paul, the apostle to the Gentiles testified to this truth saying;

"[24]So when they heard that, they raised their voice to God with one accord and said: "Lord, You are God, who made heaven and earth and the sea, and all that is in them,…""'

And again, Paul and Barnabas testified to this truth to the people of Lystra as they intended to worship (idolatry) them when they healed a crippled man in Acts 14: 14-16, saying;

"[14]But when the apostles Barnabas and Paul heard this, they tore their clothes and ran in among the multitude, crying out [15]and saying, "Men, why are you doing these things? We also are men with the same nature as you, and preach to you that you should turn from these useless things (idolatry) to the living God, who made the heaven, the earth, the sea, and all things that are in them, [16]who in bygone generations allowed all nations to walk in their own ways." (This means we are on our own, free moral agents cut off from God that is why we create our own gods.)

And in Revelation 14: 6-7, John testified this truth to the servants of Jesus Christ in his vision saying;

"[6]Then I saw another angel flying in the midst of heaven, having the everlasting gospel to preach to those who dwell on the earth— to every nation, tribe, tongue, and people— [7]saying with a loud voice, "Fear God and give glory to Him, for the hour of His judgment has come; and <u>worship Him who made heaven and earth, the sea and springs of water.</u>""

He proclaimed the end from the beginning in Isaiah 46: 9-10;
"⁹Remember the former things of old, for <u>I am God, and there is no other; I am God, and there is none like Me,</u>¹⁰declaring the end from the beginning, and from ancient times things that are not yet done, saying, 'My counsel shall stand, and I will do all My pleasure,'…""

Jesus Christ (Yeshua) is the Beginning and the End as He said in Revelation 1: 8;
"⁸"I am the Alpha and the Omega, the Beginning and the End," says the Lord, "who is and who was and who is to come, the Almighty.""

He claimed to be the only living God as Paul testified in Romans 14: 10-12 (GNT), saying;
"¹⁰…All of us will stand before God to be judged by Him. ¹¹ For the scripture says, "As surely as <u>I am the living God, says the Lord,</u> everyone will kneel before me, and everyone will confess that I am God."
¹²Every one of us, then, will have to give an account to God."

These proclamations are prophecies (history written in advance) that many have come to pass, are being fulfilled right before our very own eyes today and many more are going to be fulfilled at an accelerated rate in a heightened intensity.
And Psalms 96: 4-5, said;
"⁴For the Lord is great and greatly to be praised; He is to be feared above all gods.
⁵For <u>all the gods of the peoples are idols,</u> but the Lord made the heavens."

Except the God of the Bible, the rest of the gods of this world can be easily proven that are just human creation and imagination and can be traced back to pagan beliefs, traditions, and practices of the

Babylonish religion. Satan is the author and roots of all these idolatries because he envied God and wanted to be worshipped and be adorned also. The gods of the major religions and its offshoots in this world are already dead or does not exist. Take for example, Mary (Simiramis) and Jesus (Nimrod) as represented by mother and child deity of the Catholic Church, Allah and Muhammed of Islam, Buddha of Buddhism and Shintoism and the many gods of Hinduism, and the counterfeit Jesus of the professing Christian world who have done away the law and celebrates pagan practices and traditions. Jesus said Himself in Matthew 24: 10 that in the end time many will be offended.

This scripture is indeed very offensive to those who will not believe just as it is written in 1 Peter 2: 7-8;

"⁷Therefore, to you who believe, He is precious; but to those who are disobedient, "The stone which the builders rejected has become the chief cornerstone,"⁸and "A stone of stumbling and a rock of offense.""

But this offense is for our good so that we may wake up from our self-destructive beliefs and practices. The scripture is a warning for us to turn from our evil ways, but the word of God is a reproach to those who will not believe. Just as Jesus Christ said in Jeremiah 6: 10;

"¹⁰"To whom shall I speak and give warning, that they may hear? Indeed their ear is uncircumcised, and they cannot give heed.

Behold, the word of the Lord is a reproach to them; they have no delight in it.""

Indeed, the truth of the word of God is like a sword that pierces our heart to offend and reproach us from our evil ways just as He said in Matthew 10: 34;

"³⁴"Do not think that I came to bring peace on earth. I did not come to bring peace but a sword....""

The sword of truth that will set us free from the bondage of corruption and deceptions of Satan. The sword of truth that will cause many to be brokenhearted for we will see in the light that we have been deceived.

Jesus Christ added in Luke 12: 51 that He came to bring division between wheat and tares (Matt. 13: 24-30), good and evil, light and darkness, believers and unbelievers;

> "51"Do you suppose that I came to give peace on earth? I tell you, not at all, but rather division.""

Indeed, the word of God is like a sword that condemns those who will not believe in the light but rather love evil and darkness as what Jesus Christ said in John 3: 18-21, saying;

> "18"He who believes in Him is not condemned; but he who does not believe is condemned already, because he has not believed in the name of the only begotten Son of God. 19And this is the condemnation, that the light has come into the world, and men loved darkness rather than light, because their deeds were evil. 20For everyone practicing evil hates the light and does not come to the light, lest his deeds should be exposed. 21But he who does the truth comes to the light, that his deeds may be clearly seen, that they have been done in God.""

If we sincerely believe in God, we must go to the light so that we may see and expose our evil ways and repent from it. We must free ourselves from the prison houses (religions) that have corrupted us away from the true living God. Let the sword of truth of God pierce our heart, offend us, and be brokenhearted so that we will have hope in the healing power of the word of God.

The world is confused because of these many gods of the many religions in every corner of the world. But none of them have the truth. Only lies and deceptions. And guess who is the master and author of confusion, lies, disobedience, and deceptions? There is no other than Satan. Satan is real and very powerful. He is a powerful spirit being. Yet he cannot possess anyone without one's permission. That is why he lies, deceive, and confuse mankind to ensnare men into his traps.

Why?

Because God created mankind for special purpose. And that is to become members of God's family. Mankind is created for the purpose of becoming children of God like Jesus Christ. He is the Son of God and the only begotten Son. The angels are not created for this purpose. That is why Satan (Lucifer) and a third of the angels of heavens rebelled against God. Lucifer is one of the greatest angels of God. He was the Angel of Light until iniquity was found in him that God called him Satan the devil.

The other two greatest angels of God are Michael and Gabriel. They are in complete submission and obedience to God the Father like Jesus Christ.

Mankind on the other hand, are created a little lower than the angels (Psa. 8: 5). But God offered mankind the opportunity to be sons of God. To become member of His family as it is written in Ephesians 1: 4-5;

> "4 "…just as He chose us in Him before the foundation of the world, that we should be holy and without blame before Him in love, 5having predestined us to adoption as sons by Jesus Christ to Himself, according to the good pleasure of His will,…"

And what this sonship means to us?
We shall inherit the earth just as Matthew 5: 5 said,
"5Blessed are the meek, for they shall inherit the earth."

As co-heirs of Jesus Christ in Romans 8: 17;
"17…and if children, then heirs - heirs of God and joint heirs with Christ, if indeed we suffer with Him, that we may also be glorified together."

And co-rulers of this earth in Revelation 5: 10;
"10And have made us kings and priests to our God;
And we shall reign on the earth."

What a marvelous and wonderful opportunity that many do not know and most that do know neglected it or are deceived into another way.

Now, we have witnessed and are witnessing the darkness of our time in an increasing intensity. Lawlessness, injustice, and immorality abound in our society today. The result is more and more troubles and sufferings.

But amidst this darkness, God is calling a set of people to be lights unto the Gentiles of the world in the end times. But first He called and transformed Paul to be the light and to bring the light unto the Gentiles at the ends of the earth for the Jews have rejected the word of God as it is written in Acts : 13: 46-47, saying;

> "[46]Then Paul and Barnabas grew bold and said, "It was necessary that the word of God should be spoken to you (the Jews) first; but since you reject it, and judge yourselves unworthy of everlasting life, behold, we turn to the Gentiles. [47]For so the Lord has commanded us:
>
> 'I have set you as a light to the Gentiles, that you should be for salvation to the ends of the earth.' ""

Notice carefully how God pivot Paul and Barnabas from preaching to the Jews and into the Gentiles of the ends of the earth. It is very important to understand who and where is this code "ends of the earth" be. We will discuss, locate, and identify this biblically in detail in Chapter 3.

We should take note also that Paul and Barnabas did not literally went to the "ends of the earth" for it is a code and have prophetic implication in the end times. His teaching, preaching, and doctrines as given by Jesus Christ to be the light of the Gentiles to the "ends of the earth" in the end times.

But suffice to say for now that this code "ends of the earth" is a specific place directly connected to the isles/coastlands, the land of Ophir where there is gold, where the eagles gather who fly like a cloud and as gentle as a dove and the "east" where His glory will come from.

For the Lord have spoken to the people of the "isles" in the east through His servant Isaiah in chapter 60 verses 1-3, saying;

> "[1] "Arise, shine; for your light has come!
> And the glory of the Lord is risen upon you.
> [2]For behold, the darkness shall cover the earth, and deep darkness the people; but the Lord will arise over you, and His glory will be seen upon you.
> [3]The Gentiles shall come to your light, and kings to the brightness of your rising.""

Many ministers have written books and preaching saying that these verses pertain to the present-day nation of Israel with its true identity as the House of Judah – the Jewish people. But notice that the present-day Israel and all the tribes of Israel have already risen up in prosperity. They already have shone. But the very reason the world is descending into darkness is because they rejected their own God, their Maker – Yeshua (Jesus Christ) and have done many abominable things that are not pleasing to Him. They too like the rest of the world, and the ten lost tribes of Israel will experience or undergo the tribulation period and experienced the wrath of God. They will be scattered abroad and be put into slavery. This is called Jacob's trouble – the punishments for their abominable deeds against the Lord and the people of the earth as it is written in Jeremiah 30: 7-11, saying;

"⁷Alas! <u>For that day is great, so that none is like it</u>;
And it is the time of <u>Jacob's trouble</u>, but <u>he shall be saved out of it</u>.
⁸'For it shall come to pass in that day,' Says the Lord of hosts, 'That I will break his yoke from your neck, and will burst your bonds; Foreigners shall no more enslave them.
⁹But they shall serve the Lord their God, and David their king, whom I will raise up for them.
¹⁰'Therefore do not fear, O My servant Jacob,' says the Lord, 'nor be dismayed, O Israel; for behold, <u>I will save you from afar</u>, and your seed from the land of their captivity.
<u>Jacob shall return, have rest and be quiet</u>, and no one shall make him afraid.
¹¹For I am with you,' says the Lord, 'to save you; <u>though I make a full end of all nations where I have scattered you</u>, yet I will not make a complete end of you. But <u>I will correct you in justice</u>, and <u>will not let you go altogether unpunished</u>.'"

Jesus Christ – the Lord is talking here to the House of Jacob, the collective Israelite people. Jesus Christ is going to punished them and give them justice they deserve for their disobedience to Him. But Jesus said in verse 10 that He will save them from <u>afar</u>. Afar here is another code for the ends of the earth, the isles/coastlands, and the east (like afar east).

Jesus Christ is going to use a slave nation (domestic helpers) from afar to be His servants to accomplish this work of saving the

Israelite people and the world. That is why this people of the isles from afar east is told by God in Isaiah 60: 1 to "¹Arise, shine; For your light (Jesus Christ) has come! And the glory of the Lord is risen upon you."

And it is written in Ezekiel 43: 2, 4;

"²And behold, the glory of the God of Israel came from the way of the east. His voice was like the sound of many waters; and the earth shone with His glory.

⁴And the glory of the Lord came into the temple by way of the gate which faces toward the east."

And in Isaiah 24: 15;

"¹⁵Therefore glorify the Lord in the dawning light (east), the name of the Lord God of Israel in the coastlands (isles) of the sea."

The people whom God is talking to here have been identified as the people of the isles/coastlands in the east in verse 9 of Isaiah 60 and in the above verse. And the rest of the verses of Isaiah 60 show how God is going to comfort and save Israel (collective).

God is waking up the people of the "isles" from their deep slumber/sleep. He is bringing the light of truth to the "ends of the earth" so that we may see through the blindness of darkness of our time. And the glory of the Lord will arise over us so that His glory will be seen in us also and His light will shine upon us unto the earth in the darkness of the hour.

God is giving us the great opportunity to be his people. God's people. His servants into righteousness. Christ is righteous. God wants us to be Christ like - to be righteous that we may become his servants. Not that we are special or important people in the eyes of God least we become proud of it. But God is giving us the chance to be his servants. A lowly humble servant in righteousness amidst the unrighteousness (darkness) of this evil world.

We are not special people. We are terrible sinners like many others. We are poor and needy people. Yet we are full of pride and arrogance that we are subjected into a debased mind.

God is calling us to rise up into righteousness that we may become His servants and be called His people. To play a special role for the salvation of mankind. And that is to become God's helper in ushering and establishing the coming Kingdom of God here on earth for the salvation of mankind.

The Light will come to us now. Will you accept the Light to guide and protect you in this darkest hour? Will you allow God's righteousness to reign in your life or will you continue to live in unrighteousness under the shadow of darkness?

As the Light reveals to us His righteousness we need to decide on our own volition whether to follow and obey the guiding light or go the other way around. God created us as a free moral agent. God will not force us to do what we are not willing to do. But in every decision we make, there is always consequences. In every action we take, there is always an equal and opposite reaction.

If we accept God's calling into righteousness and the works ahead of us, He promised us His protection and abundance amidst the coming troublesome time. While the world descended into darkness full evil deeds, wars, chaos, deceptions, famine, pestilences, poverty and diseases, God will protect us from all of these if we seek and obey Him and if we allow the Light to come into our lives.

Surely, tribulation period is coming, and it is called the "terrible days" for a reason. But God is offering us his protection if we accept the job opportunity of our lifetime to be His servants. We will discuss the job descriptions in the coming chapters and also in the upcoming book – The Ophireum Manifesto.

I know it is not pleasing to be called servant or a slave because human beings are full of pride and arrogance. We want to lift ourselves above others. It feels good to be proud of something even though we have nothing. We allowed ourselves to be influenced by the feel-good society of the western world but deep inside is emptiness and loneliness because in actuality, we just lied or deceive ourselves to better up our emotions when in reality we have not accomplished anything good.

The feel-good concept is a lie. It is like a vessel, shining in the outside but empty in the inside. This belief causes the western civilization to collapse. The education system alone is a testament to this crazy concept. Real honor or reward system is no longer allowed. Now a days, everybody has honor, and everybody receive medal, making the medal supply business as a lucrative corruption avenue of the Department of Education. But everybody is happy, so nobody bothered to question what is going on.

The lessons no longer challenge the intellectual development of the kids, because it will hurt their feelings. Emotions have become more important that intellectual development. But of course, they do not want your children to learn how to think. Honors and rewards are equal to both the hardworking and lazy kids now a days in the western world (the US in particular). There is no morality in this. This is purely destructive to the future generations. And sad to say, the land of Ophir has adopted these evil doctrines of the western world. Whatever their master told them to do, they do it also in the isles. We need to end this.

What I admire is the Japanese culture. They have achieved great things in life. They have established their identity as a hardworking, disciplined, and respectful people in general. While the kids in the western world are being taught with many evil things including disregard for the law, disrespect, disobedience, racial discrimination, and gender confusion, the kids in Japan are being taught with respect, politeness, and proper demeanor even when crossing the road by themselves as young as four years old. And older people respect these children also. That is why even if the kids are in a hurry to school, they do not forget to turn their backs to bow down to the person in the car that give them the way to cross the street. They show their thanks and respect to their fellowmen.

Instead, kids in the western world are being programmed for weakness, racism, sexuality, and homosexuality, etc.. Their public school system has become an indoctrination camp for evil way of life (e.g. groomers of transgender, CRT for hatred). It becomes their utmost priority rather than developing personal development such us intellectual, physical, spiritual and health. The next western generation is on the verge of collapse by design.

On the other side of the coin, because of too much materialism, Japan is on the verge of collapse also. Economic prosperity is nothing without people. The aging and shrinking population of Japan is the consequence of too much economic focus. Everything is expensive in Japan. That is why people need to work hard to make a living, if not to survive the day-to-day struggle in life. It is so expensive in Japan that having a family became a luxury in life. That is why their population is shrinking at a very alarming level. It can be patch up temporarily through foreign workers, but eventually if their economic system remains the same, still their civilization will collapse.

Of course, there are also bad fruits in Japan such as too much work in corporate offices (causing suicide), the famous gang or mafia, etc. But the way Japanese people respect each other and their dedication to their work is admirable attitude. The bowing is showing respect and high regard for the other person. It is like showing, I am lower than you (humbleness). It is humbling and not pride and arrogance.

That is what God wants us to be. Humble and respectful to one another. In the example above we see that the humble prosper, while the proud and arrogant have a deteriorating society. Selfishness is evil, while unselfishness is of God.

As Ophirians, we have a very good characters and attitudes also. In the old times, people are respectful to each other. Our culture of blessing in the hands of the elders is an admirable one like the Japanese bowing down as a sign of respect. We are hospitable in the sense that in a poor family they will prefer their best things in their house for their visitors. Not even them use it for themselves. Prepare the best food they can offer that they themselves does not have the luxury to eat. The best food for their visitor that they can loan or barrow from their neighbor's sari -sari store. However, as we experience progress, our culture deteriorated and replaced with disrespect to our neighbors, immorality, pride and arrogance and selfishness. In the past, neighbors share food and barrow things from each other. Now, neighbors do not know and care for each other anymore in the name of privacy and security. Is this the result of progress we wanted? Instead of ascending into higher moral ground, we descended into immorality, selfishness, and unrighteousness. This is the darkness that have descended upon the earth.

Why?

Because we forgot the true Living God in our lives.

But we are fortunate people that God included us in his plans. To be called His servants and to serve according to His purpose should be a great honor for us. We should rather desire in our heart to be a servant of God rather than a servant of Satan for which we are now.

We have a lot of works to do and a very challenging time ahead of us. And that includes fighting the evil in us first and foremost and striving to get near, to seek and know God with all our hearts and soul so that we may be worthy for His blessings and protection.

If we continue to obey Satan knowingly and unknowingly through his false religions (prison houses), unrighteousness, and deceptions, we shall also suffer the darkness he is bringing up on the earth. We should remember that there are only two principalities here on earth. There is nothing in between. It's either the way of God or the way of Satan. It is either good or evil. It is either right or wrong. It is either the truth or the lies and deceptions or falsehood.

We need to decide for ourselves because we are created as a free moral agent (Acts 14: 16). This means that God have vested in us (human beings) the ability to choose how we will live our lives. In all His creation, God gave man the ability to do something that plants and animals cannot do. It is called free will. The God of the Bible promises blessings to those who obey Him and curses to those who follow and obey Satan's way of life leading us to sufferings, confusion, and eventually, death (physical and spiritual). God promised us eternal life to those who will listen and obey. Obedience to God of the Bible is the key to His blessings. While obedience to Satan is the key to destruction.

We (people of the isles) are not God's chosen people, but in this end times, He is inviting/calling us to be His servants whom He will call "My people" also as mentioned by Paul to the Gentiles quoting Hosea in Romans 9: 25, saying;

"²⁵As He says also in Hosea:

"I will call them <u>My people</u>, who were <u>not My people</u>,

And her beloved, who was not beloved.""

And God will use us (the people of the isles) to bring back his chosen people to Him so that He may be glorified in them as mentioned in Isaiah 49: 3;

"3 "...'You are My servant, O Israel,
In whom I will be glorified.'""

God promise reward according to our work (deeds). But we should not focus ourselves on the reward, but on the works that is on our hands. Our obedience to God should not be focused on the material blessings or earthly rewards, but rather our spiritual relationship with our Master, our Father and our King, the Lord Jesus Christ. Rewards are the result of our obedience to God and not the other way around as it is written in Romans 2: 5-11;

"5But in accordance with your hardness and your impenitent (unrepentant) heart you are treasuring up for yourself wrath in the day of wrath and revelation of the righteous judgment of God, 6who "will render to each one according to his deeds (work, conduct)": 7eternal life to those who by patient continuance in doing good seek for glory, honor, and immortality; 8but to those who are self-seeking and do not obey the truth, but obey unrighteousness—indignation and wrath, 9tribulation and anguish, on every soul of man who does evil, of the Jew first and also of the Greek (Gentiles); 10but glory, honor, and peace to everyone who works what is good, to the Jew first and also to the Greek. 11For there is no partiality with God."

In fact, our calling is not a walk in the park or to become a super-rich nation, but rather it is about serving our Master as a servant. It is of long suffering, lowliness, and gentleness and not proud and arrogance of our material position just as Paul preached to us in Ephesians 4: 1-6 said;

"1I, therefore, the prisoner of the Lord, beseech you to walk worthy of the calling with which you were called, 2with all lowliness and gentleness, with longsuffering, bearing with one another in love, 3endeavoring to keep the unity of the Spirit in the bond of peace. [4]There is <u>one body</u> and <u>one Spirit</u>, just as you were called in <u>one hope of your calling</u>; [5]<u>one Lord</u>, <u>one faith</u>, <u>one baptism</u>; [6]<u>one God and Father of all</u>, who is above all, and through all, and in you all."

Paul added in Collossians 1: 9-14;

"[9]For this reason we also, since the day we heard it, do not cease to pray for you, and to ask that you may <u>be filled with the knowledge of His will in all wisdom and spiritual understanding</u>; [10]that you may walk worthy of the Lord, fully pleasing Him, <u>being fruitful in every good work and increasing in the knowledge of God</u>; [11]strengthened with all might, according to His glorious power, <u>for all patience and longsuffering with joy</u>; [12]<u>giving thanks to the Father</u> who has qualified us to be partakers of the inheritance of the saints in the light. [13]He has delivered us from the power of darkness and conveyed us into the kingdom of the Son of His love, [14]in whom we have redemption through His blood, the forgiveness of sins."

Our work is not a glamourous one. For as we preach the gospel of Jesus Christ about the coming Kingdom of God in all the earth, Jesus said in Matthew 24: 9;

"[9]"Then they will deliver you up to tribulation and kill you, and <u>you will be hated by all nations for My name's sake</u>….""

And Jesus said in John 15: 18-21;

"[18]"If the world hates you, you know that it hated Me before it hated you. [19]If you were of the world, the world would love its own. Yet because you are not of the world, but <u>I chose you out of the world</u>, therefore <u>the world hates you</u>. [20]Remember the word that I said to you, '<u>A servant is not greater than his master.</u>' <u>If they persecuted Me, they will also persecute you.</u> If they kept My word, they will keep yours also. [21]But all these things they will do to you for My name's sake, because <u>they do not know Him who sent Me</u>.""

Although we are not going to focus on materialism, this does not mean that we will continue to live in poverty. The kingdom will ensure that the least of our brothers and sisters will have decent houses to dwell in and good food in their table on a daily basis. Economic opportunities will be available to everyone for us to eliminate informal settlements and poverty in our kingdom. But amidst our prosperity in the kingdom, we shall remain grounded in humbleness, lowliness, and gentleness in love to one another.

Even though, it will be hard to break away from the evil governmental system that enslaved our land, God said, "come out of her, my people" (Rev. 18: 4). It is up to us to decide to break away from the satanic shackles that put us into the bondage of corruption. And it may be impossible for us to defeat Satan and wickedness from our land, but with God, nothing is impossible.

We should also remember that God is calling us not individually but as whole nation (Matt. 24:9). The whole kingdom collectively will be hated by all nations on earth. That means that God wants us to be one.

The satanic doctrine of diversity and relativism will not and should not be in our kingdom. For it only leads us into confusion and deception. And Satan is the author of confusion and deception. We shall move us one.

We shall build our own system based on God's way of life rather than the current satanic global governmental system (the New World Order) which enslave humanity to be worshipper of Satan.

We shall be one peoples, one Kingdom, one religion, under one God.

We shall be called Ophirians from the Kingdom of Ophir.

SECTION 1

GOD

CHAPTER 1

DOES GOD EXIST?

B efore we believe in what this book is telling us, we need to prove clearly, without a doubt that what is written here is the truth and not a lie. Is there really a God? How do we know that God really exist? Should we just accept Him in faith? Or can we prove that a Supreme Almighty powerful Being have created all things that exist both seen and unseen creations?

How can we prove that there is really a God? Or who among the thousands of gods of the earth is the real God?

We need to know. We need to prove it to ourselves who and what is a real God.

What proof can bridge the gap between this Supreme Being and His creation than the visible and tangible proof of His work. The proof of work is the product. And the product is a proof that someone created the product. And that product has a user's manual – The Bible.

Therefore, the proof of God is His works (creations) and His Word (the Bible) attests to His works.

The God of the Bible Jesus Christ (Yeshua) said in John 5: 17, saying;

""17But Jesus answered them, "My Father has been working

until now, and I have been working.'"''

There is a Father and the Son that have worked and still working to this day. He declared that He is not alone. He declared the Father.

What are they working? It seems that they have not ceased the works that they have been doing since the beginning of Their work.

Is it not the same Jesus (the Son) whose name is the Lord (Isaiah 42: 8, "I am the Lord, that is My name;") who claimed to have created the heavens and the earth in Isaiah 45: 11- 12;

"'¹¹Thus says the Lord, the Holy One of Israel, and his Maker:
"Ask Me of things to come concerning My sons; and concerning the work of My hands, you command Me.
¹²I have made the earth, and created man on it.
I—My hands—stretched out the heavens, and all their host I have commanded."

And in Isaiah 42: 5;
"'⁵Thus says God the Lord,
Who created the heavens and stretched them out,
Who spread forth the earth and that which comes from it,
Who gives breath to the people on it,
And spirit to those who walk on it:"

And in Isaiah 44: 24, He also said;
"'²⁴Thus says the Lord, your Redeemer, and He who formed you from the womb:
"I am the Lord, who makes all things, Who stretches out the heavens all alone, Who spreads abroad the earth by Myself;"

And His Father proclaimed that indeed He – Jesus Christ (Yeshua) – the Lord - the Son, who claimed to have created the heavens and the earth and all the things in it did the works of creation in Hebrew 1: 5-13 (Ps. 102: 25-27);

"'⁵For to which of the angels did He ever say:
"You are My Son, today I have begotten You"?
And again:
"I will be to Him a Father, and He shall be to Me a Son"?
⁶But when He again brings the firstborn into the world, He says:

"Let all the angels of God worship Him."

[7]And of the angels He says: "Who makes His angels spirits and His ministers a flame of fire."

[8]But to the Son He says:

"Your throne, O God, is forever and ever;

A scepter of righteousness is the scepter of Your kingdom.

[9]You have loved righteousness and hated lawlessness;

Therefore God, Your God, has anointed You

With the oil of gladness more than Your companions."

[10]And:

"You, Lord, in the beginning laid the foundation of the earth,

And the heavens are the work of Your hands.

[11]They will perish, but You remain; and they will all grow old like a garment;

[12]Like a cloak You will fold them up, and they will be changed. But You are the same, and Your years will not fail."

[13]But to which of the angels has He ever said:

"Sit at My right hand,

Till I make Your enemies Your footstool"?"

The Father called His Son - God and Lord and proclaimed that indeed, He is the One who created the heavens and the earth. But the Lord Jesus Christ (Yeshua) is humble enough to recognize that His Father is greater than Him in John 14: 28, saying;

"[28]You have heard Me say to you, 'I am going away and coming back to you.' If you loved Me, you would rejoice because I said, 'I am going to the Father,' for My Father is greater than I."

And He said in John 12: 49-50;

"[49]For I have not spoken on My own authority; but the Father who sent Me gave Me a command, what I should say and what I should speak. [50]And I know that His command is everlasting life. Therefore, whatever I speak, just as the Father has told Me, so I speak.""

And in John 16: 28;

"[28]I came forth from the Father and have come into the world.

Again, I leave the world and go to the Father.'"

God the Father created all things through Jesus Christ just as it is written in John 1: 1-3, 14;

"¹In the <u>beginning</u> was <u>the Word</u>, and <u>the Word was with God</u>, and <u>the Word was God</u>. ²He was in the beginning with God. ³<u>All things were made through Him</u>, and without Him nothing was made that was made."

"¹⁴And the Word became flesh and dwelt among us, and we beheld His glory, the glory as of the <u>only begotten of the Father</u>, full of <u>grace</u> and <u>truth</u>."

And in Colossians 1: 15-18;

"¹⁵<u>He is the image of the invisible God</u>, the firstborn over all creation. ¹⁶<u>For by Him all things were created that are in heaven and that are on earth</u>, visible and invisible, whether thrones or dominions or principalities or powers. <u>All things were created through Him and for Him</u>. ¹⁷And <u>He is before all things</u>, and <u>in Him all things consist</u>. ¹⁸And He is the head of the body, the church, who is the beginning, the firstborn from the dead, that in all things He may have the preeminence."

The creation is the manifestation of the power and might and wisdom of the Creator. His Word – the Bible is the living documentation of the proof of His works, power, and might. Since Jesus Christ is the Word and the Bible is the Word of God, then we can say that the Bible is Jesus Christ in print. The creations are the products, and we are one of the products and the Bible is our user's manual.

Just think about a book that survived a hundred years and still relevant today, is a great achievement in itself. How much more the Bible which survived many attacks for thousands of years, and yet its words is much more relevant today than ever before.

And yet, mankind hated the Creator and worship the creation. Satan deceives the whole world into worshipping him by influencing mankind to create their own gods. Satan even created a fake or counterfeit Christianity that followers profess to believe in Jesus Christ and yet they are anti-Christ for they do not want to obey and believe on what the Bible say about the real Jesus Christ. All their laws and practices are opposed or against what the real Jesus commanded in His Book. They are against God's Laws and commandments, but they willfully and happily obey the traditions and practices of man which are pagan (Satanic) in nature (origin). These includes Sunday sabbath, Christmas celebration, New Year, Valentine's Day, Easter Sunday, etc. With a little research now a days, one can easily find the truth about these things if one wish to find the truth. But no. Many are too lazy to think. They just want to follow what they have been told even if it will cost their soul. All these things project their pride and arrogance against God. They do not want to obey God. They only want to obey what they believe. In fact, these practices are Satanic mockery of the real Jesus Christ (Yeshua) of the Bible because Satan is the enemy of God.

The Proof of God - the Creator

What is God?

God is a supreme being above all things who have a supreme power and might to create and govern everything. He is the Alpha and the Omega, the beginning, and the end, the first and the last, and He is from eternity.

Who is God?

God is the Creator of everything we see and feel and those we cannot see and feel and beyond our mental capacity to think and see.

God is omnipresent (All-present, present everywhere at the same time) just as it is written in Jeremiah 23: 24;

"24Can anyone hide himself in secret places,
So I shall not see him?" says the Lord;
"Do I not fill heaven and earth?" says the Lord."

And in Proverbs 15: 3;
"3The eyes of the Lord are in every place,
Keeping watch on the evil and the good."

God is omnipotent (All-powerful, having unlimited power; able to do anything) for He said in Isaiah 43: 13;

"¹³Indeed before the day was, I am He; and there is no one who can deliver out of My hand; I work, and who will reverse it?""

And Isaiah testified in Chapter 14 verse 27, saying;
"²⁷For the Lord of hosts has purposed, and who will annul it? His hand is stretched out, and who will turn it back?""

For in Daniel 4: 35 (NLT) king Nebuchadnezzar said;
"³⁵All the people of the earth are nothing compared to Him. He does as He pleases among the angels of heaven and among the people of the earth. No one can stop Him or say to Him, 'What do You mean by doing these things?'"

God is omniscient (All-knowing, knowing everything), just as He said in Isaiah 46: 9-10;

"⁹Remember the former things of old, For I am God, and there is no other; I am God, and there is none like Me, ¹⁰declaring the end from the beginning, and from ancient times things that are not yet done, saying, 'My counsel shall stand, and I will do all My pleasure,'"

And in Psalms 139: 4;
"'⁴For there is not a word in my tongue, but, lo, O LORD, thou knowest it altogether."

And in Psalms 147: 5;
"'⁵Great is our Lord, and of great power: His understanding is infinite."

Who among the gods of this world can declare such things?
Nothing! No other God can declare such things because all the gods of this world are idols (creation by man) just as it is written in 1 Chronicles 16: 25-26 (KJV);

"²⁵For great is the LORD, and greatly to be praised: He also is to be feared above all gods.
²⁶For all the gods of the people are idols: but the LORD made

the heavens."

Idolatry is the worship of god created by man's imagination. Imagine worshipping or adoring a god whom you conceive and created. Is not man foolish enough to worship his own creation? Is the creation higher than the creator?

How does God describe idolatry?

God described the foolishness of idolatry in Isaiah 44: 6-20 (NLT);

"⁶This is what the LORD says—Israel's King and Redeemer, the LORD of Heaven's Armies:

"I am the First and the Last; there is no other God.

⁷Who is like Me? Let him step forward and prove to you his power. Let him do as I have done since ancient times when I established a people and explained its future.

⁸Do not tremble; do not be afraid. Did I not proclaim my purposes for you long ago? You are my witnesses—is there any other God? No! There is no other Rock—not one!"

⁹How foolish are those who manufacture idols. These prized objects are really worthless. The people who worship idols don't know this, so they are all put to shame.

¹⁰Who but a fool would make his own god—an idol that cannot help him one bit?

¹¹All who worship idols will be disgraced along with all these craftsmen—mere humans— who claim they can make a god. They may all stand together, but they will stand in terror and shame.

¹²The blacksmith stands at his forge to make a sharp tool, pounding and shaping it with all his might. His work makes him hungry and weak. It makes him thirsty and faint.

¹³Then the wood-carver measures a block of wood and draws a pattern on it. He works with chisel and plane and carves it into a human figure. He gives it human beauty and puts it in a little shrine. ¹⁴He cuts down cedars; he selects the cypress and the oak; he plants the pine in the forest to be nourished by the rain.

¹⁵Then he uses part of the wood to make a fire. With it he warms himself and bakes his bread. Then—yes, it's true—he

takes the rest of it and makes himself a god to worship!
He makes an idol and bows down in front of it! ¹⁶He burns
part of the tree to roast his meat and to keep himself warm. He
says, "Ah, that fire feels good."
¹⁷Then he takes what's left and makes his god: a carved idol!
He falls down in front of it, worshiping and praying to it.
"Rescue me!" he says. "You are my god!"
¹⁸Such stupidity and ignorance! Their eyes are closed, and they
cannot see. Their minds are shut, and they cannot think.
¹⁹The person who made the idol never stops to reflect, "Why,
it's just a block of wood! I burned half of it for heat and used
it to bake my bread and roast my meat. How can the rest of it
be a god? Should I bow down to worship a piece of wood?"
²⁰The poor, deluded fool feeds on ashes. He trusts something
that can't help him at all. Yet he cannot bring himself to ask,
"Is this idol that I'm holding in my hand a lie?""

You see how stupid, foolish, and ignorant we are? And yet we
are so proud and arrogant in our own ways and thinking. And yet we are
blind and deaf to the truth. And we suffer the result of our own stupidity.

That is why God give us His first commandments in Exodus 20:
3-6, saying;

"³"You shall have no other gods before Me.

⁴"You shall not make for yourself a carved image—any likeness of
anything that is in heaven above, or that is in the earth beneath, or
that is in the water under the earth; ⁵you shall not bow down to
them nor serve them. For I, the Lord your God, am a jealous God,
visiting the iniquity of the fathers upon the children to the third and
fourth generations of those who hate Me, ⁶but showing mercy to
thousands, to those who love Me and keep My commandments.""

But then, those who profess to believe in the God of the Bible
said that the commandments of God were done away, and it is only
for the Israelites. Not knowing that God give the commandments
since the beginning of time. Even before Israelite become a name, God

have sanctified (made it holy) the seventh day (Gen. 2: 3) already just after the creation. It is for all mankind to keep it holy. Instead, humanity chose to disobey God. And our disobedience to God's laws and His commandments are what causing our suffering since the beginning of time until now just as Isaiah 24: 5-6 said;

> "⁵The earth is also defiled under its inhabitants, because they have transgressed the laws, changed the ordinance, broken the everlasting covenant.
> ⁶Therefore the curse has devoured the earth, and those who dwell in it are desolate."

If the laws are only for the Israelite people, then only Israelite are supposed to be cursed. But all the inhabitants of the earth are cursed because the laws apply to all. But because mankind has become so evil that God have chosen His own people through Abraham which He raise up in righteousness from the ends of the earth in the east (Isa. 41: 8-9). But then, Israelites transgressed the law and some even proclaim themselves as gods and causing havoc to humanity. Their deeds will not go unpunished. They too will undergo tribulations under the wrath of God together with the rest of the incorrigible (unrepentant) mankind in the day of the Lord. That is why God denounced Israel as His people (temporarily) and have chosen the people of the isles to be His end time servants. But God have not rejected His people as Paul said in Romans 11: 1-2;

> "¹I say then, has God cast away His people? Certainly not! For I also am an Israelite, of the seed of Abraham, of the tribe of Benjamin. ²God has not cast away His people whom He foreknew."

And in Isaiah 14: 1-2, God show His mercy upon Israel;

> "¹For the Lord will have mercy on Jacob, and will still choose Israel, and settle them in their own land. The strangers will be joined with them, and they will cling to the house of Jacob. ²Then people will take them and bring them to their place, and the house of Israel will possess them for servants and maids in the land of the Lord; they will take them captive whose captives they were, and rule over their oppressors."

Our rebelliousness, disobedience, and sinfulness to God are the real anthropomorphic causes of our sufferings, from failed states around the world governed by anarchy to increasing intensity of natural disaster such as earthquakes, storms, pestilences, and diseases. Our ever-increasing natural calamities have nothing to do with dramas and deceptions of carbon footprint or emission lies but all have to do with our failure to recognize and respect God who created and give us our lives. We are so ingrate to the One who created us that we become blind and deaf to the truth. We do not fear God even though He said is Isaiah 45: 7;

> "⁷I form the light and create darkness, I make peace and create calamity; I, the Lord, do all these things.'"

Yet in times of trouble, we call upon God consciously and unconsciously. And in times of calm, we forget and disobey Him thinking that God is just a loving God who have no bones in punishing mankind. A frail and effeminate god that can do no harm to humanity. But we are too ignorant or have forgotten what God can do and have done just as Peter said in 2 Peter 3: 5-6;

> "⁵For this they (mankind) willfully forget: that by the word of God the heavens were of old, and the earth standing out of water and in the water, ⁶by which the world that then existed perished, being flooded with water."

There was an old/ancient earth that have perished totally by flooding with water. Perish means - suffer complete ruin or destruction. This means that nothing has survived in that catastrophic event and the earth remained submerged under water. This is in contrasts to the flood in the times of Noah as God destroyed all living things on the surface of the earth through the flood once again, except those who are with him in the ark. The earth in the great flood of in the times Noah did not perish, for Noah and his family and the animals with them begin to repopulate the earth once again after one year.

And again, God destroyed Sodom and Gomorrah full of sexually immoral people (with emphasis on homosexuality in Gen. 19:

1-11). This time with fire. They have provoked God's anger and they got what they wanted.

Now mankind is provoking God's anger once again with so many abominable and detestable sinfulness such as abortion, child sacrifices and the drinking of the blood (adrenochrome) of the innocents (rampant kidnapping), homosexuality and now the more perverted version of homosexuality which is transgenderism.

This detestable act is defined in Leviticus 18: 22-23;

"22You shall not lie with a male as with a woman. It is an abomination. 23Nor shall you mate with any animal, to defile yourself with it. Nor shall any woman stand before an animal to mate with it. It is perversion."

And in Leviticus 20:13;

"13If a man lies with a male as he lies with a woman, both of them have committed an abomination. They shall surely be put to death. Their blood shall be upon them."

God's promise to those who do these sexual immorality (both who practices and those who support) is death. Their blood is in their hands. Their death both physical and spiritual is their choice as Paul explained fully how the wrath of God will come to the sons of disobedience in Romans 1: 18-32;

"18For the wrath of God is revealed from heaven against all ungodliness and unrighteousness of men, who suppress the truth in unrighteousness, 19because what may be known of God is manifest in them, for God has shown it to them. 20For since the creation of the world His invisible attributes are clearly seen, being understood by the things that are made, even His eternal power and Godhead, so that they are without excuse, 21because, although they knew God, they did not glorify Him as God, nor were thankful, but became futile in their thoughts, and their foolish hearts were darkened. 22Professing to be wise, they became fools, 23and changed the glory of the incorruptible God into an image made like corruptible man—and birds and four-footed animals and creeping things. [24]Therefore God also gave them up to uncleanness, in the lusts of their hearts, to dishonor their bodies among themselves, [25]who exchanged the truth of God for the lie, and worshiped and served the creature rather than the Creator, who is blessed forever. Amen. [26]For this reason God gave them up to vile passions. For even their women exchanged the natural use for what is against nature. [27]Likewise also the men, leaving the natural use of the woman, burned in their lust for one another, men with men committing what is shameful, and receiving in themselves the penalty of their error which was due. [28]And even as they did not like to retain God in their knowledge, God gave them over to a debased mind, to do those things which are not fitting; [29]being filled with all unrighteousness, sexual immorality, wickedness, covetousness, maliciousness; full of envy, murder, strife, deceit, evil-mindedness; they are whisperers, [30]backbiters, haters of God, violent, proud, boasters, inventors of evil things, disobedient to parents, [31]undiscerning, untrustworthy, unloving, unforgiving, unmerciful; [32]who, knowing the righteous judgment of God, that those who practice such things are deserving of death, not only do the same but also approve of those who practice them."

God have sent His warning and yet humanity have continued to walk intentionally into darkness that the world will see once again the cruelty of God just as it is written in Isaiah 13: 9;

"[9]Behold, the day of the Lord comes, Cruel, with both wrath and fierce anger, to lay the land desolate; and He will destroy its sinners from it."

If you are devastated seeing the aftermath of a hurricane or a storm, tornado, wildfire, earthquake, tsunami, and other natural disasters, wait until God show His wrath upon humanity. Disasters and sufferings that have not been seen or experienced since the beginning of time as described in 2 Peter 3: 7;

> "[7]But the heavens and the earth which are now preserved by the same word, are <u>reserved for fire</u> until the day of <u>judgment and perdition of ungodly men</u>."

And ultimately Jesus Christ said in Matthew 24: 21-22;
> "[21]For then there will be great tribulation, such as has not been since the beginning of the world until this time, no, nor ever shall be. [22]And unless those days were shortened, no flesh would be saved;…"

God will terribly punish humanity for its sinfulness. And Satan is so happy that He is successful in deceiving humanity towards rebellion and disobedience to God. He deceives humanity so that they too will partake his suffering from the penalty of his disobedience to God, his Creator.

Our present-day sufferings are because of our disobedience to God by which we allow Satan to influence our lives. Satan is real and so is God who created him (Satan) and us.

Satan as previously discussed is the present-day god and ruler of this world as Jesus Christ said to His disciples in John 14: 25-30;

> "[28]You have heard Me say to you, '<u>I am going away and coming back to you</u>.' If you loved Me, you would rejoice because I said, '<u>I am going to the Father,' for My Father is greater than I</u>.
> [29]"And now I have told you before it comes, that <u>when it does come to pass, you may believe</u>. [30]I will no longer talk much with you, <u>for the ruler of this world is coming</u>, and he has nothing in Me."

What more proof do we need in order to believe in Jesus Christ – the Creator of the heavens and the earth? For Satan is indeed the present-day god and ruler of this world. He is "the prince of the power of the air" that influence our mind that moves our attitude against God and our fellowmen. Just as it is written in Ephesians 2: 2;

> "[2]…in which you once walked according to the course of this world, according to <u>the prince of the power of the air</u>, <u>the spirit</u>

who now works in the sons of disobedience,..."

If we are disobedient to God, whom do we obey?

By its fruit you shall know (Matt. 7: 20). The result of our disobedience to God is human sufferings, lawlessness, confusion, blindness and deafness to the truth, and hopelessness. The world is hopeless apart from God. The earth is cursed because of our sinfulness. And by this we know that a Creator God does exist.

The Proof of God - the Creations

In this section, we will explore four significant creations that God has made, which demonstrate His incredible power and glory. These are the Heaven, the heavens, and the earth, plants and animals, mankind, and Lucifer – Satan the Devil. When the God of the Bible said He created all things, that means all things and that He is the only One who can claim and proclaimed His works.

The Heaven, the Heavens, and the Earth

We live in this wonderful world God called earth. From here, we see the skies by which we, human defined as earth's atmosphere. God called these atmospheres heavens. Above the earth are several layers of heavens, each one has their own function. One layer is where we get the air we breathe. Others are the one that control our temperatures and atmospheric pressures, and as our mode of transportation, etc. Another layer is the habitation of the sun and the moon, and the stars that lights the earth and so on, so forth.

Above the earth's heavens is the Heaven where the stars and other heavenly creations resides. The heavens of earth is just a subset of the Heaven (the greater heaven, firmament). It is an infinite vast space that is beyond our imagination. We cannot fully describe or grasp the magnitude of this Heaven. Perhaps, it is where God's Heaven (His habitation) is also located. But above this Heaven is an infinite space of waters. Below this Heaven (firmament) is an infinite space of waters also by which the earth resides. The earth standing out of water and in

31

the water (2 Pet. 3:5) (is in and above this water) and the gathering of this waters God called seas. This means that the earth is just part of the sea and not the sea part of the earth. The sea preexisted the earth. How vast the waters below the Heaven (firmament) and the sea is, we do not know. But like the heavens, the sea is marvelously designed by His Creator to give great benefits on the inhabitants of the earth.

- Here is how God described His creation on the first day as described in Genesis 1: 3- 5 - Day and night;

"³Then God said, "Let there be light"; and there was light. ⁴And God saw the light, that it was good; and God divided the light from the darkness. ⁵God called the light Day, and the darkness He called Night. So the evening and the morning were the first day."

So, God (Yeshua, Jesus Christ, the Lord) created the light and darkness first even before the creation of the Heaven (firmament) when everything was still waters. God gives us a glimpse of the light and darkness as He challenge and ask Job as He reveal His Omnipotence to him in Chapter 38: 19-21, 24;

"¹⁹"Where is the way to the dwelling of light? And darkness, where is its place,²⁰that you may take it to its territory, that you may know the paths to its home?

²¹Do you know it, because you were born then, or because the number of your days is great? ²⁴By what way is light diffused, or the east wind scattered over the earth?"

We cannot fathom the depths of the wisdom of how God created the light or the darkness which represented day and night later. We should remember that the day and night were created prior to the creation of sun, moon, and the stars nor even the heaven and heavens. Where did the light come from or how it is diffused? Is it not Christ the Light Himself that is why no one can hide their sins from Him?

- Genesis 1: 6-8 is the creation of the Heaven (the major heaven shall we say) on the second day;

"⁶Then God said, "Let there be a firmament in the midst of the waters, and let it divide the waters from the waters." ⁷Thus God made the firmament, and divided the waters which were under the firmament from the waters which were above the firmament; and it was so. [8]And God called the firmament Heaven. So the evening and the morning were the second day."

So, before the firmament which God called Heaven was created, everything was waters. The Heaven was to divide the waters. There are waters above and below the Heaven. And there is already day and night on the second day of creation, but there was no sun, moon, and stars yet.

And this major Heaven has minor heavens that God the Father of Jesus Christ said to His Son (the Lord) in Hebrew 1: 10, saying;

"[10]...And the heavens are the work of Your hands."

And Job said in Chapter 9: 8;
"[8]He alone spreads out the heavens,..."

And Yeshua Himself said in Isaiah 44: 24;
"[24]..."I am the Lord, who makes all things, Who stretches out the heavens all alone,..."

And He said in Isaiah 42:5;
"[5]Thus says God the Lord, Who created the heavens and stretched them out,..."

And the Lord said in Isaiah 45: 12;
"[12]...I—My hands—stretched out the heavens, and all their host I have commanded."

How does the heavens look like?
Isaiah 40: 22, said;
"[22] Who stretches out the heavens like a curtain, and spreads them out like a tent to dwell in."

And in Psalms 104: 1-2;
"[1]Bless the Lord, O my soul! O Lord my God, You are very great: You are clothed with honor and majesty, [2]Who cover Yourself with light as with a garment, Who stretch out the heavens like a curtain."

The Heaven and heavens are likened to a curtain that divide

the waters above and below the firmament (Heaven). In our mental capacity to think, the Heaven is probably rectangular in shape because we know the most common application or association of a curtain is in the window which is either rectangular or square in form. Not a sphere or a globe. How far and wide this curtain is, we do not know. It is beyond our knowledge and understanding to fathom. But we can say that the Heaven and the heavens are infinite in terms of our mental capacity to think and the One who created it is so huge and powerful beyond measure to stretch out such an infinite space.

That is why in Psalms 148: 4, said;

"⁴Praise Him, you heavens of heavens, and you <u>waters above the heavens</u>!"

- Genesis 1: 9-10 is the creation of the earth and the sea on the third day;

"⁹Then God said, "Let <u>the waters under the heavens be gathered together into one place</u>, and <u>let the dry land appear</u>"; and it was so. ¹⁰And <u>God called the dry land Earth</u>, and the <u>gathering together of the waters He called Seas</u>. And God saw that it was good."

Notice carefully in these verses the words "dry land" God refers to as Earth. The word "land" is singular – meaning one piece of land. Unlike today which are lands (several islands and continents). This changes of land to lands occurred during the great flood in the times of Noah when God said in Isaiah 24:1;

"¹Behold, the Lord makes the earth empty and makes it waste (desolate), <u>distorts its surface</u> and scatters abroad its inhabitants."

This sequence of events could probably happen only in the times of Noah because it is followed by "and scatters abroad its inhabitants". After the cataclysmic event of the great flood which resulted in a desolate and distorted surface of the earth (became lands (islands, continents)), God commanded Noah to go forth and multiply and replenish the earth (Gen. 9:1 KJV). But as they journeyed to the west from the east to the land of Shinar, they build the city and tower of Babel there as a show of their disobedience to God for His commandment. But God scattered them abroad. This is stated in Genesis 11:2, 4,

> "²And it came to pass, as they journeyed from the east, that they found a plain in the land of Shinar, and they dwelt there."
>
> "⁴And they said, "Come, let us build ourselves a city, and a tower whose top is <u>in the heavens</u>; let us make a name for ourselves, <u>lest we be scattered abroad</u> over the face of the whole earth.""

But the Lord confused their language and in verse 8, it said;

> "⁸So <u>the Lord scattered them abroad</u> from there over the face of all the earth, and they ceased building the city."

Another very important details we need to pay attention to is that God identified the earth and the sea separately. Genesis 1: 9-10 implies that the sea is not part of the earth but rather the earth is part of the sea. This is implied also by 2 Peter 3: 5, saying;

> "⁵… the earth standing out of water and in the water…"

This is impossible in a globe earth because the sea will be part of the spherical earth. And as God the creator of the earth described it in Genesis 1: 9-10, "<u>let the dry land appear</u>" and He called this dry land earth. The earth appeared in the surface of the sea (gathered waters). The sea preexisted the earth. The foundation of the earth comes from beneath the sea. The waters below and above the Heaven is infinite or beyond measure and the earth is above the waters below the Heaven and heavens. The earth can be submerged under water through the fountains of the heaven and the fountains of the deep. Just like what is described in the great flood of Noah.

God gives us a glimpse also of how He made the earth in showing His omnipotence to Job saying in chapter 38. In verse 4, Yeshua asked Job;

> "⁴"Where were you when I <u>laid the foundations of the earth</u>? Tell Me, if you have understanding."

And in Psalms 104: 5;

> "⁵You who <u>laid the foundations of the earth</u>, so that <u>it should not be moved forever</u>,…"

In Job 38: 5-6, 18, Jesus Christ continued to question Job, saying;

"⁵Who determined its measurements? Surely you know! Or who stretched the line upon it?
⁶To what were its foundations fastened? Or who laid its cornerstone,…"
"¹⁸Have you comprehended the breadth of the earth? Tell Me, if you know all this."

The earth really has a strong foundation that it cannot be moved and where it is fastened is described by Jesus Christ in Job 38: 30;

"³⁰The waters harden like stone, and the surface of the deep is frozen."

The foundation of the earth is hardened ice like a stone and is fastened in the frozen surface of the deep and not a molten lava of sort. How deep the surface of the deep is? We do not know. Even the breadth of the earth which is accessible and visible to us is described in verse 18 above is incomprehensible. We do not have the mental and physical capacity to measure the breath of the earth, how much more to comprehend of what God have created. Humans only speculates of many things on earth and make it as if it is true (idols). We create a theory, and we foolishly believe it as a fact.

Our globe earth model that described its many layers such as the crust, mantle, outer core, and inner core are just pigments of human imagination (like idolatry). For no one in reality have been there. And yet, we believe it like it is true or real. Come to think about it, the deepest hole mankind ever dug on earth is just 12 kilometers deep in Kola Superdeep Borehole in Russia. And yet scientist or so-called experts declared how thick is the crust (40 km.) or the mantle (100 to 410 km.) of the earth as if they are so certain that they have personally observed and measured the depths of the earth. How did and by what means did they measure these? And yet it is preached in schools like a solid doctrine. And people swallowed it sink, lines and sinker. What a great lie and deceptions we made to ourselves. That is why God called humanity as fools or stupid like making up something such as an idol from wood and worship it. Just as it is written in Jeremiah 51: 17 (NLT);

"¹⁷The whole human race is foolish and has no knowledge! The craftsmen are disgraced by the idols they make, for their carefully shaped works are a fraud. These idols have no breath or power."

And in Jeremiah 10: 8 (NLT);
"⁸People who worship idols are stupid and foolish. The things they worship are made of wood!"

We are indeed so stupid people. We trust on our "make believe" things and even worship them as truth. Why make an idol and worship them? Why made-up ideas or theories which is just an imagination and then believe in it as if it is true? It is just a theory and not a fact. Why believe on our fellowmen's imagination? Yet we despise the truth of God who created all things. What a pure stupidity.

And yet we cannot reconcile our brain to believe on what Jeremiah 10: 10-16 (NLT) will tell us;

"¹⁰But the LORD is the only true God. He is the living God and the everlasting King! The whole earth trembles at His anger. The nations cannot stand up to His wrath.

¹¹Say this to those who worship other gods: "Your so-called gods, who did not make the heavens and earth, will vanish from the earth and from under the heavens."

¹²But the LORD made the earth by His power, and He preserves it by his wisdom. With His own understanding He stretched out the heavens.

¹³When He speaks in the thunder, the heavens roar with rain. He causes the clouds to rise over the earth. He sends the lightning with the rain and releases the wind from his storehouses.

¹⁴The whole human race is foolish and has no knowledge!

The craftsmen are disgraced by the idols they make, for their carefully shaped works are a fraud. These idols have no breath or power.¹⁵Idols are worthless; they are ridiculous lies! On the day of reckoning they will all be destroyed.

¹⁶But the God of Israel is no idol! He is the Creator of everything that exists, including Israel, his own special possession.

The LORD of Heaven's Armies is his name!"

We cannot wrap up in our mind that an Almighty powerful being controls even the thunder, the rain, and the lightnings (the weather and climate). But who would think that wind have storehouses?

And because we cannot fathom the wisdom and workings of our Creator, we just made-up things from our imagination to anchor our belief unto something we just made up (idols) and called it science. Then worship it as truth. Pure foolishness and stupidity! Is it not?

Idols here does not only mean the idol of worship but also the so-called sciences and pseudoscience which man made-up (human centric) and worshipped as truth that only leads us to confusion and away from the true living God. This is called "anthropocentrism" which means that human beings are the central or most important entity in the universe. Mankind regard himself highly as the central or most important element of existence, especially as opposed to God. That is why mankind believe in himself that he can explain everything. And whether it is true or not, people believe it as it is true because it came from man. But when it came from God, they will not believe, or mankind become blind and deaf to God.

That is why God challenges humanity in the person of Job if they can understand or fathom God's creation. But Job, recognizing that he has no ability and capacity to give the correct answers to the prodding and challenging questions of Jesus Christ, he repented and answered Christ in chapter 42 verse 1-6, saying;

"¹Then Job answered the Lord and said:

²"I know that You can do everything, and that no purpose of Yours can be withheld from You.

³You asked, 'Who is this who hides counsel without knowledge?' Therefore I have uttered what I did not understand, Things too wonderful for me, which I did not know.

⁴Listen, please, and let me speak; You said, 'I will question you, and you shall answer Me.'

⁵"I have heard of You by the hearing of the ear, but now my eye sees You. ⁶Therefore I abhor myself, and repent in dust and ashes.'"

Remember that Job can be "you" and "me" if we allow God

to talk to us and to hear and see His wondrous power and glory in creating everything (including us, lest we forget). And if we are humble enough to ask for forgiveness of our stupidity and foolishness, we might see Him also.

God has shown us a glimpse and more details on how He created all thing and how His creation works in Job chapters 36-42, in Psalms 104, and in Psalms 148. There are many more clues and details scattered throughout the Bible that if we can connect the dots, we will be able to see the bigger picture and we will be amazed at how wonderful the works of God is and how amazing He is. The creation is described by the Creator Himself rather than just the imagination of the creature.

- Genesis 1: 14-19 describes the fourth day of heavenly creation/recreation in relation to the earth;

"¹⁴Then God said, "Let there be lights in the firmament of the heavens to divide the day from the night; and let them be for signs and seasons, and for days and years; ¹⁵and let them be for lights in the firmament of the heavens to give light on the earth"; and it was so. ¹⁶Then God made two great lights: the greater light to rule the day, and the lesser light to rule the night. He made the stars also. ¹⁷God set them in the firmament of the heavens **to give light on the earth**, ¹⁸and to rule over the day and over the night, and to divide the light from the darkness. And God saw that it was good. ¹⁹So the evening and the morning were the fourth day."

Notice very carefully here that the heavens being mentioned is the layers of heaven and some we call atmosphere which encompassed the whole earth and the sea beneath it. The heavens are below and is part of the Heaven.

We must also take note that from the very first day of creation/recreation (Gen. 1:3), God created light and divided the light from darkness by which the light He called Day and the darkness He called Night even before the firmament (Heaven) was created. There is already Day and Night prior to the creation of the sun (the greater light to rule the day), the moon (the lesser light to rule the night), and the stars on the fourth day **to give light on the earth**. God created the sun to specifically give light to earth and not to light other planets as we have been told. The sun is not a distant star from the so-called Solar System, nor it is orbiting the center of the so-called Milky Way galaxy. It is the likes of the moon but have intense light than the moon and is created to give light specifically on earth. We can have a clue of the distance of the sun to earth by the rays of the sunlight on a cloudy afternoon. By this we can have a commonsense clue that the sun is very near to earth than the so-called light years away. But that geometrical computation is not our main subject for this chapter. It is up to you to research such things and prove it to yourself.

God knows the numbers of the stars and called them by their names as stated in Psalms 147: 4;

"⁴He counts the number of the stars; He calls them all by name."

And in Job 38: 31-33;
"³¹"Can you bind the cluster of the Pleiades, or loose the belt of Orion? ³²Can you bring out Mazzaroth in its season? Or can you guide the Great Bear with its cubs? ³³Do you know the ordinances of the heavens? Can you set their dominion over the earth?""

God knows what He created. He can even count the numbers of our hairs (Matt. 10: 30, Luke 12: 7). But human science will tell us that these stars are some thousands of light years away from the earth. One light year is 5.88 trillion miles (9.46 trillion kilometers) per year according to their knowledge. Imagine that. Has anyone measured this actual distance, or it is just an assumption? A pigment of human imagination. We pretend to be wise by showing our foolishness. Trying hard to explain the unexplainable by pretending to be wise but we look like fools.

The constellations of stars mentioned above can be seen every night in almost every place on earth on the same spot as the north star called Polaris. Amazingly, a hole in the cabal's Georgia Guidestones (when it was not destroyed yet) remained permanently focused on Polaris, proving that the earth is motionless. It never moves just as God said in Psalms 104: 5, 1 Chronicles 16: 30, and in Isaiah 14: 7.

Now, the question is, if the earth is spinning at 1000 mph as it revolves around the sun at 66,600 mph while the sun shoots through space at 450,000 mph, why is it that the position of the constellations relative to earth has not changed in thousands of years? The math does not add up.

Remember that stars have been used as navigational guide for travelers on earth for thousands of years.

Mankind is so fond in creating their own idols and worship it. It is like grasping numbers from the air and concluded that that is the distance of the sun or moon to the earth. Or this and that is the age of the sun, etc. They have it figured out that the earth is orbiting the sun at this speed and the sun is orbiting in the Milky Way galaxy and put an almost realistic artist rendering of the sun in relation to the galaxy as if they have been there. They have this imagination of Big Bang Theory and Theory of Evolution and explain it as if it is really real, when in fact it is just a make-believe idea. A theory. Yet people swallowed these ideas hook, lines, and sinker. We cannot even figure out a lot of things on earth, but they can proudly say that this is the material composition of sun or moon or stars, etc. as if they really have been there.

Their physics and science can easily be disproven by common sense science and physics because you will know, if one can come to its senses that everything is just illusion and a pigment of imagination of someone tasked to create propaganda to twist and manipulate human behavior and belief system. And repeating the lies through various generations that it become as truth. But the real intention is to deny the existence of God.

Let us just look at the stars created by Jesus Christ in Genesis 1: 16. What is going to happen to these stars in the Day of the Lord as Christ open up the sixth seal from the scroll in Revelation 6: 12-13;

> "[12]I looked when He opened the sixth seal, and behold, there was a great earthquake; and the sun became black as sackcloth of hair, and the moon became like blood. [13]And the stars of heaven fell to the earth, as a fig tree drops its late figs when it is shaken by a mighty wind."

Imagine, if what the astronomers and physicist or the so-called experts' assumptions of the distance and measurements (including velocity) of the stars is true and the above verse is true, then just one piece of star is enough to vaporize the earth upon impact. But the subsequent verses 14- 17 tells us that stars (How many? We do not know) that fell upon the earth did not do much damage nor destroyed the land and its inhabitants because people are still alive and experiencing great difficulties and wanted to die but did not, as stated;

> "14Then the sky receded as a scroll when it is rolled up, and every mountain and island was moved out of its place. 15And the kings of the earth, the great men, the rich men, the commanders, the mighty men, every slave and every free man, hid themselves in the caves and in the rocks of the mountains, 16and said to the mountains and rocks, "Fall on us and hide us from the face of Him who sits on the throne and from the wrath of the Lamb! 17For the great day of His wrath has come, and who is able to stand?""

The sixth seal describes a great cosmic disturbance including the sun not giving its light on earth, the light of the moon become like a blood, and the stars falling on earth. If the science of astronomy and physics (astrophysics) is correct, then the Bible is a lie. If man is correct, then the God of the Bible is false.

But most of the premise of the sciences of man are just based on unverifiable assumptions (inconclusive observation or just pure imagination). It cannot be truly measured or in the strictest definition of scientific methodology, it cannot be tested, nor can an experiment be conducted again to verify their hypothesis or conclusion.

All of these are simply theoretical explanations or assumptions, meaning they are not necessarily based on concrete evidence. They are empirical assumptions used to create human-made knowledge, which may seem true but are ultimately just make-believe ideas generated by the human mind. Additionally, these assumptions are based on scientific theories, which are also speculative in nature. In short, they are just theories without any supporting evidence.

But why do people believe in all these theories and make it as a doctrine? Like making idols from wood and worship it. Is this not pure foolishness and stupidity?

So, everything is based on lies upon lies and fantasy of man. Even our history is also full of lies. By common sense, much scientific knowledge can be disproven easily. Yes, there may be true science, but many are pseudo-science which is a belief-at-will by the so-called authorities or experts or the so-called wisemen according to their propaganda and agenda. Science is not a god nor it is an absolute truth because everything are just based on the motives of the one creating the science.

Science can easily be manipulated at will. And never in a lifetime this statement become so obvious than the times of the scamdemic, if one just thinks and know how to ask questions. Everything in the scamdemic sciences are pseudo-science. From the science of virology, to the pandemic of PCR testing which gives 90% false positive (because it is not designed to diagnose a particular disease), to the use of mask (which are not intended to use in preventing virus in the first place as written in the label on the box), to the unreasonable lockdowns to bring down the global economy to a halt and then transfer the wealth of the ordinary people to the global cabal and the 1% that the rich have doubled or tripled their wealth in just a single year. It is an unprecedented transfer of wealth in human history. All are just based on a make-believe system, even defying the real science just to push an agenda. A pure deception at best in human history. Mankind destroying itself.

So, which are we going to believe? Our faulty brain or the One saying He created all things.

Yeshua (Jesus Christ) said in Jeremiah 17: 9-10;

"⁹"The <u>heart is deceitful above all things</u>, and <u>desperately wicked</u>; who can know it?

¹⁰I, <u>the Lord, search the heart, I test the mind</u>, even to give every man according to his ways, according to the fruit of his doings."

And in 1 Corinthians 3: 18-20;

"¹⁸Let no one deceive himself. If anyone among you seems to be wise in this age, let him become a fool that he may become wise. ¹⁹For <u>the wisdom of this world is foolishness with God</u>. For it is

43

written, "He catches the wise in their own craftiness"; [20]and again, "The Lord knows the thoughts of the wise, that they are futile.""

Indeed, the thoughts of the wise, the so-called experts, geniuses, and authorities in their fields are futile and intends to deceive and destroy humanity. The God of the Bible just allow mankind to continue in their foolishness and to made-up their own ways to their demise because of their refusal to recognize the true living God who created all things. Just as it is written in Genesis 6: 5;

> "[5]Then the Lord saw that the wickedness of man was great in the earth, and that every intent of the thoughts of his heart was only evil continually."

The time is coming that God will punish humanity once again and poured out His wrath upon the earth like in the times of Noah. But this time with fire. If still you do not fear and tremble upon the power and great authority of the God of the Bible who created all things and think that He is always a loving and forgiving God even though humanity continue in their evil ways, then just read Daniel and Revelation, and see if God will allow mankind to desecrate/defile His creation continually.

FEAR GOD!

Plants and Animals

The second proof of God's creation are plants and animals. On the third day of creation (also recreation – renewal of the face of the earth), God created the vegetations of the earth in Genesis 1: 11-13;

> "[11]Then God said, "Let the earth bring forth grass, the herb that yields seed, and the fruit tree that yields fruit according to its kind, whose seed is in itself, on the earth"; and it was so. [12]And the earth brought forth grass, the herb that yields seed according to its kind, and the tree that yields fruit, whose seed is in itself according to its kind. And God saw that it was good. [13]So the evening and the morning were the third day."

So, on the third day, God renewed the face of the earth (Psa. 104:30) because the earth was under water (Gen. 1:2) as a result of Lucifer and the earth's inhabitant's rebellion against God. He commanded the seeds of grasses, herbs, and fruit bearing trees that are already on earth from the previous creation of the earth to germinate/sprout and brings forth fruits and vegetables as food and shelter for the animal kind and mankind that He created on the fifth and sixth day. Take note once again that the sun, moon, and stars have not been created yet until the fourth day. But the seeds from the earth sprouted because there is already day and night. Remember that there is already light and darkness cycle upon the waters even before the creation of Heaven (firmament).

Are there any other gods (idols) of this world who can claim that they created every species of herbs, grasses, and fruit trees to feed the inhabitants (including animals) of the earth?

There is none that I know of. Every idolatrous book that I read is all about selfishness, pride, and violence against fellowmen and hostility against the God of the Bible. Some books of major religions copied or imitated the Bible in mockery of the word of God. The mockery of the Creator abounds in these books that man, as inspired by Satan have written. And as we know from history and what is happening now, everything leads to misery and sufferings. Disobedience and disregarding the real God only leads us to human suffering. And yet mankind continues to follow the same course or path over and over again. It seems that there are no solutions to problems humanity have been facing sense the beginning of time because we refuse to acknowledge God's solution to the chronic problems mankind is experiencing.

Just think about human health. Mankind prepares to heal themselves with man-made medicine coming from concoction of toxic chemicals rather than natural medicine prepared by God for His creation. And because human made medicine is based on greed and deceptions of the big pharma, mankind continues to suffer from a never-ending sickness and diseases making mankind dependent on the medical industry created by some savvy businessman who created a business model making mankind as his cash cow.

Despite the technological and scientific advancements in the field of the medical industry, still people suffer tremendous sickness and diseases. It seems people can no longer live without prescription drugs or the so-called maintenance medicine. People become dependent to drugs for their "health." A very good business model for the pharmaceutical industry.

Let us take a look at the cancer industry. Whether one has real cancer or not, the doctor (depending on his financial needs) will subject its patient to a chemotherapy. A procedure that has been done for many decades and have killed millions upon millions of people. And yet for whatever reason, people still allow their loved ones to be murdered slowly in front of their very own eyes until they are bankrupt. They paid doctors or hospitals to torture their loved ones to their death when in fact there are proven and effective natural ways to cure their sickness and diseases.

When I say cure, I mean totally irradicate the problem and not just the symptoms. Because the approach is from the inside out and not from the outside in. Natural healing process begins from the root cause of the problem and not just the symptoms. That is how God's healing medicine can do to our body.

But the governments around the world being owned and operated by the cabals remotely is also under the grasp of one of their tentacles which is the big pharma. The governments and the big pharma are in collusion to demonize the natural medicine coming from God's creation such as plants and animals and call those who practice and believe such natural healing power of God's creation - a quack doctor. But on the contrary the governments and the big pharma are the real quack doctors because they promoted concocted medicine made from toxic chemicals and even including human component such as fetal cells from aborted fetuses to temporarily relieve the symptoms and then create dozens of sicknesses and diseases as side effects from their concoctions or potion as it is called in witchcraft or sorcery to continuously feed their business model and control humanity.

In fact, humanity is so programmed that people become

hopeless in their sickness and diseases without the big pharma. They do not even bother to look for alternative even they know that the very medicine they are going to take from the big pharma will get them sicker or even kill them eventually. Humanity is in mass psychosis that they can no longer think of other solution than the one provided by the big pharma and sponsored by the government.

The natural medicine that has been used and have been proven to be safe and effective for thousands of years have become the alternative medicine. Natural medicine has been driven to the ground almost to its extinction. If ever it is available in the counter, it is labeled food supplement. They cannot claim their intended purpose of healing. Their natural cure target is hidden so that people will have no idea of its benefits. By this, people are so deceived into believing that only the so-called science-based medicine of the pharmaceutical industry are safe and effective.

Little did they know that this big pharma whom they put their health and lives upon are repeat offender criminals. Many times, these big pharma are repeatedly convicted of their crimes against humanity and fined by the billions of dollars. But even if they are fined two billion dollars and their annual income is $13 billion, they still have a whopping profit. That is their business model at the expense of human lives. Everything is priced in.

But why can they every so often and openly repeat their crimes against humanity without remorse or accountability?

Because the governments allowed them to be. Politicians are in their pockets and are selected by their master in Rome.

But what are their crimes you may ask? The pharmaceutical industry particularly the big pharma are in the habit of releasing products (so-called medicine) in the market with their pseudoscience experimental results (if there is any) and the governments approved these products to be legally sold for public consumption (like the covid jab). Then a few years later, they are found out that their products are harmful if not deadly to individual using it. But millions are already damage if not dead. We were taught to believe that it was science-based medicine if it comes from big pharma as conformed, attested, and verified by the approving body of the governments. But they are convicted criminals and not just a conspiracy theory.

Pharmacy comes from a Greek word *Pharmakeia* which means the use of drugs or medicines, sorcery, witchcraft. Other meaning includes poisonous potion; magic (potion). And yet they become so powerful that every human being put their trust and hope in their potion.

In the case of the cancer industry, one oncology himself realize that this chemotherapy procedures have 97% failure rate of curing cancer. Why? Because it is a concoction of harmful chemicals that poison the body of the victim slowly. It targets to poison the so-called cancer cell (if ever it is true) regardless of how it poisons and destroy the healthy cells of the body which is responsible for creating the natural immune system to fight the sickness or diseases of the body. Chemotherapy sporadically poisons the whole body like carpet bombing the whole landscape to destroy the ecosystem of the body. So as the chemotherapy spreads in the body by injecting these poisons every month, eventually the organs of the body give up because the liver, pancreas, and kidneys can no longer detoxify the body from the bombardment of these poisons. The result is death. And yet people fall into this scam repeatedly because this murder is legalized by the governments of the world. They just say, "believe in science" as if science is their god. People who allowed themselves to be victimized by this medical procedure are ignorant that they have become part of the insanity of this world. Insanity according to Albert Einstein is "doing the same thing over and over and expecting different results". And people love it.

People are so programmed to believe on the "science" of medical industry as if it is the only hope. Not knowing that it is one of the institutions owned by the Vatican to depopulate the earth to execute their agenda through their gimmick of "climate change" towards their great reset.

But there are many natural and proven cure for cancer that has been demonized by governments and the "science" of big pharma because they are the only true science, or they are the science (god) as they say. One of these cures is the Laetrile otherwise known as amygdalin or vitamin B17. Its most potent source is the apricot seeds. There are many more source of vitamin B17 such as apple seeds, grains: millet, buckwheat, barley, and flax, nuts: almonds, cashews, and macadamia, and many others. This Laetrile have been used by doctors and have been proven to cure cancer since 1840's in Russia and 1920's in the US. But the US being the god of the medical industry, demonized Laetrile and published their scrupulous fake studies declaring it as poisonous or causing toxicity in the body. The US give extra effort in insuring that it will not be available to the public in the US by banning it like illegal drugs. And they succeeded. But it is available in Mexico and still being used to cure cancer to this day. The question is why they can literally irradicate a substance that can benefit the people while they cannot do it to illegal narcotics. If they can totally eradicate the use of Laetrile and other potential natural cures through their effective policies and policing, then why can they not do it to illegal drugs (narcotics)?

Your answer could be as good as mine.

Nevertheless, in the Philippines, we have several plants or herbs that have potential cancer curing ability such as banaba, guyabano, etc. But the so-called experts in their propaganda will tell you or warn you against using those natural remedy to cure cancer. Why? Because even though those plants have been found through actual research or studies to have potential to slow, prevent or cure cancer, the gods of science will tell you that it has not been studied in humans. Therefore, there is no evidence of its safety or efficacy.

Yah, right! Because those who have been taking those herbal medicines for thousands of years are animals and not humans. And those who have been cured by those herbal medicine are not humans. But their drugs, oh, they are the best and have been studied in clinical trials and have been found safe and effective (on paper). The results of their studies are published in a fear reviewed scientific or medical journals. So, therefore their drugs are "safe and effective"? We are made to believe that their studies, when they are the ones who conducted it is reliable and true as if scientific studies and data cannot be manipulated. Not to mention those scientific or medical journals are funded by them, therefore it is directly influenced by them.

So, the government approve them and release these drugs to

the consumer as safe and effective drugs because it comes from "them". But lo and behold, after a few years of humanity using their drugs, it is found out that it is harmful to human body causing dozens of terrible side effects and death triggering class action lawsuits. Of course, the plaintiff wins in the so-called court of law because the evidence is so obvious. So, the criminal big pharma paid billions of dollars to the plaintiffs. The victims are paid $100 each while the law firm who represented them earned millions if not billions. But who knows if the law firm who represented the victims is indirectly owned by big pharma? And who knows if the purported victims are real or not? Or are they dummies of the big pharma also? Because who will participate in such shenanigans just to get a few hundred dollars that almost cost your life. We do not know.

But at the end of all of this, ... and the winner is! "Big Pharma"!

Although in reality, in the eyes of the law they are criminals, the illusion of them paying the victims portray them as sober and saints. Are they?

After a few years when the issue has cool off already, they (gov and big pharma) will release their new noble and breakthrough drugs as safe and effective. Then after a few years, people are dead if not getting sicker again. Then lawsuits. Then pay a billion dollars to the process, while pocketing tens of billion dollars in profit. The big pharma and the government make it as a cycle. It's just rinse and repeat. They do not care about human life or human health, everything is "priced in" in doing their business. What is important to them is their agenda. Their cash flow. Their business model is to make humanity dependent on them for their health needs. They are the gods of health and science, and humanity worship them.

Although this big pharma are convicted criminals, never in medical history have the government raided their laboratories or have closed their businesses. They continuously do their business as if nothing happened. And as if tens if not hundreds of billions of dollars of annual earnings from their so-called legal drugs is not enough, they create a special cash cow of pandemic. They even have the audacity to tell humanity that depending on the dictates of the market (the pandemic scam they have created) that they can create a drug on the fly at the "speed of science". Even though their drugs (Cov 19 vaccine, etc.) have not been studied or tested in humans (no clinical trials as admitted by the maker) as they normally say when attacking or demonizing natural medicine, still, together with their government cohorts, they tyrannically terrorize humanity into forcing them to accept the deadly injection. That is not to mention that these injections, test kits, and other scamdemic paraphernalia have been prepared years before the official starting date of the scam (see the Plan at stopworldcontrol.com). Now, millions have died and tens if not hundreds of millions are suffering from the irreversible side effects of this deadly injection. Yet no raid in their laboratories or businesses have occurred and the carnage continue.

Meanwhile when a clinic owned by a conscientious doctor that are really and truthfully trying to do their best to help human health by offering natural cure or the real safe and effective medicine, then the government will raid their clinic in full battle gear as if they are raiding a battalion of terrorist doctors. Although these doctors have not killed a single patient but actually given their patients a better life through better health, they are handled like criminals. Unlike those hospitals, doctors, and big pharma who actually killed millions and damaged the health of the many millions of people from their fake medicines and quackery and earned billions from their criminal activities. The governments of today are controlled by business entities and not by its people. The so-called democratically elected officials are serving the interests of their master puppeteer and its businesses rather than the people. Democracy is demagoguery. It is a fake freedom.

We are made to believe that "we, the people" is the government. But, in reality, the government are those who govern. Those who are in power to control the people according to their whims and agenda. We are the governed, the slaves. We go to work and pay our taxes. The corrupt government line up their pockets with our money. They create projects or developments in an illusion that they are doing something or cared for our welfare, but in reality, all those projects are riddled with corruption upon corruption. That is why the price tags are so high. Then it became the norm, and we have no choice but to accept the fact and say, "it is better to have a project, just don't pocket everything". We are desperate and hopeless because we have no power to police these scrupulous politicians. We just live in an illusion that in democracy the people have the power over the government, but in reality, they have the power over us. They dictate what they want us to do (knowingly and unknowingly). And this is proven how the governments of this world have treated its people during this scamdemic. Governments of this world sang like a choir following every beat of their conductor (Vatican through WHO) somewhere. Governments of this world is like a private company funded by the public (the slaves).

The Bible said that the end times will be full of lawlessness and unrighteousness. Glorifying the evil and demonizing the good. They declare evil for good and good evil. Just as it is written in Isaiah 5:20;

"[20]Woe to those who call evil good, and good evil;

Who put darkness for light, and light for darkness;

Who put bitter for sweet, and sweet for bitter!"

For thousands of years, mankind has used plants as source of medicine and people are healthy. But after a businessman named Rockefeller played god to control and profit from the health of humanity, natural medicine have been demonized and even banned. Homeopathic medicine has been demonized and even outlawed for a while. Doctors become the gods of healing, when in fact they are just a barker of the medical establishment. Yes, doctors can prescribe those pills and have cured a symptom, but the extent of curing one symptom resulted in dozens of diseases in a short term and long-term side effects. And not to consider that the education of doctors is not about human health but pharmaceutical education. And they have succeeded in deceiving humanity that people look at doctors as god. People was so programmed to just put their trust in the medical industry. People are so lazy to study and know their own personal health. They put their trust in man rather than God who gives us all the benefits coming from plants and animals as a source of our food and healing.

People rather swallow the readily made concoction of chemicals because of the belief that it is made by science but naively consider that it is an industry. A business not of healing, but a business that thrives on making people sick and miserable.

So, plants and animals are proof of God's creation. It has great benefits for us as food and for healing. But Satan, being the god of this world demonized every creation of God to deceive humanity. He created genetically modified plants such as corn, potato, etc. to project the illusion of high yield food production. Satan invented a lot of harmful chemicals that are being sprayed in the air/sky and in the plants adding to the already sick society. Animals are injected with many harmful chemicals such as antibiotics, growth hormones, and sex reversal feeds.

Satan has succeeded in destroying humanities mental capacity to think by programming because he is the prince of the power in the air. That is why the world is full of sufferings and misery. Humanity cannot solve even our most simple problem without fighting against each other. People are divided because that is what Satan wants us to be. If we are divided, we are easily conquered. And we have no way of uniting because we have nothing to cling to unite us. But the God who created us, who give us plants and animals for our benefits is the only one who can bind us together to be able to see beyond the illusion of the deceptions of Satan.

But mankind love Satan (knowingly and unknowingly) rather than the true living God who created us all and provided everything we need. That is why we are cut off from God. We are on our own for now. We love to have freedom to do whatever we want to do. But since our heart is deceptive above all things and desperately wicked (Jer. 17: 9), our actions apart from God are self-destructive. But when Jesus Christ comes back and replace Satan as the ruler of this world, He will rule us with the rod of iron to force us to have peace, become healthy, happy, and have an abundant living by departing from our evil ways under the influence of Satan.

Now, back to the marvelous wonders of plants that God have

created for us and all living organisms as a source of food, shelter, and clothing. Every living organism depends on plants. From microorganism to beasts on the land and great monster under the sea. Without plants, the earth will not be a livable land anymore. And as plants intake carbon dioxide as their food, it gives off oxygen. So aside from the great benefits God purposed the plants to serve for His creation, it is also like a janitor of the planet. It cleans the air we breathe even in our own living spaces inside the house if we have house plants. There is plant also that can clean up water in the river and in the sea. God purposed every kind of plants for the benefits of mankind.

God is so great beyond measure and understanding, even just to look at how He made the plants. The intricacies of plant design are incomprehensible. The beauty and functions for which He purposed the plants for the benefits of mankind and animal kind is a signature of a ultra-supreme (in comparison to human mind) being. Plus, the many thousands of plant species with different design is a proof of a great hands that made it. In plants alone, we can see the marvelous power and glory of a God who created it. The majesty of God can be seen in the beautiful flowers with various colors and shape.

Although we pretend to know through our so-called plant sciences (botany and biology) how plants live and function such as how plants produce food through sunlight and chlorophyll called photosynthesis, how the plants transport water and nutrients (transpiration) through their vascular vessels called xylem and phloem, how it reproduces from pollination to flowering and then become fruit and bear seeds and germinate again into a new living plant are very intricate processes that we can just wonder how magnificently brilliant the designer/planner and maker of these things, is beyond measure.

Yet, humanity chose to ignore this Supreme Being even though we see the evidence of His existence through the plants that we see on a daily basis. We rather believe on our fellowmen rather than believe on the One who is above all things. Plants are real proof of the existence of God.

We need to take note or pay closer attention to the fact that God created the earth and the plant kingdom on the third day before

He created the sun, moon, and stars on the fourth day.

On the other hand, God created animals of the water and sea (sea creatures) and birds of the air (heavens) on the fifth day in Genesis 1: 20-23;

"[20]Then God said, "Let the waters abound with an abundance of living creatures, and let birds fly above the earth across the face of the firmament of the heavens." [21]So God created great sea creatures and every living thing that moves, with which the waters abounded, according to their kind, and every winged bird according to its kind. And God saw that it was good. [22]And God blessed them, saying, "Be fruitful and multiply, and fill the waters in the seas, and let birds multiply on the earth." [23]So the evening and the morning were the fifth day."

And on the sixth day, God created man and animals on land (earth) as stated in Genesis 1: 24-26;

"[24]Then God said, "Let the earth bring forth the living creature according to its kind: cattle and creeping thing and beast of the earth, each according to its kind"; and it was so. [25]And God made the beast of the earth according to its kind, cattle according to its kind, and everything that creeps on the earth according to its kind. And God saw that it was good.
[26]Then God said, "Let Us make man in Our image, according to Our likeness; let them have dominion over the fish of the sea, over the birds of the air, and over the cattle, over all the earth and over every creeping thing that creeps on the earth.""
And God declared to men He created in Genesis 1:29-31;

"[29]And God said, "See, I have given you every herb that yields seed which is on the face of all the earth, and every tree whose fruit yields seed; to you it shall be for food. [30]Also, to every beast of the earth, to every bird of the air, and to everything that creeps on the earth, in which there is life, I have given every green herb for food"; and it was so. [31]Then God saw everything that He had made, and indeed it was very good. So the evening and the morning were the sixth day."

Is not the creation brilliantly planned and strategically executed?

The creation is not some random explosion of some kind of gas in the Big Bang Theory. From the unknown space that out of chaos comes order by itself resulting in a very organize flora and fauna of the earth and then through millions or billions of years a monkey or a gorilla or a chimpanzee evolve into a human being through their Theory of Evolution. And many people believe these theories until now and take it us a gospel or as truth even in a very sense it is a theory —just a guess without proof. Many people trust in men rather than in God.

But the Biblical order of creation will show us that there is a Master planner of everything. The Biblical account of creation makes more sense than just a random explosion out of human imagination. We cannot fathom God's mind because we are just His creation. Just as God said in Isaiah 45: 9-10;

> "[9]"Woe to him who strives with his Maker!
>
> Let the potsherd strive with the potsherds of the earth!
>
> Shall the clay say to him who forms it, 'What are you making?'
>
> Or shall your handiwork say, 'He has no hands'?
>
> [10]Woe to him who says to his father, 'What are you begetting?'
>
> Or to the woman, 'What have you brought forth?' ""

God declared in Genesis 1: 29-30 that plants and animals was created for man. But for plants to grow, there should be light and darkness, there should be water and there should be a land by which plants will grow. For animals to live there should be plants to eat. And for mankind to live, there should be plants and animals for food, clothing, and shelter. There is an order of creation because one creation will depend on another creation. Just as it is written in Psalms 104: 10-28;

> "[10]He sends the springs into the valleys; they flow among the hills. [11]They give drink to every beast of the field; the wild donkeys quench their thirst.
>
> [12]By them the birds of the heavens have their home; they sing among the branches.
>
> [13]He waters the hills from His upper chambers; the earth is satisfied with the fruit of Your works. [14]He causes the grass to

grow for the cattle, and vegetation for the service of man, that he may bring forth food from the earth, [15]and wine that makes glad the heart of man, oil to make his face shine, and bread which strengthens man's heart.

[16]The trees of the Lord are full of sap, the cedars of Lebanon which He planted, [17]where the birds make their nests; the stork has her home in the fir trees.

[18]The high hills are for the wild goats; the cliffs are a refuge for the rock badgers.

[19]He appointed the moon for seasons; the sun knows its going down.

[20]You make darkness, and it is night, In which all the beasts of the forest creep about.

[21]The young lions roar after their prey, and seek their food from God.

[22]When the sun rises, they gather together and lie down in their dens.

[23]Man goes out to his work and to his labor until the evening.

[24]O Lord, how manifold are Your works! In wisdom You have made them all. The earth is full of Your possessions—

[25]This great and wide sea, in which are innumerable teeming things, living things both small and great.

[26]There the ships sail about; there is that Leviathan which You have made to play there. [27]These all wait for You, that You may give them their food in due season.

[28]What You give them they gather in; You open Your hand, they are filled with good."

The creation is God's workmanship. The proof of His work and existence. And we should say just as verse 31 said;

"[31]May the glory of the Lord endure forever; may the Lord rejoice in His works."

Even we, humans, enjoy the works of our God. Just think about the beautiful fishes in aquariums (both big and small). How beautiful are the colors and the gracefulness of their movements. How marvelous are their sizes from the smallest to the biggest.

We have one of the smallest fish on earth called the Philippine goby (Pandaka pygmaea). We also have the biggest fish on earth called Butanding or whale shark, which is a famous attraction in Donsol, Sorsogon southern Leyte, Palawan, Cebu and other places in the country. It is believed that we are home to over 1,950 whale sharks, making it the second-largest known whale shark population in the world.

Our seas abound with so many fish in due seasons. Each kind according to each season. Fishes in the isles are so abundant that even though so many fishermen are fishing, the seas are still teeming with fish to catch. But sometimes fisherman cannot catch fish not because the sea is overfished that it runs out of fish but because God designed it to be that we should balance our diet with vegetables and meat from beasts (cows, etc.) and other animals. The supply of fish is not a problem as projected by those fearmongering godless people. The problem lays on the prices of the fish because of human greediness of the so-called law of supply and demand. We created (an idol) a lie and believe it is true. And because of this lie, prices of oil by which almost everything depends on can easily be manipulated. Even though there is no shortage of oil (as they have been barking for decades that the global reserve will be depleted by so and so years), still member countries of OPEC just connive to manipulate oil supply. The pressure in oil wells have not decreased since they started pumping. They just want to project that oil is a limited supply so that they can prop up the price every year. But each year, oil reserves can be found everywhere in the world and not just Middle East as previously projected to man. Petroleum oil is not a fossil fuel. It is God's gift to mankind as it is proven to be like a river replenished on a daily basis.

A Saudi prince said to himself that the supply of oil is like a river, contrary to what the so-called experts said that the middle east oil supply should have been depleted a few decades ago. But the pressure in their oil wells remained the same.

Let us not go farther away, let us just look at Malampaya gas field in Palawan. Their operation started in 2002. It was projected that the supply will last for 10-15 years. It is already 2023 and they are still in operation. Then they proclaimed that it will be depleted by 2024 and then move it to 2027. But they can manipulate it according to their desired outcome based on their agenda of "global warming" which was found to be a hoax then changed into a "climate change" so that they will be safe. All in the name of their "social justice" agenda to control the world into their New World Order.

In other words, the idol of law of supply and demand is a belief system to manipulate prices according to the desire of the supplier. In reality, it is not valid but a made-up scenario. Supply can be horded and sell at a high price to satisfy mankind's greediness. In short, mankind is foolish enough to fool themselves.

Likewise, in human habitation, we are made to believe that the earth, because it is round, have a very limited land and resources. We are made to believe that the earth is overpopulated and approaching its limit. Thus, the need to depopulate the earth by whatever means. Then came the scamdemics in order push the deadly injections into the unsuspecting and naive humanity to reduce the population.

Governments of the world intentionally created cities and designed it to be overcrowded and then projected to the people that earth is overpopulated. But the fact is that, our present world can even hold double or triple of the present population of 8 billion people. There are many more land that are habitable that are not being used. All we have to do is managed it properly. In today's technology, even the desert can be agriculturally productive.

But even if these people propagating their propaganda that the earth is overpopulated is true, and the God of the bible is true who commanded mankind to fill the earth, can He not make a new world to expand the earth. Just like in history that told us that previously people live in the old world (Europe, Asia, and Africa) and then they discover the new world (North America, Central America, and South America) and the population expanded to it. I am not saying that this man-made history is true. I am just giving example on the power of God to create new land if He will because the sea is vastly infinite beyond measure. God gives us limitation to our reach both vertical and horizontal space. But He can make another "dry land" to appear in the sea if He will.

Satan wants us to believe that the earth is round and has finite resources and therefore he needs to depopulate his kingdom. Or he just wants to show to God his rebelliousness by killing and destroying His creation.

But the billionaires of this world particularly the software guy who giggles into vaccinating humanity specially the children are limiting or trying to ban ranching of animals for food because it causes climate change. Instead, they want to control the production of meat in their factories so that carbon dioxide emission of animals will be limited.

So, where is the meat coming from? It will be coming from the cultured fetuses of the aborted babies from their easily accessible and free abortion clinics.

These is contrary to what God have said in Genesis 1: 26 that men will have dominion to all that God have given them;

"26 "...let them have dominion over the fish of the sea, over the birds of the air, and over the cattle, over all the earth and over every creeping thing that creeps on the earth.""

And it is to them as food in verse 30;

"30 Also, to every beast of the earth, to every bird of the air, and to everything that creeps on the earth, in which there is life, I have given every green herb for food"; and it was so."

To the satanic cult of climate change, cows cause global warming because of their dung. What a propaganda. But people believe and love it.

Nevertheless, animals aside from being source of food are also source of joy as house pet and as source of education in a zoo. Domesticated animals have many benefits to mankind as farm animals and transportation.

How God designed and purposed animals for the benefits of mankind is a marvel in itself. Each species of animals is invaluable to humans and environment. Each has its own role to play as it balances the ecosystem. Some animals pollinate the flower for the continuation of life, and some disperses the seeds to help wildlife flourish. Herbivore animals eats plants and grasses and in turn produces carbon dioxide to be used by plants for their growth and produce oxygen in the process which is needed by man and animals. This intricate relationship of plants, animals and men are like a spider web that needs to be taken care of. One missing link in the system will cause a detrimental effect to the ecosystem. So, if the cult is accusing cows and other ruminant animals are causing global warming (now climate change, previously called the "coming ice age"), what will be the catastrophic event that will happen if the beasts on the field are gone?

Plants and animals are created by God for the benefits of humanity. It is up to us to discover its benefits. Sometimes it comes to us in an instinct like food. But others we need to discover those healing power of God's creation. But Satan wants us to believe that those creation of God are useless. Satan wants to make humanity to be dependent on his manufactured foods and medicine so that he can easily manipulate human health and thinking. And governments of this world are the instruments of Satan to achieve his will.

As a proof of these satanic overreach by the government, there is a documentary produced by Gravitas in 2012 and published in November 3, 2022 titled Farmageddon in Youtube (I wonder why it is still on line and not censored yet). In their description, it states that, "The story of a mom whose son was healed from all allergies and asthma after consuming raw milk, and real food from farms. It depicts people all over the country (US) who formed food co-ops and private clubs to get these foods, and how they were raided by state and local governments.

"Farmageddon" tells the story of family farms who were providing healthy foods to their communities and were forced to stop by agents of misguided government bureaucracies."

In a very similar and recent event as reported May 2022, the US government raided and fined an Amish farm owned by Amos Miller in Pennsylvania for refusal to abandon traditional farming. A practice that did not do any harm for hundreds of years but instead give a healthy living. And during the pandemic, government is actively telling and coercing farmers to burn their produce and slaughter their farm animals.

Why would governments be very interested on how and what food people need to produce and eat if not for the purpose of demonizing humanity. And just as what Thomas Jefferson said;

"If people let the government decide what foods they eat and what medicines they take, their bodies will soon be in as sorry a state as are the souls of those who live under tyranny."

And tyranny happens according to him;

"When government fears the people, there is liberty. When the people fear the government, there is tyranny."

The governments of the world are now ruled by tyrannical people. And all forms of government be it democracy or communism paved the way to these tyrannical regimes. Now the people fear the overreach of the government.

But what can we do to alter this status quo? Thomas Jefferson added;

"Whenever any form of government becomes destructive of these ends [life, liberty, and the pursuit of happiness] it is the right of the people to alter or abolish it, and to institute new government..."

Yes, it is our right. But can right alone cause the change? No. Our enemy is so powerful that what God said in this end times that the fight according to Paul in Ephesians 6: 12;

"¹²For we do not wrestle against flesh and blood, but against principalities, against powers, against the rulers of the darkness of this age, against spiritual hosts of wickedness in the heavenly places."

Yes, we can bear arms and fight these evil governments and have a bloody revolution, but can we win the war? Certainly not. Why? Because we are fighting against spiritual principalities and flesh cannot overcome the spirit. Just as it is written Matthew 26: 40, saying;

"⁴⁰ "...The spirit indeed is willing, but the flesh is weak.""

So, what God commanded us to do in this evil world? Verse 13 of Ephesians 6 told us to;

"¹³Therefore take up the whole armor of God, that you may be able to withstand in the evil day, and having done all, to stand."

We can only attain in establishing the Ophirian Kingdom and replace our wicked and satanic government if we put the whole armor of God. The fight begins with our own wickedness before we can fight the evil principalities and rulers of our country. Our primary interest is to win our land to God and to perform the works that God have appointed us to do in this end time. Our work does not include for us to change the world, but it is of God. Our primary work is to preach the Gospel of Jesus Christ in all the earth. It is up to God to shake the wickedness out of His land and of this world.

It seems impossible, but with God, nothing is impossible.

Mankind

We are the proof that a Supreme Being (God) exist. Our body is a supreme masterpiece because we are created according to His own image (Gen. 1: 27). In His own image mean "kawangis o kamukha" and not an exact duplicate nor exact nature and characteristics. In other words, we are molded according to His forms but can have many variations in terms of physical characteristics such as color, built, and physical and mental capacity. Therefore, we can be sure that God exist because we exist as a living proof of Him in His image. But we are created a little lower than the angels as stated in Psalms 8: 4-5, saying;

"⁴What is man that You are mindful of him, and the son of man that You visit him?

⁵For You have made him a little lower than the angels,…"

Our body is an extremely complex creation. Our eyes alone is a great wonder to behold. Although humanity have tried and theorize how our eyes works, we can only try to explain in a limited way the intricacies on how our eyes work. Our science can only explain a little because the God who created us give us a limited mind. Just as Job 11: 7-8, said;

"⁷"Can you search out the deep things of God?

Can you find out the limits of the Almighty?

⁸They are higher than heaven—what can you do?

Deeper than Sheol—what can you know?"

We do not have the capacity to know the things that God have not given us the capacity to know. Similarly, we cannot have the capacity to go where God does not allow us to go. We have limits both in mind, body, and earthly territories (we are bound with certain limits (Psalms 104: 9, Acts 17: 26). We can make standards, definitions, hypotheses, and theories based on our limited capacity to think (conceive and conceptualize), but we can never fully understand or fathom what God have created nor the nature of Him. Our conception, perception, and perspective about our human body and the world by which we live in is either a folly trying to make ourselves believe on something, or we are just trying to make sense of things which we do not fully understand just to anchor our belief unto something, but in reality, we really do not understand because in Isaiah 40: 28, said;

"²⁸…His understanding is unsearchable."

And in Romans 11: 33 (NLT);
"³³Oh, how great are God's riches and wisdom and knowledge! <u>How impossible it is for us to understand</u> his decisions and his ways!"

That is why the God of the Bible is the real God, because we cannot fully understand nor comprehend Him, even His very word (the Bible) translated in many styles and languages. The many idol gods of this world can be easily understood and fathom its origin and purpose because man made it. But the God of the Bible is indeed beyond understanding.

God exist because He is the One – the all-knowing – the omniscient, omnipotent, and the omnipresent One who said in His book – the Holy Bible which is the Word of God in I Chronicles 16: 25-26 (also in Psalms 96: 4-5), saying;

"²⁵For the Lord is great and greatly to be praised; <u>He is also to be feared above all gods.</u>
²⁶<u>For all the gods of the peoples are idols</u>, but <u>the Lord made the heavens.</u>"

There it is. All the gods of this world are idols. If not the God (the Father and the Son) of the bible, then it must be an idol. But we should remember and understand also that there are many religious denominations who professed to believe in the God of the bible and yet their practices and traditions are pagan in origin and are contrary to God's laws of the bible. Those are called counterfeit or prophesying Christianity created by Satan – the anti-Christ.

Lucifer- Satan the Devil

But who created these idol gods?

There are only two principalities on earth: the real living God of the Bible and Satan who deceives the whole world (Rev. 12: 9). There is only one who wants to be God, to be worshipped and adorned and that is Satan. And since he wants to be worshipped, he introduces himself to unsuspecting human beings as the gods of this world through confusion of many religions. He deceives the whole world into worshipping and serving him knowingly and unknowingly through many confusing gods of this world.

Iniquity was found in Lucifer who later became Satan as it is written in Ezekiel 28: 14-15;

"14"You were the anointed cherub who covers; I established you; You were on the holy mountain of God; You walked back and forth in the midst of fiery stones.

15You were perfect in your ways from the day you were created, till iniquity was found in you."

Lucifer who later became Satan the Devil authored rebellion because sinfulness (iniquity) such as greediness, selfishness, envy, etc., etc. reigned in his heart. This iniquity he broadcast to humanity so that they may become like him. And Satan's declaration of his rebellion against the One who created him is documented in Isaiah 14: 12-14, saying;

"12"How you are fallen from heaven, O Lucifer, son of the morning! How you are cut down to the ground, you who weakened the nations!

13For you have said in your heart: 'I will ascend into heaven, I will exalt my throne above the stars of God; I will also sit on the mount of the congregation on the farthest sides of the north;

14I will ascend above the heights of the clouds, I will be like the Most High.'"

There it is, Lucifer who became Satan the Devil declaring he wanted to become and replace God. And to execute his sinister ambition he attempted to dethrone God by attacking Him in His habitation. But he did not even pass his fellow angels as stated in Revelation 12: 7-9;

> "⁷And <u>war broke out in heaven</u>: Michael and his angels fought with the dragon; and the dragon and his angels fought, ⁸but they did not prevail, nor was a place found for them in heaven any longer. ⁹So <u>the great dragon</u> was cast out, <u>that serpent of old</u>, called <u>the Devil and Satan</u>, who <u>deceives the whole world</u>; he was <u>cast to the earth</u>, and his angels were cast out with him."

As a result of this war, the first earth (which is also the second) perished as mentioned by Peter in 2 Peter 3: 5-6, saying;

> "'⁵For this <u>they willfully forget</u>: that by the word of God the <u>heavens were of old</u>, and the earth <u>standing out of water</u> and <u>in the water</u>, ⁶by which <u>the world that then existed perished</u>, being <u>flooded with water</u>."

Resulting into Genesis 1: 2;

> "²The earth was without form, and void; and darkness was on the face of the deep."

Satan is also a symbol of darkness. They (and his demons) were thrown back to earth as their prison and "reserve in everlasting chains under darkness (Jude 1: 6)". And God destroyed the face of the earth and its inhabitants thereof by submerging it under water and in complete darkness for how long we do not know. We can only have clue on the time the earth is under water because of the fossils of petrified trees, mollusks, and other fossils we can find in every place on earth. The sudden submersion of trees under mud and water and darkness for example preserve their imprint of their time. Examples of these are the Petrified Forest National Park in Arizona, Petrified Wood Park in Lemmon, South Dakota, and many other places in the United States. Petrified wood and fossils can also be found in Saudi Arabia, China and in almost all places on earth. These are evidence that there is a mighty powerful God who created and can destroy what He created. Fossils are evidence that a sudden cataclysmic event of flooding have occurred in the past like the Ichthyosaur fossil frozen in time while giving birth.

Petrification of trees is a very long process as we know it. And by this, we cannot say that the flood in the time of Noah caused these petrified trees to happen because the earth was only submerged under water for less than a year (human time). Plants and animals that are buried under the earth during the great flood of Noah is still subject to decay because of availability of oxygen to microorganisms that causes decomposition.

God destroy the first earth and its inhabitants through flood because Satan corrupted the earth when iniquity was found in Him. And just as Satan corrupted again the earth and God saw the wickedness of man once again in the time of Noah as stated in Genesis 6: 5, 11-12, God decided to destroy the earth once more through flood;

> "⁵Then the Lord saw that the wickedness of man was great in the earth, and that every intent of the thoughts of his heart was only evil continually.
>
> ¹¹The earth also was corrupt before God, and the earth was filled with violence. ¹²So God looked upon the earth, and indeed it was corrupt; for all flesh had corrupted their way on the earth."

So, it was the second time that God destroyed the inhabitants of the earth because of mankind's evil deeds. But the flood in the time of Noah did not cause the earth to perish because God saved the family of Noah and the animals with them.

But how can we be sure that the world that then existed as mentioned by Peter in 2 Peter 3: 6 perished with mankind in it?

Because Isaiah 45: 18 said;

> "¹⁸For thus says the Lord, Who created the heavens, Who is God, Who formed the earth and made it, Who has established it, Who did not create it in vain, Who formed it to be inhabited: "I am the Lord, and there is no other."

In other words, God created the earth perfect in its beauty (not in vain) with inhabitants in it, contrary to Genesis 1: 2 that it became "without form and void". The earth is populated with people prior to the rebellion of Lucifer. He was an angel of God. And angels according to Hebrew 1: 13-14 are ministers to those who will inherit salvation;

> "^{13}But to which of the angels has He ever said: "Sit at My right hand, till I make Your enemies Your footstool"?
> ^{14}Are they not all ministering spirits sent forth to minister for those who will inherit salvation?"

God sent Lucifer and a third of the angels of heaven to earth to minister the inhabitants of the first earth. Perhaps he is the king of the earth because Lucifer when iniquity was found in him said in Isaiah 14: 13;

> "^{13}...I will exalt my throne above the stars of God;..."

If he has a throne on earth, then he is the king of the earth. And being a king, he has subjects to reign to. Perhaps God made him the king of the earth so that he will lead mankind towards God through obedience to God's laws, ordinance, and covenant. He was supposed to be the angel of light to mankind. But when iniquity of envy was found in him because God is being worshipped by His creation, he deceives the whole world towards worshipping him instead – the creation rather than the Creator. He became the angel of darkness and the god and ruler of this world. As a result, mankind defiled the earth as stated in Isaiah 24: 5-6;

> "^{5}The earth is also defiled under its inhabitants, because they have transgressed the laws, changed the ordinance, broken the everlasting covenant.
> ^{6}Therefore the curse has devoured the earth, and those who dwell in it are desolate."

And as a result of mankind's transgression (disobedience) to God and their obedience to Satan, Isaiah 24: 1 said;

> "^{1}Behold, the Lord makes the earth empty and makes it waste,..."

In Hebrew it is *tohu* and *bohu* which means "waste and empty" just like how the earth is described in Genesis 1: 2 – "without form and void".

But after sometimes, God renewed the earth as it is written in Psalms 104: 30 saying;

"^{30}You send forth Your Spirit, they are created; and You renew the face of the earth."

Just as Genesis 1: 2 pictured the earth as it is submerged under water; "^{2}The earth was without form, and void; and darkness was on the face of the deep. And the Spirit of God was hovering over the face of the waters."

The renewed earth by which we live in is now what 2 Peter 3: 7 described as;

"^{7}But the heavens and the earth which are now preserved by the same word, are reserved for fire until the day of judgment and perdition of ungodly men."

That is why God give a covenant to Noah in Genesis 9: 11;

"^{11}Thus I establish My covenant with you: Never again shall all flesh be cut off by the waters of the flood; never again shall there be a flood to destroy the earth.""

But it is preserved for destruction through fire in the judgment day.

So, the existence of Satan and his demons that deceived the whole world (past and present) towards worshipping him knowingly and unknowingly is the very reason why there are too many sufferings, wars, violence, and wickedness in man as we are experiencing it today. The world is no longer a safe place to live in and indeed darkness have reign once again in the hearts of men. Satan as reflected in our society is a solid proof that God who created all things is real because He has a real enemy. The enemy of God is also the enemy of His followers in righteousness. Just as 1 John 3: 7-10 said;

"^{7}Little children, let no one deceive you. He who practices righteousness is righteous, just as He is righteous. ^{8}He who sins is of the devil, for the devil has sinned from the beginning. For this purpose the Son of God was manifested, that He might destroy the works of the devil. [9]Whoever has been born of God does not sin, for His seed remains in him; and he cannot sin, because he has been born of God.

[10]In this the children of God and the children of the devil are manifest: Whoever does not practice righteousness is not of God, nor is he who does not love his brother."

And in Ephesians 6: 10 – 13;

"[10]Finally, my brethren, be strong in the Lord and in the power of His might. [11]Put on the whole armor of God, that you may be able to stand against the wiles of the devil. [12]For we do not wrestle against flesh and blood, but against principalities, against powers, against the rulers of the darkness of this age, against spiritual hosts of wickedness in the heavenly places. [13]Therefore take up the whole armor of God, that you may be able to withstand in the evil day, and having done all, to stand."

In today's world, the governments of many nations have become the enemy of its own people. Satan deployed his demons in many leaders of this world that instead of making the lives of many to become abundant and at peace, they are the one making it more miserable in a very deceptive way. For instance, the recent scamdemic where many people died and are dying not from a virus that did not exist but from fear and desperation that the scam have caused. And as if that fearmongering of the governments to its people is not enough, the deadly vaccine (jab, if it qualifies for their old definition of vaccine) made another blow to the already confused and desperate people. The deadly jab killed many people almost in an instant even just a few minutes away from center where they are vaccinated. And then those who survived from the first blow suffered the irreversible adverse side effects in their body including infertility and those hard to utter medical conditions causing involuntary convulsion of the body, blood clotting, heart diseases and heart failures, myocarditis, etc. The rest of the vaccinated are suffering and are dying one by one that excess death data of 40%- 44% have never come down from the previous year's pre scamdemic era.

According to life insurance companies, they are experiencing 44% surge in their payment since the jab roll out. In their business model, 10% excess death means there is an extreme event that happened such as tornado, earthquakes, hurricane, etc., etc. It is a temporary event that give them loses and is enough to bankrupt small companies in the area hit by this disaster. But if the excess death is already at 40% to 44% it means that a catastrophic event has happened such as world war, nuclear war, or global cataclysmic event for this excess death to occur. But we know that there was no such event that occurred. The only cause of this massive excess deaths is the jab.

Could this be the clue of the billionaire software guy who wants to depopulate the earth through his jabs why he conducted the event called "Catastrophic Contagion" last October 23, 2022, to lunch his Pandemic 2.0? Remember, he is also the one who conducted the "Event 201" in November 2019 prior to Pandemic 1.0 and also conducted the monkeypox simulation event prior to its release in 2022.

He knows that catastrophic deaths are happening because of their genocide campaign against humanity through their injection. So, it is either he wants to hide from his crimes against humanity by launching Pandemic 2.0 scam or he wants to escalate the killing of people by introducing new deadly injection on the premise of what the propaganda they are doing right now (Dec. 2022) in China having a new covid surge infecting by the hundreds of millions (so it seems).

The mainstream media including the new ones (who have sold their soul to the devil) are constantly reporting that dead bodies in caskets and body bags are lining up to be cremated, hospitals and morgues are overwhelmed, and many other same old gimmickries as what China did at the start of the Pandemic 1.0 where people are falling on the street because of covid. Later it was found out that those are all staged.

But this software guy is hinting that Pandemic 2.0 is much severe that he said, "This time it will get more attention" as if Pandemic 1.0 that they created did not get much attention. What attention does he need? For the people to recognize and declare him as the god of the pandemics?

This pandemic 2.0 simulation of "Catastrophic Contagion" are planning to release their newly invented virus called SEERS defined as Severe Epidemic Enterovirus Respiratory Syndrome 2025 that will kill millions of children. Is this SEERS going to kill the children or the vaccine once again? And take note this so-called virus has an acronym of SEERS. Like a prophet perhaps? Or an all seeing god?

Take note also that this software guy profited a lot from the pandemic. He invested $50 million in the most popular vaccine of the pandemic and come out $200 million richer in just one year. He even bragged that his investment in vaccine is the most profitable investment he had ever done. He is laughing to the bank while people are dying from his deadly injections and are suffering economically.

How much attention or money does he need? The adverse effects of his deadly jab are too many to mention in this book if that is not enough attention to behold. One big pharma who manufactured such deadly injection listed a full nine pages of adverse side effects including death. This pharmaceutical company give this list when US FDA (their cohort) asks them how long they can furnish the safety data of their vaccine which they mockingly replied that it will take them 75 years to give the data. Is that how long will it take to experiment humanity of their deadly injection?

Did they not say that their vaccine is safe and effective (97%)? Where did they got those conclusions if they did not have data? Nowhere, because it is all a lie.

In fact, as an update, as of October 10, 2022 when European Parliament conducted a committee hearing on covid, a Pfizer executive (Ms. Small) admitted that their vaccine was not tested, therefore no evidence that the vaccine would or can stop transmission of the virus before releasing to the market. Tucker Carlson of the Fox News interviewed Rob Roos, a Member of the European Parliament who asked the Executive of Pfizer, "Was the Pfizer covid vaccine tested on stopping the transmission of the virus before it entered the market?"

The answer was emphatically and proudly "No". Additionally, she defended their action that they move their product to the market at the "speed of science". If there is such a thing. Is it not science based on observation and experimentation and data gathering as a proof of science?

Here is her exact answer.

"Regarding the question around, um, did we know about stopping the immunization [sic] before it entered the market? No, heh," she said.

"Uh, these, um, you know, we had to really move <u>at the speed of science</u> to really understand what is taking place in the market, and from that point of view we had to <u>do everything at risk</u>. I think Dr - the CEO (his name is not worth mentioning in this book), even though he's not here, would turn around and say to you himself, 'If not us then who?'"

Rob Roos called it scandalous. But since they (the government) are good at making up words and changing definitions on the fly, why not we call it "scamdalous"? Now the word scamdemic and plandemic become valid. Now we have two greatest scam of our time, the Covid 19 pandemic and climate change hoax.

This admission of the Pfizer executive corroborated the admission of their CEO in the early 2022 that their vaccine "offers very little protection if any" (*Censored Pfizer CEO video - #distributionbyproxy* by Banned Youtube Videos published January 12, 2022 at Bitchute.com). The same with their two booster kill shots. That is why he bragged they will create a new one. He added that, "This time it will be effective" and they have a large facility and will be able to manufacture this new vaccine and will be available by March, 2022.

See. Their science can easily say once again that, "This time it will be safe and effective" without the backing of actual data from clinical trials. They just "at will" grasp in the air and voila, they have a new safe and effective vaccine. They practice pseudoscience just how they use pseudo virus in the computer to test their deadly product.

And when asked regarding their vaccine data, the CEO said that they based their data from a pseudo-virus constructed in the lab (*Pfizer CEO (name): 'We base our data on pseudo-virus that we built in the lab.'* By "The Red Channel" published February 14, 2022 at bitchute.com). Right from the horse's mouth. And yet people love the lies and deceptions.

What? It will take sometimes to make a model of the virus in the computer than just grab it in the air because it is so deadly and highly contagious, and it is airborne. Or perhaps get it from the so called many cases or from the positive swab tests (PCR Test) or from the overwhelmed hospitals filled with covid 19 cases. The virus according to them is so contagious and deadly that even a person without a symptom can transmit it. They called it asymptomatic transmission. Then why use a newly programmed fake virus in the computer to gather their data for their vaccine? Simulation will take sometimes to develop and to gather data. It is not just a computer-generated image (CGI) to show how the virus looks like which is just an artist rendering and not an actual virus and then gather data from this imagination. So, instead of conducting a real clinical trial with real virus and real people (or animals), they worked at the "Speed of Science" using a computer program. Pure lies.

The reason why they cannot use real virus is because it does not exist. More than 200 Freedom of Information requests to 40 countries have been submitted asking for scientific proof or data showing the evidence that SARS-CoV-2 exist or have been isolated. But none have submitted proof or evidence of the virus. No government entity has any proof that the virus has been isolated and identified. In short, SARS-Cov-2 is a make-believe virus.

They magnified their scam by pure propaganda and torture using the PCR test to detect, identify, and diagnose a person of Covid 19 virus to perpetuate the illusion of a highly contagious and deadly virus. But the inventor of the PCR test said it cannot be used for diagnostic purposes nor can be used to identify a particular virus or bacteria. Dr. Kary Mullis (whom they killed (by mysterious death on Nov., 2019) prior to the scamdemic), the inventor of the PCR test said that it cannot be used for diagnosis of any infectious diseases nor can it tell that one is sick even if the test come out positive of whatever cycle the test is put into. It is just used to detect that a molecule exists in that substance being tested if it is amplified enough. But it can never identify what type or kind of molecules are being detected. The PCR test can detect molecules on anything of everything if it is amplified enough. The late Dr. Kary Mullis said.

All the government agencies and medical industry (or establishment) do not have and cannot show a proof that they have isolated the SARS-CoV-2 virus until now. Isolation of the virus takes years. Then, how come they will or can easily identify new variant almost on the fly almost every month? Again, they make an imaginary new variant at the speed of science (their science) at whim. They disregard any scientific literatures that proved that such evolution of virus in nature is impossible. It was all a hoax, fear mongering, and a test of world control as WEF confirmed. They make fun and fooled the people so hard by deep mind programming and brainwashing.

As an update (June 20, 2023) to this scamdemic, a video posted at bitchute.com entitled, *"Covid19 Scam - Dr. Scott Jensen - Mass Deletion of Propaganda (They Are Scrubbing It All...)"*, showed Senator Dr. Scott Jensen reading an article that wrote about the medical field or industry erasing their own Covid 19 era history. The article said that a group monitoring or tracking publications in scientific journals showed that a lot of original research and tests results are mysteriously disappearing. More than 300 papers and scientific articles have vanished in the past year.

These scientific papers published at major scientific and medical journals were used in their propaganda to create the illusion that the pandemic is real and science base to justify their lockdowns and protocols to oppress humanity and forcibly inject humanity with their fake and deadly injections for their depopulation agenda.

These are like the studies or papers referred to me by ChatGPT when I ask about the evidence or proof that SARS-CoV-2 virus have been isolated. ChatGPT give me four studies or published articles showing they have isolated SARS-CoV-2. All the articles are published in 2020.

By just looking at the year of publication, one who knows how to think can easily conclude that these are bogus articles/studies or publications. For how in scientific world one can isolate a virus or bacteria in less than a year. ChtGPT said that, "isolation is a complex process involving various techniques and methods. Isolation of a virus typically involves obtaining and purifying viral particles from infected individuals or cultures, which can then be used for further study and analysis."

Koch Postulates is the standard procedure for isolating any microorganisms and one year will not be enough to do these procedures. How much more writing a thorough scientific study for <u>peer review</u> and <u>publication</u> to a reputable journal?

Let us say, we get a sample from an infected person. Our body is not a monoculture of microorganisms. There are many kinds and strains of good and harmful microorganisms in our body. As one scientific fact said that one square inch of our skin is inhabited by 15 billion microorganisms. It did not mention how many hundreds or thousands of kinds, species, varieties, strains, etc. of microorganisms.

Just think about probiotics, it is already composed of many strains and billions of counts already. So, we need to isolate the microorganism we are looking from the nose swab we obtained from the infected person.

How do we isolate and identify the organism we are looking for, from the hundreds if not thousands of strains in our sample? Another problem is we do not know its actual form, shape, or characteristics. So, the only way of identifying the targeted microorganism is based on its <u>purported symptoms</u>. Let us just say, we have one hundred strains. So, we need to isolate each, and every strain found in the sample and introduced each strain to a healthy individual and see if they will exhibit the same symptoms under study. And say for the sake of shortening the conversation, we got a person that is infected and exhibit the symptoms that we are looking for, then, we will be able to characterize the organism from our previous sample. But then we need to isolate these organisms from our individuals that exhibited the symptoms. But this time it is easier because we know the characteristics of the microorganism we are looking for. Yet is will still take some time until purified sample are obtained. Maybe a few more infection to a healthy individual to verify and reverify that indeed the isolate is pure. But it is a leap of faith to do this because there are a lot of uncontrollable variables.

So, to say that a scientist was able to isolate microorganism (bacteria or virus) in just one year is purely deception and pseudoscience. Much more to say that a new variant can be identified almost every month because to say that a variant of one virus or bacteria to be identified need to undergo the same process of Koch Postulates. These are all lies.

Even Koch himself, the so-called father of virology is a liar because he is a criminal who killed a lot of people with his poisonous magic drug called Tuberculin. He was wanted in Germany for these crimes and deliberately hiding the ingredients of his deadly drug (*Germs Debunk Corona* by Spacebuster at bitchute.com). He himself did not and was not able to use the credited Koch Postulates to isolate any so-called virus which he stole the idea from Friedrich Gustav Henle. It was previously known as Henle's Postulates.

The same thing with the PCR testing. It cannot identify or diagnose a particular bacteria or virus because our nasal cavity is composed of hundreds if not thousands of strains of microorganisms. That is why the inventor of PCR Test – Kary Mullis said it is not and should not be used to diagnose any kind of disease. It can only detect molecules of any kind or anything but cannot be used to identify what kind.

This is the reason why the scientific, medical, and government industries are scrabbing their lies in their very own publications. This is like what the governments are doing in scrabbing and changing public data of deaths and adverse events to propagate their deceptions. These are the reasons why governments are refusing and ignoring to discuss the many sudden deaths occurring everywhere because of their injection.

This is how Satan worked on his deceptive moves to divide and kill humanity. (End of update)

Continuing…

Imagine that. They will be able to develop a new vaccine in less than two months while others develop and tested for ten years or more in clinical trials in the past. This is indeed a breakthrough at the speed of science. And because they have no isolate of the original virus (SARS cov 2) (which means it does not exist), they use pseudo virus (computer generated) in their experiments if ever they conducted it. Just imagine, a deadly and contagious virus which need to be avoided by social distancing of 6 feet and masking and yet cannot be captured or use an actual sample from the so-called millions of infected people to be use for their vaccine development (if ever it is true). This is not to mention that the so-called vaccine has been developed and patented years ahead of the scam. These things are not made up or a conspiracy theory (in the bad side), these are all coming from the horse's mouth and can be easily researched in stopworldcontrol.com and bitchute.com (if it still online). They themselves exposed their lies. And people swallow it sink, line, and sinker.

And lo and behold, even with this recent event of admission of Pfizer that they have not tested their vaccine for preventing transmission of the virus (if it exist) and the CEO itself admitted that it is not effective (Jan. 2022) and even as the death pile up including teens and children in the real world and as reported in the Vaccine Adverse Event Reporting System (VAERS – less than 1% reporting of actual) which are under the Center for Disease Control and Prevention (CDC) and Food and Drug Administration (FDA) of the USA, still, as of October 20, 2022, the CDC voted unanimously (15-0) for covid vaccination of children and even 6 months old baby. They will add these to the already long list of deadly vaccine schedule for children. These people are demonic to the core that they are committing genocide right in front of our very own eyes.

As an update (3-23), the same vaccine company have released their product that can cure a deadly and highly contagious C19 virus. Now their tablet can cure it. As their advertisement show, when one has fever, colds or cough, they need to buy their product because it might be covid. What a pure evil people.

Even though the VAERS data have been manipulated (reduced) by the very government who are supposed to protect the data and the reporting have almost stopped, still, there are conscientious doctors and scientist who are saying that even just one adverse event happened in the past, the vaccination program is halted immediately. But now, even there are tens of thousands already dead and millions are dying and/or suffering from the adverse effect of the vaccine as reported in VAERS, the government is still pushing for the vaccination of children, even the six-month-old. And later, even the newly born baby will be injected as the advertisement of the software guy who smirks as he openly gestures the injection into the veins of the children. This is of course in view of the illusion of saving the children or baby's life like he is a god. Even though several independent studies have been conducted by doctors and experts that showed how dangerous these vaccines are, still government are pushing these drugs to massacre its own people (just search *Vaxxed vs unvaxxed: US child vaccines are poison causing breathing, neuro & blood disorders?* in bitchute.com). This proves causation of the vaccines for children's adverse effects and even death.

But ultimately, their goal is to depopulate the earth to the "amount" of people as they wanted. I mentioned "amount" because to them (the New World Order (NWO) and World Economic Forum (WEF) people (if they are humans)), people are like their toys which they can manipulate (mRNA) or irradicate (through vaccine) as they wanted because according to them humans consume so many resources. They call them "useless eaters". As if they are gods and own the whole earth. The NWO and WEF are in the front of the Vatican's control to implement its One World Government and One World Religion.

Now, back to their safety data, when a court ruling ordered them that they should give the safety data in eight months, that is when they come out with the nine full pages of adverse side effects of their vaccine consisting of more or less 1,291 debilitating and sometimes deadly side effects. This is perhaps the list that could have been written in a very large piece of paper as an insert in the box of the vaccine that have nothing printed in it. Just a blank sheet of paper. The purpose of this paper inserts in every box of their products is to inform the user of that product of its side effects. It is called informed consent. So, a person should have read the insert of that vaccine prior to administering it to the patient. And even if the insert said that it can cause severe damage or death and the patient still consented that he/she be injected, then, the hospital, doctor or nurses, and the manufacturer are not legally bound by the adverse effect of the injection. But in the case of C19 vaccine there was no informed consent and was implemented by coercion and torture of a tyrannical government.

And that is not to mention that those boxes of the vaccine have been printed dated July 2017. And yet they have no informed consent inserts in their boxes. Only blank paper. Two years prior to the scamdemic they already have the vaccine boxes designed and printed. So are the test kits (PCR) and PPE's ordered by many country of the world as early as 2014. And yet governments around the world like the Philippines continue to peddle this deadly injection to its people. For sure many of them are part of the scam specially presidents and prime ministers and their death squad - the health department tentacles, hospitals, and doctors. Only a few leaders tried to protect their people from this deadly scam like India, some countries in Africa, and Brazil. In the Philippines, only Governor Gwen Garcia have shown opposition to the tyrannical regime of the administration. Her family is a direct victim of the medical industry and government's criminal activities. Her two brothers were killed by the medical industry and incentivized by the government.

These leaders are fully aware of how this big pharma and their god (the software guy or pedo), treated children like guinea pigs for their experimental injection (vaccines of many kinds). Many kids have been affected with irreversible side effects of their experiment. And yet this billionaire pedo guy is still at large and planning the next pandemic so that he can inject people including newborn babies with his newfound business as a medical god. He pretends and give the illusion that he cares for the health of humanity when in fact his goal is to kill as many human beings as possible and to get into their agenda of reducing the population of the world to half a billion (500M) as stated in the Georgia Guide Stone which they already destroyed to cover up their agenda. This person who pretends to protect human health is actually a eugenics believer (like his father) and he is experimenting humanity like human beings are his toys and property. The fruit of his work in playing god are deadly and devastating as experienced by India, Africa, Latin America, and the Philippines. And yet the leaders of this countries cover up this guy of his crimes through many legal means.

Now they have tried their experiment in full global scale through this covid scam. And this cabal recently admitted, this covid scam or plandemic is just a trial test or a test run.

For more or extensive explanations and evidence of this evil people agenda of depopulation, search Fallcabal at bitchute.com and stopworldcontrol.com for more information on what is happening on our world. And pay attention to their next scam – the cyber pandemic that will dwarf the outcome of the covid plandemic as announced by the head of snake of the World Economic Forum. Another man playing god. They create disaster and blame their enemy as their usual tactics or let's say antics. The videos in these websites may help every proud and arrogant Pilipino who pretends they know everything and yet know nothing. And now they are marching to their death because of their foolishness.

And even if the government of this world is just playing blind that nothing is happening, the continuous mysterious death (sudden death) or excess death is continuously high that governments called it SADS (Sudden adult death syndrome) in complete denial that healthy kids and athletes are also dying suddenly. Even if the governments are in complete denial, coroners, embalmers, and insurance companies are giving reports of unusual phenomenon of blood clotting or a coagulated unknown substance in the veins of the dead that they have a hard time injecting formalin into the body of the dead. Nowadays, they need to remove the substance from the veins manually or they need to inject the body preservatives in many different parts of the body rather than just one previously.

Meanwhile, on another scam, the climate change scam is based on the illusion that there are leaders who cares for the welfare of the earth's condition. Aside from these people (or demons) who does not believe or know God, their solutions are much more dangerous than what they are trying or pretend to solve which is the petroleum (by which they also own (petro-dollars)). They have been creating the illusion that there will be oil crisis because the oil deposits are limited. They projected previously that the world will suffer the scarcity of oil in the 1990's and yet it is already 2023 and the pressure in the wells of oil did not change. But they still create artificial shortage or crisis to manipulate the people's perceptions through wars. They paraded the lies of a greenhouse effect causing global warming brought by using petroleum in cars and energy production even to the point of blaming human consumption of beef to be the cause of their so-called global warming (change to "climate change" because the term is a hoax by all human scientific proof). Now the billionaire cabals (the tentacles of Vatican) are going to ban ranching of cows and even the normal agricultural production. Instead, they will produce every food that people will eat giving themselves complete control of every aspect of human life through their so-called carbon credit and the cashless society controlled by the global Central Bank Digital Currency (CBDC). In fact, there are billionaires who own big chunks of the US agricultural land. This is how Satan and the many upcoming plandemic will begin to control the world and implement its One World government or the New World Order (NWO) for their so-called "for the common good". And just as the World Economic Forum (WEF) admitted this September 2022, the Covid 19 hoax is just a test. They are playing a game on humanity and humanity bought into their game hook, lines, and sinker. And now millions have died and are dying from this deadly injection. Millions upon millions of people are suffering from the irreversible adverse effects and dying from sudden deaths.

Now, one or two uncensored (for now) platforms is in your fingertips to conduct your own research and prove it to yourself how Satan works in the life of men on earth. The only hindrance to the truth is one's cognitive dissonance of denying and not giving the new available information, the chance to have an informed decision or conclusion. But many will continue to believe what they want to believe because they are in denial that they have been wrong, fooled, or deceived even if is detrimental to their health.

Our educational system, the government, and the mainstream media have programmed us through their misinformation agenda to just believe what the so-called experts says and want us to do whatever they say even though our common sense dictates it is wrong. Similarly, in terms of religious prison houses, many will still believe on their religions even the God who created them have said, "all the gods of this world are idols". They will refuse or are too lazy to think for themselves and just wanted to be dictated of what they should believe or worship even if it will cost their soul.

Back to climate change hoax, their solutions such as windmills, solar panels, electric vehicles, etc., are much more destructive to earth in the long run than it solves the scam of petroleum-based economy in the name of carbon footprints. Batteries alone of the electric vehicles (EV) will cause a big catastrophic environmental problem in the very near future. Imagine, billions of unusable EV batteries lying somewhere in a dumpster or in a landfill leaking lead, lithium, and other rare earth metal juices (with unknown health effects) into our aquifers, creeks, rivers, lake, and eventually into the oceans. This is a real earth-shaking catastrophe in the making, more catastrophic than the feared danger of producing power through a nuclear power plant (more on this later) and the so-called anthropomorphic climate change because of the use of petroleum producing carbon dioxide deceptively projected to be the cause of global warming, thereby causing the flooding, stronger storms, earthquake, etc. Every environmental disaster is blamed into climate change forgetting or not knowing or they willfully ignore that there is a God who control all things including the weather. They willfully ignore that there is a God who punishes His creation because of their disobedience. God have set up a self-cleaning mechanism for carbon dioxide through grasses, oceans, plants, and even storm. Our carbon production is not even enough to touch an iota of the weather. But how human mismanaged the use of petroleum is what causes the pollution in our cities because of inefficient engines and disposal. Carbon dioxide is actually good for the planet because plants use it as their food.

On the other hand, too much carbon emissions in the cities are also detrimental to human health. But nature have its power to clean up this pollution. The storms are like janitors of the planet sweeping across all air pollution and bring it into the seas, and oceans and some are captured as food of the plants. But a dangerous chemical from batteries, spent solar panels, and broken windmill propellers seeping to our soil and into our drinking water and into the ocean, that is a formula for destroying the earth.

And if we look a little deeper at these people promoting this climate change hoax in the name of protecting the planet, they are the same people who wants to destroy the earth. This satanic people have DARPA at their disposal and spraying of Chemtrails in the atmosphere to control or influence the climate of the earth. This is called "solar geoengineering". The very people who cry for climate change is the very people destroying the earth by spraying the atmosphere with hazardous chemicals (chemtrails) that includes aluminum, and other heavy metals that affects our brain. It seeks to mask the effect of climate change by partially blocking the sun's rays from reaching the earth's surface.

Imagine if they succeed in blocking the sunlight from reaching the earth, and the natural ecosystem of the earth is altered, what is going to happen? Many species of plants and animals both in land and in water who have the natural power to sequester carbon dioxide and other pollutants produce by man will die off. Then their illusion of anthropomorphic climate change will become a reality blaming the carbon dioxide production/emission of man's fossil fuel consumption.

This destroyer/polluter of the earth is offering up false solutions to their false problems (climate change) such as the promise of geoengineering, solar panels, windmills, electric vehicles, banning farming and ranching, etc., etc. They want to solve the problem by introducing another problem. Pollution solution (geoengineering) for a pollution problem and climate change (chemtrails and DARPA) as a solution to climate change. Pandemic (of the vaccinated) solution to a pandemic problem (even though it is a hoax). More food production restrictions and regulations to a food production crisis. What an evil world we live in today.

Satan wants to depopulate the earth in direct disobedience to God's command to humanity to "go forth" and multiply and replenish the earth. Satan is making raising family as hard as it can be so that

God's wish of repopulating the earth will not happen. He is using governments of this world to implement his desire for the people to suffer and not be able to procreate as commanded by God. Through economic manipulation, a family will have a hard time raising kids.

Satan from his habitation in the Vatican uses climate change to blame humanity for a problem that does not exist so that they will have reason to kill as many people as they want. He has his population control agenda also. They cry out overpopulation when we still have so much land that we can use even our population today doubled or tripled. That is not to mention that God, the Creator of the heavens and the earth can expand or contract the earth as He like it. They cried out that if the population today continue to grow that we will have food and water crisis ahead. But they forgot to tell us that we have so much arable land that are not being utilized because the rich own it. We have unlimited fresh water to drink, even just from the air and yet they created water crisis scenario everywhere so that life for people become so difficult and therefore become dependent to their businesses. They intentionally mismanaged water resources so that they can create problems they can only solve through their businesses. And since people are dependent to their businesses, they can dictate their terms.

By these, we should start to realize that this climate change hoax is not about saving the earth for the welfare of the people, but it is an illusion with main goal of destroying the earth. Like depopulating the earth.

God created the earth perfect in beauty and with all its mechanism in place for its sustainability and Satan wants to destroy what God have created including humanity. Satan does not want us to know our potential under God's reign that is why he deceives the whole world with many deceptions from religions, governments, false freedom, education, economics, health, plandemics, to climate change hoax. And the Vatican is behind all of these deceptions because it owns majority of the businesses and governments of this world. It is the one pushing this climate change agenda as a precursor to Satan's one world government and one world religion otherwise known as the New World Order. Now, they are going to connect their new series of plandemic with their climate change agenda. Satan wants to deceive the whole world in his final attempt to make humanity worship and serve him to provoke God once again to destroy the earth and its inhabitants like what happened to the first earth, the great flood in the times of Noah, and the event in Sodom and Gomorrah. That is why Satan is the god and king of this present world. He manipulates our mind and thinking because he is the prince of the power of the air.

But the Bible said in Revelation 11: 18;

"[18]...And should destroy those who destroy the earth.'"

God will surely punish those who destroy the earth as He said in Isaiah 13: 11, saying;

"[11]"I will punish the world for its evil, and the wicked for their iniquity; <u>I will halt the arrogance of the proud</u>, and will lay low the haughtiness of the terrible.'"

Satan is the enemy of God and he will always find a way to deceive humanity into destroying God's creation. Even human body is being transformed by Satan from medical industry (vaccination to become transhuman) to the simple act of tattooing and piercing to transgenderism that even a six-year-old kid are now being mutilated both in mind and physical body under the operating table to change their gender identity physically at the expense of taxpayers money. Yes, they can change the mental and physical perception of what their gender is, but they cannot change the reality that they are only either male or female. Yes, they can think they are a non-bisexual wood in one moment and then a bisexual tree or an electric pole after a few moments, but the reality is still they are human being created by God. These are just all a perversion of the mind influenced by Satan because he is the prince of the power of the air who influence people who are disobedient to God. He broadcast his evil nature to mankind and mankind knowingly and unknowingly obeyed Satan rather than God. People become self-centered and lovers of themselves because Satan is self-centered. This is contrary to what Christ said to His disciples in John 15: 12 and 11 that has become a children's song in Sunday schools, saying;

"¹²This is My commandment, that you <u>love one another</u> as I have loved you. ¹¹... that your joy may be full."

And while Satan is teaching us to love yourself before others, Philippians 2: 3-4 (NLT) told us to love others before ourselves;

"³<u>Don't be selfish;</u> don't try to impress others. <u>Be humble, thinking of others as better than yourselves.</u> ⁴Don't look out only for your own interests, but <u>take an interest in others, too.</u>"

Satan being the god and ruler of this world do the opposite and telling his subject (humanity) to be lover and be proud of yourself. Just as it is written in 2 Timothy 3: 1-5, saying;

"¹But know this, that <u>in the last days</u> perilous times will come: ²For <u>men will be lovers of themselves,</u> lovers of money, boasters, <u>proud,</u> blasphemers, disobedient to parents, unthankful, unholy, ³unloving, unforgiving, slanderers, without self-control, brutal, despisers of good, ⁴traitors, headstrong, haughty, <u>lovers of pleasure rather than lovers of God,</u> ⁵<u>having a form of godliness but denying its power.</u>"

These are exactly what is happening to the peoples of the isles and of the world. All of these are the influences of Satan. As a living proof of his present-day influence is the Sodomite movement whose alphabet is not worthy to be mentioned in this book. Satan empowered (1-2%) and declared June as their pride month. And the 98% percent of the world are afraid to rebuke or offend these perverts. But Satan knows that God hates those who practice and support these practices as mentioned by Paul in Romans 1: 24-28;

"²⁴Therefore God also gave them up to uncleanness, in the lusts of their hearts, to dishonor their bodies among themselves, ²⁵who <u>exchanged the truth of God for the lie,</u> and <u>worshiped and served the creature rather than the Creator,</u> who is blessed forever. Amen. ²⁶For this reason God gave them up to <u>vile passions.</u> For even <u>their women exchanged the natural use for what is against nature.</u> ²⁷<u>Likewise also the men, leaving the natural use of the woman, burned in their lust for one another, men with men committing</u>

<u>what is shameful, and receiving in themselves the penalty of their</u> <u>error which was due.</u>

[28]And even as <u>they did not like to retain God in their knowledge,</u> God gave them over to a <u>debased mind,</u> to do those <u>things which</u> <u>are not fitting</u>; …"

And because there are only two principalities on earth which is God and Satan, then if you do not have God in your knowledge, you have Satan. That is why in Jeremiah 17: 9;

"[9]"The heart is deceitful above all things, and desperately wicked; Who can know it?""

If you are not of good, then you are of evil. If you are not a slave to God, then you are slave of Satan. We cannot serve two masters just as Jesus Christ said in Matthew 6: 24;

"[24]"No one can serve two masters; for either he will hate the one and love the other, or else he will be loyal to the one and despise the other. You cannot serve God and mammon.""

The intensifying resurgence of Sodomy today is a fulfilled prophecy that before the Creator God comes back to replace the current ruler of this world many will be proud and lovers of themselves. And this transgenderism is not only about sexual immorality nor a gender issue but rather it is a satanic religion - a cult that their ultimate goal is to worship Satan (Moloch) (This was proven during the 2023 Grammy's award). And they are creeping (influencing, grooming) in schools so that they will have an abundant supply of children for sacrifice to their god. Gender issue is just an illusion and just as God said, those who practice and support these detestable practices are worthy of death. Their blood is in their hands.

If we have the light, we can see the working of darkness. But if you are in darkness, you will not recognize the light because you are blinded by darkness.

If we love righteousness, we will hate unrighteousness (lawlessness, wickedness, iniquity) just as the Father God said to His Son Jesus Christ in Hebrew 1: 9;

"⁹You have loved righteousness and hated lawlessness;
Therefore God, Your God, has anointed You…"

Satan is a living proof that God – the Supreme being and the Creator of all things exist.

God exist, so are His creations.

The Proof of God – His Word - the Bible

The Bible is the word of God. The Word is Jesus Christ (Yeshua) as mentioned in John 1:1-5;

"¹In the beginning was the <u>Word</u>, and the Word was with God, and the Word was God. ²He was in the beginning with God. ³<u>All things were made through Him, and without Him nothing was made that was made.</u> ⁴In Him was life, and the life was <u>the light of men</u>. ⁵And the light shines in the darkness, and the darkness did not comprehend it."

As a proof that Jesus Christ is the Word that created all things, God the Father Himself declared His Son in Hebrew 1: 10;

"¹⁰And: "You, Lord, in the beginning laid the foundation of the <u>earth</u>, and the <u>heavens</u> are the <u>work of Your hands.</u>""

The Bible is Jesus Christ in print. And the Word is the light unto men. Just as it is written in Psalms 199: 105;

"¹⁰⁵Your word is a lamp to my feet and a light to my path."

And in John 8: 12, Jesus said;

"¹²Then <u>Jesus</u> spoke to them again, saying, "<u>I am the light of the world</u>. He who follows Me shall not walk in darkness, but have the light of life.""

Therefore, the Bible is the guiding light in the darkness of this world. The world is full of darkness because the ruler of this world is the god of darkness. The Bible shines into the world because it is the all-time bestseller book. It is present in almost every house in the Philippines. But people love darkness rather than light, that is why humanity did not and cannot comprehend the light. Few pay attention or care for the light but each one does according to their own will. But the Word said in John 15: 5 (NLT);

"⁵ …For apart from me you can do nothing."

That is why all human problems cannot be solved by human foolishness. We have the light, but we deliberately ignore the light. But the Light is coming and have come, and He prophesied all these things in His Word – the Bible.

Prophecy is one proof that God is what He say He is.

Prophecy

Prophecy is the future written in advance. But who can give us prophecy than the One who is from the Beginning and the End. No other gods of this world have ever claimed that they are the beginning and the end than our Lord Jesus Christ as He said in Revelation 22: 13;

"¹³I am the Alpha and the Omega, the <u>Beginning</u> and <u>the End</u>, the First and the Last."

Jesus Christ has no beginning and no end because He is the Beginning and the End just like Melchizedek as stated in Hebrews 7: 1-3 because He is Melchizedek;

"¹For this Melchizedek, king of Salem, <u>priest of the Most High God</u>, who met Abraham returning from the slaughter of the kings and blessed him, ²to whom also Abraham gave a tenth part of all, first being translated "<u>king of righteousness</u>," and then also king of Salem, meaning "<u>king of peace</u>," ³without father, without mother, without genealogy, <u>having neither beginning of days nor end of life</u>, but made like the <u>Son of God</u>, remains a priest continually."

Just as Jesus said in John 8:58, saying;

"⁵⁶ "Your father Abraham rejoiced to see My day, and he saw it and was glad.""

But His very own people – the Jews did not believe Him and they ask in verse 57;

"⁵⁷Then the Jews said to Him, "You are not yet fifty years old, and have You seen Abraham?""

And Jesus answered them in verse 58, saying;
"⁵⁸Jesus said to them, "Most assuredly, I say to you, <u>before Abraham was, I AM</u>."" (He is the Great I AM of the Old Testament.)

And if we still do not believe in Jesus Christ, would you not believe the Father who proclaimed in Hebrews 5: 5-6, saying;
"⁵So also Christ did not glorify Himself to become High Priest, but it was He (the Father) who said to Him (Yeshua):

"You are My Son,
Today I have begotten You."

⁶As He also says in another place:

"You are a priest forever
According to the order of Melchizedek";"

- This is the fulfillment of the prophecy in Isaiah 53:3 as <u>He was rejected by His own people, the Jews</u>;
"³He is despised and rejected by men, a Man of sorrows and acquainted with grief. And we hid, as it were, our faces from Him; He was despised, and we did not esteem Him."

Just as John said in Chapter 1 verse 11;
"¹¹He came to His own, and His own did not receive Him."

And in Luke 23:18;
"¹⁸And they (Jews) all cried out at once, saying, "Away with this Man, and release to us Barabbas" —"

This fulfilled prophecy is great evidence that the God of the Bible is the real God because it is a well-known fact that majority of the Jews do not believe that Jesus Christ is the Messiah, the Prophet, or even the Son of God. They are blinded for now by the scales in their eyes- the spirit of stupor just as it is written in Romans 11: 25-27 as Paul talking to the Gentiles saying;
"²⁵For I do not desire, brethren, that you should be ignorant of this

mystery, lest you should be wise in your own opinion, that <u>blindness in part has happened to Israel</u> until the fullness of the Gentiles has come in. [26]And so all Israel will be saved, as it is written:

"The Deliverer will come out of Zion, and He will turn away ungodliness from Jacob;

[27]For this is <u>My covenant</u> with them, when I take away their sins.""

The Bible also prophesied that the nations of Israel would undergo the <u>tribulation period</u> including Jerusalem. But at the end of the day, all Israel will be saved, and God said in Hebrews 8: 10;

"[10]For this is <u>the covenant</u> that I will make with the house of Israel <u>after those days</u>, says the Lord: I will put My laws in their mind and write them on their hearts; and I will be their God, and they shall be My people."

God will call them "My people" once again. But not now, many of them are indulge in disobedience and unbelief that grieves that heart of God. Just as it is written in Isaiah 63: 10;

"[10]But they rebelled and grieved His Holy Spirit; so He turned Himself against them as an enemy, and He fought against them."

Many governments of the nations of Israel such as the USA, Britain, present day Israel, Canada, Australia, New Zealand, etc. are at the forefront of implementing the satanic New World Order. They are enslaving their own people towards worshipping and serving Satan. They are ushering the darkness in all the earth making people the slaves of Satan rather than of God. That is why they will undergo the tribulation period which the Bible called as Jacob's Trouble (Jer. 30: 7). It is a collective trouble for both the House of Israel and the House of Judah (present day Israel – Jewish people).

But in 2 Chronicles 21: 7, said;

"[7]Yet the Lord would not destroy the house of David, because of the covenant that He had made with David, and since He had promised to give <u>a lamp</u> to him and to his sons forever."

Now, let us look at some of the prophecies fulfilled pertaining to the coming of the Word in flesh to fulfill the work given to Him by

His Father.

In the above verse, the lamp or the light is prophesied or promised to come from the line or a descendant of David just as it is written in Jeremiah 23: 5;

"⁵"Behold, the days are coming," says the Lord,
"That I will raise to David a <u>Branch of righteousness</u>;
A King shall reign and prosper, and execute judgment and righteousness in the earth.""

And in John 7: 42;

"⁴²For the Scriptures clearly state that the Messiah will be born of the royal line of David, in Bethlehem, the village where King David was born."

- Isaiah 9: 7 is the prophetic scripture of the Messiah as <u>heir to the throne of David</u>;

"⁷Of the increase of His government and peace there will be no end, upon the throne of David and over His kingdom, to order it and establish it with judgment and justice from that time forward, even forever. The zeal of the Lord of hosts will perform this."

This is confirmed by God to David as He speak to him through Nathan in 2 Samuel 7: 16;

"¹⁶ "...And your house and your kingdom shall be established forever before you. Your throne shall be established forever.""
Jesus Christ fulfilled this prophecy in Luke 1:31-33, saying;

"³¹And behold, you will conceive in your womb and bring forth a Son, and shall call His name Jesus. ³²He will be great, and will be called the <u>Son of the Highest</u>; and <u>the Lord God</u> will <u>give Him the throne of His father David</u>. ³³And He will reign over the house of Jacob forever, and of His kingdom there will be no end.""

And Jesus said in Revelation 22: 16;

"¹⁶"I, Jesus, have sent My angel to testify to you these things in the churches. I am the Root and the Offspring of David, the Bright and Morning Star.""

And many believers called Him the Son of David :

"¹The book of the genealogy of Jesus Christ, the <u>Son of David</u>, the Son of Abraham:" - Matthew 1:1

"²²And behold, a woman of Canaan came from that region and cried out to Him, saying, "Have mercy on me, O Lord, <u>Son of David</u>!" - Matthew 15: 22

"⁹Then the multitudes who went before and those who followed cried out, saying:
"Hosanna to the <u>Son of David</u>! 'Blessed is He who comes in the name of the Lord!' Hosanna in the highest!"" - Matthew 21: 9

"⁴⁷And when he heard that it was Jesus of Nazareth, he began to cry out and say, "<u>Jesus, Son of David</u>, have mercy on me!"
⁴⁸Then many warned him to be quiet; but he cried out all the more, "<u>Son of David</u>, have mercy on me!"" - Mark 10: 47-48

Jesus being the Root and the offspring - Son of David is a figurative mystery. In another chapter, we will learn why Jesus is also the root of David and all humanity.

But ultimately, Jesus Christ will reign on earth from the throne of David when He comes back as King of kings and Lord of lords. The mystery of whereabouts of the throne of David if it was prophesied to last forever warrants another lengthy discussion. But suffice to say for now that the throne of David is the present-day throne of the monarchy of Britain which is the tribe of Ephraim the son of Joseph. The British monarchy is the only kingdom on earth that use the throne of David and Davidic ceremony during the coronation of their kings and queens. Let us see if the coronation of King Charles III on May 6, 2023 will still use the throne of David known today as the Coronation Chair and Stone of Scone in their ceremony (Update-They used it). The Stone of Scone also known as the Stone of Destiny.

- Isaiah 7: 14 is another prophetic scripture foretelling of the coming Messiah to be born <u>of a virgin</u>;

"¹⁴Therefore the Lord Himself will give you a sign: behold, <u>the</u>

virgin shall conceive and bear a Son, and shall call His name Immanuel."

The fulfillment of this prophecy is written in Luke 1: 26-31, saying; "²⁶Now in the sixth month the angel Gabriel was sent by God to a city of Galilee named Nazareth, ²⁷to a virgin betrothed to a man whose name was Joseph, of the house of David. The virgin's name was Mary. ²⁸And having come in, the angel said to her, "Rejoice, highly favored one, the Lord is with you; blessed are you among women!" ²⁹But when she saw him, she was troubled at his saying, and considered what manner of greeting this was. ³⁰Then the angel said to her, "Do not be afraid, Mary, for you have found favor with God. ³¹And behold, you will conceive in your womb and bring forth a Son, and shall call His name Jesus."

Many know or believed that Jesus is indeed a Son of the virgin Mary, but few knows that He has brothers and sisters in flesh as stated in Matthew 13: 54-56;

> "⁵⁴When He had come to His own country, He taught them in their synagogue, so that they were astonished and said, "Where did this Man get this wisdom and these mighty works? ⁵⁵Is this not the carpenter's son? Is not His mother called Mary? And His brothers James, Joses, Simon, and Judas? ⁵⁶And His sisters, are they not all with us? Where then did this Man get all these things?""

- And although Christ has an earthly family, His real and spiritual Father which is in heaven declared in prophetic scripture in Psalms 2: 7 confirming that indeed He is the Messiah – the Son of God;

> "⁷"I will declare the decree: The Lord has said to Me,
> 'You are My Son, today I have begotten You....""

This prophecy concerning Jesus as the Son of God was confirmed in Matthew 3: 17, saying;

> "¹⁷And suddenly a voice came from heaven, saying, "This is My beloved Son, in whom I am well pleased.""

- Aside from being the Son of God, the prophetic scripture of Deuteronomy 18: 15, 17-18 foretold that the Messiah will also be called as a Prophet;

"[15]"The Lord your God will raise up for you a Prophet like me from your midst, from your brethren. Him you shall hear,…

[17]"And the Lord said to me: 'What they have spoken is good. [18]I will raise up for them a Prophet like you from among their brethren, and will put My words in His mouth, and He shall speak to them all that I command Him."

Paul in Acts 3: 20-23 confirmed this prophecy saying;

"[20]and that He may send Jesus Christ, who was preached to you before, [21]whom heaven must receive until the times of restoration of all things, which God has spoken by the mouth of all His holy prophets since the world began. [22]For Moses truly said to the fathers, 'The Lord your God will raise up for you a Prophet like me from your brethren. Him you shall hear in all things, whatever He says to you. [23]And it shall be that every soul who will not hear that Prophet shall be utterly destroyed from among the people.'"

And Jesus Christ Himself confirmed this prophecy fulfilled in Himself in John 14: 31;

"[31]But that the world may know that I love the Father, and as the Father gave Me commandment, so I do. Arise, let us go from here."

And Jesus confirmed this further in the following verses;

"[49]For I have not spoken on My own authority; but the Father who sent Me gave Me a command, what I should say and what I should speak. [50]And I know that His command is everlasting life. Therefore, whatever I speak, just as the Father has told Me, so I speak."" - John 12: 49-50

"[4]I must work the works of Him who sent Me while it is day; the night is coming when no one can work." - John 9: 4

"[38]For I have come down from heaven, not to do My own will, but the will of Him who sent Me." - John 6: 38

"¹⁹Then Jesus answered and said to them, "Most assuredly, I say to you, the Son can do nothing of Himself, but what He sees the Father do; for whatever He does, the Son also does in like manner…."""
"³⁰I can of Myself do nothing. As I hear, I judge; and My judgment is righteous, because I do not seek My own will but the will of the Father who sent Me." - John 5: 19, 30

"²⁸Then Jesus said to them, "When you lift up the Son of Man, then you will know that I am He, and that I do nothing of Myself; but as My Father taught Me, I speak these things. 29And He who sent Me is with Me. The Father has not left Me alone, for I always do those things that please Him."" - John 8: 28-29

"⁷"If you had known Me, you would have known My Father also; and from now on you know Him and have seen Him." ⁸Philip said to Him, "Lord, show us the Father, and it is sufficient for us." ⁹Jesus said to him, "Have I been with you so long, and yet you have not known Me, Philip? He who has seen Me has seen the Father; so how can you say, 'Show us the Father'? ¹⁰Do you not believe that I am in the Father, and the Father in Me? The words that I speak to you I do not speak on My own authority; but the Father who dwells in Me does the works. ¹¹Believe Me that I am in the Father and the Father in Me, or else believe Me for the sake of the works themselves."" - John 14: 7-11

And finally in John 10: 30, Jesus said;
"³⁰I and My Father are one."

And in John 14: 6;
"⁶ "…No one comes to the Father except through Me….""

Although they are two personas, they are one in Spirit and in Truth. That is why those who mock or despise Jesus Christ as just an imagination, a myth, an ordinary person, or just a prophet and pretends to directly worship God the Father are deceived. For Jesus and the

Father are one. We cannot pray or worship the Father except through Jesus Christ.

And the greatest or culminating prophecy of Jesus Christ is His testimony to His end time servants as given to Him by His Father and sent and signified it by His angel to His servant John, of events that must shortly take place in the end times.

So, we can say from this fulfilled prophecy regarding the Messiah -the Prophet that:

1. The real Jesus Christ (Yeshua) of the Bible is the prophesied Messiah, the Son of David, the Son of God,
2. He and the Father are one,
3. He is "The Prophet" of the Almighty Father for or all the prophecy in the Old Testament up to Revelation is His Word,
4. He is a very loyal "Servant of God" that He followed the order of His Father to the letter, no more, no less,
5. He came in the image of God (2 Cor. 4: 4) for indeed mankind are created in their own image (Gen. 1: 26-27).

So, just as the Son is loyal and obedient to His Father, we must also be loyal and obedient servants to our God (Master) and serve Him only with all our heart, with all our mind and soul. That is why we need to work hard to be Christ-like for this is the whole duty of man just as it is written in Ecclesiastes 12: 13-14 (KJV), saying;

"[13]Let us hear the conclusion of the whole matter: Fear God, and keep his commandments: for this is the whole duty of man. [14]For God shall bring every work into judgment, with every secret thing, whether it be good, or whether it be evil."

Jesus Christ feared His Father and God that is why He is in absolute obedience to Him and His commandments. He recognizes the authority of His Father over Himself. This result into perfect harmony that they become two persona in one. Jesus Christ have faith in His Father and the Father have faith in Him. And they work together in harmony resulting into beautiful creation. He is a perfect Son and a Servant.

- It is well known to the Christian world that Christ, the Messiah have died, was buried, and <u>was resurrected</u> from the dead just as the prophetic scriptures said in Psalms 16: 10;

"¹⁰For You will not leave my soul in Sheol, nor will You allow Your Holy One to see corruption."

And in Psalms 49: 15;
"¹⁵But God will redeem My soul from the power of the grave, for He shall receive Me. Selah"

This prophecy was testified that have come to pass in Mark 16: 6-7; "⁶But he said to them, "Do not be alarmed. You seek Jesus of Nazareth, who was crucified. He is risen! He is not here. See the place where they laid Him. ⁷But go, tell His disciples—and Peter—that He is going before you into Galilee; there you will see Him, as He said to you.""

And when Mary Magdalene have seen the risen Lord, He did not allow to touch Him because He have not ascended yet to His Father as written in John 20: 17;
"¹⁷Jesus said to her, "<u>Do not cling to Me</u>, for I have not yet ascended to My Father; but go to My brethren and say to them, '<u>I am ascending to My Father</u> and your Father, and to My God and your God.' ""

But on the same day He appeared to His disciples in verses 19-20; "¹⁹Then, the same day at <u>evening</u>, being the <u>first day</u> of the week, when the doors were shut where the disciples were assembled, for fear of the Jews, Jesus came and stood in the midst, and said to them, "Peace be with you." ²⁰When He had said this, He showed them His hands and His side. Then the disciples were glad when they saw the Lord."

Perhaps He already ascended into heaven and have comeback and allowed Himself to be touched by His disciples to prove that He is real just like what He allowed Thomas (one of the disciples who was not with them during His first appearance) to do in verses 24-29;

"²⁴Now Thomas, called the Twin, one of the twelve, was not with them when Jesus came. ²⁵The other disciples therefore said to him, "We have seen the Lord."

So he said to them, "Unless I see in His hands the print of the nails, and put my finger into the print of the nails, and put my hand into His side, I will not believe."

²⁶And <u>after eight days</u> His disciples were again inside, and Thomas with them. <u>Jesus came, the doors being shut,</u> and stood in the midst, and said, "Peace to you!" ²⁷Then He said to Thomas, "Reach your finger here, and look at My hands; and reach your hand here, and put it into My side. Do not be unbelieving, but believing."

²⁸And Thomas answered and said to Him, "My Lord and my God!"

²⁹Jesus said to him, "Thomas, because you have seen Me, you have believed. <u>Blessed are those who have not seen and yet have believed.</u>"

- It was also prophesied in the prophetic scripture of Psalms 68: 18 that the Messiah will <u>ascend into the right hand of God;</u>

"¹⁸You have <u>ascended on high,</u> You have led captivity captive; You have received gifts among men, even from the rebellious, That the Lord God might dwell there."

This prophecy was confirmed in Mark 16: 19;

"¹⁹So then, after the Lord had spoken to them, He was received up into heaven, and sat down at the right hand of God."

This is His final ascension as seen by His disciples in Luke 24: 50-51;

"⁵⁰And He led them out as far as Bethany, and He lifted up His hands and blessed them. ⁵¹Now it came to pass, while He blessed them, that He was parted from them and carried up into heaven."

These are some of the prophecies that the Christian world popularly knows. But there are many more prophecies that even the prophesying Christians does not know or understand.

Prophecies Observable in the Secular World

But what if you do not know or have not heard, or believe in Christ or the God of the Bible because you are non-Christian believer, how can the prophecy of the Bible as the word of God be a proof of God's existence?

There are prophecies that are relatable to all mankind regardless of religion or beliefs that will show us or tell us the mystery and majesty of the God of the Bible. And one of those is fulfilled prophecies is the Information Technology. Everyone has cellphone and have internet access one way or another in almost every corner of the earth. And the abundance of information whether good or evil is available to us at our fingertips. And that fulfilled prophecy which applied to all mankind regardless of belief is written in Daniel 12: 4, saying;

> "'"But you, Daniel, shut up the words, and seal the book until <u>the time of the end</u>; many shall <u>run to and fro, and knowledge shall increase</u>.""'"

❶The proliferation of knowledge or information is one of the signs that we are at the end time. End time here means the end of Satan's time as the god and ruler of this world. At the end or culmination of Satan's kingdom here on earth is the beginning of Jesus Christ Millennial Kingdom (The Kingdom of God). The sorrows that were inflicted by Satan and humanity to himself will end and will usher the new millennia with Jesus Christ ruling the earth with the rod of iron to force humanity to have real peace, joy, happiness, and prosperity.

The internet is full of good and evil knowledge (not to mention the dark web). And people have information overload that deciding between what is good and what is bad information really needs to be sifted out by going back and forth (run to and fro, browsing) to those information. It is now more apparent when Youtube and Google became heavily censored specially to mislead people during the scamdemic. Most of the information shown or promoted in these platforms are in favor of the conspiratorial narrative against humanity specifically promoting medical tyranny that resulted to millions of deaths from the jab and millions upon millions of people are suffering from the adverse side effects and economic loses. Good or unbiased information questioning the narrative of the governmental conspiracy to commit crimes against humanity become disinformation and those biased information become or projected as the good information. That is why new video platforms such as bitchute.com, rumble, etc. have arisen to counter this information monopoly so that people will be given an informed decision. People will have a chance to think and weigh in the information they read or view and decide for themselves whether it is truth or evil. That is why we are in the information war. Those who are telling the truth or questioning the narrative of the few are levelled misinformation and name called as terrorists. And those who control the world whose intention to humanity is evil (to lie and deceive to depopulate the earth) is projected as the good guys. One really need to literally "run to and fro" between these platforms or from one browser to another to see the needed knowledge (good or bad) to have an informed decision.

If this information age is not the fulfilment of the above prophecy, I don't know what. Everyone can relate because everyone has used internet in almost every place on earth. Billions have smartphone capable of browsing to and fro in the internet.

If you have read this prophecy in the 1980's, you would not believe because we have no clue how knowledge will abound in the end times. At that time, we only have snail mails, books, newspapers which could distribute information but in a very slow manner that exchanging information may take weeks or months. Then, a few decades later, we have the emails which we can share information in an instant. Communication have become very cheap and way faster than before. But it become much much faster like the speed of light with the advent of many social media platforms. Now we can just share a link to a website or information sources that will explode knowledge of the subject we want to research whether it is good or evil. Indeed, we are at the end times.

❷ Another observable prophecy that every human being can see or experience whether they believe or not in the Bible is Jesus Christ prophecy of the end times. This prophecy is called Olivet

Prophecy because He revealed this prophecy to His disciples in the Mount of Olives as written in Matthew 24: 3-12;

> "³Now as He sat on the Mount of Olives, the disciples came to Him privately, saying, "Tell us, when will these things be? And what will be the sign of <u>Your coming, and of the end of the age?</u>"
>
> ⁴And Jesus answered and said to them: "Take heed that no one deceives you. ⁵For <u>many will come in My name, saying, 'I am the Christ,' and will deceive many</u>. ⁶And <u>you will hear of wars and rumors of wars</u>. See that you are not troubled; for all these things must come to pass, but the end is not yet. ⁷For <u>nation will rise against nation, and kingdom against kingdom</u>. And <u>there will be famines, pestilences, and earthquakes in various places</u>. ⁸All these are the <u>beginning of sorrows</u>.
>
> ⁹"Then they will deliver you up to tribulation and kill you, and you will be hated by all nations for My name's sake. ¹⁰And then <u>many will be offended, will betray one another, and will hate one another</u>. ¹¹Then <u>many false prophets will rise up and deceive many</u>. ¹²And because <u>lawlessness will abound, the love of many will grow cold</u>.""

There are seven very important prophecies in these verses that every man regardless of beliefs can attests to the authority of the Bible proclaiming these events that have happened and are happening right in front of our very own eyes. These are;

1. Many will come in My name, saying, 'I am the Christ,' and will deceive many,
2. You will hear of wars and rumors of wars,
3. Nation will rise against nation, and kingdom against kingdom,
4. There will be famines, pestilences, and earthquakes in various places,
5. Many will be offended, will betray one another, and will hate one another,
6. Many false prophets will rise up and deceive many,
7. Lawlessness will abound, the love of many will grow cold.

Jesus Christ (Yeshua) Himself give us the events to come prior to His return to rule the earth. Number one tell us that there are many counterfeit Christian religions professing to believe in Christ, but they worshipped another Jesus (2 Cor. 11: 4) because they do not even want to believe and obey what Jesus Christ Himself told them to do to those who profess to follow Him. Instead, they chose to obey what they want instead of what Jesus Christ wants which is self-righteousness. And the many so-called Christian religions composed of many denominations observed and practices pagan traditions rather than biblical traditions. As a result, billions upon billions of people have been deceived by these many counterfeits and professing Christianity.

Examples of this deceptions are the many man-made gospels such as the gospel of grace, the gospel of salvation, the gospels about Jesus Christ rather than the gospel of Jesus Christ which is about the coming Kingdom of God, the gospel about God's Laws being done away, the gospel of salvation by penance and penitence, the gospel of praying repetitive prayers for salvation, prosperity gospel, and many other gospels that are not actually written in the Bible but made up by man (idolatry) to make their own narrative and agenda.

Number two is very much being fulfilled in our very own eyes. We have ongoing wars right now in Ukraine and Russia (Made up war of 2022), information war between good and evil (censorship of information in favor of the narrative or agenda of the few through their propaganda machines), we have currency war played by many countries against the US dollar, we have silent war between governments and its own people (enslaving them to serve the master in Rome), people are silently at war with government sponsored poverty, prostitution, child trafficking, human trafficking, drug addiction and its cartels, corruptions, etc., etc. Too many to mention if we care.

Then we have humors of wars between China versus the US, the Philippines, Japan, Vietnam, and many other countries victimized by China in its deceptive business dealing of "debt traps". Humors of wars persistently can be heard between Israel and its surrounding nations specially Iran with its proxy in Syria and Palestine. There are also humors of wars created or instigated by the US government (through CIA) for a regime change in any country at anytime and anywhere they want. Of course, these are under the duress of their master in Rome. And these wars and humors of wars will continue to pop up at any moment at any place on earth until Jesus come.

Number three is correlated with the wars and humors of wars of nations and kingdoms fighting against each other. But the main reason of these fighting against each other is the stupidity and foolishness of man. We detached ourselves from God who created us and forgot that we came from one family – the family of Noah. We are actually brothers and sisters. And Satan have successfully divided and conquered us because we do not believe in the God of the Bible who created us. That is why we all lost our root and identity, and we fight with each other like we are strangers to one another. And because we lost our root and foundation, Satan easily manipulated us into fighting with each other. In a family, there are wars between siblings whether it is silent or real fighting for whatever reason. Even the very unit of the society is divided against each other because of our own stupidity and foolishness just as God said we are (Ps. 92: 6). Now Satan have programmed the minds of every human being on earth to be hostile to each other. This programming is brought by the Satanic machines of propaganda through the mainstream media, big tech, movie and music industry and the governments of Satan all over the earth. Each nation and kingdom are supposed to be family and helping one another. But instead, we fight with each other like fools.

And as if human stupidity and foolishness is not enough, the World Economic Forum (WEF) is trying to change human species into a cyborg or transhuman where human being is treated as data (hackable) that can be controlled by the ruling elites. The sad thing is the main proponent of this stupidity and insanity is a professor at the Hebrew University (HU) which means he is a Jew. The software guy is also a Jew. The others who are at the forefront of this satanic New World Order are coming from the various tribes of Israel. That is why there will be a coming Jacob's Trouble for their stupidity and outright disobedience to their very own God.

The Fourth Industrial Revolution of WEF aims to subject

humanity under the control of world ruling cyborg elites. The US is perhaps the first nation on earth ruled by a cyborg. Transhumanism has begun using the C19 injection with the nano technology chips implanted on every human being that allowed themselves to be an experimental guinea pigs of this technology. Every human activity of the injected will be and can be collected as data, even their dreams. Humans are now hackable animals as they say. They can be switch on and off if they desire. Free will according to them will be over. Life to them is meaningless. To them, humans are just useless eater.

This is not some kind of conspiracy theory to those who create conspiracy against humanity. Well, decades ago it was a conspiracy theory against them (the elites, the 1%). But now, they are openly talking about it in their summit at the World Economic Forum. The head of the WEF and its minions are openly discussing their intention to enslave and depopulate the earth under the pretense of their so-called science. They decide who lives and who will die. Some even openly admitted that they are excited to become a cyborg. These people are playing gods even up to the point of saying they are greater than the God of the Bible because they made a new species of human out of what God have created (according to this HU professor). If that is not pure stupidity and foolishness, then it is insanity of the few (the 1%). How can one claim he is greater than the creator when he just innovates on the creation out of what the original creator have created? Pure insanity. And that is where we are now as one family. These are verifiable and searchable information. If you want to see and hear directly from the horse's mouth, then watch "The Plan" in stopworldcontrol.com before it is gone.

But we have not heard it from the news, nor our government informed us of what is going on. The scamdemic as the head of WEF said, is just a test. A beginning of sorrow. Meaning there are more tests coming to perfect their technology in humanity. And people will love it and even proud of it as if they are really like hypnotized. Or in our words, "na gayuma". People played and will play their role as sheep in this insane drama of the elites and the Vatican. And as the proverbial saying goes, "the world is a stage". There are actors and actresses and there are directors and producers. The sad thing is the actors, and the actresses have no talent fee (TF). Instead, they will pay with their life in playing the role as a sheep in this drama of insanity and stupidity.

This is the very reason why Christ is coming back soon. To save mankind from its own self-destructive ways of foolishness and stupidity. He needs to rule humanity with the rod of iron to curve us out of our foolishness and stupid mentality. Because people love darkness than light. People love lies and illusion rather than the truth and the reality. We refuse to recognize the real God who created and give us our life and instead worship Satan who is also just a creation.

With this there, will be silent and constant war (cold war) between the one that knows the truth and the one that do not. There is even war going on between neighbors because of the mistrust to one another. Nobody knows their neighbor's stand on any issue. Everyone lives in animosity with each other. Each neighbor become a threat to each other, suspecting one another. That is why humanity become vulnerable and weak because we are divided. Only the government will know "who is who" because they have the data to implement total control and surveillance through the nano technology injected in the body and other surveillance technology.

Those who do not and does not want to know the truth are controlled and programmed to be the subject of this Satanic one world government and one world religion otherwise known as the New World Order. The WEF is as they claim are the one who will control or determine the future of the world. Under this WEF is the UN and WHO and other tentacles in every government of the world. WHO alone have the global power to take over the sovereignty of any country in times of global health problems or pandemic if they want to create one. They have the power to take control of the police and the military in case of global emergency to enforce their vaccination agenda. Wars are eminent before this will come to reality.

In fact, wars are already going on between governments and its people. Of course, we already know that these tyrannical governments already exist in communist and socialist government like China, Iran, some African nation warring with its own people. But not at the level of the United States of America where government treat its people as enemy. Like a terrorist. Anyone who question or disagree with their policies whether it is right or wrong are considered domestic terrorists. This includes people who question the result of elections, satanic school policies, farming policies, etc. Those parents who argue with school boards regarding vaccination, masking, school sexualization, etc. are now domestic terrorist. Even a very popular former US president was treated like a terrorist. But the real enemy, the real terrorists and criminals are pouring in on their border freely with US government sponsor of free hotel, free air fare to their destination/sponsor, and free allowance/pocket money. All-expense paid by taxpayers' money. And people can do nothing about it. Where is the so-called democracy, they are so proud about? There is none because democracy is just an illusion. It protects the corrupt and the criminals of the highest order. The law only applies to the weak and the poor.

We are made to believe that wars and fighting against each other will be gone in a civilized or educated society. But we are wrong. Wars and fighting against each other just transform into a different form from stone axe, bow and arrow to high caliber guns to nuclear bombs. As we develop towards the so-called materialistic progress, we become more and more savaged to one another. And those who have accumulated material wealth specially the one percenter became insane people to think that they become different from the rest of us. They put up wars against the "useless eaters" as their disposable property and children as their sex slaves. They have no regards to human life because they feel they are gods.

If these are not insanity going on in this world, I do not know what.

Number four prophecy of Jesus that applies or affect everyone on earth is, "There will be famines, pestilences, and earthquakes in various places".

Many of us will automatically picture a very skinny with a large head black African children when we heard the word famine. We almost immediately think of Africa when we heard the word famine because that is the mainstream media and governments have programmed as to believe. As if famine is only happening in Africa. But believe it or not, famine is experienced by each country in the world even USA. There are people who do not have food to eat in the US for whatever reasons. And one of that is homelessness/poverty. But there are organizations who at least provide them food such as Food Banks. But in other countries who are starving, children are malnourished and in our own language "butot balat" (bone and skin) only. But governments do not do something about this problem. Instead, they just supply food temporarily and after that, nothing. They do not guide or educate people how to make their own food supply. They have this so-called superficial aid that just come and go. Of course, why would governments help their people when that is exactly what they want to happen. Program people to be dependent to government so that they can easily manipulate and control the people. Remember election and taxation day?

Recent data showed that 821 million people experience chronic hunger while another 135 million people face "crisis levels of hunger or worse". If only one percent of those 135 million people died of starvation, then that would mean 1,350,000 more people died of starvation in 2020 than in 2019. But all those deaths suddenly become covid deaths.

On the other hand, pestilences can be associated with the stories that occurred when God was redeeming the Israelite people from the bondage of Egyptian slavery in the time of Moses. Pestilence is a deadly disaster, usually a disease or pests that affects an entire community of either plants, animals, human or all of them at the same time. Pestilence also known as plague. It is contagious, virulent, and devastating in nature.

When Pharaoh during the time of Moses refused to let go of the Israelite people, God sent 10 plagues to Egypt. These are the 10 Plagues of Egypt: water turning to blood, frogs, lice, flies, livestock pestilence, boils, hail, locusts, darkness, and the killing of firstborn children.

Farmers are always at constant fight against pests and diseases of crops and from time-to-time locust do attack fields with great economic damages. Agricultural sectors occasionally suffer pestilences such as pest and diseases to both plants and animals.

Those are the natural pestilences. But there are man-made pestilences created to kill mankind. Example of this is the Spanish Flu that did not originate from Spain but from USA. The name is a smoke screen to hide the truth. The deaths were not caused by some kind of flu virus but also from the vaccination. We were made to believe that there was a virus that killed 50 million people from this plague. But the truth is, those people died from the injections they receive from and administered by the government. It will be too long to discuss this in this book. But one can easily find the truth with a little research. The Spanish flu scam is a man-made genocide at that time. It is C19 in our time. The tactic and methodology of this scam is very similar to the scamdemic that happened in our time. There was no proof presented that people died of the so called deadly and highly contagious covid 19 virus. All those declared death of covid are just an illusion to the fact that they just attached "with" to those who died from other causes or co-morbidities. Imagine those who died from a gunshot and declared covid death. Very obvious lies and deceptions. But people ignore it. Instead, they love it.

Now, millions upon millions of people are dead and are dying from the injections. Life Insurance companies are the best source of data to prove that the fake virus was not deadly or does not exist, but the injection is. The extreme limit of life insurance companies is 10% excess deaths. And they considered this percentage as an indicator that a very disastrous event has occurred such as tsunami, earthquakes, hurricane, etc. But as of November 2022, the excess death is already at 44% which means a catastrophic event have occurred. But we never heard these things from mainstream media or from the government except from certain platforms and private documentaries such as "Sudden Death" by Peter Stew.

Perhaps this is what actually the mainstream media and the government have been barking that millions will die if they do not flatten the curve, if lockdown will not be implemented, if people will not wear masks or observe social distancing and ultimately if people are not vaccinated. And from the onset of the scam, particularly in Wuhan, China where crisis actors are falling in the streets in the early 2020's but never happened anywhere else in the world even though governments are barking about the millions of cases in each of their country. Instead, they have been acting to intimidate, coerce, and deceive people into taking the jab (fearmongering). Everything was a premonition of what is about to happen after the jab. And indeed, it has happened and is happening to this day. People are dying and falling like flies in the streets, political events, sports fields, homes, news anchors, etc., etc. And people are so naïve that they think that these sudden deaths are just normal deaths. The governments psychological operations (Psyop) of creating mass formation psychosis to humanity is very successful that people, even the most educated one have subjected themselves to these unknown injections and mind manipulation. Many are even proud about it, and many are dead.

The government are calling this deaths "Sudden Adult Death Syndromes" (SADS) similar to SIDS or "Sudden Infant Death Syndromes" for babies who are from day one injected with there so called life saving vaccines. There is already an independent study conducted that prove causation that vaccine schedules from day one to teenage are the cause of chronic illnesses. This study was conducted in ten-year period. Watch this in Bitchute.com titled *"Vaxxed Vs Unvaxxed: Us Child Vaccines Are Poison Causing Breathing, Neuro & Blood Disorders?"*. There is a need to access this information as soon as possible before it will be taken down.

Other links in the descriptions of the video will show us how the government are poisoning the brain with ethyl mercury from day one which exposes the baby to 46 times over the guidelines of EPA for mercury intake. At two months the same baby will be expose to 138 times over the guidelines and so on and so forth. But the problem is the guidelines being used here is based on organic methyl mercury and not the synthetic ethyl mercury (thimerosal) used in the vaccines. And according to the documentary, an Italian published study on the effect of thimerosal on cells showed that ethyl mercury is 50 times toxic than methyl mercury. Methyl mercury is an organic mercury that can be taken from eating fish. On the other hand, thimerosal containing the ethyl mercury is the main suspect of children autism which is currently at 1 in every 30 kids in the US are autistic. Other ratio showed 1 in 40 depending on what government agency you are looking at. But the projection of 1 in 2 by 2025 if the trend continue is very much alarming. Yet governments all over the world are still pushing these vaccines to children from day one. But who cares about children anyway? Pocket and power are more important to them than human life.

And so, chronic diseases are ingrained in human's life from day one because of vaccination. This is just man-made (as influenced by Satan) self-inflict pestilence and not yet pestilences that God will inflict upon humanity because of hard headedness.

Including in the fourth prophecy mentioned are earthquakes in various places on earth. It is estimated that there are 50 earthquakes every day and there are 500,000 earthquakes detected every year all over the earth and 100 of these earthquakes can cause severe damages. Earthquakes become so devastating when it hits heavily populated area or if the epicenter is near the seashore which is enough to cause a tsunami. It seems that earthquakes today are increasing in magnitude and frequency. And this devastation is very sorrowful to those affected and even to the observers. This is just part of the beginning of sorrows. But the time will come that the earth will be shaken out of its place because of God's anger just as it is written in Isaiah 13: 11, 13;

> "[11]"I will punish the world for its evil, and the wicked for their iniquity; I will halt the arrogance of the proud, and will lay low the haughtiness of the terrible.
> [13]Therefore I will shake the heavens, and the earth will move out of her place, in the wrath of the Lord of hosts and in the day of His fierce anger."

Imagine how terrible the wrath of God be when He shakes the heavens and the earth (Job 9:6). The whole earth. All nations (Hag. 2: 7).

How devastating would it be that Revelation 6: 12-17 describes the result of opening the sixth seal as;

"[12]I looked when He opened the sixth seal, and behold, there was <u>a great earthquake</u>; and the sun became black as sackcloth of hair, and the moon became like blood. [13]And the stars of heaven fell to the earth, as a fig tree drops its late figs when it is shaken by a mighty wind. [14]Then the sky receded as a scroll when it is rolled up, and <u>every mountain and island was moved out of its place</u>. [15]And the kings of the earth, the great men, the rich men, the commanders, the mighty men, every slave and every free man, hid themselves in the caves and in the rocks of the mountains, [16]and said to the mountains and rocks, "Fall on us and hide us from the face of Him who sits on the throne and from <u>the wrath of the Lamb</u>! [17]For <u>the great day of His wrath</u> has come, and who is able to stand?""

The wrath of God or the wrath of the Lamb (Jesus Christ) is for all unrepentant humanity great and small. It is indeed an unmatched cataclysmic event in human history just as Jesus Christ said in Matthew 24: 21-22, saying;

"[21]For then there will be great tribulation, such as has not been since the beginning of the world until this time, no, nor ever shall be. [22]And unless those days were shortened, no flesh would be saved; but for the elect's sake those days will be shortened."

Terrible, terrible days are coming. And what Satan is doing right now with his deceptive Great Reset, human alteration through medical establishment (e.g., mRNA vaccines, transgenderism, transhumanism, etc.), and the destruction of the earth through the deceptive hoax of climate change, will dwarf in comparison to what God is about to do to the unrepentant humanity.

If you will not fear God, but fear Satan instead, think for a second. For if we are real, God is more real than us.

The fifth prophecy that apply and are observable in our present time is, "Many will be offended, will betray one another, and will hate one another,…"

Are these not what is happening in all humanity today. There are people pretending to be offended by even the mention of the word "god". Even they themselves do not know who and what is god being mentioned. People now a days are so sensitive to little things even to mention one's skin color. What if one has black, white, yellow, red or brown skin color? We cannot deny that because that is the truth. Why do we make offend about that when that is the reality. Because one think that one skin color is greater or lesser than the other and we do not want to accept that that is the fact? There are brown or black people who want to be white and there are white people who wants to be brown. It all depends on one's perception to think that there is always greater and lesser person than yourself. So, why make offence of what is reality.

Then there is this insanity about gender issues of what pronouns one person need to be called. They would pretend to be offended if one called them by a pronoun, they do not deem they are at the moment. But deep inside them, they are still he or she. They are just nurturing the insanity of faking themselves for what they are not. All are perversion of the mind.

As a result of this easily offended generation, many indeed is betraying and hating one another even among siblings and neighbors. Truly, the distrust and mistrust upon one another have not been greater than in today's society of the so-called civilized and highly educated people. This is what we have become. This is our so-called progress. Progress forward materialistically, and progress backward humanistically.

The sixth prophecy of Jesus Christ that applies to all mankind is, "Many false prophets will rise up and deceive many". This prophecy has happened, is happening, and will happen in a very obvious way to those who are watching and preparing. We can look at this from the perspective of professing Christianity and from non-Christian point of view.

In the world of professing Christianity, many denominations (by the thousands in fact) proclaimed that they believe in Christ. Yet, they refuse to obey what Christ of the Bible have said and commanded. In fact, they do not even know who is Yeshua of the Bible. Instead, they made up their own doctrines, gospels, laws, and traditions. And now, there is even a denomination which are focus on their man-made gospel of prosperity who outrightly creating their own bible interpretation (even twisting the verses) to serve their narrative of loving money and materialistic things.

These false prophets and false teachers will be more and more visible (like mega super churches) as they continue to deceive many towards worshipping another Jesus.

In the non-Christian world, many false prophets have deceived many towards worshipping man-made gods. Many of these belong to the so-called major religions. Each has their own gods and belief system. Some directly and secretly worship Satan, like most secret societies who are part of ruling the world. These too have deceived billions upon billions of unsuspecting followers/believers.

The seventh prophecy that applied and observable by all mankind as preached by Jesus Christ to His disciples in the Mt. of Olives is, "Lawlessness will abound, the love of many will grow cold".

Never in the history of mankind where rampant and very obvious lawlessness have happened than in today's society. People are helpless against this lawlessness. Justice system only applies to the poor and the lowly. The rich can do whatever they want including child trafficking for sex slaves, drug and human trafficking and they can just continue their business as if there is no law that applies to them. Instead, the evil is rewarded and glorified and good are demonized and persecuted with the law. In the US alone, violent rioting is viewed by the government and mainstream media as a noble activity and claimed to be their rights and mainly peaceful as buildings are burning in the background and rioters have destroyed billions worth of private and public property. Even if these rioting causes billions upon billions of damages on private properties and businesses, yet nobody has been persecuted to this day. But the almost peaceful protest in the US Capitol on January 6 was declared as worse than civil war or 911. If the January 6 is really worse than US civil war, could the Capitol should have burned down to the ground? No, it cannot be burned because the perpetrators are inside. The violence arises only from the paid actors and federal agents operating the scenario complete with communication equipment. It was a controlled operation to deliver their deceptive narrative.

But were these operators persecuted? No. Even though these people can be and have been identified as feds and members of BLM and Antifa and not Trump supporters, no one have been persecuted. But the real protesters who support Trump and love their country, actually fight the operators breaking the door and windows, walking calmly inside the Capitol, and taking selfie. They respected the place and did not burn it to the ground. They have no intention to do that because their intention is just peaceful protest of the election steal. But these protestors have been declared as terrorist. Some of them are rotting in solitary confinement because wearing a weird costume and carrying a flag pole as a deadly weapon, and walking peacefully inside the Capitol during that day is a terroristic act comparable to 911 attack or even worse than a civil war. And as if the government is not satisfied yet of their perversion, they still intend to arrest thousands more they have identified that do not belong to the operators. But those operators whose faces are clearly seen in the hidden/forbidden videos were not arrested or persecuted at all. In fact, the leading operator pretending to be Trump supporter was protected by them. Imagine that, they said all January 6 protester are terrorist but they single out this man seen in video footage actually encouraging protestor to attack the Capitol as if he is in command.

Such lawlessness we are in today. To think that this is happening to the most developed and prosperous and purveyor of the so-called democracy.

On the other hand, if a parent inquires or object to the evil educational system being implemented in public schools, they are outrightly persecuted and declared as domestic terrorist as if they have the desire to burn a whole city than the rioters. Meanwhile, government officials (politicians) are outrightly lying to the people whom they swear to serve. There is no accountability to them. Law does not apply to them. They are the law.

Even independent farmers who are just trying to make a living are persecuted like criminals if they do not belong or obey the mandates of the cabals to burn or destroy their crops and slaughter their livestock.

This lawlessness is more pronounced in this scamdemic times. No presidents, prime ministers, health officials, police officials, employers, etc., etc. have been persecuted under the law for committing genocide against their own people. Millions upon millions of deaths are filing up with a 44% excess death rate. Millions are suffering from the permanent adverse effects of this injection. Yet, the government and the mainstream media are silent like a cold-blooded criminal as if nothing is happening. They even called this death phenomenon as Sudden Adult Death Syndrome or SADS and blame it on climate change, or sex, or spider. This is blatant crime against humanity to the core. And yet there is no justice, and the people love it.

Perhaps the reason why this prophecy involves the law and love will grow cold because the family of the dead does not care to think of what is going on and does not want to seek justice for their loved ones who is murdered by injection by the government and the medical industry. But where can you seek justice when the government is the law and the law does not apply to all. It is pure lawlessness.

As the popular slogan of then President Ramon Magsaysay said, "Those who have less in life, should have more in law".

Although he might have mean to say that the poor should have more protection and benefits from the law, but what is happening in these days of lawlessness is that the poor is heavily subjected under the law than the rich. The poor who is hungry and have no choice but to steal a can of sardines to provide for his family will be imprisoned for many years. Meanwhile, many politicians who are corrupt to the core, steal billions upon billions and yet they are still scotch free and living in luxury from the sweat and tears of the people. Justice and laws does not apply to them. Because for all we know, they are all brothers and sister in the secret society of the Vatican.

That is why this genocide committed by the governments of the world will not be brought to justice because they are the law. People are dying like flies, and they do not even know what hits them.

Or they do not even want to know what hits their love ones as if they do not care. The love of many indeed have grown cold. Very few wants to seek justice. But they are weakened because we are divided.

People are so lazy to think what is going on. They just accept that their loved one died from a natural cause. Even it is very obvious that only the injection could have caused these people to die suddenly. Even the very young and healthy kids and athletes suddenly died from unknown reason other than vaccination. Even just looking at social media, we can notice easily that there is something going on because there are many posted condolences of sudden death of their "friends" or family members on their pages. Some have more than dozens death condolences at some point after the rollout of the jab. But this has never happened in the past even during the heightened hype of the scamdemic.

These deaths are not just isolated cases. It is happening all over the world just after the vaccination of the governments of this evil world.

But people have no interest in seeking justice for their loved ones who perished. It is fine to those people who are even proud and arrogant brandishing that they have gotten the jab in their social media profiles. Their blood is on their hands. But those who are coerced or tortured (mentally/psychologically) to take the jab because they will lose their livelihood need to have justice. Their blood is on the hand of those who ordered and those who execute the injection. They are all liable criminals because they are all participants in Satan's masterplan.

But we have no working law, and criminal justice system is highjacked by the very people who need to be persecuted of these crimes they have committed against humanity. Except of course to those who allowed or voluntarily allowed themselves to be butchered by these criminals.

The love of the living loved ones left behind are so cold to seek justice for the death of their loved ones. They are by the thousands if not millions that should seek justice for their dead. Their loses are just in vain because they are in cognitive dissonance to accept that they have been deceived, fooled, or lied upon. Their pride and arrogance are more important than their loved one's life. Their love is indeed cold. But as Mark Twain said;

"It's easier to fool people than to convince them that they have been fooled."

Another fulfilled prophecy observable by all man is what Paul wrote in 2 Timothy 3: 1-5, saying;

"[1]But know this, that <u>in the last days perilous times will come</u>: [2]For men will be lovers of themselves, lovers of money, boasters, proud, blasphemers, disobedient to parents, unthankful, unholy, [3]unloving, unforgiving, slanderers, without self-control, brutal, despisers of good, [4]traitors, headstrong, haughty, lovers of pleasure rather than lovers of God, [5]<u>having a form of godliness but denying its power.</u> And from such people turn away!"

There is no need for further elaboration of these verses because it has become so common specially in the new generations. That is why humanity is descending farther into a very dangerous world we live in today. Perilous times indeed.

But even those who profess to believe in God and professing to be Christians – "having the form of godliness" and yet denying the power and truth of the Bible by creating their own doctrines and traditions. Even denying the law of God that have been repeated many times in the Bible that is very important to be kept and observe.

Just as Jesus said Himself in John 14: 15;

"[15]"If you love Me, keep <u>My commandments</u>....""

If he nailed the commandments in the cross and people are not required to observe it, why would He preach that the commandments is prerequisite to loving Him? Take note that He said "My commandments". It is His, given or commanded by His Father that He Himself obeyed and obeying to this time forth and forevermore.

But professing Christians denied the power that is embodied in obeying the commandments of God. And that is the love of God. And for this, they become blind and deaf to the truth that even Paul preached to the Gentiles in Romans 2: 13, saying;

"13(for not the hearers of the law are just in the sight of God, but the doers of the law will be justified;…)"

And in 1 John 2: 3-4;

"3Now by this we know that we <u>know Him</u>, if we <u>keep His commandments</u>. 4He who says, "I know Him," and <u>does not keep His commandments, is a liar, and the truth is not in him</u>."

See, the power of the law is a prerequisite for us to be justified in the eyes of God. It has not been done away. For without obedience to the law, we do not show fear towards God, and without fear towards God we will not have godly wisdom, knowledge, and understanding because the Holy Spirit which will guide us towards the truth will not be granted to <u>disobedient people</u>. That is why even the thousands of professing Christian denominations, many are still confused and deceived. The truth is not in them. How much more the secularist mega churches whose focus is not about God but materialism. They invented their own gospel – the prosperity gospel.

It is very clear in the above verse that he who keeps His commandments know Him. But those who profess to know Him but does not want to obey His commandments are liars. If one lie to another, he is against that person. And if one is against that person, he is anti- that person. Therefore, if one is against Christ commandments that person is anti-Christ. Anti or against the real Christ and worshipping another Jesus.

So, whether you are a professing Christian or a Non- Christian, the evidence of the truthfulness of the God of the bible is the fulfillment of His prophecies that have happened and is currently happening right before our very own eyes.

If you still will not believe the God of the Bible based on this realistic evidences presented by God – Jesus Christ (Yeshua) in His words for our present time for whatever reason, whether it is pure foolishness or stupidity (as God called us to be), then how much more you will not believe the warning about the coming dreadful day of the Lord.

But for us Ophirians -the people of the isles in the east ends of the earth, we are accounted for to hear and obey the calling of God for His purpose. We should not remain to be in our foolishness and stupid state of mind, pretending that we are not deceived when we do not believe and obey the Word of God. God is calling us to be His servants into righteousness. And we should be thankful to God that even though we are weak, meek and poor, proud and arrogant people, He have chosen us to be His end time servants for the salvation of mankind. And as Hebrews 3: 15 said;

"¹⁵"Today, if you will hear His voice, do not harden your hearts as in the rebellion.""

Rebellion against God is pure foolishness and stupidity because no one can win against God. It is clearly said in Acts 5: 29;

"²⁹"We ought to obey God rather than men....""

For as Jesus Christ read the prophecy in Isaiah 61: 1-2 in Luke 4: 18-19 for us Ophirians saying;

"¹⁸"The Spirit of the Lord is upon Me, because He has anointed Me to preach the gospel to the poor; He has sent Me to heal the brokenhearted, to proclaim liberty to the captives and recovery of sight to the blind, to set at liberty those who are oppressed; ¹⁹To proclaim the acceptable year of the Lord."

And in Luke 4: 21, Jesus claimed that He fulfilled this prophecy upon reading the book of Isaiah saying;

"²¹..."Today this Scripture is fulfilled in your hearing.""

We must understand that Isaiah is particularly talking to three identities namely, Israel (both collective and the House of Israel (the ten lost tribes)), the House of Judah particularly Jerusalem (signifying Jewish People, Levites, and Benjaminite's), and the Gentile peoples of the isles from the ends of the earth in the east.

Of the three, only the Gentile peoples of the isles have not heard the gospel. Jesus Christ and His disciples have preached the gospel to Israel. But they did not believe.

Of the three, only the Gentile peoples of the isles is poor

(present day), will be brokenhearted (upon reading this book because we will realize that we have been deceived and we worship another Jesus although we sincerely believe in God. The truth may hurt for a little while, but lies hurts forever.), as such, we need liberty from Satan's captivity that is causing our blindness resulting for us to live in darkness (That is why the Light will come to us in Isa. 60: 1). When one is deceived or betrayed by someone specially those whom they love, they become brokenhearted. People of the world love and serve Satan (knowingly and unknowingly), thinking that he is telling the truth. But he is the great deceiver. And it will break our hearts knowing that we have been deceived all along.

The phrase "and recovery of sight to the blind, to set at liberty those who are oppressed;" in Luke 4:18 is written as, "and the opening of the prison to those who are bound;" in Isaiah 61: 1. What does this mean?

Of the three, only the <u>Gentile peoples of the isles</u> have been bound by Satan's prison houses of many religious denominations for a long - long time even before God took Abraham from the Ur of the Chaldean. The House of Israel have been recently captured by Satan's prison houses through their diversity, religious tolerance and political correctness.

We will call the Gentile peoples of the isles – Ophirians.

Now we know that the prophecy of Isaiah 61 is and will be fulfilled by Jesus Christ to the Ophirian people. Why? Because God is calling us into righteousness so that we may become His end time servants. And we may become worthy to be called His people also.

So, how will Jesus Christ preach the gospel, open the blind eyes, free up from prison houses of Satan to the Ophirian people?

God uses His prophets, disciples, apostles, servants, and messengers to accomplish His plans. Now, Jesus Christ used His humble servant to preach the message of truth to His future people.

So, it is said, "Today this Scripture is fulfilled in your hearing and reading of this book".

Jesus Christ (Yeshua) commissioned Paul to preach the gospel to the Gentiles. Paul is a former anti-Christ. He persecuted the Church.

But he became the apostle of Jesus Christ by the will of God to preach good tidings unto the Gentiles in former times and in our present time. He became the prisoner of Jesus rather than him imprisoning and persecuting those who follow Jesus.

Let us hear the preaching of Jesus Christ to the Gentiles (present day Ophirians) through Paul in Ephesians 4: 1-24;

"¹I, therefore, the prisoner of the Lord, beseech you <u>to walk worthy of the calling with which you were called</u>, ²with all <u>lowliness</u> and <u>gentleness</u>, with <u>longsuffering</u>, <u>bearing with one another in love</u>, ³endeavoring to keep the unity of the Spirit in the bond of peace. ⁴There is <u>one body and one Spirit</u>, just as you were called in <u>one hope</u> of your calling; ⁵<u>one Lord</u>, <u>one faith</u>, <u>one baptism</u>; ⁶<u>one God and Father of all</u>, who is above all, and through all, and in you all.

⁷But to each one of us <u>grace was given</u> according to the measure of Christ's gift. ⁸Therefore He says:

"When He ascended on high,

He led captivity captive,

And gave gifts to men."

⁹(Now this, "He ascended"—what does it mean but that He also first descended into the lower parts of the earth? ¹⁰He who descended is also <u>the One who ascended far above all the heavens</u>, that He might fill all things.)

¹¹And He Himself gave some to be apostles, some prophets, some evangelists, and some pastors and teachers, ¹²for the <u>equipping of the saints for the work of ministry</u>, for the <u>edifying of the body of Christ</u>, ¹³till <u>we all come to the unity of the faith and of the knowledge of the Son of God</u>, to <u>a perfect man</u>, to the measure of the stature of the fullness of Christ; ¹⁴<u>that we should no longer be children, tossed to and fro and carried about with every wind of doctrine, by the trickery of men</u>, in the cunning craftiness of deceitful plotting, ¹⁵but, speaking the truth in love, may grow up in all things into Him who is the head—Christ— ¹⁶from whom the whole body,

joined and knit together by what every joint supplies, according to the effective working by which every part does its share, causes growth of the body for the edifying of itself in love. [17]This I say, therefore, and testify in the Lord, that <u>you should no longer walk as the rest of the Gentiles walk, in the futility of their mind,</u> [18]having their understanding darkened, being alienated from the life of God, <u>because of the ignorance that is in them, because of the blindness of their heart;</u> [19]who, being past feeling, <u>have given themselves over to lewdness, to work all uncleanness with greediness.</u>

[20]But you have not so learned Christ, [21]if indeed you have heard Him and have been taught by Him, as the truth is in Jesus: [22]that <u>you put off, concerning your former conduct, the old man which grows corrupt according to the deceitful lusts,</u> [23]and <u>be renewed in the spirit of your mind,</u> [24]and that <u>you put on the new man which was created according to God,</u> <u>in true righteousness and holiness.</u>"

This is a very powerful message for us Ophirians and this is the very essence of God's calling for us that we may depart from our former conducts and as Jesus Christ Himself told His servants in Revelation 18: 4, "Come out of her, my people,…".

Notice very carefully also that Satan is working hard to discredit Apostle Paul as a false prophet so that the Epistles of Paul will be excluded from the Bible. It is being projected that the gospel and doctrines, Paul is preaching, appeared to be his own personal account and not coming from the revelation of Jesus Christ as His chosen minister for the Gentiles. Let us make it very clear that Paul's preaching as revealed to him by Jesus Christ for the Gentiles (past, present (Ophirians), and future (the rest of the world other than Israelites)). This is Satan's attempt to hide the truth about the mystery stored/prepared for the Gentile peoples of the isles (present and future) so that they may not know their works and their future in God's masterplan.

This is the mystery as revealed by Paul in Ephesians 3: 1-21;

"[1]For this reason I, Paul, the prisoner of Christ Jesus for you Gentiles- [2]if indeed you have heard of <u>the dispensation of the grace of God</u> which was <u>given to me for you</u>, [3]how that <u>by revelation</u> He <u>made known to me</u> the mystery (as I have briefly written already, [4]by which, when you read, you may understand my knowledge in the mystery of Christ), [5]which in <u>other ages was not made known to the sons of men</u>, as it has now been revealed by the Spirit to His holy apostles and prophets: [6]that <u>the Gentiles should be fellow heirs, of the same body, and partakers of His promise in Christ through the gospel</u>,[7]of which I became a minister <u>according to the gift of the grace of God</u> given to me by the effective working of His power.

[8]To me, who am less than the least of all the saints, this grace was given, that I should <u>preach among the Gentiles the unsearchable riches of Christ</u>, [9]and <u>to make all see what is the fellowship of the mystery</u>, which from the beginning of the ages has been hidden in <u>God who created all things through Jesus Christ</u>; [10]to the intent that now the manifold wisdom of God might <u>be made known by the church</u> to the principalities and powers in the heavenly places, [11]according to the eternal purpose which He accomplished in Christ Jesus our Lord, [12]in whom we have boldness and access with confidence through faith in Him. [13]Therefore I ask that you do not lose heart at my tribulations for you, which is your glory.

[14]For this reason I bow my knees to the Father of our Lord Jesus Christ, [15]from whom the whole family in heaven and earth is named, [16]that <u>He would grant you, according to the riches of His glory, to be strengthened with might through His Spirit in the inner man</u>, [17]<u>that Christ may dwell in your hearts through faith</u>; that you, being rooted and grounded in love, [18]may be able to comprehend with all the saints what is the width and length and depth and height— [19]<u>to know the love of Christ</u> which passes knowledge; that you may be filled with all the fullness of God.

[20]Now to Him who is able to do exceedingly abundantly above all that we ask or think, according to the power that works in us,[21]to Him be glory in the church by Christ Jesus to all generations, forever and ever. Amen."

In our part, we will call the church as the "Ophirian Church of God".

There are many more preaching of Jesus Christ through the epistles of Paul that we need to study to fully understand what God has in store for us to do for His Kingdom and His glory. The Church will be preaching more of this when we, "the Ophirians" begin to recognize the power and glory of the True Living God of the Bible.

SECTION 2

THE ENEMY

CHAPTER 2

KNOWING THE ENEMY

The Physical Enemy

Who is our enemy?

Many of us will think immediately that our greatest enemy is Satan the devil. In reality, our greatest enemy is ourselves. Satan has no power over us unless we allowed him to be. Satan just present the temptations to sin. He will lie to us. He will deceive us. He will coerce us to the furthest extent, but he can never enforce his will upon us.

Just like God our maker, He does not enforce his will upon us. He created us as a free moral agent. We are creation with free choice. We decide on our own. As the saying goes "we are the captain of our soul". God did not create us as a fiat human being.

And as a free-moral agents, God had given us a choice. It's either we choose God's way or Satan's way. In God's way, he promised us real peace, joy, happiness, and prosperity in His Kingdom. While Satan, being the great liar, deceiver, and ruler of this world, will tell us that God is a liar, or is not true, or does not exist. Instead, he leads us to his way promising peace, happiness, and material abundance. But as we know it for centuries that Satan's material abundance comes with a price. Satan's way actually resulted in wars, unrest, sufferings, diseases, sadness, depression, poverty, and lawlessness. And ultimately, Satan's way is the way to death (both physical and spiritual – he deceives the whole world). While God's way is the way to life (physically and spiritually).

Does Satan enforce his will upon us? No. Humanity had decided to follow him voluntarily because we believe in his lies and deceptions. We despise God's truth, and we love to be lied and deceived. It has been since time to this day. We are easily deceived, and Satan loves it and laughed hard on us because we believe on his empty promises. Like politicians perhaps?

On the other hand, God is grieving on what we are doing in our lives. He wants to give us good life and yet we choose the way of death. He hated our way of choice, that he wanted to destroy humanity once again. But in John 3:16 said, "For God so love the world, so much that He give his only begotten Son, that whosoever believe in Him should not perish but have everlasting life".

Instead, humanity continue to choose Satan's way of death. God is not saving us from Satan! He is saving us from ourselves - our greatest enemy. From our self-destructive choices. From our wickedness.

But we are so powerless to fight the enemy from within because Jesus said in John 15: 5;

"⁵...for without Me you can do nothing."

If we do not choose the way of God, we can do nothing to better up our human conditions. For we are pure evil as written in Jeremiah 17: 9-10;

"⁹"The heart is deceitful above all things, and desperately wicked".

God knows our heart and mind.

"¹⁰ "I, the Lord, search the heart, I test the mind, even to give every man according to his ways, and according to the fruit of his doing."

God knows our wickedness. Yet he is a just God. We are on our own free- will. We decide what we like for our lives to be. But we have a choice to make between good and evil, between life and death, between light and darkness, between righteousness and unrighteousness, between selfishness or outgoing concern for others, between right and wrong, between the way of God (giving) and the way of Satan(getting).

That is why God declared in Jeremiah 17:13;

"¹³O Lord, the hope of Israel, all who forsake You shall be ashamed. "Those who depart from Me shall be written in the earth, because they have forsaken the Lord, the fountain of living waters.'"

Most of humanity have departed and forsaken God – his Maker. Instead, they serve and worshipped Satan the devil, knowingly and unknowingly. But the time of reckoning is near. Tribulation period is in the horizon. The wrath of God is sure to come. Humanity is about to experience the greatest sufferings and troubles no man have experienced since the beginning of time. The world is about to meet the wrath of his Maker just as Jesus said in Matthew 24: 21;

"²¹ "For then there will be great tribulation, such as has not been since the beginning of the world until this time, no, nor ever shall be.'"

God is grieving for humanity's wickedness (Gen. 6: 6). That is why He condemns those who are incorrigible that forsake Him when He come just as He said in John 16: 8-9;

"⁸And when He has come, He will convict the world of sin, and of righteousness, and of judgment: ⁹of sin, because they do not believe in Me;…"

Can you feel the heart of God on how He is grieving because of our hardheadedness and disobedience? Let us put our feet on His shoes; We are a good father like our God. We want the best for our family. We want to guide our children to what we think will be best for them to take, so that they will have a blessed and fruitful future. We know it because we have been there, and we have committed mistakes that we do not want them to commit too, so that they can advance faster and more efficiently. We at least know what the best for them. So, we become their guiding light, and their compass in starting their journey in life. Yet our children are hardheaded and disobedient. They decide to do things on their own without capitalizing the precious experiences of their parents that can lead them to happiness and less troublesome life.

The happy family we dreamed to build starting to crumble because our children chose the wayward way of disobedience and self-righteousness. We know that the path they are taking is a very dangerous path, yet we can do nothing about it because that is their choice.

Some of us as parents strive and tried our vey best to discipline and guide them to the proper way that will be best for them according to our knowledge. And some of us give up on them early on. We lack the knowledge, courage, and determination to guide them. We easily give in to their will. We let them go early on because we do not like to struggle in disciplining and training them. Perhaps because we do not know how to raise children. And we do not know how to pray to God for guidance. We rely on ourselves thinking without proper guidance. And so, we give up on them very easily. But this is our family. They are our responsibility – to God and our society.

Raising a family is not easy. It is not just about sex or infatuated love from the very start. It is about responsibility. It is full of struggles and sacrifices. We fight hard so that Satan cannot ensnare our children to his traps. Yet most of the children chose the way of Satan than our way as their father who loved them and care for them. And yet, with this caring and loving heart as a father, it grieved us most seeing our children walking in the way of darkness that will make them suffer in life.

It troubles us to our grave. We worried and suffered the weirdest feeling we can ever have. And we ask ourselves, where did we go wrong? We blame ourselves as a failure parent for what our children have become. It is a gut-wrenching feeling tormenting us day and night.

When they went away from us to go to college or for whatever reason, we worried for them. We ask ourselves, how are they doing? Are they okey? Do they have food to eat or are they safe?

On the other hand, it is our joy to see our children become successful in life. Their success is our success. Although they do it on their own, they succeeded in life because they listen, obey, and respect their parents. These are the three fundamental attitudes in life that will "honor thy mother and thy father" (Exod. 20:12) which lead to long and happy life.

This is the most basic human way on how we can understand God's feeling towards us. He grieved to those disobedient children, and he rejoiced on those who chose to listen and obey His commandments.

Gone Astray

Indeed, Isaiah 53:6 said;

"⁶All we like sheep have gone astray; we have turned, everyone, to his own way; and the Lord has laid on Him the iniquity of us all."

All humanity has gone astray. We have transgressed God. We have sinned against God. And the penalty of sin is death (Rom. 6: 23). Eternal death. Because we refuse to seek and obey God's way. We suffer the consequences of our own making. But God is a gracious and a loving Father. He sacrifices His only begotten Son to die for our iniquities. God, the Almighty Father put our iniquities on Yeshua (Jesus Christ) so that He will be the one to suffer and die for our sins. He was stricken and afflicted because of our sins. He died on behalf of our transgressions. And that is the greatest grace of the Almighty Father. To sacrifice His very own for the salvation of filthy, ingrate, and disobedient human beings.

If we come to think about it, we are not worthy for this sacrifice because we are useless and evil to the core. We are the worse of the worse that cannot even be compared to a filthy rug, because we forsake and despises our own Maker, our Father. We deserve to die and be vanished. That is why God's salvation for mankind is by grace because the price of the sacrifice is too expensive just to pay for our sins. When in fact, we are worthless and not worthy for this grace. That is why we should not take God's grace in mockery. Not because it is by grace it is free. It comes with a great price. And with that great price comes with great responsibilities on our part so that we may be worthy to accept the grace being offered to us for free. We need to voluntarily take it and own it, including all the conditions in receiving that grace. This grace is contingent on the obedience of His commandments. This grace is given so that we can perform a great work in God's family and not as an ultimate passport to have an ultimate everlasting vacation grandee in heaven.

The book of Isaiah gives us the great lamentation of God on how His very own people – Israel have transgressed Him. Yet He is sending His Servant and the servants of His Servant to save Israel and mankind in the end times.

The Disobedient Enemy

Now we know that we are our own greatest enemy because we are disobedient children. Hardheaded and we harden our hearts with pride and arrogance. Pretending that we know the best for us better than our father. And so, our pride and arrogance has blinded us to the bigger picture of what is good. We became fools trying to do it on our own without capitalizing the experience and wisdom of those who came before us. And so, fools breeds fools and the world become a pool of fools just as it is written in 1 Corinthians 3: 18-21, said;

> "¹⁸Let no one deceive himself. If anyone among you seems to be wise in this age, let him become a fool that he may become wise. ¹⁹For the wisdom of this world is foolishness with God. For it is written, "He catches the wise in their own craftiness"; ²⁰and again, "The Lord knows the thoughts of the wise, that they are futile." ²¹Therefore let no one boast in men."

Humanity despises godly wisdom. We love foolishness. We love to experiment things and ideas we thought it is new and exciting. Little do we know that these ideas have preexisted since the ancient of times. It might be in different forms but the same main idea.

These bad ideas originate from Satan the devil. And these evil ideas if we just look back and learn from history ended up in more disaster, troubles, and suffering.

Now we are in it again. Humanity is busy promoting and practicing homosexuality and experimentation of transgenderism. To the point that even them are confused on what they will call

THE PHILIPPINES IN BIBLE PROPHECY

themselves. They want and are willing to be called and confused themselves to any kind of invented identity just not to be called man or woman, boys or girls or classified as male or female. "Call me anything, but not this" mentality. They despise to belong to what God have designed them to be. They are missing the grand design big time. And they feel good about it trying to disobey God. Yet, they are so confused of what to call themselves. To them, there is a great spectrum of identity between male and female. They would invent it. It can be millions or even billions of identities that they can create for themselves just to disobey God who created them and obey and worship Satan as their god who confused and troubled them. What a foolishness to behold.

Humanity is too perverted in sexual immorality that homosexuality become an accepted norm in almost every society in the world. But the most disgusting and dangerous about this sexual immorality is that it is hard to distinguish some of then anymore. Some male homosexuals are very handsome, some are masculine (not effeminate) and some are even bearded that we will not recognize that they are practicing homosexual until they make advances or intentions to their fellow male. Some male homos change their appearance to look like a real woman. They augment their breast, facial features, and bodily forms even up to hormonal level. Many of them work in hospitality/prostitution industry. And many of them have been killed by their customers. What a tragic event as a result of their foolishness.

On the other hand, beautiful woman whom men will admire, and desire are hard to recognize whether they are practicing lesbians or not. Some homosexual women who's desire is to become or act and practice like a man try to change their appearance through their hair cut and manly clothing. At least they became recognizable.

These homosexual practices are not new. It has been in the world since the ancient of times. And God hated and despises those who practice homosexuality. How much more the new age transgenderism acts. The Bible explicitly said that these acts are abominable to God. Those who practice and support this sexual immorality they cannot enter the kingdom of God just as it is written in 1 Corinthians 6: 9-10;

> "⁹Do you not know that the unrighteous will not inherit the kingdom of God? Do not be deceived. Neither fornicators, nor idolaters, nor adulterers, nor homosexuals, nor sodomites, ¹⁰nor thieves, nor covetous, nor drunkards, nor revilers, nor extortioners will inherit the kingdom of God."

Sodomites here is now the present-day transgenderism. But the root cause of all of this is idolatry. In Romans 1: 24-29, those who practice idolatry are subjected into debased mind;

> "²⁴Therefore God also gave them up to uncleanness, in the lusts of their hearts, to dishonor their bodies among themselves, ²⁵who exchanged the truth of God for the lie, and worshiped and served the creature rather than the Creator, who is blessed forever. Amen. ²⁶For this reason God gave them up to vile passions. For even their women exchanged the natural use for what is against nature. ²⁷Likewise also the men, leaving the natural use of the woman, burned in their lust for one another, men with men committing what is shameful, and receiving in themselves the penalty of their error which was due.
> ²⁸And even as they did not like to retain God in their knowledge, God gave them over to a debased mind, to do those things which are not fitting; ²⁹being filled with all unrighteousness, sexual immorality, wickedness,…"

They will not be able to distinguish what is good and what is evil for they are blinded by their unrighteousness and wickedness.

There are many more evil practices humanity are addicted to. But in this section, I focused on homosexuality and sodomy because this is the sign of the impending punishment to humanity – the wrath of God.

God had promised to Noah after the flood that he will never destroy the earth again with water in Genesis 9: 11;

> "¹¹"…Thus I establish My covenant with you: Never again

shall all flesh be cut off by the waters of the flood; never again shall there be a flood to destroy the earth.""

But with fire as it is written in 2 Peter 3: 6-7;
"⁶"...by which the world that then existed perished, being flooded with water. ⁷But the heavens and the earth which are now preserved by the same word, are <u>reserved for fire until the day of judgment</u> and perdition of ungodly men.""

And the precedent of this coming event is Sodom and Gomorrah. It was burned in brimstone and hell fire as it is written in Genesis 19: 24-25 (Deut. 29: 23, Luke 17: 29);
"²⁴Then the Lord rained brimstone and fire on Sodom and Gomorrah, from the Lord out of the heavens. ²⁵So He overthrew those cities, all the plain, all the inhabitants of the cities, and what grew on the ground."

And finally, during the tribulation period as it is written in Revelation 9: 18;
"¹⁸By these three plagues a third of mankind was killed—by the fire and the smoke and the brimstone which came out of their mouths."

Surely, because of mankind's hardheadedness, the wrath of God is coming.

The Spiritual Enemy

The enemy of God is Satan.

If we are to become servants of God, we should declare Satan as our enemy also. By this, we should know the workings, ways, and characteristics of our enemy. But Satan have deceived the whole world. The world has been blinded by Satan that in the eyes and mind of man, good became evil and evil became good. Right became wrong and wrong became right. Now a days, evil deeds are rewarded, and good deeds are punished. This is the sign that we have indeed descended into darkness. And the world is loving it, even if the result is suffering, poverty, diseases, and confusion. Insanity reigning in the world today.

We should declare war against our enemy. For how can we win the war without fighting the war?

But our enemy is so powerful. We cannot win the war on our own flesh. Just as Jesus said in Matthew 26: 41;

""41"... The spirit indeed is willing, but the flesh is weak.""

That is why Jesus Christ fought and won the battle for us. All we must do now is say NO to our enemy. Satan has no power over us unless we allow him to do so. But how can we use Christ's victory against our enemy?

FEAR GOD!

In Psalms 111:10 said;

""10The fear of the Lord is the beginning of wisdom; a good understanding have all those who do His commandments."

That is right, winning the war against Satan starts by fearing God and not by fearing Satan.

But humanity fear Satan more than they fear God. People of the earth are not bothered to disobey God's commandments. For most people, the Creator God is not real. To some, it is whatever they can think and conceive of. To those who believe that there is a God, they think that He is always a forgiving, merciful and loving Father that is why it is okey to disobey and even mock Him. God is taken for granted and even treated like their slave when they pray. Lord, give me this, give me that. Do this, do that...

Humanity have become blinded because of our sinfulness, and we forget or have not known the true nature of our Creator God. His creation is at His mercy. He can do whatever He want to do with His creation. He is an all-powerful God that can send catastrophe, kill people, allow sickness and diseases and all the bad things that had happened and is happening and going to happen to us because of our disobedience to Him since the time of Adam. And yet, people will say there is no God for how can He allow these bad things to happen to His creation. People forget that the wickedness of men will not go unpunished just as it is written in Proverbs 11: 21;

> "²¹Though they join forces, <u>the wicked will not go unpunished</u>; But the posterity of the righteous will be delivered."

And the Lord said in Isaiah 13: 11;

> "¹¹"<u>I will punish the world for its evil</u>, and <u>the wicked for their iniquity</u>; I will halt <u>the arrogance of the proud</u>, and will lay low the haughtiness of the terrible...."

Humanity forgot that we have wronged God because Satan deceived the whole world. And for that we deserve punishments and death. There is no justification for our wickedness. What we are experiencing are just warnings and a solid proof that a real God do exist. He controls everything and He can do whatever He wants.

We have not known that God killed the entire civilization of the first earth. And again, He wiped out the entire humanity through flood from Adam's time to Noah. All because of our wickedness, sinfulness and disregard for our Maker. And the time is coming that billions of people (3/4 of population) will suffer and die from the wrath of God and from the wrath of Satan. But Satan can kill our body but cannot kill our soul. Only God can kill both body and soul.

In reality, majority of the people do not know the true living God and we do not care knowing God until we experience trouble in our lives. We do not fear Him that is why we disobey His commandments which is the most important aspect in life that will lead us to have wisdom, knowledge and understanding of the true nature of our God. The fear of God will open our eyes to be able to identify and see beyond the illusion of the trickery of our enemy. The fear of God will give us the armor we need to protect us against our enemy. The fear of God will give us wisdom, knowledge and understanding on how to defeat our enemy. And ultimately, the fear of the Lord will give us the wisdom, knowledge and understanding to empower us to be able to listen and obey God and declare His glory.

The key to defeating Satan is fearing God. Through God we will have the power to defeat Satan in our lives and to free us from his prison houses (religions). But to claim God's victory in our live, we need to go to Him. Approach Him with fear and trembling to obey His Laws and commandments that we may have wisdom, knowledge, and understanding to know His ways and be able to win our war with Satan. Apart from God, we can do nothing.

So, seek Him with all our might and soul just as it is written in Deuteronomy 4: 29;

> "²⁹But from there you will <u>seek the Lord your God</u>, and you will find Him if you <u>seek Him with all your heart and with all your soul</u>."

Knowing How the Enemy Operates

Knowing how the enemy operates is vital to winning the war. Knowing the strength and weaknesses of our enemy is one deciding factor how to attack our enemy.

Satan's weakness is if we get near to God and gain wisdom, knowledge, and understanding of God. That is how we see and recognize Satan's evil working and strategies.

Satan's strength is his great lies, and deceptions. We have witness this in almost every human government on earth. Through lies and deceptions, nations and kingdoms are divided. The pro and the anti of whatever political ideology divides a nation and its people in democracy. Constant fighting and confusion happen among politicians and the people. Bickering here and there. Fake news here and fake news there. No moral ascendency among leaders and people. And they call it a healthy government. A healthy nation in democracy. The same with any other form of governments and religions. They call it freedom and diversity. And this is how Satan weakened the nations (Isa. 14: 12).

Is democracy really healthy? If a family is divided against each other, how can they stand strong and function effectively if there is always bickering and fighting with each other? They will be fighting all the time like what is happening to every so-called democratic country today. Fighting among family members will be frequent and it does not feel good to belong to a family full of animosity. This situation will result in rebellion eventually among family members. And this is where Satan is expert at. *Divide et impera* (divide and conquer). Satan divide nations, people and families because a divided nation cannot stand just as Jesus Christ said in Mathew 12: 25-26;

> "²⁵But Jesus knew their thoughts, and said to them: "<u>Every kingdom divided against itself is brought to desolation</u>, and every city or house divided against itself will not stand. ²⁶If Satan casts out Satan, he is divided against himself. How then will his kingdom stand?"""

In a divided organization, the enemy can easily penetrate the defenses and eventually conquer it. A very popular example of this is our nation (Philippines) and the USA. The bastion of the so-called democracy was conquered by their very own enemy without a single shot fired in a battlefield. From the time Abraham Lincoln was assassinated, the American people became the slaves of their enemy to this day. That is why democracy is a failure form of government because in actuality, it enslaves the people through the illusion of freedom.

Just think about it for a second, the government of the USA is sending money to the corrupt government of Ukraine, funding the illegal immigrants, funding wars in any part of the world, etc., etc. without the approval of the people. In fact, it is against the will of the people because they are the one who will bear the burden of paying the great debt, the present (2022) government is giving them. But they can do nothing about it even though they themselves are suffering from double digit inflation brought by deliberate economic and foreign policy sabotage by their very own government.

The American people (Manasseh), one of the tribes of the chosen people of God is being used by Satan (Vatican) to destroy themselves and the world. Satan is operating and attacking the nation of the USA from within by the many deceptions through his American minions who are traitors to their own country. The kids have been destroyed and being destroyed by dozens of vaccines from the time they were born creating chronic illnesses (when and if they grow up), brain damages (autism, etc.), and death. Education is being demonized so that people will never learn how to think and can be easily manipulated and controlled.

The same thing happened and is happening in the Philippines. Mind manipulation as the result of their long-term predictive programming and propaganda became more obvious (to those who are able to think) during the scamdemic where government oppressed the people of their so-called human rights and the rampant corruptions of the politicians, government establishments, and the medical industry. Killing was even incentivized for the sake of covid propaganda.

Satan use human emotion as a tool to confuse people into his plans. Satan is the author of rebellion, confusion, and division. He likes people to be confused so that they become paralyzed and therefore not able to think and fight back.

"A nation divided cannot stand." What happened to our country and the USA is a proof that this thesis is true. This is the very strength of Satan in attacking us. It is so subtle that we do not even know what hits us. Satan used our mental and emotional weaknesses to turn ourselves into an enemy of our own. He creates his army from within. He attacks nations from within and win the war without a single fire shot just by turning people to be traitors against their own land using his secret societies.

He hates people who knows how to think, people who are united and who loves harmony. Because he knows that mankind can accomplish amazing things if we work together. So, he divided us. Divide and conquer. Divided, we become our own enemy. And that is freedom, diversity, and relativism all about. Satan weaponizes these ideas to raise confusion and division among people.

Knowing Satan's ways, tools, and weapons and avoiding them can make us get closer to God.

How does Satan use freedom, diversity, and relativism to confused and deceive many?

Through the so-called civil rights. By this evil concept, people are made to believe that everyone is free to do whatever they want to do, believe whatever they want to believe, practice whatever they want to practice. This freedom is relative to every individual's perception and belief. Through relativism, there is no right and wrong. Everyone is free to do whatever they want to do without the bounds of a righteous law. By this concept, diversity is healthy in every home, groups, organizations, or in a nation.

We know this evil concept is wrong and it causes division and troubles to everyone's life. It is masquerading as protection of the people - their human rights. We know for a fact that the beneficiary of this so-called human rights are the evil people. Those who are in power and corrupt oligarchs. It is not for the welfare or protection of the ordinary people; it is for their protection. This is similar to the justice system. Justice system is not just broken but is rigged for their protection. But for ordinary people, there is no justice. Justice is for sale. Those who have money can have justice. But those have not, suffer even if they are not the one who did the crime they are accused of. I know poor people who were killed that did not get justice because they do not have money to hire a lawyer just to file a case. Even if police or authorities know who the killer is, justice still is not served because nobody complained. Or even the living family of the victim who have money to hire a lawyer will still be hesitant or will have a second though of filing a case because the criminals are protected by the politicians or the rich. Still justice cannot be served. Our justice system is fake like the illusion of the so-called freedom, and human rights.

There is no real freedom apart from the laws that is equally applied to all. Similarly, there is no real prosperity apart from having a financial system that allow equal opportunity to all and not just the wealthy and the few.

These are just the few examples of systems where Satan works to deceive the many. His main ploy is for the protection and welfare of the people. But underneath is his evil plan to deceive and make great sufferings for the people. These are just a few characteristics and strategies of Satan to play on the minds of humanity.

But we can do nothing about it because Satan is a powerful

spirit being. He knows our weakness is our emotion. When he deals with our emotions, everything falls apart. In a sense, the first line of attack of the enemy is ourselves.

We are the one who empowers Satan in our lives because we allow ourselves to be manipulated by him. We are so weak to fight or think when the illusion being presented to us looks so good for our feelings, but the final result is actually the opposite. We are blinded by the material and physical gratification. But the end is suffering and misery. Not only for ourselves but also to those around us. Our loved ones.

Many are deceived because we cannot see. We cannot see because we do not have God in our lives. If we have God, it is the wrong god that we believe and worship. The gods of this world is Satan's creation. Those are actually Satan's representation so that humanity will worship him. We should remember that Satan wanted to be worshipped. He wanted to be the God who created him. Satan wanted to replace the Almighty God in heaven that is why he attempted to attack God in His throne in heaven. But Satan and his demons were defeated by the angels of God through the leadership of Michael and Gabriel.

Chaos, confusion, and destruction are the result of Lucifer's rebellion against God - his maker. Lucifer later becomes Satan the Devil who deceives the whole world (Rev. 12: 9).

Notice very carefully that the deception of Satan is the whole world. If you belong to a religion who have hundreds of thousands, or millions or billions of followers, ask yourself, am I deceived?

The beautiful creation of God the Heaven, the heavens, and the earth was destroyed because of this war in heaven. And so the creation is subjected into desolation but not on their own will. That is why the creation is groaning and waiting for the sons of God for their redemption. That their beauty and life may be restored once more as Paul said in Romans 8: 19-22;

"[19]For the earnest expectation of the creation eagerly waits for the revealing of the sons of God. [20]For the creation was subjected to futility, not willingly, but because of Him who subjected it in hope; [21]because the creation itself also will be delivered from the bondage of corruption into the glorious liberty of the children of God. [22]For we know that the whole creation groans and labors with birth pangs together until now."

This is one of the great human potentials that God has in store for us to do when we become sons of God. For the redemption of the creation under the bondage of corruption or destruction. So, the sons of God will recreate and beautify the creation once more into its former glory.

And that is why Satan is so eager to deceive humanity to blind us from this incredible human potential.

The creative mind we have as a human being is just the tip of the iceberg. Imagine how powerful and creative we will be when we become children of God. What will be the magnitude of our accomplishments and achievements under our Almighty Father.

Remember that the universe as far as the human eyes can see was perceived by astronomers and scientists that are approximately composed of 13 trillion earthlike planets based on their computation a planet's distance from the stars like the sun in the solar system. And that is only based on the visible two-dimensional space of the universe. What about 3D or 4D or who knows how many dimensions the universe has. And the universe is still growing by the day.

Our human perception is so limited, yet this number human mind can conceive is so mind boggling already. But I am not saying that this is really true or witness to its validity. Because who can really know the numbers and distance of the stars? We can only speculate or assume. Only God knows how His government is going to grow whether it is vertical or horizontal.

But one thing is sure that He said in Isaiah 9: 7;

"[7]Of the increase of His government and peace there will be no end,..."

As Ophirians, would you not fear God of His great power and majesty that is bestowed upon you today?

God is calling us to serve Him, to be His servants in accomplishing God's master plan of saving mankind and showing them their greatest potential under the true living God who created us.

In God's Kingdom, we can really have the real peace, joy, happiness, and prosperity if we allow ourselves to be governed by God.

And just as Paul preached to the Gentiles for our time in 2 Thessalonians 2: 13-14;

> "[13]But we are bound to give thanks to God always for you, brethren beloved by the Lord, because God from the beginning chose you for salvation through sanctification by the Spirit and belief in the truth, [14]to which He called you by our gospel, for the obtaining of the glory of our Lord Jesus Christ."

And just as Jesus Christ said to His disciples in John 15: 16;

> "[16]You did not choose Me, but I chose you and appointed you that you should go and bear fruit, and that your fruit should remain, that whatever you ask the Father in My name He may give you."

God have chosen us from the beginning to be his helper, servants, disciples in this end times. Not that we are special or anything. In fact, we are poor and needy that we enslave ourselves to many nations on earth. That is why, pride and arrogance should have no place in our hearts and mind, but rather, we should humble ourselves in humility before God. God give us the mind of a slave that we may know how to serve our master. And in the very near future, we shall have the greatest job opportunity of our lifetime, and that is to become the servant of God. He will sanctify us by the Spirit and in believing in this truth.

The following are our potential job descriptions;

First, in preaching the gospel of the coming Kingdom of God for the salvation of mankind in all the earth. And then the end shall come. And Jesus will come to us as light that He may become the Light unto the Gentiles through us.

Second, we will bring God's gold and silver and help rebuild the temple and to restore the daily sacrifices for the fulfillment of this prophecy. The isles is the custodian of God's gold, silver and precious stones.

Third, God will protect our land and His bride the Church, His chosen people, and those who will believe in the preaching for the coming great tribulation and the wrath of God on earth. We will serve them like our brothers and sisters.

Fourth, God will send us to restore the desolate places after the tribulation period and the wrath of God and bring back his sons and daughters to designated places.

These are just some of the major works ahead of us. We have many works to do, and we need to prepare for it that we may become worthy and trained in accomplishing these things.

But first we need to work on ourselves in turning to God and away from Satan.

Satan the god of this World

Why God allows Satan to become the god of this world?

First of all, God is not a creator of fiat things. He does not create things in a magical way. God is a God of process. Everything is a process. For instance, God created man as a free moral agent. He did not create Adam as an eternal being immediately, even if He can do it. Instead, He gave Adam a choice. It is commanded to Adam and Eve that they can eat every tree in the garden except the tree of the knowledge of good and evil. For in the day that they will eat of that fruit they shall surely die as God said in Genesis 2: 16-17;

> "[16]And the Lord God commanded the man, saying, "Of every tree of the garden you may freely eat; [17]but of the tree of the knowledge of good and evil you shall not eat, for in the day that you eat of it you shall surely die.""

This is the first commandment of God given to Adam. He pointed out immediately what is wrong and how to avoid it. Everything in that garden was good except for that very particular tree. God did not point out the tree of life to Adam. Perhaps it will be a reward for them if they continue to live their life in obedience to God. But instead, they disobey God and obey Satan. They are supposed to be seeking the tree of life which will give them an internal life and the rest of their offspring. But they were cut off from the opportunity to eat the fruit of "the tree of life" which can give them eternal life.

From that time on, mankind is cursed and cut off from God and punished for 6000 years. We are at the end time of this. In this period, mankind is on his own. He decides on his own whatever he wanted to do and suffer the consequences of sin. This period of human history is full of sufferings, death, tears, heartaches, and Satan's deceptions. But because God is a loving Father, He will give mankind a rest from these sufferings and Satan's manipulations. He will give mankind 1000 years to decide to obey His laws and commandments and follow God's way in the absence of Satan during the coming Millennial Kingdom of God when Jesus Christ will reign on earth as the King of kings and Lord of lords. He will reign humanity with a rod of iron to force them to experience real peace, joy, happiness, and prosperity. But mankind is still a free moral agent. They can still decide whether to obey God or not. But at that time no mind manipulation and deceptions from Satan. So, the consequence of our action is solely in our hands.

Even in the presence of God here on earth and in the absence of Satan, many will still choose to disobey God when He release Satan for a short time by the end of the Millennial Kingdom. And at the White Throne Judgment by the end of the millennial Kingdom many names will not be written in the Book of Life because they chose to obey Satan even though they already heard and know the truth and experience the love of God firsthand.

Those names that are not written in the Book of Life will be thrown into the lake of fire called hell for them to be consumed by fire eternally. They will be gone forever and ever as their second death just Christ said in Revelation 21: 7-8;

"⁷ "...He who overcomes shall inherit all things, and I will be his God and he shall be My son. ⁸But the cowardly, unbelieving, abominable, murderers, sexually immoral, sorcerers, idolaters, and all liars shall have their part in the lake which burns with fire and brimstone, which is the second death.""

This is contrary to common belief that hell is an eternal punishment for those who obey Satan rather than God. Hell is a consuming fire to remove or banish people (eternal death) who are not worthy to receive eternal life from the Tree of Life which will be available once again to those who choose to seek and obey God. Just as John testified to its truth in Revelation 22: 1-2, saying;

> "¹And he showed me a pure river of water of life, clear as crystal, proceeding from the throne of God and of the Lamb. ²In the middle of its street, and on either side of the river, was <u>the tree of life</u>, which bore twelve fruits, each tree yielding its fruit every month. The leaves of the tree were for the healing of the nations."

Who then have the right to eat of the tree of life?
Jesus said in Revelation 2: 7;

> "⁷"He who has an ear, let him hear what the Spirit says to the churches. To him <u>who overcomes</u> I will give to eat from the <u>tree of life</u>, which is in the midst of the Paradise of God." ""

And in Revelation 22: 14 -15;

> "¹⁴Blessed are those who <u>do His commandments</u>, that they may have the right to the <u>tree of life</u>, and may enter through the gates into the city. ¹⁵But outside are dogs and sorcerers and sexually immoral and murderers and idolaters, and whoever loves and practices a lie."

Notice very carefully that the privilege and opportunity to partake in "the tree of life" will be given to those who will <u>overcome this world</u> and <u>obey His commandments</u>. This is the very privilege and opportunity given to Adam and Eve in the Garden of Eden to have an eternal life. To be sons of God.

Obedience to the commandments of God have not been done away. It is a prerequisite to having an eternal life.

God created mankind as a mortal being and as free moral agent so that those who are incorrigible (continuously disobedient), who choose evil rather than good can be banished through hell fire forever.

God is a loving Father. He is not cruel to punish those who disobey Him in an eternal fire. God sentence them to the second death through the consuming fire in hell. They will be gone forever, and their soul destroyed.

Unlike Satan and his demons, they will be punished eternally in hell because they are spirit beings (immortals) and therefore they cannot die.

Second, Satan and his demons was cast down to the earth when his rebellion against God was defeated by God's angels in heaven. Satan became the god of this world. But God is still in control.

God has a master plan in saving mankind from the penalty of sins which is eternal death (second death) and saving the world from Satan's influences and deceptions.

But God's masterplan depends on every individual's response whether to choose God's way or Satan's way of life. But God when He will end the 6000-year punishment for mankind will give a rest from Satan and be given the chance to know and learn the truth.

In the Millennial Kingdom – the Kingdom of God, under the rulership of Jesus Christ, Satan will be bound for 1000 years (Rev. 20: 2). He can no longer influence people. He is no longer the god and ruler of this world. So, people will have the freedom to decide whether to obey God or not. There will be no more excuses of mind manipulation and deception. It is all up to their own volition.

As Ophirians today, we are heavily under the influence and control of the many prison houses of Satan. That is why we need to do a hard work to get to know and obey the true living God. There will always be a resistance in the hearts and mind of man because of our evil nature since the time of Adam. The so-called cognitive dissonance will kick in to deny the truth and depend on the current belief system whether one has in-depth knowledge about that belief system or just a blind follower. That is why it will be harder for us to choose the truth. We are accustomed to believing lies and deceptions. Our resistance in accepting the truth being revealed to us today will be strong at first. But when we come to our senses and we will know that there is no other choice than God to end up our misery, we will turn to God. This time, the truth will prevail as God promised. I hope and pray that we do not harden our hearts, lest we enter into a great tribulation or great catastrophe before we seek God.

But God knows also that we are waiting for Him as He said in Isaiah 60: 9(KJV);

"⁹Surely <u>the isles</u> shall wait for Me,…"

And we are awaiting for His law in Isaiah 42: 4 (KJV);

"⁴…and <u>the isles</u> shall wait for His law."

And we see His truth, His laws, and commandments and feared Him and get closer to Him as written in Isaiah 41: 5 (KJV);

"⁵The <u>isles</u> saw it, and feared; the <u>ends of the earth</u> were afraid, drew near, and came."

And God will surely make it happen as He said in Isaiah 60: 21-22;

"²¹ "…Also your people shall all be righteous; they shall inherit the land forever, the <u>branch of My planting</u>, <u>the work of My hands</u>, that I may be glorified.

²²A little one shall become a thousand, and a small one a strong nation.

<u>I, the Lord, will hasten it in its time</u>.""

And God said in Isaiah 46: 11-13;

"¹¹ "…Indeed I have spoken it; I will also bring it to pass.
I have purposed it; I will also do it."

¹²"Listen to Me, <u>you stubborn-hearted</u>, who are <u>far from righteousness</u>:

¹³<u>I bring My righteousness near</u>, it shall not be far off;
My salvation shall not linger.""

The question is whether we will make it happen the easy way or the hard way. It is up to us. If we resist and hardened our hearts, then surely disaster will come upon us until we bow down on our knees and submit to God our Maker. Just like what is going to happen to the world during the tribulation period and the wrath of God. Shall we harden our hearts and wait for the wicked to be shaken out of us? Or shall we open our hearts to the truth and open our eyes to the light and righteousness of our God? But surely, Christ will come to reign on earth with the rod of iron.

I hope and pray that we all shall become servants of our God for the salvation of mankind (our brothers and sisters), and to be one kingdom, one people, united under one God.

Satan Control the Whole World

Satan is a spirit being. Meaning, he is an immortal being. He cannot die like all the angels of God. He is a very powerful creature and yet he needs to use an instrument to execute his evil plans. He uses human beings to spread his lies and deceptions even though he is the prince of the power of the air (Eph. 2: 2). His mind control, mind programming and subliminal messages of deceit is done through man. Through music, mass media, screen time, government propaganda, etc. And the global powerful entity he uses to project his power and influences to control the whole world is the Vatican his habitation. It is described in Revelation 17: 1-6 as;

"¹Then one of the seven angels who had the seven bowls came and talked with me, saying to me, "Come, I will show you the judgment of the great harlot who sits on many waters, ²with whom the kings of the earth committed fornication, and the inhabitants of the earth were made drunk with the wine of her fornication."

³So he carried me away in the Spirit into the wilderness. And I saw a woman sitting on a scarlet beast which was full of names of blasphemy, having seven heads and ten horns. ⁴The woman was arrayed in purple and scarlet, and adorned with gold and precious stones and pearls, having in her hand a golden cup full of abominations and the filthiness of her fornication. ⁵And on her forehead a name was written:

MYSTERY, BABYLON THE GREAT,
THE MOTHER OF HARLOTS
AND OF THE ABOMINATIONS
OF THE EARTH.

⁶I saw the woman, drunk with the blood of the saints and with the blood of the martyrs of Jesus. And when I saw her, I marveled with great amazement."

The great harlot here is the woman (the church- Vatican) who is the mother of all the harlots (world's religions and governments). She controls (sits) the people of the whole world (many waters) as interpreted in verse 15 saying;

"15... "The waters which you saw, where the harlot sits, are peoples, multitudes, nations, and tongues...."""

The Vatican controls the people of the world through her many religions and her fornication (manipulation and control through her secret societies) of the governments of the world working for her in their agenda. It will appear today that there are many various religions (major and minor) and cults that are against each other. But that is how Satan works – divide and conquer. That is how he operates – by confusion and division. That is how he weakens family and nations.

There is no other great city on earth that sits between seven hills or mountains and controls the whole world than the Vatican as stated in verse 9 and 18, saying;

"9"Here is the mind which has wisdom: The seven heads are seven mountains on which the woman sits."

18And the woman whom you saw is that great city which reigns over the kings of the earth."""

It is the one going to persecute and murder many Ophirians and believers as we preach the gospel in all the earth through her many religions and governments on earth. Remember he is the ruler of this world.

Vatican control the whole world's education system, financial system, medical industry, entertainment industry, food industry, judicial system, military and intelligence system, through her control of the global elites (the cabal) and majority of the global government leadership (political system). She can strengthen or weaken a nation according to her liking. In a flick of her finger, her minions will execute her will accordingly. Such events include regime changes, economic collapse and even pandemic. Her actions affect every human being here on earth through her many religious systems, business entities and governmental tentacles called the deep state. The deep state operates through the power of the secret societies that supervise them.

The Vatican sits at the center of the Holy Roman Empire (the Beast of Revelation) past and present. The Holy Roman Empire have come and gone (v. 8) and have been prophesied to come for a final revival in Daniel 7 and Revelation 17. The Holy Roman Empire is the fourth beast of Daniel 7 and is already alive once again and for the last time. It is called today as the European Union under the leadership of Germany. EU was intentionally designed to collapse to give way to the ten horns which are the ten kings (Rev. 17: 12). It will wreck great havoc in the world before its time is over. It is the instrument of Satan because he knows that he has but a short time also.

"The [European] Community is living largely by the heritage of the Holy Roman Empire, though the great majority of the people who live by it don't know by what heritage they live."—Otto von Habsburg

The Holy Roman Empire is not just bound to EU. It is a global empire that controls all the nations of the world particularly the big players such as the US, Britain, China, Russia and the rest of the nations of Israel.

The fake pandemic of 2020 is a clear visual proof of its power around the world. It is so subtle, but it shows us that she is in control. She was able to control the wealthiest and most powerful country in the world (USA) and the poorest of the poor in Asia and Africa.

Under her pretense of pandemic - a trial for global mind control of humanity. The next stage now is being set up in the name of another scam – the continuation and intensification of the climate change hoax (formerly ice age, then global warming), and the remaining nine plandemics in their table until 2030. Then after this is her global reeducation program as stipulated in Francis of the Vatican encyclical called "Laudato si'". It is the reeducation of the global population towards total satanic control of one world government and one world religion. Some of the common tagline we can hear often from this campaign are, "for the common good", "build back better", "build build build", to name a few. Notice carefully that the last two examples have an abbreviation of bbb which is 666 – the number of the beast. The above examples are commonly used by many countries around the world such as the US, Britain, and the Philippines.

One of the major goals of Laudato si' is to reeducate the religious and political leaders of the world to come back to their common mother church and government. The mother church is the Catholic Church (Vatican- the mother of harlots (Rev. 17: 5) and the religions and cults of this world are her daughters. Their reunification is called "ecumenism". Some of the major religions that have joined already in the Ecumenical Churches are the Orthodox (particularly eastern), Protestants, Islam, Hinduism, Buddhism and many other religions on their way to signing the concordance in the Vatican.

And when all the daughters have come back to their mother, then she will proclaim Sunday as their sabbath day in direct defiance to the sabbath day of God which is Saturday. By this time, no one can buy or sell unless one has the mark of the beast – their sabbath. And this will happen through their deliberate collapsing of the banking system (2023) and slowly replace it with their Central Bank Digital Currency where they can dictate how much money you can use or not use through your "social credit score". This social credit score is based on your obedience to their commands that are hinge on your carbon credits measured by how you obey or participate in their climate change propaganda.

Many of us, whatever our religions or beliefs sincerely believe in the god we were taught since we were kids. We are sincere in our prayers and beliefs, but we are sincerely deceived. Just as our Maker said in Revelation 12: 9;

> "⁹So the great dragon was cast out, that serpent of old, called the Devil and <u>Satan, who deceives the whole world</u>;..."

It said, the whole world is deceived by Satan. It is not possible that all the thousands of gods of this world are true God. These are all deceptions. There is only one true God that knows very well His creation that said in Romans 3: 9-18 (NLT);

> "⁹Well then, should we conclude that we Jews are better than others? No, not at all, for we have already shown that all

people, whether Jews or Gentiles, <u>are under the power of sin</u>.
¹⁰As the Scriptures say,

"<u>No one is righteous— not even one</u>.
¹¹No one is truly wise; no one is seeking God.
¹²All have turned away; all have become useless. No one does good, not a single one."
¹³"Their talk is foul, like the stench from an open grave. Their tongues are filled with lies."
"Snake venom drips from their lips."
¹⁴"Their mouths are full of cursing and bitterness."
¹⁵"They rush to commit murder.
¹⁶Destruction and misery always follow them.
¹⁷They don't know where to find peace."
¹⁸"They have <u>no fear of God at all</u>.""

Who other gods can describe humanity exactly as we are? There is no other god than the God of the Bible. Indeed, "no one is righteous, not even one" because we are deceived by Satan into unrighteousness and self-righteousness creating our own gods/idols and worship it. And for this, the true living God called us stubborn, fools, and stupid. And in Jeremiah 17: 9, He said;

"⁹"The heart is deceitful above all things, and desperately wicked;...""

We are wicked people that we do not fear the God of the Bible who have given us this user's manual. We do not seek the righteousness of God because we are busy seeking our own self-righteousness. Our own self-destructive ways.

And because we are not wise in seeking God, we live in misery. We are in constant fear of what the governments or other people will do to us. We have no peace of mind. Indeed, we cannot find peace on earth, even if everyone is looking for peace and our destruction will come as it is written in Ezekiel 7: 25-27;

"²⁵Destruction comes; <u>They will seek peace, but there shall be none</u>.²⁶Disaster will come upon disaster, and rumor will be upon rumor. Then they will seek a vision from a prophet; but the law will perish from the priest, and counsel from the elders.

[27]"The king will mourn, the prince will be clothed with desolation, and the hands of the common people will tremble. <u>I will do to them according to their way</u>, and <u>according to what they deserve I will judge them</u>; Then <u>they shall know that I am the Lord!</u>' "'"

We will be judge under the laws of God and not from our own self-made humanistic laws and we shall all be found guilty as it is written in Romans 3: 19-20;

"[19]Now we know that whatever the law says, it says to those who are under the law, that every mouth may be stopped, and <u>all the world may become guilty before God</u>. [20]Therefore by the deeds of the law no flesh will be justified in His sight, for <u>by the law is the knowledge of sin</u>."

Therefore, recognize that we are sinners and seek God and His law so that we may begin to see the light and see beyond the illusion of Satan's deceptions.

Satan always counterfeit God's plan, from the institution of a family to establishment of one world government and one world religion. Satan wants to destroy God's instituted family through marriage by perverted minds of counterfeit sexuality such as homosexuality, transgederism, pedophilia and many others. Through sexual immorality leading up to abortion, sexually transmitted diseases, breakup of the family, premarital sex, etc. Imagine if these continue for generations after generations. Eventually humanity will be instinct by their own making even without the nuclear war. Truly, the way to death is wide and easy and seems enjoyable at first. But at the end it is full of trouble, unhappiness, destruction, and death.

God will establish one world kingdom under the reign of Jesus Christ as the King of kings and Lord of lords for a thousand year (The Millennial Kingdom). He will rule humanity with the rod of iron so that they will be forced to have real peace, joy, happiness, and prosperity by serving the One True God. But Satan is busy now in showing his one world government that control the whole world for a long time. He wants to assert his control over the people of the world through his minions from his bastion in Vatican and through the cabal that controls the businesses and governments of the world. While God's one world government is about salvation of mankind from their self-destructive ways, Satan's government is about enslavement of the people to his lies and deceptions so that they will not be able to know their God given human potential of becoming children of God, thereby making them hopeless, poor, and needy and be reliant to him as their god resulting to more violence, suffering, trouble, and confusion.

Jesus Christ will be establishing a one world religion during the Millennial Kingdom to proclaim the glory of the Almighty Father as the One true God. Satan on the other hand, has been busy establishing his one world religion by uniting his many deceptive religions (prison houses) he himself created into coming back to the Catholic Church which is called ecumenism. This will be the council of ecumenical churches of Satan so that together they will have one god (Satan) and will proclaim and institute his day of worship (counterfeit sabbath) which is Sunday all throughout the world.

Satan will rule the world with the rod of iron also so that humanity will be in complete submission to his deceptive one world government and one world religion. No one will be able to buy or sell without his mark that will be instituted or implemented by the Holy Roman Empire (currently called European Union) in all the earth as the one world government of Satan. And this is the mark of the beast, for the empire is the beast.

The 2020 vision of pandemic is the pretext of this coming events (the Great Reset and the New World Order). This event is a test for the final determination of action to implement their plans. The test is to see the quantity and quality of people who knows how to think and see beyond their illusion and how many are blind followers - the sheeple. This are the people who are too lazy to think or are deeply blinded and are willing to gobble up whatever they are commanded to do or are told to eat. Tragically, most of these people belong to the group of the so called highly educated people who allow themselves to be programmed and are not willing to think. They are the product of miseducation that we have been told to get since our childhood. Sadly, I was one of them before, until I humble myself before God and seek His guiding light to see beyond the darkness of our time.

This pandemic test is a quantitative and qualitative study of the global population of the resistance they will face towards the determination of the final outcome of their plan. In their rehearsal, the only problem they were not able to totally solve is the resistance or the civil unrest. Nevertheless, they were able to pull out a win-win scenario for their agenda. Only God can put a standard against Satan's master plan of deceiving the people and putting the world into total darkness. Unless the people of the isles accept the job and the coming of light we will remain in darkness and continue to live a miserable life under the rulership of Satan.

But the hardest part is that people do not want to wake up or see the truth. They are deep into Satan's deception that they cannot discern what is right from what is wrong. And the pharmaceutical industry have a big role to play in destroying the minds of the people through their vaccination program early in life to the yearly vaccination for the common flu.

People chose to live in ignorance deliberately than challenging their brain to think even just a little bit. There is a saying that, "The illiterate of the 21st century will not be those who cannot read or write, but those who cannot unlearn the many lies that they have been conditioned to believe and seek out the hidden knowledge that they have been conditioned to reject." And, "If the truth offends you, it is most likely because you are deceived."

The Religious Tentacles

What can be more effective in controlling the people than to conquer their spirituality. In every human being, there is this little-small voice that tells us that there is a supreme being that created us and that we need to seek and obey Him. But Satan being the "Prince of the power of the air," said no. Instead, he/she (whatever gender he wanted to be) entice people to worship and obey him knowingly and unknowingly. He became the god of this world through many forms of religions. If 38,000 plus religions and denominations will not confuse you, I do not know what will. But one thing for sure, Satan is the author of confusion. Just as he/she confused Eve by putting a doubtful question in her mind with regards to God's command to them. Just as the world today is confused whether God's commandments and laws are still enforced to this day.

The two major religions that Vatican created to conquer the whole world were Catholicism and Islam. These two major religions are full of bloody history of conquering humanity by the sword. In the surface, these two religions have very different belief system and culture. But deep inside is their murderous history and a common denominator of idolatry and the lies and deceptions of human civilization. But now, they have merge back into one through ecumenism.

These two major religions have their own kingdom and territories. But how did these two majors religions come out?

The image of a man in king Nebuchadnezzar's dream in Daniel 2 explains everything. Daniel 2: 36-45 interpreted to the king his dream about the three successive kingdoms after him until all the kingdoms is replaced by the Kingdom of God here on earth. The four kingdoms in this image are Babylonian Empire, Medo-Persian Empire, Grecian Empire, and the Holy Roman Empire. Among these empires or beasts, the fourth is different from them all as described in Daniel 7: 7, 23-25;

"⁷"After this I saw in the night visions, and behold, a fourth beast, dreadful and terrible, exceedingly strong. It had huge iron teeth; it was devouring, breaking in pieces, and trampling the residue with its feet. It was different from all the beasts that were before it, and it had ten horns.

²³"Thus he said:

'The fourth beast shall be a fourth kingdom on earth, which shall be different from all other kingdoms, and shall devour the whole earth, trample it and break it in pieces.

²⁴The ten horns are ten kings who shall arise from this kingdom. And another shall rise after them; he shall be different from the

first ones, and shall subdue three kings.

[25]He shall speak pompous words against the Most High, shall persecute the saints of the Most High, and shall intend to change times and law.

Then the saints shall be given into his hand for a time and times and half a time."

The fourth beast or the Holy Roman Empire is very different from the rest of the beasts because it is Satan's instrument in deceiving, controlling, confusing, and dividing the whole world. It is weak yet, is strong. It is one, yet it is divided. And this empire has come and go and have come back again (Dan. 7: 19-27).

It breaks or divide the whole world into pieces because Satan's dividing scheme is up to family level. Families are broken even among family members or siblings. They are divided in their beliefs. Some wants to seek the truth, and some are just followers and some just want to be told or dictated what to do. The scamdemic tear apart family members because some are worshipper of doctors and are blind followers of the government and the medical industry and some seek the truth beyond the illusion. That is why Satan easily implements his deceptions because a divided, unsuspecting, gullible, and ignorant people cannot stand his attacks. Remember, he deceives the whole world.

But the progress of the subsequent kingdoms become less and less valuable from precious gold to silver, to bronze, to iron, and then finally into to mixed iron and clay. The Bible prophesied in that dream that the fourth kingdom of this world will be split into two represented by its two legs. One kingdom but split into two. The final kingdom is represented by feet and toes made up of mixed iron and clay. They have two capitals namely, Rome and Constantinople. These are the political capitals of these kingdoms. But each one has their own religious component – Catholicism and Islam. Until these kingdoms are destroyed by the stone representing the Kingdom of God as it written in Daniel 2: 41-45, saying;

"[41] "...Whereas you saw the feet and toes, partly of potter's clay and partly of iron, the kingdom shall be divided; yet the strength of the iron shall be in it, just as you saw the iron mixed with ceramic clay. [42]And as the toes of the feet were partly of iron and partly of clay, so the kingdom shall be partly strong and partly fragile. [43]As you saw iron mixed with ceramic clay, they will mingle with the seed of men; but <u>they will not adhere to one another</u>, just as <u>iron does not mix with clay</u>. [44]And in the days of these kings <u>the God of heaven will set up a kingdom which shall never be destroyed</u>; and the kingdom shall not be left to other people; it shall break in pieces and consume all these kingdoms, and it shall stand forever. [45]Inasmuch as you saw that <u>the stone was cut out of the mountain without hands</u>, and that it broke in pieces the iron, the bronze, the clay, the silver, and the gold—the great God has made known to the king what will come to pass after this. The dream is certain, and its interpretation is sure.'"

Notice that Catholicism is split into two - Catholics and Protestants. Islam is also split into two - Sunni and Shia. Each one does not agree with one another on their religious practices and beliefs. They are all confused and divided like the kingdoms of this world under the rulership of the Holy Roman Empire. That is why there are always wars and humors of wars and "nation will rise against nation, and kingdom against kingdom" just as Jesus said in Matthew 24: 7 at the end times. The feet and toes symbolize the end times of the kingdoms of the beast. And we are in it today because humanity is like iron and clay. We cannot go along with each other because of many divisive belief systems.

But before it became Vatican and Catholicism, it started as a pagan religion in Babylon – the Nimrod-Semiramis couple/mother and child tandem is the Babylonish system of religion (idolatry). It is the worship of Satan in the form of Nimrod. Paganism became the main religion of Babylon and of the world, even to this day. Although the names are different today, their customs and traditions are the same. Its practices are the most horrendous and abominable to God which includes child sacrifices. These satanic sacrifices which we think are things of the past, are being practiced to this day at an accelerated rate. Kidnapping of children is becoming frequent these days. But with the open border policy of the current US administration (2021), they have an abundant supply of soldiers, women, and children as young as two years old. These are abundant supply from illegal immigrants crossing the borders of the USA and Europe.

Wonder why immigration laws does not apply to them and they are well funded? That is the main benefit of allowing these people to pour in into their borders unrestricted. All of these are funded by people's money under the operation and supervision of the Catholic Church through her minions in the governments (deep state) and Catholic's Non-Governmental Organizations (NGO's). These Catholic NGO's are at the forefront of financing and facilitating this illegal immigration around the world with its cartel networks. Remember who operates the Communist Party of the Philippines and the various Muslim Rebel groups in Mindanao? It is all brought to you by the Catholic Church through her NGO's.

How Catholicism Became the Counterfeit Christianity?

The followers of Jesus Christ are called Christians as mentioned in Acts 11: 26, saying;

"²⁶And when he had found him, he brought him to Antioch. So it was that for a whole year they assembled with the church and taught a great many people. And the disciples were first called Christians in Antioch."

During the time of Jesus, Jerusalem and almost the entire world is under the control of the Holy Roman Empire. Paganism is the religion imposed throughout the empire. But other religious practices were also allowed such as Judaism.

During the time of the disciples of Jesus Christ, a man called Simon Peter Magus – the Sorcerer (not the Simon Peter the disciple, note Satan's counterfeit already), became a follower of the religion founded by Jesus Christ which is called Christianity. Simon the sorcerer became follower of the disciples not because of the teaching of Jesus Christ but because of the power that the disciples have. This power includes healing and other miraculous things that the disciples performed. Simon the Sorcerer attempted to buy this power from the disciples thinking that those power can be given away by the disciples. This act is called simony, or paying for position, named after Simon Magus who tried to buy his way into the power of the Apostles.

The disciple Peter rebuke him knowing that this Simon the Sorcerer are not one of them but of Satan. Simon Peter the Sorcerer, did not understand that the power he is buying is the gift of God to His disciples who loved, obeyed, and served Him. It was free. Unlike Satan's power through sorcery and witchcraftcy that is for sale and the cost is one's soul. This is written in Acts 8: 9-24;

> "⁹But there was a certain man called Simon, who previously practiced sorcery in the city and astonished the people of Samaria, claiming that he was someone great, ¹⁰to whom they all gave heed, from the least to the greatest, saying, "This man is the great power of God." ¹¹And they heeded him because he had astonished them with his sorceries for a long time. ¹²But when they believed Philip as he preached the things concerning the kingdom of God and the name of Jesus Christ, both men and women were baptized. ¹³Then Simon himself also believed; and when he was baptized he continued with Philip, and was amazed, seeing the miracles and signs which were done.
>
> ¹⁴Now when the apostles who were at Jerusalem heard that Samaria had received the word of God, they sent Peter and John to them, ¹⁵who, when they had come down, prayed for them that they might receive the Holy Spirit. ¹⁶For as yet He had fallen upon none of them. They had only been baptized in the name of the Lord Jesus. ¹⁷Then they laid hands on them, and they received the Holy Spirit.
>
> ¹⁸And when Simon saw that through the laying on of the apostles' hands the Holy Spirit was given, he offered them money, ¹⁹saying, "Give me this power also, that anyone on

whom I lay hands may receive the Holy Spirit."

²⁰But Peter said to him, "Your money perish with you, because you thought that the gift of God could be purchased with money! ²¹You have neither part nor portion in this matter, for your heart is not right in the sight of God. ²²Repent therefore of this your wickedness, and pray God if perhaps the thought of your heart may be forgiven you. ²³For I see that you are poisoned by bitterness and bound by iniquity."

²⁴Then Simon answered and said, "Pray to the Lord for me, that none of the things which you have spoken may come upon me.'""

The history of Christianity founded by Jesus Christ was not known or missing. The true Christians at that time was heavily persecuted and they went into hiding underground literally and figuratively. This missing history of Christianity has a gap of a 100 years (Rawlings). This is called the 100-year darkness of Christian history. No one knows what really happened to them during this 100-year period. Perhaps the written document of this dark history can be found in the underground archive library in the Vatican or in the writings of John.

But after 100 years, Christianity resurfaced. But this time, it was completely different from what it was before. Pagan practices, customs, and traditions became Christianized. It will later become known as Catholicism who created other religions whose common denominator is centered on these Paganic practices, customs, and traditions.

Catholicism is a Christianized form of Paganism. They replaced pagan gods and goddesses' names or identity corresponding to Christian history. Their idol gods Isis and Horis for example, became Jesus (and baby Jesus). Semiramis and Venus became Mary (the mother of Jesus in flesh). Simon Peter the Sorcerer became the Simon Peter the disciple which is now edified in the Vatican. This is the reason why the Bible told us in 2 Corinthians 11: 4 that we worship another Jesus;

"⁴For if he who comes preaches another Jesus whom we have not preached, or if you receive a different spirit which you have not received, or a different gospel which you have not accepted—you may well put up with it!"

164

They also Christianized the pagan dates of celebration. Their day of worshipping the sun, which is Sunday (the other religion is Friday), became the counterfeit sabbath of the Bible which is Saturday. They change the day and time (Dan. 7 : 25) of God's instituted sabbath day from Saturday to Sunday in the council of Nicea in 354 AD. Many died when the Holy Roman Empire implemented this edict until all submitted to this counterfeit sabbath. In this end time, Satan, once again will assert to reestablish this Sunday sabbath for all humanity on earth. That is why they implemented their plan of pandemic and then the climate change and the global policy of the Vatican of reeducating the world under his ecumenical churches. That means that Satan wants to have full control of the people of the world so that they will be fully deceived and worship him before his time is over. He is just playing humanity through their own folly and stupidity.

Another significant date which is an abomination to God is December 25. This is the winter solstice. A big day celebration for sorcerer and witchcraftcy that became the designated birthday of Jesus Christ for the counterfeit Christianity. But if the Bible did not clearly state the day of birth of the author Himself, should we put importance to that unknown date that we need to celebrate? No! The fact that it was not written nor commanded to be celebrated means that it is not important. In fact, nowhere in the Bible did Jesus Christ nor His disciples celebrated their birthday except the pagan kings of the Holy Roman Empire. Therefore, if Christ Himself did not command this celebration, then who's birthday are the pagans celebrating or worshipping on this day? I am pretty sure by now that you know who the Great Counterfeiter is and who wanted to be worshipped since the time of the first earth.

There are many more dates that the counterfeit Christianity and other religions celebrate that are of pagan origin. And by doing so, they knowingly or unknowingly worshipped Satan instead of their God who created them and give them life. These dates include Valentine's Day, Halloween (all souls and all saints day), easter Sunday, and many other Christianize pagan celebration (e.g. feasts). These, we really need to repent and ask for forgiveness to our Creator God for we have been deceived knowingly and unknowingly.

Read "The Two Babylons" by Alexander Hislop for more information of Pagan dates and holidays and the root of Catholicism in "50 Years in the Church of Rome" by Charles Chiniquy. All these can only be found in the Chick Publications website. You need to wake up and see the truth.

But why did the Holy Roman Empire Christianize paganism?

It is because, true Christians at that time, even though they are heavily persecuted and being crushed to the ground, still its influence was still increasing even to the Arab world. The Pagan religion(later became the Catholic Church) created Islam to prevent Christianity in spreading to the Middle East or Arab nations so that they will have complete control of that region. This is because the Empire is worried that true Christians may revolt in the future if they become many and it will become a very dangerous scenario for their kingdom. But Satan, being the master of lies, and deceptions and the god of paganism, created the grand scheme of Christianizing paganism. So, many true Christians and non-Christians eventually look at Catholicism as Christianity. And those faithful true Christians were either hiding or were martyred by the new religious system.

For a more complete explanation of how Catholicism created Islam, read "The Prophet", Alberto Part Six, Volume 17 of the Crusaders by Chick Publications.

True Christianity was becoming a threat to the empire. But as Satan and many evil politicians say, "never let a crisis go to waste". And because Satan wanted to be god and be worshipped like God, he deceived many into believing that paganism is Christianity by hiding the truth about what those idols really represents.

The Empire was facing another crisis in the Arab World. True Christianity is spreading fast in the Arab lands. But the Holy Roman Empire have no control of that area. And what can be more effective in controlling the people than human spirituality. And, in order for this crisis not to go to waste, why not create another religion so that it will create more confusion and fighting. And so, the persecution of the true Christians in the hand of the Babylonish religion (the Catholic and Islam) murdered tens of millions of Bible believing people throughout that century. Today, Islam is confused that the modern-day Christians (of various denominations) are still their enemy, not knowing that these religious sects and them are one and the same. As we know it, Satan is the author of confusion and rebellion. He is playing the lives and mind of humanity so that we remain deceived, and we will not know or discover our real potential and the reason why God have created us.

To control true Christianity from spreading into the Arab world, the Holy Roman Empire created a grand schema of another religion through a wealthy Arabian Lady who is a devout Catholic called Khadijah.

Since Vatican have no control in the Arab world, a devoted Arab Catholic and a faithful follower of the Pope became the means of achieving their goal. Khadijah, who is a widow, had a cousin named Waraquah who is also a faithful Catholic, was placed by the Vatican as Muhammad's main advisor. Their main mission is to "find a young brilliant man who could be used by the Vatican to create a new religion and become the messiah for the children of Ishmael".

Muhammad was 25 years old when he married Khadijah who is 40 years old.

According to Alberto's account, "Rome had found their man, and money was no object. Teachers were sent to young Muhammad, and he underwent intensive training. Muhammad devoured the works of "Saint" Augustine under Waraquah's teaching and became a devotee of his works. This was preparing him for his "great calling".

They controlled Muhammad and designated him as the Prophet of Islam. Like many Catholics and other professing Christians, Muslims are very eager to defend their faith or belief even though they do not know their own religion. Even to the point of killing fellow men to defend their belief which they themselves do not know. They just follow and obey and are happy with it. They do not seek the truth if what they obey, and follow is right or wrong. They do not care seeking the truth. What is important to them is the sense of belongingness and the pride of brotherhood. And so, humanity is easily deceived because they put more importance to their pride and emotions and not on reason or morality or seeking the truth. And because of these pride and arrogance, people are easily offended and do not want to see the other side of the coin.

Like pagan Catholicism, Islam is also a paganic religion based on idolatry. The main god of Islam is Allah. It was randomly selected from thousands of wooden piles of rejected idols of the Babylonish religion's – pagan gods. Islam is not as extensive as Catholicism in terms of idolatry. It only involves Allah, the five meteorites which became the daughters of Allah and became the symbols of the five pillars of Islam. Other idolatry practices that connect Islam to Catholicism is Fatima. But the common denominator of the two is idolatry.

Like Catholicism, Islam also based their religious practices and methodology through the Bible. The only major difference is, they distorted the meaning of the Bible to use it to lie and deceived the whole world into idolatry.

Islam was founded on blood and violence. Like their projected founder Muhammad, he is a very violent man in the Arab world. That is why he fits the job descriptions of the Babylonish religion of the Catholic Church. But as we know it, he is not the founder of the religion, but his wife and her cousin did. Similarly, the Babylonish religion was not founded by Nimrod himself but by his wife Semiramis.

For more information of the history and purpose of Islam, read the books: "Anatomy of the Qur'an" and "Who is this Allah?". These books can only be found in the Chick Publications website.

The main mission of creating the religion was to stop, destroy, and persecute the spread of true Christianity in the Arab region. And as the history will tell us, it was a blood bath.

Satan used these two major world religions to wage war against the Church that Jesus Christ Himself founded when He was on earth. Satan drive Christianity into the verge of extinction through their heavy persecution.

True enough, real Christians (the elects) today is very few

compared to major religions and mega churches of today. Although the true Church of God have some presence in some countries, their members do not even exceed a thousand. The Church was also attacked by Satan and was broken into many splinter churches with doctrinal and spiritual problems and differences. Many true believers were deceived by Satan to go back to their previous (vomits) major religious belief system.

Again, as the Roman Empire was prophesied in the Bible that it will be divided into two, two capital emerges. The capital in Rome and the capital in Constantinople with its own major religion. Catholicism and Vatican in Rome and Islam in Constantinople. Later, Islam became the main religion in the Arab world to this day. And Satan being the god of confusion and deceptions, Muslims still believe that their enemy is the fake Christianity of Catholicism or Protestants, etc. Not knowing that they are one and the same but different gods and belief system. But Satan's main goal is to oppress and control people into his evil ways so that they will not know God and disobey Him. And because of this ignorance and disobedience, people are blinded and lived in darkness under the reign of Satan. He wants people to suffer from violence, poverty, immorality, and misery so that people will be disenfranchised and confused to hide their true potential in God's Masterplan for mankind.

This is the common denominator of the countries under the influence of Islam and Catholicism and other major religions of the world – POVERTY. This breeds into drug addiction, misery, and violence and corruption. These two major religions control the world and if we notice, they do not want to solve the problem of violence and poverty. That is because they are the one causing it because Satan wants us to live in a miserable life. God allow this to happen to humanity as a punishment or consequence for obeying and worshipping Satan knowingly and unknowingly.

Countries such as the Philippines (named as the only Christian/Catholic nation in Asia), and many countries in Latin America (South America) such as Argentina, Brazil, Columbia, Guatemala,

Mexico, Nicaragua, Venezuela, and many other countries in that region have one thing in common – they are Catholic nation and ravage with poverty, drug addiction, and violence. One can only wonder why. The religion that has enslaved them are supposed to be godly and not be full of evil. But there they are, in complete submission to this religion yet it is the one subjecting them to utter human disaster.

Similarly, countries in Africa and the Middle East which is the bastion of Islam have been in utter poverty and violence. The people continue to live in constant suffering and fear from each other. Fighting against each other without regard for the future of the next generation. Oppression upon one another is common especially those that are empowered by this religion. They think they are gods over their fellow Muslims.

Does anyone think that these two major religions cannot solve the poverty and violence of their people? Can they not give peace and prosperity to humanity?

Of course, they can, because they are the government and the economy. They are the power behind every government and every major business in the world. And yet through these power and great influence in the society, they chose to confuse and subject humanity into adverse life situation so that they will remain in their prison houses (churches, synagogues, mosque, congregations, governments, etc.) and blinded by the darkness of evil so that they will not know their true and real potential which God our Creator have in store for us to do. Satan is the god of this world for now. He reigns over the nations on earth.

The evil Catholic church even instigated a genocide in Rwanda in 1994, killing more than 800,000 people with participation of nuns and priests hacking and beheading people with machetes literally. This was admitted by the Vatican in 2017 apologizing for their involvement in the genocide as reported in one prominent mainstream media whose name is not worthy to be written in this book, said to then President Paul Kagame, "Pope Francis acknowledged that priests, nuns and members of the Catholic church had succumbed to hatred and violence in Rwanda, "betraying their own evangelical mission," the Vatican said.

These priest and nuns did not succumb to their evil nature, they are commanded to do so. Vatican is the root cause of many civil wars, world wars, regime changes, and pandemics in the world for many centuries. They are the author of the American civil war for which Abraham Lincoln know so well that British and American will not fight with each other without the hand of the Vatican. He was assassinated like JFK who was fighting with the same entity. The Vatican also cause the downfall of the Philippines during the time of then President Marcos.

Like many civil wars in the world, the CIA which is one of the intelligence tentacles of the Vatican, divide the countries people through ethnic, color, ideology, or politics. Then, regime change happens either in the so-called peaceful revolution such as the fake Edsa Revolution of the Pilipino people in 1986 or a bloody genocide in Rwanda in 1994, and many bloody revolutions in the Latin Americas such as Argentina, Peru, Guatemala, etc. All the outcome of these regime changes is poverty, violence, and sufferings. The common denominator that emerges is that these countries, including those in the Middle East like Iraq and Libya, have all come under the influence of the Catholic Church after the war. All these things happen under the hands of one or two Catholic Jesuits CIA agents. Imagine one or two persons have the power to infuse their poison to destroy a country. All in the name of conquest, lies, and deceptions of an evil religion.

The American Civil War of 1861 is a great testament to the evil reach of the Vatican conquest through its Jesuits operatives when President Abraham Lincoln told Charles Chiniquy the following;

"This war would never have been possible without the sinister influence of the Jesuits. We owe it to popery that we now see our land reddened with the blood of her noblest sons. Though there were great differences in opinion between the South and the North on the question of slavery, neither Jeff Davis nor any of the leading men of the Confederacy would have dared to attack the North, had they not relied on the promises of the Jesuits, that, under the mask of democracy, the money and the arms of the Roman Catholics, even the

171

arms of France, were at their disposal, if they would attack us. I pity the priests, the bishops and the monks of Rome in the United States, when the people realize that they are, in great part, responsible for the tears and blood shed in this war. I conceal what I know, for if the people knew the whole truth, this war would turn into a religious war, and at once, take a tenfold more savage and bloody character. It would become merciless as all religious wars are. It would become a war of extermination on both sides." (Charles Chiniquy. 50 Years in the Church of Rome, Chapter 55 pp. 296-297. Chick Publication, 1985).

Our intention in exposing the evil of the Vatican is not to create religious wars but rather to show humanity specially the people of the isles, who the enemy is and be able to say no to its deceptive lies and manipulations anymore and begun to turn to the real living God of the Bible. Individually, we shall begin to open our eyes and see the light. And with the help of God, free us from the many prison houses (religions) of Satan. Then we shall have wisdom, knowledge and understanding of the truth if we fear and seek the real living God. We shall be able to think and see beyond the illusion of how the enemy operates to destroy and confuse mankind and to think for ourselves instead of allowing Satan to program humanity's mind through its medical, entertainment, mass media, religious, and political industries.

The following excerpts from Charles Chiniquy book "50 Years in the Church of Rome", will give us a glance how the Vatican conquered the United States of America, and in parallel, the Philippines and the world as a whole. This was narrated to him in 1851 by an Irishman D'Arcy McGee, editor of The Freeman's Journal, an official Journal of the Bishop of New York.

"We are also determined to take possession of the United States; but we must proceed with the utmost secrecy and wisdom. What does a skillful general do when he wants to conquer a country? Does he scatter his soldiers over the farmlands, and spend their energy in plowing the fields? No! He keeps them close to his flanks and marching toward the strongholds: the rich and powerful cities. The farming countries then submit and become the price of this victory without moving a finger to subdue them.

"So, it is with us. Silently and patiently, we must mass our Roman Catholics in the great cities of the United States, remembering that the vote of a poor journeyman, though he be covered with rags, has as much weight in the scale of power as the millionaire Astor, and that if we have two votes against his one, he will become as powerless as an oyster. Let us then multiply our votes; let us call our poor but faithful Irish Catholics from every corner of the world, and gather them into the very hearts of the cities of Washington, New York, Boston, Chicago, Buffalo, Albany, Troy, Cincinnati, etc.

"Under the shadows of those great cities, the Americans consider themselves a giant unconquerable race. They look upon the Irish Catholics with supreme contempt, as only fit to dig their canals, sweep their streets and work in their kitchens. Let no one awake those sleeping lions, today. Let us pray god that they continue to sleep a few years longer, waking only to find their votes outnumbered as we will turn them forever, out of every position of honor, power and profit! When not a single judge or policeman, will be elected if he be not devoted Irish Catholic! What will those so-called giants think when not a single senator or member of Congress will be chosen, unless he has submitted to our holy father the pope!

"We will not only elect the president, but fill and command the armies, man the navies, and hold keys of the public treasury. It will then be a time for our faithful Irish people to give up their grog shops, to become the judges and governors of the land.

"Then, yes! Then, we will rule the United States, and lay them at the feet of the Vicar of Jesus Christ (the pope and their Christ is another Jesus, emphasis mine), that he may put an end to their godless system of education, and impious laws of liberty of conscience which are an insult to god and man!"

Chiniquy added that, "In order to more easily drill the Roman Catholics and prepare them for this struggle, the Jesuits have organized them into a great number of secret societies..." (Chapter 54, pp 281-283).

It is more evident today that the United States is run by the Cabal Establishments (WEF, UN, WHO, etc.) which own everything from food production down to most politician in the country and of the whole world. The law and economy are at Catholics Church mercy. The deep states under the supervision and operation of the secret societies (particularly the Jesuits and the Masons) operate deep down the superficial government of the US and of the world.

Similarly, the final conquest of the Philippines in 1986 was executed perfectly by the Vatican's operatives (CIA, nuns, and priests) and Catholic minions of their secret societies. They do not want the country to prosper under the Marcos regime so that people will remain ignorant of their true identity and purpose, if people will become prosperous and be able to learn how to think.

The so called Irish Catholic politicians and CIA operatives in the US masterminded the whole operations involving their congress. This operation is no different than regime changes the United States of Vatican have conducted all throughout the world like the case of Guatemala which has very similar pattern or blueprint to that of the Philippine regime change of the Marcos administration. I will discuss extensively Vatican's involvement in the coup d' etat in the Philippines under the Marcos regime in the next book – The Opherium Manifesto.

Today, if people know how to think, this pandemic hoax will directly link to Vatican as their operatives are all Jesuits and members of secret society billionaires. It will be very clear to us how the Vatican conquered the whole world through its political tentacles all over the nations on earth. The nations on earth get their command from UN and WHO who's leaders have very questionable backgrounds. That is why the world have only one voice just as planned and rehearsed in Events 201 in 2019 from the inception of pandemic plan in 2005. The leaders in most of the countries in the world are like choir members. They sing the same song every time the Vatican through its tentacles told them to sing. We can count in one hand those leaders who stand for their people against this tyrannical pandemic and some of them are dead or in great danger.

All things lead to Vatican if we follow the money since it owns almost all big businesses in all the world from pharmaceutical companies supplying the deadly injections, to mind manipulation of the people through big tech and mainstream media to every government politician on earth who basically terrorize its people more than the so-called virus.

Likewise, as one meme goes, "I tried to follow the science, but it was simply not there. I followed the money, that's where I found the science."

The governments of the earth have become basically the enemy of the people whom supposedly they protect from the enemy. But then, they became the enemy of its people. Under the pretext of a non-existent virus and their vision of a global pandemic, they have suppressed their people, aiming to subjugate nations through genocide, with their ultimate goal to depopulate the world and assert absolute control over the population. All in the name of their science god. Or should we say, puppet master?

We must not forget also that the Vatican is the architect of World Wars One and Two. Now, their involvement in the many man-made pandemics scam is starting to unravel. Their ploy of the Covid 19 pandemic exposes their lies and deceptions in killing humanity every now and then. Their tentacles and agents may be different in some period of time, but their goal is the same – depopulate the world (Eugenics). A con man billionaire is the one spearheading this event right now. He is achieving his goals of eugenics and at the same time earning from its injections at a profit margin of 1:20. The pandemics the Vatican have instituted from century ago to this day have killed more people than civil wars, and world wars combined. It is a very subtle deceptions yet very effective in killing a lot of people. The outcome always come to one point in these pandemics, people died not of virus or bacteria but from injection. It is a win-win for them, kill people while destroying the economy of the people. The money flow back to them easily which the people are willingly giving them even their life without a fight.

Similarly, Islam causes a lot of troubles and sufferings to every places it conquered to. There is something in this religion that causes people to change behaviorally. Just as the goal of Islam to bring the world back to dark ages, so are their followers thinking, as well as their living condition. And just like Catholicism, those who experience good life are those who belong to their elite group that comprises of the leaders down to their priest (Imam) and Mutawa while the rest of the members suffer in abject poverty, violence, and religious abuses (oppression). But people feared them and are helpless and are willing followers.

This is not an Islamophobia; it is the reality on the ground. In Mindanao alone particularly Basilan, Sulu, and Tawi Tawi, they are in deep poverty and in constant violence. The same thing in Africa. People are driven to commit terrorism and piracy because of the great economic depression in society.

If these two major religions will use its power and wealth in the right way, they can easily solve poverty and sufferings in the world very easily. But no. Their goal is to subjugate people into submission so that they will have power and control over the people if they remain poor and without peace. In other words, their followers are their prisoners and slaves. Humanity have been imprisoned by Satan in darkness.

I am not sorry to offend anyone by telling the truth. But I abhor everyone to listen and think and pray to our Creator God that we maybe enlightened in our current situation – living in prison of darkness. We need to seek the light so that we will see the truth. And we shall know the truth and the truth will set us free from our prison houses. We shall set ourselves free from the influence of darkness. We shall get near to the light that will lead us to the way of righteousness and freedom from Satan's influences. For it is written in Psalms 96:5;

"⁵ "For all the gods of the peoples are idols,…""

We have exposed the true colors and doctrines of these two major religions and how Satan is their author.

I focused in these two major religions because these are the roots of almost all other religions (daughters) and have a bloody, deceptive, and violent history.

Nevertheless, like the people of the isles, the world's poor (meek) have potential to inherit the earth just like what Jesus Christ said in Matthew 5: 5-6;

> "⁵ "Blessed are the meek, for they shall inherit the earth.
>
> ⁶ "Blessed are those who <u>hunger and thirst for righteousness,</u> for they shall be satisfied…"""

The people who have been oppressed by Satan through its various deceptive religions have this potential to inherit the earth if we seek God and His righteousness. But if one is willingly obeying, Satan rather than God, then surely there is a place in hell for those incorrigible people just like what God is going to do to the evildoers in Psalms 37:1-2, 9-11;

> "¹ "Do not fret because of evildoers, nor be envious of the workers of iniquity.
>
> ² For they shall soon be cut down like the grass, and wither as the green herb."
>
> ⁹"For evildoers shall be cut off: but <u>those that wait upon the LORD</u>, they <u>shall inherit the earth</u>."
>
> ¹⁰For yet a little while and the wicked shall be no more; Indeed, you will look carefully for his place, but it shall be no more.
>
> ¹¹But <u>the meek shall inherit the earth,</u> and shall delight themselves in the abundance of peace."

The coming Kingdom of God will give us real peace, joy, happiness, and prosperity. God will give humanity a rest from Satan's lies and deceptions causing so many troubles and suffering. The coming Millennial Kingdom of God is the Sabbath day of the Lord. It is His gift to humanity. For a thousand years which is one day to God (2 Peter 3:8), every human being (both the living and the dead) will be given a chance to learn the truth and be saved from internal damnation. Jesus Christ will rule the whole earth with the rod of iron and humanity will be forced to obey Him so that peace, happiness, and prosperity shall abound on earth. Christ will be our King of kings and Lord of lords (Rev. 19: 16). In Him we shall have rest. For as Jesus Christ said in Matthew11:28-30;

> "[28] "Come unto Me, all you who are weary and burdened, and I will give you rest. [29]Take My yoke upon you and learn from Me; for I am gentle and humble in heart, and you will find rest for your souls. [30]For My yoke is easy and My burden is light.""

As we approach God, we should be like little children and learn from Him just as Jesus Christ said in Matthew 18: 3-5;

> "[3]"Assuredly, I say to you, unless you are converted and become as little children, you will by no means enter the kingdom of heaven. [4]Therefore whoever humbles himself as this little child is the greatest in the kingdom of heaven. [5]Whoever receives one little child like this in My name receives Me....""

What is a little child?

Little children do not pretend they already know everything. Little children want to read and learn new things. Little children do think and strive hard to get what they wanted or what hey want to do. And they have great faith and confidence. Little children are great imitators. So, Paul told the Gentile peoples of the isles in Ephesians 5: 1-2;

> "[1]Therefore be imitators of God as dear children. [2]And walk in love, as Christ also has loved us and given Himself for us, an offering and a sacrifice to God for a sweet-smelling aroma."

A little child is without prejudice and are eager and willing to learn new things. Unlike adult's mind who think they know everything when in fact they know nothing but a deceived mind. Just as it is written in 1 Corinthians 8:2;

> "[2] "And if anyone thinks that he knows anything, he knows nothing yet as he ought to know.""

And in 1 Corinthians 3:18-19;

> "[18] "Let no one deceive himself. If any of you thinks he is wise in this age, he should become a fool, so that he may become wise. [19]For the wisdom of this world is foolishness in God's

sight. As it is written: "He catches the wise in their craftiness.""""

The pride and arrogance of mankind made us easily deceived just as the Lord said in Proverbs 8:13-14;

"¹³The <u>fear of the Lord</u> is to hate evil; <u>pride and arrogance</u> and the evil way and the perverse mouth I hate.

¹⁴Counsel is mine, and <u>sound wisdom</u>; I am <u>understanding</u>, I have strength."

And the key to have knowledge and understanding of God is to fear the Lord as stated in psalms 111:10;

"¹⁰ "<u>The fear of the Lord is the beginning of wisdom</u>;

A good understanding have all those who <u>do His commandments</u>. His praise endures forever.""""

If we fear God, we need to obey His commandments. But Satan deceived the whole world with his many lies including the lie that God's laws and commandments have been done away or buried in the cross. Even to the point of saying there is no God. A perfect way for the enemy to lie so that people will not see the truth (the light, Christ) and remain slaves to sin and unrighteousness full of darkness and suffering.

Jesus Christ said in John 8: 32, 34;

"³² "...And you shall know the truth, and the truth shall make you free.""""

Free from what?

"³⁴Jesus answered them, "Most assuredly, I say to you, <u>whoever commits sin</u> is a slave of sin. ³⁵And a slave does not abide in the house forever, but a son abides forever. ³⁶Therefore if the Son makes you free, you shall be free indeed...."

The truth and the light is godly wisdom. And in order to have wisdom, we begin to fear God and obey His commandments. And then the truth shall set us free from the bondage and corruption of Satan. But first we need to make an effort to open our eyes so that we may see the light. For Jesus said in John 8: 12;

"¹²Then <u>Jesus</u> spoke to them again, saying, "<u>I am the light of the world</u>. He who <u>follows Me</u> shall not walk in darkness, but have the light of life.'"''

We need to follow Jesus so that we may see. On the other hand, Satan wants us to despise Jesus Christ and lied to us of many things about Him in many of his religious prison houses of this world so that we will not see the light. Satan told the world that Christ is just a man, or a prophet, or just a fiction, a myth, or preached another Jesus with a vicar in the church of Rome. Satan blinded us in darkness about the truth that Jesus Christ is our maker as stated in John 1: 3-5;

> "'3All things were made through Him, and without Him nothing was made that was made. 4In Him was life, and the life was the light of men. 5And the light shines in the darkness, and the darkness did not comprehend it."

Paul testified to this truth in Colosians 1: 15 -18 that;

> "'15 "He is the image of the invisible God, the firstborn over all creation. 16For by Him all things were created that are in heaven and that are on earth, visible and invisible, whether thrones or dominions or principalities or powers. All things were created through Him and for Him. 17And He is before all things, and in Him all things consist. 18And He is the head of the body, the church, who is the beginning, the firstborn from the dead, that in all things He may have the preeminence.'"''

Everything was created through Him and for Him. He was before everything. But we were told that He was born on December 25 and He exist only as God and Lord of the New Testament. When in fact He is the God and Lord of both New and Old Testament. It is one.

And yet, humanity hates the truth and the light. Instead, they loved darkness and evil things. People love to be lied and believe in lies of the enemy and loved it. But why, we may ask?

Jesus Christ answered in John 3: 19-21;

> "'19 "And this is the condemnation, that the light has come into the world, and men loved darkness rather than light, because their deeds were evil. 20For everyone practicing evil hates the light and does not come to the light, lest his deeds should be

exposed. ²¹But he who does the truth comes to the light, that his deeds may be clearly seen, that they have been done in God.'"

And even when Jesus Christ comes back to establish the Millennial Kingdom of God here on earth to give rest and replace Satan as the god of this world, still humanity will hate Him as it is written in Revelation 11: 17-18 saying;

"¹⁷ "We give You thanks, O Lord God Almighty,
The One who is and who was and who is to come,
Because You have taken Your great power and <u>reigned</u>.
¹⁸<u>The nations were angry, and Your wrath has come,</u>
And the time of the dead, that they should be judged,…'"

Humanity love darkness so much that they do not want to see or be exposed to light. They are so blinded that it is easy for them to believe in lies and deceptions rather than to make them realize that they have been lied to. That is why Christ need to rule humanity with the rod of iron to forced them to see the light and have real peace, happiness, joy, and prosperity. Mankind will resist at first when Christ come. Just like my fellow Evangelical Christians who refuse to accept the truth of the many doctrinal errors of being born again now, once save forever saved, of going to heaven or hell when one die and observing, practicing, celebrating paganic customs and traditions (will discuss this in another chapter).

It is beyond my imagination how these so-called professing Christians do not see the truth even if it is clearly written in the Bible. How much more the Pilipino people who are full of pride and arrogance and confused in many religions turn to the truth or the light of God. In my limited mind it is impossible. But I believe, that with God nothing is impossible.

When He called us to be His servants and He will call us His people, I have doubt on the people, but I believe God will make a way. When He said in Isaiah 60: 1-3 that He will come to us as our light and we will rise us up;

"¹Arise, shine; for your light has come!

And the glory of the Lord is risen upon you.

²For behold, the darkness shall cover the earth,

And deep darkness the people; but the Lord will arise over you,

And His glory will be seen upon you.

³The Gentiles shall come to your light, and kings to the brightness of your rising."

I have doubt on the Pilipino people if they are willing to see the light and will be interested to know the truth. Because most of the Pilipino people are so proud and believe that they are "wise" and are "self-righteous". Their cognitive dissonance immediately kicks in and easily closes their brain when their beliefs are contradicted with new information. Their brain easily shuts down and immediately disregard any rational evidence that contradicts what they previously regarded as the truth. They are so proud to be adults. Nevertheless, I will deliver the message. For who am I to judge the peoples and to disobey God? But He said in Isaiah 51: 4-5;

"⁴ "Listen to Me, My people; and give ear to Me, O My nation: For law will proceed from Me, and I will make My justice rest as a light of the peoples.

⁵My righteousness is near, My salvation has gone forth, and My arms will judge the peoples; the isles/coastlands will wait upon Me, and on My arm they will trust.""

And Psalms 98: 3 said;

"³ "…All the ends of the earth have seen the salvation of our God.""

For in Isaiah 24:14-16 said;

"¹⁴ "They shall lift up their voice, they shall sing; for the majesty of the Lord they shall cry aloud from the sea.

¹⁵Therefore glorify the Lord in the dawning light (east), the name of the Lord God of Israel in the isles of the sea.

¹⁶From the ends of the earth we have heard songs: "Glory to the righteous!""""

If God said this to us, then who am I to doubt? But as a human being with a faint and unfaithful heart, I always have a doubt on myself. I ask myself how can I deliver Your message to your hardheaded prospective servants? Am no body. Will they accept your message and the job You are offering to us? How can I lead them to You? Who will help me, if ever? I only ask God to forgive me of my unbelief.

Although I have the joy and that I am sure God has chosen us to be His servants in this end times and to be called His people and nation also, I have no idea what the future will bring or hold for us. But He said in Isaiah 45:13;

"13 "I have raised him up in righteousness, and I will direct all his ways;""

And as He said In Isaiah 60:22;

"22A little one shall become a thousand, and a small one a strong nation. I, the Lord, will hasten it in its time.""

He has a plan. And we need to trust in His plan. It maybe challenging, but for sure it will be worthwhile. And He will be our guide and strength.

As we have identified our enemy and our weaknesses, we can first approach God by crushing our pride and arrogance and let us humble ourselves before the Lord. This is the starting point to defeating our enemy. The fight maybe long, but it is a fight worth fighting for.

We may have nothing to offer before the Lord, but He said in Psalms 51: 17 that "a broken spirit and a contrite heart He will not despise." Let Psalms 51 be our arduous prayer for forgiveness of our sinfulness to the Lord so that we may defeat our enemy. For it is written in Proverbs 22:4;

"4 "By humility and the fear of the Lord are riches and honor and life.""

And finally, brethren, Paul said in Ephesians 5: 8-14;

"8For you were once darkness, but now you are light in the Lord. Walk as children of light 9(for the fruit of the Spirit is in all goodness, righteousness, and truth), 10finding out what is acceptable to the Lord. [11]And <u>have no fellowship with the unfruitful works of darkness</u>, but rather <u>expose them</u>. [12]For it is shameful even to speak of those things which are done by them in secret. [13]<u>But all things that are exposed are made manifest by the light, for whatever makes manifest is light.</u> [14]Therefore He says:

> "Awake, you who sleep, arise from the dead,
> and Christ will give you light.""

SECTION 3

THE PEOPLE

CHAPTER 3

TRACING THE REAL IDENTITY

The Biblical Perspective of Human History

As humans, our cognitive abilities to think are quite restricted. Our thinking processes is full of errors. The outcomes of our educated guesses, assumptions, hypotheses and testing their validity, show how our society and the earth have evolved to its current state. The human brain is susceptible to corruption by evil rather than being inclined towards goodness.

The history of mankind has always been in a disintegrating process. From the time of Adam to Noah, God destroyed humanity because mankind has become so evil that even the Creator regretted putting them on earth as stated in Genesis 6: 6-7;

> "⁶And <u>the Lord was sorry that He had made man on the earth</u>, and <u>He was grieved in His heart</u>. ⁷So the Lord said, "<u>I will destroy man whom I have created from the face of the earth</u>, both man and beast, creeping thing and birds of the air, for I am sorry that I have made them."

Even from the time of Noah to our time today, God will destroy humanity once again through the "tribulation" period and the "wrath of God". During this time period, a significant number of individuals will pass away, potentially more than half of the population by the time it is finished. It is a time of great turmoil, chaos, pain, and suffering that has not been experienced since the beginning of time as it is written in Matthew 24:21;

"²¹For then there will be great tribulation, such as has not been since the beginning of the world until this time, no, nor ever shall be."

But even these great sufferings, God will not totally eradicate humanity. He will continuously give people a chance to believe in Him specially His chosen people – Israel. In the end, Christ will rule over the remaining humanity in the Kingdom of God here on earth.

Perhaps, this is what happened also to the first earth (Rev. 21: 1) when it was under the influence of Satan. God destroyed the first earth and all humanity on it.

Our own mental capacity is not sufficient to fully understand and comprehend the wisdom and depth of God, our Creator. Given our limited understanding, some may falsely conclude that God does not exist, and therefore they do not seek to understand or know Him.

Instead of submitting to a Supreme Being whose mind, ways and nature are beyond our comprehension, we reject His existence and dismiss Him as nonexistent. We declare that He does not exist based on our limited cognitive abilities.

Instead, we declare ourselves as supreme beings capable of resolving our own problems and making our own gods. And in our own lies, we pretend that if one has a higher education (based on our current educational system), we become an expert or an authority of something we believe is right, even though it is wrong. Many individuals who consider themselves experts, theorists, philosophers, and academics have written books or dissertations and present their ideas (hypothesis/theory) as if they are absolute truths. However, it has become apparent that these theories and philosophical human wisdom are proving to be unreliable and crumbling by the day.

What does this mean? Our human mind is flawed and can

easily be deceived, even by our own thoughts. An optical illusion is an example of this, as it demonstrates how our mind can be deceived by what we perceive. We understand that a visual representation of something we see, or experience is not real, yet our brain and eyes perceive it and believe it to be true, despite it being an illusion. This is also true in the real world, which is filled with illusions and deceptions. Many people tend to believe what they are told by individuals they perceive as authoritative figures, even if it contradicts the reality. They do not take the time to question or verify the information. This could be due to laziness or a lack of critical thinking skills.

Why did I present this statement or idea as a foundation? I want to make it clear that as an ordinary human being with a limited cognitive ability, like many others, I do not take credit for the ideas and information presented here. They are not the result of my own intelligence. In fact, I am amazed by how the pieces of the puzzle of human civilization found in the Bible come together to answer questions that no one has been able to answer before. I do not claim that God directly speaks to me or reveals these things to me, as that would be prideful and arrogant. However, I am sure that there is a divine guidance that led me to learn these things that is beyond my comprehension. I am simply writing what I have come to understand through this guidance.

Therefore, I want to encourage you to not take what I have written here as absolute truth or the correct understanding, as this is a spiritual matter. It is important to question every idea presented in this book in terms of biblical proof and not rely solely on philosophical or logical reasoning. The only way to do this is to earnestly pray to God, the God of the Bible, for knowledge, wisdom, and understanding. We must humble ourselves and approach Him with the eagerness of a child excited to learn new things. I am confident that He will grant us our request as this message is intended for us.

As it is written in 1 Thessalonians 5: 21;

"[21]Prove all things; hold fast that which is good."

We must always strive to overcome our natural tendency to be easily deceived and deny the truth. Even though I pray earnestly to God for His Holy Spirit to guide me and give me knowledge, wisdom, and understanding to understand His Word, I still doubt myself that He has revealed these things to me. For who am I to Him?

On the other hand, who am I to deny this truth? I am just a servant, a messenger and a scribe for His people.

I do not doubt God, but I doubt myself, recognizing my limitations and human nature that only God can bridge the gap for me to tap into His knowledge, wisdom, and understanding, to connect the spiritual truth to our physical existence. That is why I constantly pray, "Lord, let not my own thoughts or ideas be recorded in this book, but let only Your message to Your people be written upon this book. Not my words, but Your Words."

Although I have wondered how this knowledge and understanding of His Words have come to me, I still doubt myself. But how God guided me to the verses as pieces of the puzzle in bringing the pictures of His wonderful plan for humanity is really beyond my capability. That is why, I cannot say that what I wrote here comes from my own mental capacity. Nor I can claim that God talked to me, nor He reveal these things to me personally, as that would be viewed as prideful and arrogant. I am simply a humble servant who places my trust and hope solely in His mercy.

Writing these things may be my calling and likely just a small part of a larger picture, a piece of a beautiful and grand schema of life.

As previously stated, my theories or assumptions expressed with words such as "perhaps" or "maybe" should not be taken as absolute truth. The reader should also examine them not in a philosophical way but in a biblical manner, as they might just be another piece of the puzzle or the beginning of something bigger that has not been revealed yet. In other words, it might be the tip of the iceberg, the start of another biblical truth. To fully understand what is written, we must pray to God for His Holy Spirit to guide us in understanding spiritual matters.

So, in any of my theoretical propositions when I say "perhaps" or "maybe", I will try my best to support it with Biblical verses and try to avoid too much opinion.

The purpose of this book is not to spark debate or argue with others' opinions, but rather to draw us closer to God, marvel at His power and might, and surrender ourselves to Him in righteousness, and to fear and obey Him. If you have doubts or questions, I encourage you to re-read the book multiple times and seek answers by studying the verses of the Bible provided more in-depth. You may have a "eureka" moments also like me as God speaks to you through His Word - the Bible.

I cannot explain everything in one book, nor I know everything of the things of the past and things of the future. But God will reveal to us things that we need to know and do, one day at a time. In His time.

With all that said, let us begin our journey in discovering human history in Biblical perspective and where the isles of the present-day Philippines came from.

First, let us take a look at the so-called "Gap Theory". This theory argues that there is a time gap between verse 1 and 2 in the creation day in Genesis 1 (KJV);

> "¹In the beginning God created the heaven and the earth. ²And the earth was without form, and void; and darkness was upon the face of the deep. And the Spirit of God moved upon the face of the waters."

Most professing Christians do not believe that there is a big gap between verse 1 and verse 2. They just read it as it is. Perhaps, they are just lazy to dig deeper into the knowledge of God. Or perhaps they fail to realize that the Bible is a compressed historical event of creation and coded messages of God. Or perhaps the truth has not been revealed yet in their time.

The Bible is so compressed that just one verse can have a multi-dimensional meaning and jumping from one event to another. Although some verses may look like there is a gap, yet it will be filled by other verses from another book. The Bible interprets itself. That alone is a testament of the gaps in the Bible yet interconnected (matrix) to each other that the mystery of the Word of God is like a puzzle as described in Isaiah 28: 13:

"13But the word of the Lord was to them, "Precept upon precept, precept upon precept, line upon line, line upon line, here a little, there a little,...""

And as you will notice, some of the verses in the Bible suddenly jumps into another topic or subject, and that is why we suddenly lost the understanding and the flow of thoughts. Yet when you lift up some of the important words, it will show you the connections of things. In other words, it is a coded messages or a piece of the puzzle that without the help of the Holy Spirit of God, we cannot understand or be able to connect the dots. Apart from the Holy Spirit of God, we cannot decipher His Words. For on their own, many have tried, but failed to understand.

One of the proofs that there is a gap or missing information between verses 1 and 2 of Genesis 1 is when God created something, it is very good and beautiful as stated in Genesis 1: 31;

"31Then God saw everything that He had made, and indeed it was very good."

But you may say that this verse does not address the gap because it pertains to the creation. That will be answered by our second proof that there is a missing event between verses 1 and 2.

But let us examine Isaiah 45: 18 (KJV) first;

"18For thus saith the LORD that created the heavens; God himself that formed the earth and made it; He hath established it, He created it not in vain, He formed it to be inhabited: I am the LORD; and there is none else."

It is very clear in this verse that God Himself formed and established the earth, not in vain (not empty, not void nor formless) for the purpose of human and angelic habitation.

Compare this to Genesis 1: 1-2 (KJV);

"1In the beginning God created the heaven and the earth. 2And the earth was without form, and void; and darkness was upon the face of the deep. And the Spirit of God moved upon the face of the waters."

Verse 2 is the exact opposite of Isaiah 45: 18. After verse 1 in Genesis 1, it becomes without form and void – dark and empty. Submerged under water.

Evangelicals who reject the idea of a gap between verse 1 and 2 argue that verse 2 describes the condition of the earth prior to its creation, and therefore, there is no gap or missing information. It is like a clay before it is made into a pot.

But notice the element of darkness in verse two. What does darkness symbolize?

Satan symbolizes darkness, emptiness, chaos, and confusion while God symbolizes light, harmony, beauty, goodness, and order as in 1 John 1: 5;

> "⁵This is the message which we have heard from Him and declare to you, that God is light and in Him is no darkness at all."

So, if God the Father and Jesus Christ is Light, why would They start creating the earth from darkness, emptiness, and chaos (without form and void)?

They did not, because Christ created all things in light and it was very good (Isaiah 45: 18). Verse 2 immediately contrasted by verse 3 and 4;

> "³Then God said, "Let there be light"; and there was light. ⁴And God saw the light, that it was good; and God divided the light from the darkness."

Clearly, these verses are testament that God did not like darkness. God do not represent darkness and cannot make the earth or any of His creations out of darkness (1 John 1: 5). And as Jesus Christ accomplished His mission in the last book of the Bible and the New Jerusalem come down from Heaven (Rev. 21:2), John proclaimed the glory of the New Jerusalem in Revelation 21: 23;

> "²³The city had no need of the sun or of the moon to shine in it, for the glory of God illuminated it. The Lamb is its light."

It is clear in this verse that Jesus Christ – the Lamb, is the Light. Yet to those who will not believe these verses, do you think God dwells in darkness before He created all things? Not at all. It is exactly the opposite because He is the Light.

But when did darkness started on earth?

It started when Lucifer, the "angel of light", "shinning star of the dawn", or the "Bringer of light", rebelled against God, his Creator.

Lucifer is one of the three Archangels of God. The two other Cherubs (Archangels) are Michael, and Gabriel. They are the supreme masterpieces of God's creative power of the angelic world. They are spirit beings and cannot die (immortal).

Lucifer was created perfect in beauty, power, mind, knowledge, intellect and wisdom, until he rebelled against God in Ezekiel 28: 12-15;

"¹²You were the seal of perfection, full of wisdom and perfect in beauty. ¹³You were in Eden, the garden of God; every precious stone was your covering: The sardius, topaz, and diamond, beryl, onyx, and jasper, sapphire, turquoise, and emerald with gold. The workmanship of your timbrels and pipes was prepared for you on the day you were created.
¹⁴You were the anointed cherub who covers; I established you; You were on the holy mountain of God; you walked back and forth in the midst of fiery stones.
"¹⁵You were perfect in your ways from the day you were created, till iniquity was found in you."

Take note of the connecting word "established" when God created the earth in Isaiah 45: 18 and when He put Lucifer in- charge of the earth in verse 14 of Ezekiel 28.

When God first created the first heavens and earth, it was perfect in beauty. It was very good. Like Lucifer who was created perfect in his ways. There was no darkness at that time.

God is perfectionist. When He said, He created the heavens and the earth, He reveals Himself as Creator of perfection, beauty, and light.

When God created the earth in Job 38: 4,7, all the angels rejoiced;

"⁴Where were you when I laid the foundations of the earth?
Tell Me, if you have understanding.

[7]When the morning stars (angels) sang together, and all the sons of God (angels- created sons of God) shouted for joy?"

Sons of God here pertains to angels. Angels are created sons of God, while Jesus Christ became a Son of God by birth (begotten) when He was sent to earth, and the saints by adoption.

The above verses show us that angels including Lucifer were created prior to the creation of earth.

Then God assigned Lucifer and a third of the heavenly angels to take charge of the earth and its inhabitants for His purpose. Angels like Lucifer were created to be ministers, agents, and helpers in God's creation. They were created to be servants of God.

Perhaps Lucifer and his angels was supposed to beautify the earth and led the inhabitants to God. To enhance its beauty further and to be functional. The earth must be like a house. It was built beautifully, but needs embellishments such as furniture, functional kitchen, lighting, landscaping the surroundings of the house, etc. Besides the house, the environment needs to have beautiful scenery and be productive.

And Lucifer was the perfect leader to do the job as described in Ezekiel 28: 12-13 when he was on earth as a perfect angelic creation of God.

This verse tells us that Lucifer was somewhat special to God. He made him king over the whole earth as he described himself in Isaiah 14: 12;

"[13]For you (Lucifer) have said in your heart: 'I will ascend into heaven, I will exalt my throne above the stars (angels) of God;...'"

If he is the king of the earth (because he has a throne) and angels are created to be ministers, agents, and helpers to God's creation, could God have created human beings already on earth as the subject of Lucifer's kingdom? And humans at that time are what the angels supposed to minister to?

It is not explicitly stated in the Bible that Lucifer governed human beings during the first creation of the earth. However, there is a very mysterious verse in Genesis 1: 27-28 (KJV);

"²⁷So God created man in his own image, in the image of God created he him; male and female created he them. ²⁸And God blessed them, and God said unto them, be fruitful, and multiply, and replenish the earth, and subdue it;…"

The word "replenish" in this verse only mean that something needs to be replaced. And a similar object that pre-existed need to be present again or to be put in place again because the former (or first earth (Rev. 21:1) is gone or have vanished under water (submerge)).

Notice very carefully that this blessing of God to the mankind (*he him; male and female created he them*) He created is very different mood from the cursing He cast unto Adam and Eve. It could not be possible that God blessed Adam and at the same time cursed them. The former humans were to easily multiply for their mission of repopulating the earth almost without a problem. Meanwhile, Adam and Eve will struggle to give birth and will struggle to feed themselves. Very different scenario.

Similarly, this God's command to the former human beings to "replenish" the earth was repeated to Noah after God destroyed humanity from the face of the earth through flood in Genesis 9:1 (KJV);

"¹And God blessed Noah and his sons, and said unto them, be fruitful, and multiply, and <u>replenish the earth</u>."

Some translations replaced the original text of the word "replenish" to just "fill". But based on what God had said to Noah, "to replenish the earth" in Genesis 9: 1, we know that God killed millions or even billions of people that ever live on earth from the time of Adam (or perhaps even prior to Adam) to the time of the flood. God only saved eight. And now, their mission is also to repopulate the earth and subdue it also.

Therefore, we can infer (but not conclusively because we are not there, and we have no solid verse to support the claim yet) that Mankind pre-existed prior to the creation of man in Genesis 1: 27 and therefore there is habitable earth that existed prior to becoming in the state described in Genesis 1:2;

"²The earth was without form, and void;..."

And with this inference, we can say that Lucifer, have human subjects during his reign on the first earth (Rev. 21: 1) prior to his rebellion to God in Isaiah 14: 12-14;

"¹²How you are fallen from heaven, O <u>Lucifer, son of the morning</u>! How <u>you are cut down to the ground</u>, you <u>who weakened the nations</u>!

¹³For you have said in your heart: '<u>I will ascend into heaven</u>, I will exalt <u>my throne</u> above the stars of God; I will also sit on the mount of the congregation on the farthest sides of the north; ¹⁴I will ascend above the heights of the clouds, I will be like the Most High.'"

We must take note that <u>Lucifer has throne</u> on earth in verse 13 and therefore, the earth is his kingdom for he said that he will ascend into the heaven and exalt his throne above the stars of God. But when he was defeated, he was cast down to the ground. This ground means earth because he weakened the nations of the past and present earth. At present, he is still the god and ruler of this world.

Lucifer literally wants to become God. He wants to dethrone his Master and Maker. He wants to exalt himself – to be worshipped and be served like God. Lucifer, also known as Satan the Devil, was once considered the "bringer of light". But due to his rebellion and disobedience to God, he became known as the author of darkness. Now, darkness reign upon the whole earth because he was cast down to the earth.

Satan, the Devil, is the author of rebellion and have influenced many people to rebel against God, family, and their country. He is thought to be a genius who has become twisted in his thinking, actions, and being. He is believed to have introduced self-centeredness or vanity, lust (including perverted sexual immorality such as transgenderism, adultery, homosexuality, pedophilia, etc.), greed, envy, jealousy, the spirit of competition, hatred of what is good, violence and destruction, and darkness and error. He is said to have brought darkness instead of light and truth, and ugliness instead of beauty.

As result of the iniquities in his mind, Lucifer (the dragon) and his angels with him, wedge war against God in heaven as described in Revelation 12: 7-9;

> "⁷And war broke out in heaven: Michael and his angels fought with the dragon; and the dragon and his angels fought, ⁸but they did not prevail, nor was a place found for them in heaven any longer. ⁹So the great dragon was cast out, that serpent of old, called the Devil and Satan, who deceives the whole world; he was cast to the earth, and his angels were cast out with him."

According to the verses mentioned, Satan had human subjects on Earth prior to the war in heaven. He is believed to have deceived the entire world with his iniquities. And after his defeat in his failed attempt to overthrow God, he was cast back down to Earth and bound to it as his prison. He no longer has the ability or power to return to heaven. He is now symbolized as the serpent (of old) who tempted Eve when God put Adam in the garden of Eden.

So as a result of this futile and destructive war in heaven, the creation was subjected into bondage of destruction (corruption) and decay in Romans 8: 19-20;

> "¹⁹For the earnest expectation of the creation eagerly waits for the revealing of the sons of God. ²⁰For the creation was subjected to futility, not willingly, but because of Him who subjected it in hope; ²¹because the creation itself also will be delivered from the bondage of corruption into the glorious liberty of the children of God."

The rebellion caused by Lucifer is the main reason why God destroyed the first earth and its inhabitants that it became "without form, and void (empty)", in Genesis 1:2. The earth became flooded or submerged under water and became the habitation of darkness, of chaos, confusion, Satan the Devil and his sinning angels. For God does not represent darkness (John 1: 5).

The creation is waiting for the sons of God for them to be restored to its former glory in Romans 8: 22;

"²²For we know that the whole creation groans and labors with birth pangs together until now."

The rebellion or iniquities of Lucifer did not only subject the former earth into darkness and destruction, but the whole creation – the entire universe we may say.

Instead of the creation radiating with light and beauty, it become darkness and destruction.

But God restored the earth and created mankind (*he him; male and female created he them*) for the purpose of becoming the sons of God who will deliver the creation from the bondage of corruption. But Satan corrupted mankind once again and lead them to rebel against God. Then He created Adam as a savior type, but failed God.

This is the gap or the event missing between Genesis 1 verses 1 and 2. And this will bring us to the second proof that the gap existed as testified by Peter in 2 Peter 3: 5-7;

"⁵For this they willfully forget: that by the word of God the heavens were of old, and the earth standing out of water and in the water, ⁶by which the world that then existed perished, being flooded with water. ⁷But the heavens and the earth which are now preserved by the same word, are reserved for fire until the day of judgment and perdition of ungodly men."

If we pay close attention to the verses above, we note that;

1. The scoffers of this days, who are walking according to their own lust, willfully forget or are ignorant that the heavens existed long time ago (of Old) and that there is a former world (first earth) that previously existed but perished through flood. This is the first earth that Lucifer and his angels were assigned to minister to its inhabitants.

    This is a different earth (but the same earth (created and recreated)) that was subjected by God to flooding during the time of Noah. The former or first earth perished – meaning totally destroyed (without form and void (empty) and full of darkness (habitation of Satan). Submerge under water for a long time.

The second earth (which is also the first became the recreated earth) at the time of the Great Flood of Noah did not perish but was transformed or distorted by God (Isaiah 24: 1) after it was submerged under water for a little while.

If the earth that Peter is referring to is the same as the earth during the Great Flood in the time of Noah, then he and his family would not have existed because the whole earth have perished. Perish means to suffer complete ruin or destruction.

During the Great Flood, God destroyed all living things on the face of the earth except the family of Noah and those who are with them. God did not destroy (perish) the earth totally as mentioned in Genesis 7: 23 but;

> "²³So He destroyed all living things which were on the face of the ground: both man and cattle, creeping thing and bird of the air. They were destroyed from the earth. Only Noah and those who were with him in the ark remained alive."

God's covenant with Noah indicates that God have formerly destroyed all flesh on earth in Genesis 9:15;

> "¹⁵ "...and I will remember My covenant which is between Me and you and every living creature of all flesh; the waters shall never again become a flood to destroy all flesh.""

God have done it before. He destroyed all flesh (no exemption) as also testified by Peter in 2 Peter 3: 6:

> "⁶ "...by which the world that then existed perished, being flooded with water.""

The Great Flood did not destroy all flesh on the face of the earth. Although God said to Noah that He will destroy all living things on earth, He made a covenant to save Noah and his family and all the pairs of every living things he will bring into the ark in Genesis 6: 17-19;

"[17]And behold, I Myself am bringing floodwaters on the earth, <u>to destroy from under heaven all flesh in which is the breath of life</u>; <u>everything that is on the earth shall die</u>. [18]But I will establish My covenant with you; and you shall go into the ark—you, your sons, your wife, and your sons' wives with you. [19]And of every living thing of all flesh you shall bring two of every sort into the ark, to keep them alive with you; they shall be male and female."

This time, God wants to destroy all mankind and all living creatures in the face of the earth, except Noah and all flesh with him. The second earth did not perish during the Great Flood. It was a sort of clean up (clean slate) and start all over again or a new birth (rebirth).

2. Peter testified to the recreation of the earth in 2 Peter 3: 7 (KJV);

"[7]But the heavens and the <u>earth, which are now, by the same word are kept in store</u>, reserved unto fire against the day of judgment and perdition of ungodly men."

From verse 6 which the "<u>world that then existed – perished</u>", to verse 7 "<u>the earth which now exist</u>", indicates that the former world was gone and a new earth has come (Rev. 21 : 1). Note carefully that the second earth will no longer be destroyed by flooding (Gen. 9:15) but with fire in verse 7 and detailed in the books of Daniel and Revelation in the very near future.

Take note also that not only the earth perished but also the heavens. That is why during the time of recreation there was a total darkness because the sun, the moon, and stars also perished.

By what way then was the world recreated?

By the "same word" that made the former (verse 7).

The word here may have multiple meanings. It means

the same God, the Word who is Jesus Christ recreated the earth. And "the same word" (procedure) as in Genesis 1 created and recreated the Heaven, the heavens, and the earth. All these might have been damage by the war in heaven.

Let us take a look at it in the perspective of God recreating the earth.

A. The word pertains to the Maker, the Word in John 1: 1-5, 10, 14, as the Creator of all things which is Yeshua (Jesus Christ);

"¹In the beginning was the Word, and the Word was with God, and the Word was God. ²He was in the beginning with God. ³All things were made through Him, and without Him nothing was made that was made. ⁴In Him was life, and the life was the light of men. ⁵And the light shines in the darkness, and the darkness did not comprehend it.

¹⁰He was in the world, and the world was made through Him, and the world did not know Him. ¹¹He came to His own, and His own did not receive Him.

¹⁴And the Word became flesh and dwelt among us, and we beheld His glory, the glory as of the only begotten of the Father, full of grace and truth."

Please take note verse 5 as the light shines into darkness and compare it to Genesis 1: 2-3;

"² "…and darkness was on the face of the deep…."

³Then God said, 'Let there be light"; and there was light."

And this is the beginning of the creation/recreation of the ancient world – the world of old and the world a new.

B. The "word" pertains to the making or the process of making as in Genesis 1: 2-30;

This is the first week of creation/recreation. As Peter said, the same process in recreating the present earth is the same process when the former earth was created. But unlike the former world, which was destroyed through water, the present earth will be destroyed through fire.

And in verse 8 of 2 Peter 3 (KJV), he reminded us that; "[8]But, beloved, be not ignorant of this one thing, that one day is with the Lord as a thousand years, and a thousand years as one day."

Now that we have seen the missing links of the gap theory through the testimony of Peter and John (in Revelation 21), the gap between verses 1 and 2 of Genesis is now complete. And the closer examination of this gap is not to accommodate the theory of evolution (as some skeptics may say) for this is a Satanic deception, but rather in seeking to find answers to the mystery, might and power of our God, our Creator. For after all, the Almighty Father is not only confined from Genesis to Revelation. God is greater than the Bible (His Word) and we can only think or imagine what God can do and have done and is doing in our very limited mental capacity to think. Perhaps God created many universes, or earths in the vastness of the firmament and each of these universes/earths have Jesus Christ type of His Son. This we do not know for sure (until we become children of God). But Jesus Christ is the only begotten Son of God. What we know for sure is that God – the Almighty Father will dwell on the new earth as the headquarter of His Kingdom (Rev. 21).

God give us the Word of God – the Bible as in "a need-to-know" basis concerning us as human beings, starting from Adam, and ending with Jesus Christ. But He give us also tiny bits of clue to see (a glimpse) what is beyond.

The Bible is a compressed historical event but a very precise and concise instruction as to how mankind should behave (to conduct oneself) and obey God. The Bible is an instructional or user's manual for mankind to have a good life that humanity have ignored. But those that does not concern us yet are not given in details.

The Bible gives us (human beings) our specific duty or work in Ecclesiastes 12: 13 (KJV);

"[13] "Let us hear the conclusion of the whole matter:

Fear God, and keep his commandments:

for this is the whole duty of man.""

It is very clear what we need to do. That plain and simple. But humanity complicate this thing and have hard time obeying it. We are blinded by the darkness (Satan) that have "deceived the whole world" in Revelation 12: 9 (KJV);

> "⁹So the great dragon was cast out, that serpent of old, called the Devil and Satan, who deceives the whole world; he was cast to the earth, and his angels were cast out with him."

And have "weakened the nations" in Isaiah 14: 12;

> "¹²"How you are fallen from heaven, O <u>Lucifer, son of the morning</u>! How you are cut down to the ground, you who <u>weakened the nations</u>!""

We see, we have a hard time seeing and obeying, nor understanding the things that concerns us at the present, why are we so hypocrite concerning ourselves of things that are of the past and that are of the future that are unseen?

In other words, if we are having a hard time grasping the things that is bestowed upon us in our time, how much more of the things that are hidden. For John the Apostle testified to this fact in John 21: 25;

> "²⁵And there are also many other things that Jesus did, which if they were written one by one, I suppose that even the world itself could not contain the books that would be written. Amen."

For instance, in our limited mind, we can marvel how many books will be written about the anatomy of creating the human body. What, how, where, when, and why from conception to death and every human organs and cells of our body and the functions and purpose of each is a large volume of books in itself. Added to that are the thousands of species of every plant and animal according to its kind created by Jesus Christ one by one. Each created in a special passion, beauty, and purpose we can only marvel at. How much more of the creation of the entire universe?

For in fact, God said in Ecclesiastes 12: 12;

> "¹²And further, my son, be admonished by these. Of making many books there is no end,…"

Now let us look at the mystery of the creation of man.

Jesus Christ (Yeshua) testifies to us through John in Revelation 21:1 that there was a first heaven and a first earth that passed away. Meaning that it perished and was destroyed;

"¹Now I saw a new heaven and a new earth, for the first heaven and the first earth had passed away. Also there was no more sea."

This was confirmed and seconded by Peter in his 2nd epistle chapter 3 verse 5 to 7 (KJV);

"⁵For this they willingly are ignorant of, that by the word of God the heavens were of old, and the earth standing out of the water and in the water: ⁶Whereby the world that then was, being overflowed with water, perished: ⁷But the heavens and the earth, which are now, by the same word are kept in store, reserved unto fire against the day of judgment and perdition of ungodly men."

These verse clearly is telling us that there was a former heavens and earth that previously existed and have perished and then replaced by the second one for which we are now according to Peter.

The first earth mentioned here is not the earth before Noah's flood for the earth before the flood did not perish or destroyed but was transformed into its present form today from a single piece of dry land (Gen. 1:9) distorted by God (Isaiah 24:1) into many islands and continents. The lands of the present earth are like pieces of a puzzle that can be put back together as one piece of land. Like a circle perhaps?

Were there human beings on the first earth when it was destroyed by God?

Let us investigate further and look at the possible reasons why mankind existed on the first earth.

First, Revelation 21: 1 mentioned;

"¹ "…Also there was no more sea.""

Why would God mention "sea" when the first earth already passed away? Could the sea mean literal sea or does it have a symbolic meaning?

If the "sea" in this verse is literal for the new earth, then we might ask, why will God remove a beautiful and functional element of design in the landscape of the new earth. It is a source of food, recreation, and beautiful scenery. Besides, we should remember that in Genesis 1: 9-10 indicates that the sea is not part of the earth but the earth is part of the sea. This is also confirmed by Peter in 2 Peter 3: 5 saying, "the earth standing out of the water and in the water:". It seems in this verse that the earth is not just floating in the waters (which is called by God as "seas") but also standing out of the water which implied that it has feet or foundation. And the sea is perhaps infinite or so vast compared to earth.

We should remember that the Bible is a very compressed word of God. It could have multiple meanings and also have multi-dimensional pictures and perhaps coded messages.

But let us connect the dot as to what is the Biblical meaning of "sea" in the verse above. Let the Bible interprets itself.

In Genesis 1: 10, God called the gathering of waters as sea;

"¹⁰And God called the dry land Earth, and the gathering together of the waters He called Seas."

Here, the waters is also called seas. They are one and the same. And Revelation 17: 15 give the symbolic or figurative meaning of "sea" as "waters";

"¹⁵Then he said to me, "The waters which you saw, where the harlot sits, are peoples, multitudes, nations, and tongues.""

We also have an expression describing a multitude of people attending a rally or a concert as "sea of people".

Now, we have decoded the meaning of the "sea" in Revelation 21:1 as inhabitants of the first earth which also perished when it was destroyed by God through flood resulting into the state of the earth mentioned in Genesis 1:2. God did not create the first earth "without form and empty". When He first created the earth it is beautiful and complete to be inhabited by man just as said in Isaiah 45: 18;

"¹⁸ "For thus says the Lord, Who created the heavens, Who is God, Who formed the earth and made it, Who has established it, Who did not create it in vain, Who formed it to be inhabited:

"I am the Lord, and there is no other…"'"

Second, Peter said in his second Epistle 3:7;
"⁷ "But the heavens and the earth, which are now, by the same word are kept in store,…"'"

The "word" here may mean Jesus Christ the Creator of heavens and earth as mentioned in John 1:1-3, 14;
"¹In the beginning was the Word, and the Word was with God, and the Word was God. ²He was in the beginning with God. ³All things were made through Him, and without Him nothing was made that was made."

The Word is Jesus Christ, the only begotten Son of God.
"¹⁴And the Word became flesh and dwelt among us, and we beheld His glory, the glory as of the only begotten of the Father, full of grace and truth."

The word also may mean the same process of recreating or restoring the heavens and the earth as in Genesis 1: 3-31 – the first week of recreation with emphasis on the creation of man in verse 27-28 (KJV);
"²⁷So God created man in his own image, in the image of God created he him; male and female created he them. ²⁸And God blessed them, and God said unto them, Be fruitful, and multiply, and replenish the earth, and subdue it:…"

Most of the translation replaced the word "replenish" or refill the earth in King James Version (KJV) to only "fill" the earth, which is a wrong translation because they did it also in Genesis 9:1(NKJV);
"¹So God blessed Noah and his sons, and said to them: "Be fruitful and multiply, and <u>fill the earth</u>."

But Genesis 9:1 in King James Version is;
"¹And God blessed Noah and his sons, and said unto them, be fruitful, and multiply, and <u>replenish the earth</u>."

Clearly, it should be "refill" or "replenish" the earth because this verse also references Genesis 1: 28 and God said in Genesis 6:7;

> "⁷So the Lord said, "I will destroy man whom I have created from the face of the earth, both man and beast, creeping thing and birds of the air, for I am sorry that I have made them.""

God destroyed mankind from the face of the earth, except Noah's family (8) and those who are with him (animals). So, there mission is to repopulate (replenish) the earth because there were people previously living before and with them on earth. So, was the first earth.

The third reason why mankind already exist on the first earth is because God created the angels to be ministers and agents of His creation on earth. Just as it is written in Hebrew 1: 13-14 (KJV) said;

> "¹³But to which of the angels said he at any time, sit on my right hand, until I make thine enemies thy footstool?
> ¹⁴Are they not all ministering spirits, sent forth to minister for them who shall be heirs of salvation?"

Why would God send Lucifer and a third of the angels of heaven to earth if they have nobody to minister and be an agent to?

Perhaps, mankind whom the angels are ministering to, became the reason why iniquities was found in Lucifer (Ez. 28:15). His iniquities include greed, envy, self-centeredness, jealousy, and many others as his mind continuously to be corrupted by sin. Lucifer envy and rebel against God because His creation worshipped and served Him. Lucifer desired to be worshipped and served too. He is also jealous to mankind because God give them opportunity to become sons of God. Therefore, he declared he wanted to become god and replace God which is in heaven.

Then Lucifer became Satan the Devil who deceives the whole world. He did it before, he is doing it again.

Now, we have seen from the Word of God that there were human inhabitants on the first earth that was destroyed. Our next question is, who are the male and female and them that God said He created in the first week of recreation in Genesis 1: 27-28? Was it Adam and Eve? Or a different group of people?

Was there a group of people created by God prior to Adam's

creation?

Let us examine the Word of God and consider some facts about creation of man in Genesis 1: 27-28 and compare it to Genesis 2: 7 and Genesis 3: 16 and 17.

If we look at Genesis 1: 27-28 (KJV);

"²⁷So God created man in his own image, in the image of <u>God created he him; male and female created He them</u>. ²⁸And <u>God blessed them</u>, and God said unto them, be fruitful, and multiply, and <u>replenish the earth</u>, and subdue it:…"

And compare it to Genesis 2: 7(KJV);

"⁷And the LORD God formed man of the dust of the ground, and breathed into his nostrils the <u>breath of life</u>; and man became <u>a living soul</u>."

And the curses to Adam and Eve when they were driven out of the Garden of Eden in Genesis 3: 16- 17 (KJV);

"¹⁶"Unto the woman he said, I will greatly multiply thy sorrow and thy conception; in sorrow thou shalt bring forth children; and thy desire shall be to thy husband, and he shall rule over thee.

¹⁷And unto Adam he said, because thou hast hearkened unto the voice of thy wife, and hast eaten of the tree, of which I commanded thee, saying, thou shalt not eat of it: "<u>cursed is the ground for thy sake</u>; in sorrow shalt thou eat of it all the days of thy life;""

First, if we consider chronological order in this aspect of the Bible, we can say that there were two sets of people that was created. One is the "male and female and them" that God created simultaneously/together in the sixth day of recreation or creation (first week) and the other was Adam on the eighth day (second week).

We must remember that to God, one day is a thousand years and a thousand years as one day to God (2 Peter 3: 8).

Second consideration is how God declared the creation of man. In Genesis 1:27, God declared that He "<u>created them male and female</u>" at the same time/simultaneously. On the other hand, on the next day following His declaration of the seventh day as His Sabbath,

He created Adam first. <u>Eve was not created independently</u> but she was taken from Adam in Genesis 2: 21-23;

> "²¹And the Lord God caused a deep sleep to fall on Adam, and he slept; and <u>He took one of his ribs</u>, and closed up the flesh in its place. ²²Then <u>the rib which the Lord God had taken from man He made into a woman</u>, and He brought her to the man. ²³And Adam said: "This is now bone of my bones and flesh of my flesh; she shall be called Woman, because she was taken out of Man.""

Well, we can philosophically argue that they are one and the same male and female described on the sixth day of creation. But if we dig a little bit deeper, we can see that there is a big difference in the way they were created. One is that the "male and female and them" was described as created at the same time. While Adam and Eve's creation is separate and have time gap between Adam's creation and the time Eve was taken from Adam. One originates from the other and was not created separately. One was blessed, the other one was cursed.

Third consideration is the "Breath of Life". The first male and female were not specifically mentioned if they have the "Breath of Life" like Adam as mentioned in Genesis 2:7. On the other hand, we need to ask the question, why God also put the "tree of life" in the garden of Eden and then places Adam there too? And then in 1 Corinthians 15: 45-47 said;

> "⁴⁵And so it is written, "The <u>first man Adam</u> became a living being." <u>The last Adam</u> became a life-giving spirit.
> ⁴⁶However, the spiritual is not first, but the natural, and afterward the spiritual. ⁴⁷<u>The first man was of the earth, made of dust; the second Man is the Lord from heaven</u>."

The first man pertaining to Adam could not necessarily mean literally the first man on earth because obviously Jesus Christ is not just the second man. The "first man and second Man (The last Adam)" can be figurative meaning of the "savior" type.

It could be that if Adam did not disobey God and he found the "tree of life" and eat of the fruit of it, then he will be the savior of mankind before him (*he him; male and female created he them*). He could have been the "life-giving spirit" instead of Yeshua (Jesus Christ). But he failed God.

So, God the Almighty Father have to make a supreme sacrifice by sending His only begotten Son just to save mankind from the penalty of their sins which is death (by grace). Adam was a savior type like Jesus Christ that is why the comparison was made (1 Cor. 15: 45). Adam failed God. Christ successfully accomplished His mission as the Servant of God. Just Christ Himself said in Mark 10: 45;

> "[45]"...For even the Son of Man did not come to be served, but to serve, and to give His life a ransom for many.""

And Peter said in Acts 3: 13 and 26;

> "[13] "The God of Abraham, Isaac, and Jacob, the God of our fathers, glorified His Servant Jesus, whom you delivered up and denied in the presence of Pilate, when he was determined to let Him go.
>
> [26]To you first, God, having raised up His Servant Jesus, sent Him to bless you, in turning away every one of you from your iniquities.""

We must remember that God is trying to save mankind from their own destructive ways so that they may become sons of God because the creation is awaiting the revelation of the sons of God.

The fourth consideration is the curses and blessings. The "male and female and them" created by God in Genesis 1: 27 were blessed by God to go forth and multiply and to replenish the earth. It seems that food and reproduction (giving birth) was not their problem.

Now, compare this to the curses given by God to Adam and Eve for their disobedience.

1. Adam is to toil or till the ground in order for them to eat.
2. Eve's sorrows and pain in conception and giving birth was greatly multiplied.

There must be a basis for these increased sorrow and pain that

Eve is going to experience during the process of reproduction or giving birth. If not, then how can it be multiplied?

Adam and Eve were cursed and driven away from the garden. They were not blessed. Cursed and blessing cannot be given at the same time. Otherwise, one has no effect over the other.

These are just a few considerations we can think about. There are many more that can connect the dots. The main reason we are discussing this is not to really prove if there is a separate man aside from Adam, but rather to give emphasis to the majesty, mystery, and power of our God that our limited mind can barely scratch or fathom. That there is really a Supreme Being who designed and orchestrated everything since the ancient of times up to this day.

The Great Flood

From the time of Adam to the time of Noah, humanity's wickedness had become so severe that God decided to destroy all humans once again, as stated in Genesis 6:5-7:

> "⁵Then the Lord saw that the wickedness of man was great in the earth, and that every intent of the thoughts of his heart was only evil continually. ⁶And the Lord was sorry that He had made man on the earth, and He was grieved in His heart. ⁷So the Lord said, "I will destroy man whom I have created from the face of the earth, both man and beast, creeping thing and birds of the air, for I am sorry that I have made them." ⁸But Noah found grace in the eyes of the Lord."

So, God saved Noah and his family of eight and all the living creatures that are with them to replenish the earth once more when God finishes the cleansing of the earth with flood (deluge).

The great flood is like a process of giving birth or a rebirth for the earth. The ark is like an egg or a fetus. The fetus inside the mother's womb is surrounded with water for cushion and protection from the elements. And as God curse the woman (Eve) in Genesis 3:16;

> "¹⁶To the woman He said: "I will greatly multiply your sorrow and

your conception; in pain you shall bring forth children;…""

Indeed, giving birth of a woman is painful and involves great energy – a violent event that stops only after the baby is delivered. And so, God told us His pain and agony in giving birth to a new set of humanity on earth in the times of Noah as He said in Isaiah 42: 14-15;

> ""[14]"I have held My peace a long time, I have been still and restrained Myself.
>
> Now I will cry like a woman in labor, I will pant and gasp at once. [15]I will lay waste the mountains and hills, and dry up all their vegetation; I will make the rivers coastlands (isles), and I will dry up the pools.""

We see in these verses how God poured out His indignation against humanity, against His enemies. He unleashes His anger to the earth like a woman giving birth.

First, the water broke and then the violent transformation (distortion) of the earth as in a woman travailing in pain during the labor of giving birth. There is a ripping and gnashing of teeth like the ripping apart of the land of the earth (Ps. 112: 10) creating severe tectonic plates movements resulting into continents and mountains grinding against each other. From a single piece of land (Gen. 1: 9, circle of the earth (Isaiah 40:22)) to several islands and continents separated by bodies of water after the flood. He divided the earth with rivers (Oceans and Seas) (Hab. 3: 9). But God made a special mention about the rivers whom He turned into islands (isles, coastlands).

Before the flood, God only mentioned one river, which came from Eden and watered the garden in the east. This river then split into four branches that flowed to the ends of the earth in the east. (Gen. 2: 10). In other words, the rivers mentioned by God before the flood were located at the easternmost parts of the earth and their waters flowed into the eastern sea.

We can imagine that initially, a river originated from the center of a circular piece of dry land and flowed to the ends of the earth in the east, providing water for a garden. It then divided into four distinct rivers. But during the flood, God changed the earth, breaking it apart like puzzle pieces. He also made mention that the rivers located at the ends of the earth were transformed into islands.

As previously stated, when God references directions in His speech, He likely uses the Temple in Jerusalem as a point of reference. This is because the Temple has doors facing precisely towards the four cardinal directions, similar to a compass. This is the reason why these rivers are located directly east of Jerusalem when the earth was just one piece of dry land. Then it became the islands of the present-day Philippines which moved south from its original location in the present-day mainland China when God distorted the face of the earth. These are like pieces of a puzzle that fits exactly together when we look at the map. The rock formation in Palawan is one of the clues to its connectivity in the land of the present-day China.

But, while looking at the map of the world, one might wonder why of all the places, country island nations, only the Philippines have a very distinct arrangement. The island formation of the Philippines resembles the shape of a woman, yet it is not. It also looks like a tent or perhaps a lamb. It has a very mysterious arrangement and yet beautifully and artistic in appearance. Why?

Because God created it himself or arranged it Himself in Isaiah 40: 28;

"28Have you not known? Have you not heard?
The everlasting God, the Lord, the Creator of the ends of the earth, neither faints nor is weary. His understanding is unsearchable."

God specifically mentioned that He is the Creator of the ends of the earth. The "ends of the earth" is a code name for the isles in the east. He specially arranged the islands in an artistic way. Just as he mentioned, He is the Creator of Israel in Isaiah 43: 15;

"15I am the LORD, your Holy One, the Creator of Israel, your King."

And the Builder of Jerusalem in Psalms 147: 2;
"2The Lord builds up Jerusalem;..."

This is the connection of Israel and the present – day Philippines, that these are His special land and possessions and His people as we will discuss later.

But it said the "ends of the earth" (in Isaiah 40: 28) and did not mention "islands", you may say.

But if we read a little bit farther in verse 5 of the next chapter (41 KJV) and use the principle of the Bible mentioning two different words or phrases yet have one and the same meaning, we will see that the codes "ends of the earth" and the "isles (islands, coastlands)" are one and the same.

"⁵The isles saw it, and feared; the ends of the earth were afraid, drew near, and came."

Take not also that at the beginning of Isaiah 41:1(KJV), God is talking to the isles, and verse 5 is the reaction of the isles to God's calling;

"¹Keep silence before Me, O islands (isles); and let the people renew their strength: let them come near; then let them speak: let us come near together to judgment."

The "ends of the earth" and the "isles" are not only locator and identifier respectively, but it also pertains to its people as "they drew near and came" (in NKJV). God is calling the people of "the ends of the earth/isles" to come and to draw near to Him and join Him in the judgement of this generation.

God is calling the peoples of the "ends of the earth" to renew their strength in the Lord. For He is the giver of power and strength to those who are weak (nation/people) so that they may be able to perform the works and be able to "let them speak" – preach the Gospel of Jesus Christ in all the earth just as it is written in Isaiah 40: 29 and 31;

"²⁹He gives power to the weak, and to those who have no might He increases strength."

Specially this pandemic hoax, our people have become more helpless and weaker, because our very own government have weakened us further by serving the "woman" rather than its people. We are also weakened by our pride and arrogance that we become deaf and blind to the truth. And yet, God promised in verse 31 that;

"³¹But those who wait on the Lord shall renew their strength; they shall mount up with wings like eagles, they shall run and not be weary, they shall walk and not faint."

This verse identified us farther by the word "eagle". There is no other magnificent eagle in the east than our very own majestic "Philippine Eagle".

If we take all the important words in the verses we have already read, it will appear that the terms "ends of the earth," "east (for the ends of the earth is in the east)," "isles (islands, coastlands)," "weak," and "eagle" will surely identify and characterize the Ophirians or the Pilipino people.

Now, after the flood in the times of Noah, the Bible first mentioned the "isles" (islands) in Genesis 10:5;

"⁵From these the coastland (isles, islands) peoples of the Gentiles were separated into their lands, everyone according to his language, according to their families, into their nations."

No wonder why we have hundreds of languages, and ethnic groups. Each have their own territories and culture up to this day.

Notice that succeeding generations (descendants) of Noah were previously in and from the isles/islands/coastlands and not from the mountains of Ararat because they migrated to the west in the land of Shinar from the isles in the east. And, what and where exactly are these isles?

It is the "rivers" in the east that God turned or made into the isles mentioned in Isaiah 42:15 after He distorted (Isaiah 24:1) the face of the earth (during the flood). It is clear that the "isles, islands" (mentioned in Gen.10: 5) is in the east at the ends of the earth where the Ark of Noah settled after the flood.

That is right, the ark of Noah landed in the isles because that was what Genesis 10:5 told us so. The generations of Noah started in the isles and not from the Mountains of Turkey near Armenia nor in the Middle East or Mesopotamia. And God is so wise enough to start the new set of living things on earth on a tropical climate, than in a harsh environment of a desert, nor in the harsh cold and snowy climate of Mt. Ararat in Turkey (now Türkiye).

In a tropical climate, people and animals can easily adopt to the new environment before they migrate to their own environment that suits them. Every livable place on earth experience summer heat (except polar regions). But not every livable place experience extreme cold (snowy) season.

Now we ask again, could the Mt. Ararat mentioned in Genesis 8: 4 was mistranslated instead of Mt.Arayat in Pampanga? Or could it be a code, hiding the real identity until the appointed time?

"⁴Then the ark rested in the seventh month, the seventeenth day of the month, on the mountains of Ararat."

Of course, translators of the Bible do not know the islands of the Philippines. Some translators (translations) of the Bible changes the original words to fit their belief or interpretations according to their background in their geography and history of their civilization. Like for example changing the names of the four rivers to Niles, Blue Nile, Tigris, and Euphrates rivers because of their belief that the ancient world or the beginning of civilization is only confined in the Middle East particularly Mesopotamia which was believed to be the cradle of civilization. So, they change the actual words of the Bible according to their historical and geographical backgrounds.

But they forgot the facts that these rivers are located at the "ends of the earth" in the "east". At the corner of the earth and not in the center or middle of the earth. Besides, the actual rivers no longer exist because God turned it into islands, and the earth is no longer the same form before the flood for He distorted it (Isaiah 24:1).

But it is okey, because God hide things to those whom he did not called to understand yet. And He reveals things in His time. Because even though He revealed Himself already to humanity, still they did not believe Him. How much more those things that are hidden in mystery. But the time is coming where He will reveal His glory on earth just as He said in Isaiah 40: 5;

"⁵The glory of the Lord shall be revealed, and all flesh shall see it together; for the mouth of the Lord has spoken."

And so, humanity started again in the isles in the east. Then, they travelled to the west in Genesis 11:2;

"²And it came to pass, as they journeyed <u>from the east</u>, that they found a plain in the land of Shinar, and they dwelt there."

Where is the land of Shinar?

It is in the west of the isles because they travelled from the east and it is believed to be the land of Mesopotamia. For how long they stayed or dwelt there before they build the tower of Babel, we do not know.

Some locate Shinar in the Southern Mesopotamia and called it Sumer. But for our discussion let us just locate it as in the whole land of Mesopotamia for it is called the Fertile Cresent as we have been told.

The Tower of Babel mentioned in Genesis 11 is the symbol of disobedience or rebellion against God's will of the descendants of Noah. Instead of obeying God's command in Genesis 9:1 to, "Be fruitful and multiply and <u>replenish</u> the earth", they hardened their hearts and said in Genesis 11: 4;

"⁴ "Come, let us build ourselves a city, and a tower whose top is in the heavens; let us make a name for ourselves, lest we be scattered abroad over the face of the whole earth.""

This is a direct disrespect and disobedience to God's command for them to "go forth and multiply and replenish the earth". Perhaps this is the very reason why they migrated westward towards the land of Shinar. They just want to be together and not be separated from one another. Perhaps, they were thinking that if they moved west, they could get away from God in the isles of the east. Because remember that the isles is God's land/nation for He personally emphasize that He created it like Israel.

Perhaps, the descendants of Japheth or Japheth himself is the one leading to build the Tower of Babel because he is the youngest and he does not want to be separated from his other siblings and descendants (this can mean literally and figuratively). As we have discussed, Japheth's descendants move southward of the isles after they returned from the land of Shinar. They move to the larger islands known today as the Indonesian and Malaysian Archipelago. From these territories, Noah's blessing to Japheth was fulfilled in Genesis 9: 27;

"[27]May God enlarge Japheth, and may he dwell in the tents of Shem; and may Canaan be his servant."

If we look at the map, Indonesia and Malaysia is literally under the tents (plural, perhaps islands) of the isles (Philippines) and they are enlarged islands. They become larger than the tents. Perhaps, the tents from the top to the bottom including all the islands in the Pacific up to Hawaii, was just one kingdom until they separated from one another and become independent nations or smaller kingdoms.

One of the proofs of this is the now considered oldest (so far) ziggurat or pyramid found in Indonesia's West Java province called Gunung Pandang. It is believed to have been built dating back to 10,000 B.C. or earlier. Although I do not believe in this dating methodology, still it is the oldest by their standard. So, from the pyramids in Egypt and Central America that are usually considered to be the oldest in the world, cannot stand anymore. With the recent result of the study of the Gunung Padang, the timeline of history taught in our schools and universities for the last hundred years can no longer stand. Added to that are the pyramids or ziggurats found and China that are much larger and older than the one in Egypt and central America. We can now also say that the cradle of civilization did not begin in Mesopotamia, for this pyramid is a proof that human civilization started far earlier than assumed today. This prove that the Bible is not confined in the Middle East and that the new human civilization most likely started from the east. The ziggurats and pyramids of Egyptian, the Mayans of Mexico and Central America, the Aztecs of Mesoamerica, and the Incas of Peru and other places on earth such as China are just products of Japheth's descendants of the art and technology of tower building such as the tower of Babel.

But as we know in Genesis 11: 7-9, God destroyed their plans and God said;

"⁷Come, let Us go down and there confuse their language, that they may not understand one another's speech." ⁸So the Lord scattered them abroad from there over the face of all the earth, and they ceased building the city. ⁹Therefore its name is called Babel, because there the Lord confused the language of all the earth; and from there the Lord scattered them abroad over the face of all the earth."

This scattering abroad of the people is not an instant like we can imagine that it is just a flick of the finger of God and everyone were distributed in all their places. It is a process that took several decades or even centuries based on the days of Peleg (Gen. 10: 25). But the Tower of Babel is the beginning of God's working on His plan that the whole earth be inhabited once again. Showing that He is God, and no one can destroy His plan.

As we can see in Genesis 10: 30 (KJV), the family of Shem with emphasis on Eber, travelled back to the east;

"³⁰And their dwelling was from Mesha, as thou goest unto Sephar a mount of the east."

Perhaps, this Mesha is now the Mashad, Iran. Iran is part of the ancient Mesopotamian region (Iraq, Iran area). Or it could be Jordan today because of the Mesha Stele or Moabite Stone containing the name of King Mesha of Moab which is in the kingdom of Jordan today. Nevertheless, both are within the vicinity of the Land of Shinar. The important thing about the places mentioned in verse 30 is that this are locational and directional marker of a movement of people or migration pattern. One is from the west as they moved to the east. To clearly state, they are moving back to east (Mt. Sephar) after travelling from east to west (Shinar).

The general direction of emigration of the family of Shem went from Mesopotamia or the Land of Shinar back to the east. Remember, they (descendants of Noah) came (immigrated) from the east in the Isles of the Gentiles in Genesis 10: 5 to the Land of Shinar (west). And perhaps, Japhet's went back with them. Being the youngest brother of

Shem, Japheth was to dwell in the tents of Shem (Gen. 9: 27). Meaning he will be under the care or custody of Shem until he is enlarged.

Genesis 10: 21 indicates that Japheth was with Shem;

"²¹And children were born also to Shem, the father of all the children of Eber, the brother of Japheth the elder."

Why is this verse mentioning Japheth when it is supposed to be about the family of Shem? And this verse does not mean that Japheth is the eldest, but rather, Shem as the elder brother of Japheth. For we know in Genesis 10: 1 that the genealogy of Noah is in the order of Shem, Ham, and Japheth. Shem being the oldest and Japheth being the youngest.

The above verse indicates that Japheth's family was with or among the family of Shem who travelled back to the east (Mt. Sephar), in the isles as indicated in Genesis 10: 2 and 5;

"²The sons of Japheth were Gomer, Magog, Madai, Javan, Tubal, Meshech, and Tiras. ³The sons of Gomer were Ashkenaz, Riphath, and Togarmah.

⁵From these the coastland (isles, islands) peoples of the Gentiles were separated into their lands, everyone according to his language, according to their families, into their nations."

Verse five can have a dual meaning. One being the original point of origin of the family of Noah and two being the point of dispersion of the family of Japheth. Ham was no longer mentioned because they remained in the land of Shinar.

We should remember once again that the islands mentioned here came from the four riverheads that God made into islands (Isaiah 42:15) in the east. It is where they came from when they travelled or immigrated westward to the Land of Shinar, and it is where Shem and Japheth emigrated back to the islands in the east. And from these islands that they were separated and divided each to his own family, languages and nations or territories. And from this, Japheth's descendants were enlarged and scattered abroad. Some as far as Russia (Gog (Gomer) and Magog) and some remained as Javan with its territory in Java, Indonesia. Perhaps, Japan is also the descendants of Javan. Perhaps, Japheth is also the origin of the Oriental People of the east. The eyes are their connection.

Shem have remained in the isles and were not promised to be enlarged as Japheth's until God called Abraham from the idolatrous nations of the isles from the land of the Chaldeans to inherit the land of Canaan in the Middle East.

Hams family remained in Mesopotamian Region in the Land of Shinar from which Nimrod, the son of Cush, the son of Ham, build his kingdom as stated in Genesis 10: 9-10;

> "⁹He was a mighty hunter before the Lord; therefore it is said, "Like Nimrod the mighty hunter before the Lord." And the beginning of his kingdom was Babel, Erech, Accad, and Calneh, in the land of Shinar."

Ham is the father of Arabian (Dedan) and African people.

Perhaps, some of Shem's descendants spread to the Americas and Latin America. My ancestors look like Native American they called today. My ancestors according to my father (side) are fishermen who are tall and copper-toned skin. And my uncles in my father side looks like Native American Indian.

Most of the people in Latin America can also be found in the Philippines. Almost all type of people can be found in the Philippines. We have Mestizos and Mestizas even in places that are remote (islands) from Spanish colonization. It is wrong to say that the Mestizos and Mestizas in the Philippines are all product of Spanish colonization because there are Mestizos and Mestizas royalty already in the isles prior to the arrival of Spaniards as pictured in the Boxer Codex.

There are shorter people in Mexico that are similar to some people in Lucban, Quezon. The tribes in the jungles of Amazon forest are very similar to our Negritos, Tasadays, Mangyans, and Aaetas.

Few years ago, I suspected that the Negritos and others were brought from the Amazon for deceptions of our true history and identity until I recently learned from the Bible that Noah landed in the isles in the east which by default became the origin of the new civilization after the Great Flood. All the origin of the people on earth came from the isles (Gen. 10: 5) that is why almost all kind of people are represented in the isles. A few giants and dwarfs are with us too.

Mount Sephar in the East

But where is this mountain of Sephar in the east located?

We must remember that the family of Shem went back (Gen. 10:30) to the isles in the east and one of them is Joktan, one of the two sons of Eber (Gen. 10: 25) who have thirteen sons and three of them were <u>Sheba</u>, Ophir, and Havilah in Genesis 10: 26-30;

"²⁶Joktan begot Almodad, Sheleph, Hazarmaveth, Jerah, ²⁷Hadoram, Uzal, Diklah, ²⁸Obal, Abimael, <u>Sheba</u>, ²⁹<u>Ophir</u>, <u>Havilah</u>, and Jobab. All these were the sons of Joktan. ³⁰And <u>their dwelling place</u> was from Mesha as you go toward <u>Sephar, the mountain of the east</u>."

The location of Mt. Sephar can be determined by identifying the location of Sheba. It is the missing link in determining the location of Mt. Sephar. Sheba, with Ophir, Havilah, and the rest of the descendants of Shem, are believed to be located in the east. It should be noted that there are also regions of Sheba and Havilah located in the west, from among the descendants of Ham who remained in the land of Shinar.

1 Kings 10: 1- 2, tells us a clue that Sheba is a kingdom in the east; "¹Now when <u>the queen of Sheba</u> heard of the fame of Solomon concerning the name of the Lord, <u>she came</u> to test him with hard questions. ²She came <u>to Jerusalem</u> with a very great retinue, with camels that bore spices, very much gold, and precious stones; and when she came to Solomon, she spoke with him about all that was in her heart."

She came to Jerusalem to see and hear the wisdom of Solomon as it is written in verses 4 and 6:

"⁴And when <u>the queen of Sheba had seen all the wisdom of Solomon</u>, the house that he had built, ⁶then she said to the king: "It was a true report which I heard in my own land about your words and your wisdom."

Notice that in order for the Queen of Sheba to test the wisdom and knowledge concerning the name of the Lord, they must believe in the same Lord or God. For how can one prove of something if they do not believe in the same thing.?

But where is the location of Sheba? It is stated in Matthew 12: 42; ""42The queen of the South will rise up in the judgment with this generation and condemn it, for she came from the ends of the earth to hear the wisdom of Solomon;..."

The queen of the South is a code name for the Queen of Sheba, for both seek to hear and see the wisdom of Solomon. They are both queens. They are one and the same and she came from the "ends of the earth". As we have previously proven, the "ends of the earth" is a code name for the "isles" in the east. The isles is located at the ends of the earth in the east. Therefore, the kingdom of Sheba is located in the isles in the east at the ends of the earth. This is not the Sheba in the west from the line of Ham.

So, we can infer that Mt. of Sephar is also in the isles at the ends of the earth in the east because this is where the family of Shem (including Sheba) migrated back.

Perhaps, God intended to use the mountain to indicate an edge or a boundary or a marker as He used it to describe the boundaries of Canaan to Moses in Number 34: 7-8;

"7"And this shall be your northern border: From the Great Sea you shall mark out your border line to Mount Hor; 8from Mount Hor you shall mark out your border to the entrance of Hamath; then the direction of the border shall be toward Zedad;"

Similarly, the mountain of Sephar could be the boundary, edge or marker of the east at the ends of the earth.

Notice that at this time, the ends of the earth (isles, Philippines) which is represented by the Queen of Sheba also believed in the same God of Abraham, Isaac, and Jacob (Israel). The "ends of the earth" must be knowledgeable about God. For how can the Queen of Sheba test the knowledge and wisdom of Solomon concerning the name of the Lord if she is not equally or greater than in knowledge, wisdom and understanding regarding the Lord. She is also wise to test King Solomon's knowledge and wisdom of the same God whom they both believe. And she was glad and satisfied that it is. Perhaps, they (the ends of the earth) are waiting for the Messiah like the wisemen from the east who visited and give gifts to the King Yeshua (Jesus Christ) when He was about two years old. Perhaps the Queen of Sheba went there to see if King Solomon is the Messiah or not because she knows the prophecy in Isaiah 9: 6-7 where it implied that the Messiah is the "Son of David";

> "⁶For unto us a Child is born, unto us a Son is given; and the government will be upon His shoulder. And His name will be called Wonderful, Counselor, Mighty God, Everlasting Father, Prince of Peace.
>
> ⁷Of the increase of His government and peace there will be no end, upon the throne of David and over His kingdom, to order it and establish it with judgment and justice from that time forward, even forever. The zeal of the Lord of hosts will perform this."

From this, those who are waiting for the Lord Yeshua believes He will be the "Son of David" just as the two blind men who followed Jesus called Him in Matthew 9: 27;

> "²⁷When Jesus departed from there, two blind men followed Him, crying out and saying, "Son of David, have mercy on us!""

But Isaiah lives almost two centuries (200 years) after King Solomon - the son of David. How could the Queen of Sheba have known the prophecy? Perhaps she has known it from the Psalms of David, since King David have trading relationship with the "ends of the earth" particularly Ophir, Sheba, Tarshish, and Havilah through King Hiram. For it is written in Psalms 132: 11;

> "¹¹The Lord has sworn in truth to David; He will not turn from it: "I will set upon your throne the fruit of your body...."

That is why Matthew 1:1 in the beginning of Christ earthly

mission in flesh said;

> "¹The book of the genealogy of Jesus Christ, the Son of David, the Son of Abraham:…"

Just as the first book of the New Testament proclaimed that Jesus Christ is the Son of David, so is the last book of the New Testament revealed the meaning of this mystery in Revelation 22: 16;

> "¹⁶"I, Jesus, have sent My angel to testify to you these things in the churches. I am the Root and the Offspring of David, the Bright and Morning Star.""

Jesus Christ declared that He is the Creator of mankind (the root (the beginning of all things)) from Adam, to Noah, to Shem, to Abraham, Isaac, and Jacob. And finally, to Judah, the Jews where David and Jesus Christ came from, in flesh.

Why this is important? This is because most of the secular historians sexualize the visit of the Queen of Sheba to King Solomon and demonize it into adultery rather than the quest for wisdom regarding the name of the Lord. It is most likely that the Queen of Sheba is a wise woman who is already advance in age because she is also full of wisdom. Wisdom comes with age and experience unless one is gifted by the Lord such as Solomon.

The second reason is that this establishes the fact that the "ends of the earth" has relationship with Israel and is waiting for the coming of the Messiah like the "Wisemen" who visited, give gifts, and worshipped the Messiah when He eventually come to earth. This wisemen also come from the ends of the earth, from the east, from afar like the Chaldeans who are also called wisemen (Dan. 2:2) and where Abraham came from.

Chaldeans are known also to be wisemen. But by the time God took Abram from the Ur of the Chaldeans, the land is so sinful, full of idolatry and abominable practices against God. But perhaps, the Ur of the Chaldeans at the ends of the earth was punished by God and have repented. And those who did not want to repent were brought by God to Babylon as fugitives (Isa. 43: 14). Perhaps, the "ends of the earth" (isles) repented, believed, and worshipped the true living God of the

Bible until Satan brought his two major deceiving religions – Catholicism and Islam by blood and conquest to propagate their deceptions until now. God is once again calling on the peoples of the isles to repent and turn to Him, as our ancestors did in the past.

The location of Mt. Sephar can be located by tracing the connection of the Queen of Sheba to the "ends of the earth" in the east. This is because the descendants of Shem returned to the east from the land of Shinar, specifically from Mesha, which is believed to be the present-day Mashhad, Iran. Mt. Sephar is referred to as the easternmost boundary in the ancient texts. In other words, it is the "ends of the earth" in the east literally.

The Other Names of the Isles

Now, we have known that the isles/coastlands is at the ends of the earth in the east. This we know for sure because even our modern-day map will show that among the four ends of the earth namely north, south, west, and east only the east has many islands. The north and south ends of the earth the Arctic and Antarctic respectively are inhabitable places because they are mostly frigid zones of ice. The other end in the west (California side) is not composed of islands. The only ends of the earth with islands is in the east. And when we speak about directions, we are speaking here of the point of reference from the Temple in Jerusalem, unless otherwise specified.

Now, if we use the modern map and compass from Jerusalem the exact location eastward point is between Japan and the Philippines. But one university in Israel is studying archeological artifacts dug near Jerusalem and they want to find out the ancient magnetic north. I said to myself, "What! Is there such a thing?" I thought we are already using the true magnetic north. But who knows. Perhaps the ancient true magnetic north will pinpoint exactly where the isles is in the Bible. (Take note how this thinking progressed as God reveal the truth in another chapter.)

It will be great if the isles mentioned in the Bible collectively includes Japan for, we have a great friendly relationship now with them. But as we know it, Japan has its own religion which does not believe in the God of the Bible. On the other hand, the Philippines believe in the God of the Bible. But they do not know or serve the God of the Bible. In fact, there are hundreds of fake religions professing to believe in the God of the Bible and yet, knowingly, and unknowingly worship another god. They rather believe and obey the commandments and traditions created by men based on pagan practices than believe and obey what is written in the Word of God. They created their own doctrines based on twisted understanding and interpretations of the Bible and came up with their own conclusions and do whatever they want (self-righteousness).

There is this professing Christian group to which I previously belong after coming out from the clouts of Catholicism who proclaim they believe and accepted Jesus Christ as their Lord and Savior. In yet worship another Jesus by twisting what is written in the Bible and celebrate and worship Jesus using paganic practices and traditions.

For Jesus said in Matthew 15: 3 and 8 to 9;

"³He answered and said to them, "Why do you also transgress the commandment of God because of your tradition?

⁸These people draw near to Me with their mouth, and honor Me with their lips, but their heart is far from Me.

⁹And in vain they worship Me, teaching as doctrines the commandments of men.""

Similarly, God said in Isaiah 29: 13-14;

"¹³Therefore the Lord said: "Inasmuch as these people <u>draw near with their mouths and honor Me with their lips, but have removed their hearts far from Me</u>, and <u>their fear toward Me is taught by the commandment of men</u>,¹⁴therefore, behold, <u>I will again do a marvelous work among this people</u>, a marvelous work and a wonder; for the wisdom of their wise men shall perish, and the understanding of their prudent men shall be hidden."

And in Mark 7: 9, 13;

"⁹He said to them, "All too well <u>you reject the commandment</u> <u>of God, that you may keep your tradition</u>.

¹³…making the word of God of no effect through your tradition which you have handed down. And many such things you do."

We profess to believe in God, but when He said do not do the way of the heathen (pagans), we just disregard God and continue to practice the way of the heathen. Even Christianize it.

We continue to praise and worship another god on a pagan sabbath on Sunday instead of worshipping the true God on His Sabbath on Saturday reasoning that the commandments were done away. And we proclaim that the day is not important but <u>what is in the</u> <u>heart</u> that counts! Such foolishness and stupidity indeed.

Have you not heard or listen to God in Jeremiah 17:9?

"⁹The <u>heart</u> is <u>deceitful</u> above all things, and desperately <u>wicked</u>; who can know it?"

And yes, we celebrate birthday, Christmas, Halloween, valentines, easter, and all souls and saints' day and many more pagan traditions that worship Satan. And then we justify it by saying that "it's the heart that counts". People have a hard time doing it away for it is the tradition of man, the way of the heathen. People do these abominable practices and worship Satan knowingly and unknowingly.

But now, God will reveal to us the truth so that we shall judge and condemn ourselves how we have wronged God. We shall repent and turn to God before we can perform the tasks that God has stored upon us. For Yeshua said in Luke 11: 30-32;

"³⁰For as <u>Jonah</u> became <u>a sign</u> to the Ninevites, so also <u>the Son of</u> <u>Man will be to this generation</u>.

³¹<u>The queen of the South</u> will *rise up* in the <u>judgment with the men</u> <u>of this generation and condemn them</u>, for <u>she came from the</u> <u>ends of the earth</u> to hear the wisdom of Solomon; and indeed a greater than Solomon is here.

³²The <u>men of Nineveh</u> will *rise up* in the <u>judgment with this</u> <u>generation and condemn it</u>, for <u>they repented at the preaching of</u>

<u>Jonah</u>; and indeed a greater than Jonah is here."

The queen of the South is a code name for the Queen of Sheba that came from the "ends of the earth" in the east. The "ends of the earth is a code for the "isles" in the east. The "isles" is a code name for the present-day Philippines. We are like Ninevites who are so sinful, and yet God sent a Jonah like person to minister to us. And as it is prophesied, we shall repent at the preaching of Jonah and we shall judge and condemn this generation including ourselves.

Jesus Christ is the Light (John 8: 12) and the sign for this generation. He will come to us so we may see and free us from the prison we are in right now. We must repent and obey Him so that we become good and faithful servants. That we may become light also to the Gentiles and free them from their prison houses also.

Another mark why the Philippines is the isles being mentioned in the Bible is, it has the remnant of the Church of God that Christ founded when He was in flesh here on earth. It is just composed of a few hundred or thousand members, and a very few knows about them. And while the Church have many issues also like the churches in New Testament as exemplified in many Gospels and in Revelation, still, the light, the truth and the righteousness of God is with them.

Now notice Luke 11, particularly verse 31.

Who is the queen of the south who came from the ends of the earth to hear the wisdom of Solomon?

We have discussed and proven that the ends of the earth is a locational code for the isles, which is located in the east. It is also where Abraham came from. When the Bible talks about the ends of the earth with people, it is certainly pertaining to the east. For no account in the Bible have discussed the ends of the earth in the west concerning people or civilization at that time. The east had been mentioned directly or implied in the Bible many times.

There is no other queen directly mentioned in the Bible that visited Jerusalem to hear the wisdom of King Solomon concerning the name of the Lord, than the Queen of Sheba in 1Kings 10: 1, 3-6;

"¹Now when the queen of Sheba heard of the fame of

Solomon <u>concerning the name of the Lord</u>, she came to test him with hard questions.

³So Solomon answered all her questions; there was nothing so difficult for the king that he could not explain it to her.

⁴And when the queen of Sheba had seen all the wisdom of Solomon, the house that he had built, ⁵the food on his table, the seating of his servants, the service of his waiters and their apparel, his cupbearers, and his entryway by which he went up to the house of the Lord, there was no more spirit in her.

⁶Then she said to the king: "It was a true report which I heard in my own land about your words and your wisdom."

The wisdom of King Solomon is very well known in the land of Sheba. But who is the Queen of Sheba to be given a high regard by a famous king to question him regarding his wisdom, knowledge, and understanding of the Lord? Why does she need to prove him regarding his wisdom of the Lord? Why does the wisdom of King Solomon matter to the people of the ends of the earth? Is it just about gossips? (for the peoples of the ends of the earth loves gossips) Or is it something else? What is the relationship of Israel to the ends of the earth, aside from being its merchants or the source of gold and precious stones? There must be a reason why God mentioned the Queen of Sheba (ends of the earth) and King Solomon (Israel).

These are a few of the questions regarding Chapter 10 of first Kings. Let us try to understand its connection to Isaiah 41:2-9, that said God raised up Abraham from the east, and He took him from the ends of the earth.

Abraham, and the Queen of Sheba both came from the ends of the Earth (Isles). Abraham is the father of Isaac who is the father of Jacob who became Israel.

Perhaps this is the reason why the people of the Isles have an affinity to Israel. Some people even claim or believe they are Israelites because many of our words have Hebraic meaning and practice Hebraic traditions. It does not mean that one is Israelite if one has a Hebraic root because Jacob (Israel) came, long after Eber was gone.

He is the root of the word Hebrew. Eber have two sons, Peleg and Joktan. Abraham came from the line of Peleg. There are many more descendants from Eber and perhaps they speak Hebrew even before Israel (Jacob) was born.

Hebrew is both an olden (ancient if it may be) and a modern language spoken by Jewish people, specifically the tribe of Judah, which includes the tribes of Benjamin and Levi. However, the other ten tribes of Israel have lost not only their identity, but also their traditional language.

The olden language spoken in afar-off place of the ends of the earth where Abraham came from in the east is called Alibata. It has some similarities to Hebrew. Alibata is considered the oldest language because it has only 17 letters in its alphabet. It's believed that the fewer letters a language has, the less developed it is, and therefore, much older than languages with more letters, like Hebrew, which has 22 letters.

Alibata is an ancient writing system used in the Philippines before the arrival of the Spanish in the 16th century. It is also known or interchangeably referred to as Baybayin, which means in Tagalog as "to write" or "spell". The script was primarily used for writing Tagalog, Ilocano, and Pangasinan, but it was also used by other languages in the Philippines. The script is syllabic, with each symbol representing a syllable, and it is written from left to right. The script fell out of use after the Spanish colonized the Philippines and introduced the Latin alphabet.

There is a contention that Alibata and Baybayin (e.g. Monreal Stone found in Monreal, Ticao, Masbate) is not the same for the reason that Baybayin could have not been derived from the Arabic Language which resembles Alibata. This is most likely true because Alibata did not come from Baybayin because it came from Alibata.

Although Alibata is just a coined word by Verzosa in 1914, it is a standard set to identify the ancient script used by the people of the "ends of the earth". Perhaps this is the pure language (Zep. 3: 9) or script used by Noah and was retained by the olden peoples of the isles including Ophir, Sheba, Havillah, and Tarshish, then Eber, and perhaps even Abraham.

But the missing puzzle in this understanding is our conception that civilization begun in Mesopotamia sometimes referred to as the Arab World. But the Bible stated that civilization come from the isles in Genesis 10: 5 after the flood. Therefore, let just accept that the name of the ancient script or language used by Noah and its descendants prior to the destruction of the Tower of Babel is Alibata. Then we can say that it is the root of Hebrew, Arabic, and Baybayin language. The common denominator for this is their similarity in script or character letters.

Since, Abraham, who came from the "ends of the earth", the people of the "ends of the earth" and the Israelite people share a common ancestry that can be traced back to Noah. So are the root of their language and scripts.

We all came from the line of Shem who begot Elam, Ashur, Arphaxad, Lud, and Aram (Genesis 10:22). Arphaxad is where Eber came from who begot Peleg and Joktan. Peleg is the root of Abraham. Joktan on the other hand, is the root of Sheba, Ophir, and Havilah and other brothers.

They lived back or migrated back to the east after God confused their language when they were building the city and tower of Babel in the land of Shinar in the west as stated in Genesis 10:30;

"³⁰And their <u>dwelling place</u> was from Mesha as you <u>go toward Sephar</u>, the mountain of the <u>east</u>."

We should consider the idea that perhaps the east mentioned here may not only be directional in meaning but as coded name for the isles as previously discussed. Another connection is the word Chaldeans because Flavius Josephus, a Jewish historian of the 1st century CE, wrote about the descendants of Shem, Ham and Japheth and their territories in his work "Antiquities of the Jews". In his account, he mentioned that Chaldeans descended from Arphaxad. And as we have previously shown, God brought the Chaldeans from the east to Babylon through their ships and by the mighty waters.

Now, let us examine the line of Eber, the root of Sheba, Ophir, and Havilah, and Abraham in Genesis 10:24-29;

"²⁴Arphaxad begot Salah, and Salah begot Eber.

²⁵To Eber were born two sons: the name of one was Peleg, for in

his days the earth was divided; and his brother's name was Joktan.
²⁶Joktan begot Almodad, Sheleph, Hazarmaveth, Jerah,
²⁷Hadoram, Uzal, Diklah,
²⁸Obal, Abimael, <u>Sheba</u>,
²⁹<u>Ophir</u>, <u>Havilah</u>, and Jobab. All these were the sons of Joktan."

We should emphasize that Joktan, the younger brother of Peleg is the father of Sheba, Ophir, and Havilah. And if Sheba was in the "ends of the earth" in the east, so there is a big probability that Ophir and Havilah were also in the ends of the earth in the east. This will be very important in understanding our future discussions.

Now the side of Peleg was laid out in Genesis 11:18, 20,22,24,26;

"¹⁸Peleg lived thirty years, and begot Reu.
²⁰Reu lived thirty-two years, and begot Serug.
²²Serug lived thirty years, and begot Nahor.
²⁴Nahor lived twenty-nine years, and begot Terah.
²⁶Now <u>Terah</u> lived seventy years, and begot <u>Abram</u>, Nahor, and Haran."

The line of Jacob (Israel) from Abram in Canaan as shown in Genesis 21:5;

"⁵Now Abraham was one hundred years old when his son Isaac was born to him."

Isaac was sixty years old when he begot Essau and Jacob as a twin (Genesis 25: 26).

And God change Jacob's name to Israel in Genesis 32:28;

"²⁸And He said, "Your name shall no longer be called Jacob, but Israel; for you have struggled with God and with men, and have prevailed.""

Perhaps, this genealogy of Eber is the reason why king Solomon give high regard to the Queen of Sheba to allow her to asked pressing questions concerning the Lord. Another reason might be that he recognizes or know that the people of Sheba and of the ends of the earth is his distant relatives. This is why they know and worship the same God. That is why they both understand and speak the same language (Aramaic). Their ancient or common language perhaps? For we do not know if through time their languages have change due to their interactions to other races with different languages.

Now, the common denominator between Sheba, Ophir, Havilah and Abraham are:

1. They all come from the line of Shem,
2. They are from the "ends of the earth",
3. In the east,
4. The "ends of the earth" is composed of many islands (isles),
5. Gold. Except for Abraham – Sheba, Ophir, And Havilah are places well known for its gold, while Abraham is a big holder of gold (Gen. 13: 2, Gen. 24:35).

Israel (Jacob) on the other hand originate from Canaan because God brought Abraham from the Ur of the Chaldeans (other side of the River, ends of the earth) to inherit the land.

So, the Queen of Sheba comes from the ends of the earth to hear the wisdom of Solomon (Luke 11:31) in Canaan that later became the land of Israel.

In Luke 11:31, the queen of Sheba was called the queen of the South for two reasons;

One, she and her retinue (dromedaries) arrived at the Port of Ezion Geber which is south of Israel. This port was described in 1 Kings 9: 26;

"²⁶King Solomon also built a fleet of ships at Ezion Geber, which is near Elath on the shore of the Red Sea, in the land of Edom."

Compare this to how God brought the Chaldeans as 'fugitives' to Babylon. They "rejoice", or they love their ships and God brought them to Southern Mesopotamia through the shoreline of the Persian gulf by the way of the sea and paths through the mighty waters. This means they pass through ocean and seas. Let us call this the Persian Sea in parallel to the Red Sea. Ezion Geber in the northern Red Sea is very near to Jerusalem than when Abraham and his family first arrived in Southern Mesopotamia to the promised land – the land of Canaan.

Ezion Geber is south of Jerusalem. Perhaps the people of Jerusalem call her the Queen of the South because she arrived in Jerusalem from the south with a large retinue or caravan that exudes wealth and riches in 1 Kings 10:2;

> "²She came to Jerusalem with a very great retinue, with camels that bore spices, very much gold, and precious stones; and when she came to Solomon, she spoke with him about all that was in her heart."

The "Queen of the South" here not only have this literal meaning of coming from the south of Jerusalem but also have coded mystery in one of the islands at the ends of the earth in the east as we will see later.

Some people claimed that the Queen of Sheba comes from Ethiopia or other regions of Africa because she travelled through camels. This is because they ignored the facts that prior to her arrival in 1 Kings 10: 1, the port at Ezion Geber was introduced or mentioned already in 1 Kings 9: 26;

> "²⁶King Solomon also built a fleet of ships at Ezion Geber, which is near Elath on the shore of the Red Sea, in the land of Edom."

This is the port used by King Hiram to bring gold from the land of Ophir to King Solomon. The Queen of Sheba and the fleets of Hiram both used the same port for docking at the ports of Ezion Geber since both Sheba and Ophir were located at the ends of the earth. There is also the possibility that the Queen of Sheba and her entourage boarded one of Hiram's ships.

There must be a reason why the Word of God mention that series of events, it's a hint for those who seek understanding.

It does not mean that one use camels or dromedaries as the mode of transportation from point A to point B that one just travels by land. The camels are the modern "taxi" at that time. So, with the great loads and cargoes and people that the queen brought with her entourage, she certainly needs transport system to carry them to Jerusalem. It is still a long distance from Ezion Geber to Jerusalem. And even if the queen did not used camels as taxi at that time, for sure, king Solomon must have sent his fleets of camels and chariots to fetch an honorable dignitary from another kingdom. For what is the use of being the richest and the wisest man on earth (2 Chron. 9:22) if he cannot provide a comfortable and hassle-free transportation for the Queen of Sheba.

Besides, 1 Kings 9:27 to 28 gives us farther clue as to where she came from after mentioning Ezion Geber in verse 26;

> "[27]Then Hiram sent his servants with the fleet, seamen who knew the sea, to work with the servants of Solomon. [28]And they went to Ophir, and acquired four hundred and twenty talents of gold from there, and brought it to King Solomon."

Now, let us compare this to 1 Kings 10: 10 after she questioned King Solomon;

> "[10]Then she gave the king one hundred and twenty talents of gold, spices in great quantity, and precious stones. There never again came such abundance of spices as the Queen of Sheba gave to King Solomon."

So, the land or kingdom of Sheba is abundant with spices and gold? Is it not the reason why the Portuguese and Spaniards sent by the Vatican as explorers and conquistadores went to Moluccas and then "accidentally" discovered the islands they later called the Philippines? Of course, the historians did not say what was their real purpose. Is it to find spices or to get gold or to destroy the identity of the isles? Perhaps, abundant evidence to the identity and historicity of the isles lies in the underground pavements of the more than 56 kilometers Vatican Achieve. Wink wink.

We just need to wonder why history portrayed us like a primitive ignorant people living in the jungle when in fact some of the artifacts that was hidden under the face of the earth that was later found showed that the isles is far more advance even before Portugal or Spain or Vatican became a nation.

But notice how verse 11 suddenly became about the ships of Hiram, gold, and Ophir.

"¹¹Also, the <u>ships</u> of Hiram, which brought <u>gold</u> from Ophir, brought great quantities of almug wood and precious stones from Ophir."

Compare this to 2 Chronicles 9: 21;

"²¹For the king's ships went to Tarshish with the servants of Hiram. Once every three years the merchant ships came, bringing gold, silver, ivory, apes, and monkeys."

Why use the word <u>also</u> in verse 11?

It is a connective word which connects or portray a relationship to one another. In this case, we can infer that the Queen of Sheba used the ships of Hiram to travel to Israel (the land of Canaan) through the port in Ezion Geber from the land of Ophir. Besides, Sheba and Ophir are brothers from the lines of Eber, the sons of Joktan whose dwelling places is in the east (Gen. 10:25-30). They are in the same place. And if the queen of the south in Luke 11 comes from the "ends of the earth", then, Ophir is also at the "ends of the earth" where there is plenty of gold and spices like the land of Havilah (Gen. 2: 11-12) - their brother.

This is a different Sheba from the lines of Cush (the father of Nimrod), the son of Raamah (Gen. 10: 7-8). Cush descendants remained in the plain of Shinar (v. 10) and then later spread through the lands of Arabia (Dedan) and Africa. The Sheba of Africa or Arabia is not from the ends of the earth in the east but is of the south of Jerusalem.

We should take note also that the queen brought spices in great abundance. This might give us a clue, that perhaps the travel time is long as stated in 2 Chronicles 9: 21. That is why she brought a lot of spices to King Solomon in her one time visit to Jerusalem. This is also confirmed in 1 Kings 10: 22;

"²²For the king had merchant ships at sea with the fleet of Hiram. <u>Once every three years</u> the merchant ships came bringing gold, silver, ivory, apes, and monkeys."

Please take note the big difference in these two verses. The mention of the word Tarshish. It is mentioned in 2 Chronicles 9: 21, but not in 1 Kings 10: 22. Perhaps this is the collective name of Sheba, Ophir, and Havilah as a trading entity which we are going to discuss later in another chapter.

So, every three years is the cycle of commerce between Israel and Ophir or Tarshish. This time includes all the back-and-forth travel, perhaps stops to other ports along the way, and the time to upload and unload merchandise. For sure, this endeavor does not only involve one ship but a fleet of ships. A balangay or barangay, perhaps? Balangay is composed of at least 26 boats with variable sizes.

Could the discovery of Butuan boats be God's confirmation that the isles in the east at the ends of the earth is indeed the location of Sheba, Ophir, Havilah, and Tarshish?

We should also remember that the "ends of the earth" is also the Isles. Islands. This brings us to our second reason why the Queen of Sheba is called the queen of the south.

Two. Coincidentally, there is an island in the Philippines that is called the Queen of the South. That island is the island of Cebu. If we stretch a little bit, Cebu and Sheba might have similar phonetic sound. Or perhaps, Cebu was also Sebu or Seba prior to the modern inclusion of the letter C in the alphabet.

Now, we know that God took Abraham from the Ur of the Chaldeans which is also the other side of the River, also the "ends of the earth" in the east which is also the isles or coastlands in other translations.

Since the Queen of Sheba is also the Queen of the South that came from the "ends of the earth", we can say that she came from the isles/coastlands in the east where Ophir and Havilah are also located for they are brothers. Plus, gold is the uniting element of the three.

These are very important symbolism to understand and remember, in order for us to grasp the magnitude of the works God have prophesied for us to do before, during, and after the tribulation period.

But first, let us try to understand the mystery of Havilah.

Havilah was first mentioned in the Bible after God created a garden eastward of Eden in Genesis 2: 8;

"⁸The Lord God planted a garden eastward in Eden, and there He put the man whom He had formed."

Now, He created a river to water the garden in Eden in verse 10;

"¹⁰Now a river went out of Eden to water the garden, and from there it parted and became four riverheads."

So, at the other end (side) of the River (which is the garden), the River became four rivers. We need to understand that this period is pre-flood. Before God flooded the earth during the time of Noah. So, we can infer that the earth is just a large mass of land surrounded by water as explained in Genesis 1: 9-10;

"⁹Then God said, "Let the waters under the heavens be gathered together into one place, and let the dry land appear"; and it was so. ¹⁰And God called the dry land Earth, and the gathering together of the waters He called Seas. And God saw that it was good."

If am I the Landscape Designer or the Landscape Architect, and tasked by God to make a design as instructed in the above verse, then, I will propose to Him two plans. One, the land is in one side and the waters on the other side. The second plan would be a large mass of land would appear at the center of the waters. It can be a circle, square, rectangle, or triangle.

Perhaps God approved the circle because Isaiah 40:22 said;

"²²It is He who sits above the circle of the earth,…"

Circle is different from sphere and globe. It denotes two dimensionality while sphere and globe are three dimensions. If the earth is a globe, the Bible is false because a sphere will not have ends of the earth. Although this book is not about whether the earth is flat or a globe, we should note that in verse 10, God specifically called the dry land Earth and the gathering of waters He called Seas. Seas are not part of the Earth but Earth sits above the waters as stated in Psalms 136: 6;

"⁶To Him who laid out the earth above the waters,…"

Verse 10 also specifically stated singular dry land and not lands as we are today. Perhaps circular land is more appropriate for a single piece of land.

This makes sense because most of the ancient maps almost resembles a circular form. Although we do not know if the drawing is affected by limitations such a paper size or lack of knowledge as to the real form of the earth. In addition, most of the map renderings today are post floods which definitely changed the landscape of the earth from which God created the earth originally - being a single mass of land surrounded by waters.

Besides, in Job 38: 14 said;

"¹⁴It (earth) takes on form like clay under a seal, and stands out like a garment."

A clay seal impression (called a *bulla*) is an imperfect circle like the seal of Isaiah (see front cover of hardcover jacket) and the seal of Hezekiah that was excavated by Dr. Eilat Mazar. During the excavations led by Dr. Eilat Mazar at the southern edge of the Temple Mount, they found a clay seal impression known as a bulla. These bullae, including the one that had Isaiah's name on it, were commonly utilized for sealing documents and storage containers, as well as acting as receipts. Dr. Mazar's very important work in discovering many biblical artifacts including the location of King David's palace was cut short when she died after the vaccine rule out in the present-day Israel.

Indeed, the former earth is like a single circular seal that have corrugated surface like a garment represented by planes, hills and mountains. Perhaps, God called this circular earth as Eden where He formed the man. And God planted a garden eastward of Eden (Gen. 2:8) and brought the man in the garden. Perhaps a river came out from the center of Eden to water the garden in the east. In the garden, this river become four river heads after it watered the garden.

The first river is called Pishon in Genesis 2: 11-12;

"¹¹The name of the first is Pison: that is it which compasseth the whole land of Havilah, where there is gold; ^{12}And the gold of that land is good: there is bdellium and the onyx stone."

It is very mysterious why God mentioned the land of Havilah very early on, even if it was first mentioned in Genesis 10: 7 as the son of Cush after the flood;

"^{7}And the sons of Cush; Seba, and Havilah, and Sabtah, and Raamah, and Sabtecha: and the sons of Raamah; Sheba, and Dedan."

Cush is the son of Ham and brother to Mizraim, Put, and Canaan. Ham is the son of Noah and brother to Shem and Japhet.

Four generations from Shem, Joktan, the son of Eber, brother to Peleg which is the lineage of Abraham, named one of his sons Havilah also in Genesis 10: 26-29;

"^{26}Joktan begot Almodad, Sheleph, Hazarmaveth, Jerah, ^{27}Hadoram, Uzal, Diklah, ^{28}Obal, Abimael, Sheba, ^{29}Ophir, Havilah, and Jobab. All these were the sons of Joktan."

Let us try to understand which land of Havilah, God pertains to in Genesis 2: 11. What is the significance of Havilah? Why God mentioned his name even he was not yet born.

Noah lived 350 years after the flood (Gen. 9:28), with a total of 950 years before he died (v. 29).

Based on the genealogy of Shem, Noah was approximately 892 years old when Abram was born.

Noah have witnessed many generations after the flood. Perhaps Noah was able to witness how God changes the language of his family to many languages and how they were scattered abroad through time.

According to Genesis 11: 1, the multi-generational family of Noah composed the whole earth and have one language;

"^{1}Now the whole earth had one language and one speech."

Noah's ark must be in the east because their family move to the west in verse 2;

"^{2}And it came to pass, as they journeyed from the east, that they found a plain in the land of Shinar, and they dwelt there."

241

I just wonder why they need to move towards the west. Why not towards the east? Perhaps it is already a large body of water? Or is it the end of the earth in the east? So, when it is already the end, there is nowhere to go to but to the opposite side. This is probably the reason why they moved towards the west.

And so, the multi-generational family of Noah move to the west into the plain land of Shinar. The plain of Shinar is sometimes called by modern history as Sumer. But to be exact, it is the Fertile Crescent or the whole land of Mesopotamia – called by the modern-day historians as the cradle of civilization, because their history only started in the Tower of Babel. Some historians claimed that Noah landed in Mount Ararat in the mountains of Armenia or Turkey and then they migrated to the plain of Shinar. But this narrative failed to account that the plain of Shinar is south of either Armenia or Turkey.

The multi-generational family of Noah build the Tower of Babel in the plain of Shinar because they do not want to be scattered abroad in Genesis 11: 4;

> "⁴And they said, "Come, let us build ourselves a city, and a tower whose top is in the heavens; let us make a name for ourselves, lest we be scattered abroad over the face of the whole earth.""

They want to be united forever contrary to what God commanded them to do in Genesis 9: 1;

> "¹And God blessed Noah and his sons, and said unto them, be fruitful, and multiply, and replenish the earth."

Note that this verse is also similar to Genesis 1: 28 as God blesses the new mankind during the recreation of the earth.

Their mission is to repopulate the earth and subdue it; "have dominion over the fish of the sea, over the birds of the air, and over every living thing that moves on the earth." Genesis 1: 28, 9: 2.

So, God destroyed their plans and scattered them abroad as mentioned in Genesis 11: 7-9;

> "⁷Come, let Us go down and there confuse their language, that they may not understand one another's speech." ⁸So the Lord

scattered them abroad from there over the face of all the earth, and they ceased building the city. ⁹Therefore its name is called Babel, because there the Lord confused the language of all the earth; and from there the Lord scattered them abroad over the face of all the earth.”

Now, because of their disobedience, they are not only scattered abroad, but they cannot understand each other also. Each family have their own language and put into their own nation.

God called the family of Noah who went and dwelt in the plain of Shinar, “the isles/coastlands peoples of the Gentiles” in Genesis 10:5;

“⁵By these were <u>the isles of the Gentiles</u> divided in their lands; every one after his tongue, after their families, in their nations.”

“The isles/coastlands people of the Gentiles” is definitely the family of Noah that is mentioned in this verse. They were scattered abroad according to their nation, family, and languages. This is the time that God begin to divide the earth during the days of Peleg (Gen. 10: 25), beginning when God destroyed the Tower of Babel.

This is the first time the Bible mentioned the words isles/coastlands and Gentiles. Therefore, the family of Noah previously resides in the isles in the east for they moved to the west to the plain of Shinar. They are called Gentiles. All the people of the earth are called Gentiles until God created Israel to be His chosen people and nation. But in a prophetic future, the Gentiles pertains to the peoples of the isles.

So, when God begin to scatter the people, the family of Shem moved back to east as stated in Genesis 10: 30-31 (KJV);

“³⁰And their dwelling was from Mesha, as thou goest unto Sephar a mount of the east. ³¹These are the sons of Shem, after their families, after their tongues, in their lands, after their nations.”

Mesha is thought to be the present-day Mashhad in Iran. Perhaps the plain of Shinar is located within or is the present-day Iran, Iraq area which is the region of Mesopotamia. For this place was also the Babylonian area where the Babylonish religion originated. Their god head is Nimrod which is the son of Cush.

Perhaps, the family of Cush and Ham remained or are scattered around Africa and the Middle-East area. But Nimrod, the son of Cush (Gen.10: 8) definitely remained or have returned to the land of Shinar as stated in Genesis 10:8-10;

> "⁸And Cush begat Nimrod: he began to be a mighty one in the earth. ⁹He was a mighty hunter before the LORD: wherefore it is said, Even as Nimrod the mighty hunter before the LORD. ¹⁰And the beginning of his kingdom was Babel, and Erech, and Accad, and Calneh, in the land of Shinar."

There is no clear indication as to where the family of Japheth went to, except a clue in Genesis 9: 27 as Noah blessed Shem and Japheth;

> "²⁷God shall <u>enlarge Japheth</u>, and he <u>shall dwell in the tents of Shem</u>;…"

And in Genesis 10: 2-4, after giving the genealogy of Japheth, verse 5 mentioned for the first time the words isles and Gentiles;

> "²The sons of Japheth; Gomer, and Magog, and Madai, and Javan, and Tubal, and Meshech, and Tiras. ³And the sons of Gomer; Ashkenaz, and Riphath, and Togarmah. ⁴And the sons of Javan; Elishah, and Tarshish, Kittim, and Dodanim. ⁵By these were <u>the isles of the Gentiles</u> divided in their lands; every one after his tongue, after their families, in their nations."

Could enlarge in verse 27 mean larger isles and larger territories under Shem? Could Japhet have gone with Shem to go back to the isles in the east and then, they occupy the larger islands in the east which is currently Indonesia and Malaysia?

If we stretch our imagination a little bit and look at the map of Indonesia and Malaysia, they look like under the tent of the Philippines as the islands from Luzon flared into a wider base of islands down towards Indonesia and Malaysia. This does not mean that the Philippines is superior to them in anyways. In fact, we are presently inferior to these countries economically, politically, and culturally. We are the sick man of Asia – sick of our sinfulness and of our pride and arrogance.

Another interesting connection of Japheth to the isles is Javan and Tarshish. Javan might be the Java, Indonesia, and Tarshish is also indicated to be in the east. It can also be Japan.

Other than these guesses and inferences, there is no clear indication as to where Japheth went for now.

There is no biblical basis on Strong's Concordance claim that Japheth is "His descendants occupy Asia Minor and Europe" nor Javan being identified as Greece.

But we do not know if they spread out also around the world, like the descendants of Shem, the root of Abraham who have become the father of many prosperous nations – the Tribes of Israel.

Perhaps, some of Japhets's sons became the peoples of India, Bangladesh, Madagascar, and other countries that became the British colony. Perhaps, this is the fulfillment of Noah's blessings to Shem and Japheth (Gen. 9:27), that Japheth to dwell in the tents of Shem in the modern day Shemites. Britain is the modern day tribe of Ephraim, the younger brother of Manasseh (USA), the sons of Joseph, the son of Jacob, the son of Isaac, the son of Abraham, the son of Terah, the son of Nahor, the son of Serug, the son of Reu, the son of Peleg, the brother of Joktan, the sons of Eber, the son of Salah, the son of Arphaxad, the son of Shem, the elder brother of Ham, and Japheth, the sons of Noah.

Ephraim was blessed by Jacob to become multitude or commonwealth of nations in Genesis 48: 19;

"¹⁹But his father refused and said, "I know, my son, I know. He also shall become a people, and he also shall be great; but truly his younger brother shall be greater than he, and his descendants shall become a multitude of nations.""

Ephraim is the younger brother of Manasseh. They inherited the name Israel as Jacob adopted and blessed them in Genesis 48:16;

"¹⁶...Bless the lads; let my name be named upon them, and the name of my fathers Abraham and Isaac; and let them grow into a multitude in the midst of the earth.""

There is no other nation on earth that have become a great

multitude or commonwealth of nations in the history of the modern world than Ephraim who is Britain and Manasseh who is the USA who become a single great and most powerful and prosperous nation on earth today (for now).

British colonization of Indonesia, Malaysia, India, Singapore and Hong Kong made them a prosperous nation. Even the discovery and extraction of oil in the middle east is caused by Britain.

Britain have prospered many nations on earth in all the history of mankind. At his prime, more than a third of the earth were under the British Empire.

But not the isles/coastlands, of all people. The isles was just colonized for a short period of time by both Britain and the USA. Not enough to be prosperous nation such as Hong Kong and Singapore. I wonder why. To think that the isles is their roots. But if they have lost their identity, how much more their roots. Or perhaps, God have hidden the truth for His purpose. According to His plan and timeframe.

Now, we know that the family of Noah after the flood was called the "isles people of the Gentiles in Genesis 10:5;

> "⁵From these the <u>coastland/isles peoples of the Gentiles</u> were separated into their lands, everyone according to his language, according to their families, into their nations."

Notice that the Bible called the new inhabitants of the earth, Gentiles. And also, they lived or dwell in the isles. Take note also that this is the first time the Bible mentioned the word Gentiles and isles or in other translations – coastlands or islands. These islands are located in the east because they moved to west to the land of Shinar in genesis 11: 2;

> "²And it came to pass, as they journeyed from the east, that they found a plain in the land of Shinar, and they dwelt there."

It was not specified here what mode of transportation they used to travel to the land of Shinar. Did they walk on foot by land, or did they used vessels such as ships? They already have an idea about ship building because Noah builds the ark. Besides, they live in islands besides the sea. On the other hand, it will be hard for them to travel by foot because of the unknown terrains along the way into to the land of Shinar. There is no clear pathway towards their destination. Not to mention the wild animals and the rugged terrain of the mountains along the way. But perhaps, God lead them the way through a path in the sea and the mighty waters (Isaiah 43: 16) from the isles to the land of Shinar or Mesopotamia just as God brought the Chaldeans to Babylon who loved their ships (Isaiah 43: 14). Note that Mesopotamia became the Babylonian Empire later on.

The Gentiles moved as one multi-generational family of Noah because they do not want to be separated from each other. That is why they build a tower in the land of Shinar as mentioned in Genesis 11: 4;

> "⁴And they said, "Come, let us build ourselves a city, and a tower whose top is in the heavens; let us make a name for ourselves, lest we be scattered abroad over the face of the whole earth.""

As usual, human beings are hardheaded and disobedient to God. They do not want to separate from each other, contrary to what God have commanded them to do – "go forth and multiply and replenish the earth". To repopulate the earth in Gensis 9: 1;

> "¹And God blessed Noah and his sons, and said unto them, be fruitful, and multiply, and replenish the earth."

So, what did God do?

Genesis 11: 7-9 said that God confused their language and scattered them abroad;

> "⁷Come, let Us go down and there confuse their language, that they may not understand one another's speech." ⁸So the Lord scattered them abroad from there over the face of all the earth, and they ceased building the city. ⁹Therefore its name is called Babel, because there the Lord confused the language of all the earth; and from there the Lord scattered them abroad over the face of all the earth."

But this scattering is not instant like magically every tongue or family transported or teleported suddenly into many nations or places on earth. God is a God of process. So is the scattering of the peoples

247

of the earth as indicated in Genesis 10:25;

"²⁵To Eber were born two sons: the name of one was Peleg, for in his days the earth was divided;…"

So, the division of the earth and the scattering of the people according to their language into their nations, happened in the days of Peleg. Many days and years. We do not know at what age of Peleg the division of the earth started. But Peleg lived for 239 years (Gen. 11:18-19). Almost two and a half centuries.

The tribes of Shem (with emphasis to the tribes of Peleg and Joktan, the sons of Eber) and perhaps some of the family of Japheth went back to the east, particularly in the isles where they came from. This is because Abraham came from the isles in the east at the ends of the earth as was previously discussed. Abraham is a Shemites like Arphaxad who is associated with the Chaldeans as per Josephus.

But let us trace the origin of this isles/coastlands in the east and why this is important.

When God created/recreated the earth in Genesis 1: 10, it was just a dry land (singular – one piece) and described as circular in shape in Proverbs 8:27;

"²⁷When He prepared the heavens, I was there, when He drew a circle on the face of the deep,…"

And in Isaiah 40: 21-22;

"²¹…Have you not understood from the foundations of the earth? ²² It is He who sits above the circle of the earth,…"

No mention of any body of waters such as lakes, rivers, etc in the earth, but the gathering of the waters Ha called Seas (Genesis 1: 10).

Until He planted a garden eastward of Eden (Gen.2:8). Then He created a River from Eden to water the garden. From the garden, the River parted into four heads. We need to be clear on this because many so-called expert's opinions are making people confused because they are giving conclusions or firm statements so that the four rivers will fit into their narrative that the garden of Eden is in the Middle-East where Tigris and Euphrates are presently located. They willfully forget or did not understand that the earth prior to the flood is not composed of seven continents but just one single piece of land. The landscape of the earth when it was called by God as Eden prior to the flood is very different from the landscape after the flood. They willfully replaced two of the rivers name in the Bible translations into Tigris (Hiddekel) and Euphrates (Perat/Pherat) even though it is not true. They interpreted the other two rivers as Pishon, the Nile River and Gihon as the Blue Nile. This is Bible misrepresentation. This humanly interpretations cannot withstand the truth of what the Bible said. The Bible said in Genesis 2: 10 that a river went out from Eden to water the garden of Eden in the east because God planted the garden eastward of Eden. Then, it became four heads.

For many reasons, these experts/scholars' interpretation is false.

First, the four rivers they are trying to portray as the four rivers in the garden of Eden is too much of a stretch of imagination. The four rivers in the Middle East namely Tigris, Euphrates, Nile, and Blue Nile have no common point of origin contrary to what the Bible said that it parted into four heads from one main River.

Second, these rivers specially Tigris and Euphrates flow southwards and not eastwards. If this is the case, their Eden is in the north and their garden is in the south in Mesopotamia which is contrary to what God said in the Bible. I wonder who the god of these historians and experts/scholars is, feeding us with lies.

Third, if their interpretation is correct, the four riverheads became longer than the main River based on the current location of Tigris and Euphrates rivers.

There are many more reasons that what we believe today as the portrayed location of the garden of Eden is in the Middle East is false. But there is a saying that "all rivers eventually flow to the ocean" if we try to understand.

We should also remember that these rivers are pre-flood in Noah's time. After the flood, the earth became a different landscape that we are today. We cannot see the garden of Eden nor the rivers anymore. Perhaps it was hidden by God into another dimension beyond human eyes or God destroyed it during the great flood in Noah's time.

Could God have given us a clue to the potential or previous location of the garden? What happened to the rivers after the flood?

Isaiah 42: 15 gives us the clue or the answer as to what happened to the rivers;

"¹⁵…I will make the rivers isles/islands/coastlands…"

We should take note that the Lord in Isaiah 42 is talking to the isles/coastlands. And in verse 15, He pointed out the original form of the isles. The isles/coastlands were originally rivers. What rivers? Why should it become isles/coastlands? What is the connection of rivers and isles/coastlands?

As we know it, the Word of God (the Bible) is a very compressed message of God for humanity. It has multi-dimensional meaning and is like a matrix that one verse has multiple connections to another verse or sentence or even a word throughout the Bible. That is why the Bible is not for private interpretation, but the Bible interprets itself if the Holy Spirit of God guide us to those matrixes.

This phrase in verse 15 for instance is a code and symbols to the origin of the isles/coastlands and as a piece of the puzzle as to why the isles in the east is important to God. He elects the isles to be His servants, as a temporary replacement of His servants Israel who disobeyed Him because it is involved from the very beginning of creation particularly in creating Adam and to the end of the last Adam (Yeshua) (1 Cor. 15: 45).

Verse 14 and 15 of Isaiah 42 is the fury of the Lord that wants to destroy the whole earth because of how mankind has become so evil. If not for the sake of Noah in Genesis 6: 5-8, God could have obliterated the earth once again.

"⁵Then the Lord saw that the wickedness of man was great in the earth, and that every intent of the thoughts of his heart was only evil continually. ⁶And the Lord was sorry that He had made man on the earth, and He was grieved in His heart. ⁷So the Lord said, "I will destroy man whom I have created from the face of the earth, both man and beast, creeping thing and birds of the air, for I am sorry that I have made them." ⁸But

Noah found grace in the eyes of the Lord."

You see how human become so evil that even the One who created them want to destroy them if not for the sake of one. Genesis 6: 11-13;

"11The earth also was corrupt before God, and the earth was filled with violence. 12So God looked upon the earth, and indeed it was corrupt; for all flesh had corrupted their way on the earth. 13And God said to Noah, "The end of all flesh has come before Me, for the earth is filled with violence through them; and behold, I will destroy them with the earth."

Let us try to understand these verses.

The Lord and God in this chapter is Yeshua (Jesus Christ). He is always the One communicating to His chosen elects – the prophets, disciples, and apostles. He is the Messenger of God the Father as He said in John 12: 49-50;

"49I have not spoken on My own, but the Father who sent Me has commanded Me what to say and how to say it. 50And I know that His command leads to eternal life. So I speak exactly what the Father has told Me to say.""

And in John 14: 24;

"24Whoever does not love Me does not keep My words. The word that you hear is not My own, but it is from the Father who sent Me."

Yeshua is the One sent by God to give the commandments of God to Moses, just as stated in Malachi 3: 1;

"1 ""Behold, I send My messenger, and he will prepare the way before Me. And the Lord, whom you seek, will suddenly come to His temple, even the Messenger of the covenant, in whom you delight. Behold, He is coming," says the Lord of hosts."

Although this verse has multi-dimensional meaning that transcends different periods of time, like the messenger who prepared the way when Yeshua came as a flesh in the person of John the Baptist, the end time messenger who will prepare the way of Yeshua to establish the coming Kingdom of God, and Yeshua being the Messenger to prepare the way during the Millennial Kingdom of the coming of the Father to dwell here on earth (Rev. 21: 3-5), we can say that the One who "is coming" is also the One "who is and who was and who is to come" (Rev. 1: 8) is also the "Messenger of the covenant" who give the Ten Commandments to Moses in Mount Sinai in Arabia (Gal. 4: 25).

Yeshua is also the Creator of all things as God the Father told Him to do (Rev. 4: 11). Everything was created by Him and through Him as stated in John1: 1-4;

> "¹In the beginning was the Word, and the Word was with God, and the Word was God. ²He was in the beginning with God. ³All things were made through Him, and without Him nothing was made that was made. ⁴In Him was life, and the life was the light of men."

The Light, Life, and the Word is Yeshua (Jesus Christ). He became flesh and came to His own – the Jewish people- the tribe of Judah from which David came from. But the Jewish people rejected Him and did not know Him. John 1: 10-11, said;

> "¹⁰He was in the world, and the world was made through Him, and the world did not know Him. ¹¹He came to His own, and His own did not receive Him."

Mankind was created by and through Yeshua. But because mankind has become so evil that He intends to destroy it. He consulted His Father about His plan. And God the Father looked down on earth and was convinced that the earth is indeed full of evil and need to be destroyed. But perhaps, Yeshua hesitated and told His Father that there is one righteous man among them and ask, "shall we also destroy him with the earth?"

Perhaps, the Father answered to Him like He answered Abraham in Genesis 18: 23 as he intercedes for Sodom;

> "²³And Abraham came near and said, "Would You also destroy the righteous with the wicked?"

After several persuasive questionings or prodding of Abraham to the Lord as to how many people are needed in order for Him not to destroy Sodom, Abraham arrived at ten from fifty. And the Lord answered him in Genesis 18: 32 saying;

> "³²Then he said, "Let not the Lord be angry, and I will speak but once more: Suppose ten should be found there?" And He said, "I will not destroy it for the sake of ten.""

Similarly, God did not destroy the whole earth for the sake of Noah. But God saved Noah from His fury that He unleash on the face of the earth through the flood in Isaiah 42: 14-15;

> "¹⁴"I have held My peace a long time, I have been still and restrained Myself. Now I will cry like a woman in labor, I will pant and gasp at once. ¹⁵I will lay waste the mountains and hills, and dry up all their vegetation; I will make the rivers coastlands, and I will dry up the pools."

And then He turned the rivers (the rivers that water the garden?) into isles or coastlands where the ark of Noah landed in Mt. Ararat (perhaps, Mt. Arayat?) after the flood. The family of Noah multiplied in the isles where they are called, "the isles peoples of the Gentiles" (Gen.10:5). All the peoples of the post flood earth were called Gentiles and they all reside in the isles in the east before they move to the land of Shinar in the west (Genesis 11:2).

The isles is the key to understanding the possible previous location of the garden of Eden and the four rivers after the garden are the clue to understanding the location of the isles/coastlands.

We need to bear in mind the mystery behind why God uses the locator River, rivers, gold, bdellium, and onyx stones. And also, the name of the lands to which the rivers were associated. Cush and Havilah were not yet born when God created the garden of Eden. Of course, God declared the end from the beginning (Is. 46: 10).

Let us examine a little closer these four rivers that came from one main river that water the garden in the east of Eden in Genesis 2: 10-14;

"¹⁰Now <u>a river</u> went out of Eden to water the garden, and from there it parted and <u>became four riverheads</u>."

We need to fully understand verse 10 first before we proceed. The main river flowed from west to the east. But which west? Perhaps God is talking from the center of the earth's perspective. It makes sense because He divided the earth into four corners (Isaiah 11:12). North-South, West-East. And in Isaiah 40: 21-22, the earth is described as a circle;

"²¹ "Have you not known? Have you not heard?

Has it not been told you from the beginning?

Have you not understood from the foundations of the earth?

²²It is He who sits above the <u>circle of the earth</u>,…"""

So when God recreated the earth (because the first earth become without form and void (Gen.1: 2) and submerged under the water (flood) after the war in heaven (Rev. 12: 7-10) in Genesis1: 9-10;

"⁹Then God said, "Let the waters under the heavens be gathered together into one place, and let the dry land appear"; and it was so. ¹⁰And God called the dry <u>land</u> Earth, and the gathering together of the waters He called Seas. And God saw that it was good."

The earth was a circular mass of dry land surrounded by the seas (waters) before the flood. Take note again that the earth was previously one piece of land. The seas are not part of the earth as we believe today, but the earth is in the seas, above the waters as in Psalms 136: 6;

"⁶To Him who laid out <u>the earth above the waters</u>,…"

And because God might have been speaking from the center of the earth, the River must have originated from there. But where is the center of the earth?

The land of Canaan, now known as the land of Israel, is most likely the center of the earth. It is the point of reference when the Bible talks about directions. As a matter of fact, the temple in Jerusalem is like a compass that have four gates that points to north, south, west, and east. No other Biblical references mentioned in the Bible pointing to the four corners of the earth except the temple.

In our modern map (after the flood) which look like a puzzle pieces, if we reconnect them all together, Israel will be the center of the earth in a flat map. For me, it makes more sense that Israel is the center of the earth because it is the land that God called His own and He will reign on earth from Jerusalem. He gives it as inheritance to Abraham. Of course, the whole creation is His own that is why He can give it to anybody He wanted to give. But, the land of Canaan that became Israel (Jerusalem) which He said He personally built in Isaiah 43:15;

"¹⁵I am the Lord, your Holy One, the Creator of Israel, your King."

So, if you are the creator of everything, why not build your own land or your throne or temple at the center of all your creation. Israel is very special piece of real estate to God and in His glorious master plan for the salvation of all His creation.

We may say that perhaps the whole circle of the earth is Eden and God particularly planted a garden in the east of Eden. Or maybe the land of Canaan is the Eden. There was no rain at that time (because He did not cause it yet to rain on earth (Gen. 2:5)). So He made a river to water the garden in the east. And because God is in the center of the earth in Canaan, particularly in Jerusalem (His Land) Israel, the ancient river might have originated from Jerusalem which is west of the garden. But God give us a concrete clue to where the River came from in 2 Chronicles 9:26;

"²⁶So he reigned over all the kings from the River to the land of the Philistines,..."

King Solomon reign from the River to the land of Philistines. It is a coded verse but verses 25 and 27 interpret this verse that the beginning of the River is in Jerusalem. And we know for a fact that King Solomon reigned in Jerusalem and so is our Lord Yeshua be, just as Psalm 72:8 said;

"⁸He shall have dominion also from sea to sea, and from the River to the ends of the earth."

Could the Philistines in verse 26 above a code for the present-day Philippines as it is similarly worded in verse 8 above and replaced with "the ends of the earth"?

Because God is the author of beautiful creations, perhaps He made the River a beautiful meandering river to the east end of the earth. And as the water travel from the center of the earth, it gathered a lot of gold and minerals and deposited those concentrations along the head waters at the bottom of the four rivers particularly in the land of Havilah and Ophir.

So, from the garden, the main River parted into four riverheads. In my simple understanding, riverheads connote short distance from the main river. It has a short distance from its origin to its end (head) like deltas. Perhaps, because it is near the end of the earth in the east? And the water at the heads of the four rivers flowed to the sea or ocean? We will see. Remember the circle of the earth?

This information is very important in order to contrast the interpretations of other experts that the rivers are in the Middle-East (Mesopotamian region) or to some, it is under water of the oceans that flowed to the whole earth.

Now, let us go back to the four rivers in verse 11 to 14:

"^{11}The name of the first is Pishon; it is the one which skirts the whole <u>land of Havilah</u>, where there is <u>gold</u>. ^{12}And the gold of that land is good. <u>Bdellium</u> and the <u>onyx</u> stone are there. ^{13}The name of the second river is Gihon; it is the one which goes around the whole land of Cush. ^{14}The name of the third river is Hiddekel; it is the one which goes toward the east of Assyria. The fourth river is the Euphrates (Pherat)."

Let us first talk about the last two rivers – the river Hiddekel and the river Pherat or Perat because this is where the greatest confusion arises.

These two rivers are not only mistranslated but most of all, misrepresented. Modern translations of the Bible intentionally replaced or have footnotes that the river Hiddekel is Tigris River and the river Perat is Euphrates River. They also misrepresented the directional flow of Hiddekel River to Assyria.

They also misrepresented the location of Gihon River by changing the land of Cush into Ethiopia. Although the land of Cush and Ethiopia have relationship or connection to each other which we will discuss later, it is not the one that this verse is pertaining to.

This misrepresentation in the translation of the Bible as previously discussed, happened to fit their narrative or belief that the garden of Eden was in the region of Mesopotamia (Iran-Iraq area). But the rivers in that region does not fit to what the Bible said that the four rivers originate from one river, the main river flowed to the east and the four rivers was turned into islands by the Lord (Isaiah 42:15) after the flood.

That is right, the rivers were turned into islands according to Isaiah 42:15. Verse 14 and 15 showed us how God wanted to unleash His fury upon the earth. He holds it until Noah fulfilled all that He instructed him. Then the destruction of the earth by flood happened once more. And the landscape of the earth changed since its recreation. Perhaps, the ancient magnetic North have change also to where we are now. Just perhaps.

Because if we look back, the direction of the Bible is coded based on the original creation when the earth was just one mass of land resembling to that of a circle (2D) (Isaiah 40:22) if we remove our preconceptions that the earth is a sphere (3D). I know it is very controversial topic. But that is what the Bible tell us. The earth is a circle, symbolic of an infinity for expansion horizontally above the waters. While sphere is close system, finite and bound to explode if expanded.

The islands of Philippines will be exactly in the east of Jerusalem when the islands of Borneo and the Philippines goes back to the sides of Vietnam and China respectively as it fits perfectly like a piece of the puzzle. Many of the lands or continents (intercontinental shelf) in a flat map resembles pieces of puzzle that can fit together to form a larger singular mass of land if they are rejoined or reconnected to each other. This gives us a clue to the validity of Isaiah 40: 22 regarding the earth being a circle when God first created it before He

distorted, the face of the earth in Isaiah 24: 1;

> "'Behold, the Lord makes the earth empty and makes it waste, <u>distorts its surface</u> and scatters abroad its inhabitants.'"

This verse transcends periods of time from the moment God expresses His regret in creating man on earth and intended to destroy humanity from the face of the earth, except Noah (Gen.6: 6-8) to the time of the flood when He distorted the face of the earth that we are now (composed of continents and many islands), to the time that the earth became empty and desolate after the flood, and to the time when the descendants of Noah became many and build the tower of Babel in the land of Shinar (Gen.11:1-9). And from there, God scattered abroad the new inhabitants of the earth for approximately 239 years (the lifetime of Peleg (Gen. 10: 25)).

The distortion of the face of the earth included the time when God turn the rivers into islands (Isaiah 42:15) and at the same time a wilderness (Isaiah 50:2) at the ends of the earth in the east which He specifically mentioned that he created like Israel (Isaiah 40:28). For this is where He placed Noah and his family as new inhabitants of the earth and called them "the island (isle) peoples of the Gentiles" (Gen. 10:5). From these islands will come once more a new beginning, a new inhabitant that will light up the earth and spread God's righteousness in this end time and usher in the coming Kingdom of God.

We may ask why God allowed these misrepresentations and substitutions of the Bible. Perhaps God wanted to hide the truth to humanity until the appointed time, which is now. Or perhaps, God wanted to hide the identity of the people whom He will be calling to be His servants in the end times, until now.

The Bible hides the mysteries of God that are revealed only to those people whom He chose to make it understand His mystery. But of course, to those who are willing to listen and obey and with a humble heart.

The word of God is multi-dimensional in nature and have multiple meaning and applications to one's life. Perhaps God compressed the multi-volume of books into one book – the Bible to convey His message into codes and puzzle pieces, and parables that to whom He called my understand and unravel the mysteries in His time. But to those who are proud and arrogant He hides His Truth.

Now let us continue to try to decode the mystery of the rivers in Genesis 2. But first, let us understand the importance of this rivers into the end time prophecy of the Lord.

These rivers became islands after the flood as mentioned in Isaiah 42:15. The Bible often refer to it as the isles, islands, or coastlands (NKJV) in other translations. The location of these ancient rivers which became islands in the east (Gen. 2:8-10), is at the ends of the circle of the earth (Isaiah 40:22). The end time peoples of the isles will be called by God to be His servants (Isaiah 42, 49), to prepare His way and serve Him in His coming Kingdom here on earth. The isles is composed of many ancient nations or kingdoms because God divided the land by the rivers in Isaiah 18: 7 (KJV) (be careful, NKJV have a very different translation);

> "⁷In that time shall the present be brought unto the LORD of hosts of <u>a people scattered</u> and <u>peeled</u>, and from <u>a people terrible from their beginning</u> hitherto; <u>a nation meted out and trodden under foot, whose land the rivers have spoiled</u>, to the place of the name of the LORD of hosts, the mount Zion."

> Now, from one main river, it became four rivers in Genesis 1:10;
> "¹⁰Now a river went out of Eden to water the garden, and from there it parted and became four riverheads."

It is very clear from this verse that the four rivers originated from the garden after the main river watered the garden. The four rivers are at the other end of or at the other side of the main river. Perhaps, these four rivers are in itself inside the garden.

The first river mentioned in verse 11 is called Pishon. It encompasses the whole land of Havilah. The same "encompasses" word was also used when verse 12 described the second river called Gihon which "encompasses" the whole land of Cush. Cush in other translations is written as Ethiopia.

"Encompasses" here might mean a boundary or enclosure. The order by which the rivers are mentioned are perhaps not meant to be a sequential order but rather in terms of significance. The first two rivers are the two major rivers that establishes the boundary by which these four rivers occupy. It is like a close and open parenthesis engulfing the other two rivers – the third river Hiddekel and the fourth river Perat.

The river Pishon is the upper or northern enclosure of the river bounded by the land of Havilah and the river Gihon is the lower or southern enclosure bounded by the land of Cush.

We should remember three important things in understanding these four-river system.

1. Havilah and Cush were not yet born at this point in time of creation.
2. The four riverheads is flowing to the east end of the earth eventually ending up to the sea like a delta.
3. The description of these riverheads is before the flood (pre-flood) of the times of Noah. Before these rivers was turned by God into islands (Isaiah 42:15).

These verses are so mysterious to understand as to why God mentioned already the name of Cush and Havilah even if they are not yet born. And Havilah of all names. Which Havilah? Is it the son of Cush or is it the son of Joktan?

But Havilah, the son of Joktan is five generations away from Shem. And Havilah the son of Cush is just the second generation from Ham the younger brother of Shem.

The family of Cush, the son of Ham and the father of Havilah, the brother of Nimrod remained in the land of Shinar (perhaps now known as Mesopotamia). Therefore, Havilah the son of Cush is no longer in the isles. They remained in the land of Shinar. This is perhaps the reason why Cush and Havilah are related to Ethiopia.

God give us solid evidence that the Havilah being associated with the first river Pishon is not the son of Cush (in Africa) but the son of Joktan, the son of Eber from the line of Shem because they went back to the isles in the east. And this evidence is the word Bdellium (Gen.2:12).

What is bdellium?

Some define it as an aromatic resin from a tree like frankincense and myrrh and some define it as a pearl.

Which is which?

Using common sense and not philosophical argumentation, it is clearly a pearl.

Why?

Because verse 11 and 12 of Genesis 2 mentioned gold, bdellium and onyx stone. It is not logical to mention gold and onyx stone – a well-known hard objects, then suddenly mention aromatic resin or gum which is soft. Both gold and onyx are associated with the ground of the earth, and suddenly compare it to a resin from the sap of a tree? It does not make sense.

All the three stones mentioned are of ground origin and with significant beauty and therefore with great value.

So, the bdellium mentioned in verse 12 is pearl. The Bible gives us also the clue as to what color the bdellium is in Numbers 11: 7;

"⁷Now the manna was like coriander seed, and its color like the color of bdellium."

Some translations literally change the word bdellium from the original text to gum resin.

Exodus 16: 31 give us exactly what the color of manna is;

"³¹And the house of Israel called its name Manna. And it was like white coriander seed, and the taste of it was like wafers made with honey."

Now we can say that the color of bdellium is white, like pearl. It cannot be aromatic resin or gum resin because as resin becomes old it turns into amber color. The most aromatic white resin I have seen is the one coming from Pili nut tree. It is called "salung" in our place in Bicol. It is also known as Manila Copal. It is gummy white when fresh and turns into crystalline amber when old. My father and I usually gather "salung" to sell in the market or use it in lighting firewood in our dirty kitchen.

Other aromatic resins like frankincense and myrrh are amber or darker colored crystalline resins.

So, bdellium is pearl. Pearl as we know it is a precious stone like gold. It is formed inside the mother of pearl or oyster shell. Originally, pearl is just white. But with the new technology, it can be made into black, pinkish, yellowish, and other colors can be made in a cultured pearl.

But God is so great to give us a clue where this bdellium is located. The biggest pearls can only be found in Palawan, Philippines. Nowhere else in the world can we find pearl such as the latest and largest pearl called, "Pearl of Puerto" weighing 75 pounds (35 kgs) and valued at $100 million. The second largest pearl is the "Giga Pearl" weighing 61 pounds (27.7 kgs) and valued at $90 million. The biggest pearl in my elementary years was the "Pearl of Lao Tze" which weigh less than 14.2 pounds (6.4 kgs) now valued at $35 million. There are other smaller ones that are still way bigger than the normal pearl used in jewelry. All these pearls are found only in Palawan.

Gold and onyx stones can be found in many parts of the world, but God give a distinction in the land of Havilah, and that is bdellium – pearl. Pearl can be cultured also in many parts of the world that suits its habitat. But the Palawan pearls are natural, the biggest and therefore the ancient ones.

This is a specific indication of the location of the land of Havilah, which is bordered by the Pishon river that originates from the garden. As God turned the rivers (Isaiah 42: 15) into islands, the Pishon river perhaps became the island of Palawan and possibly even extending to the islands of Luzon and Japan.

Now, the river that borders the south is the Gihon river that encompasses the whole land of Cush (Gen.2: 13).

Other translations of this verse replaced Cush into Ethiopia. This is to fit the narrative that Eden and the garden of Eden is in the regions of Mesopotamia or Africa because of the Nile and Blue Nile rivers can be found in that region. This is because at that time, the so called "Bible Scholars and Experts" have not known yet or God have not revealed yet that He made the rivers into islands in Isaiah 42: 15. That was God's intention before the flood as He was angry and intends to destroy mankind from the face of the earth. And that was what God did. He destroyed mankind from the face of the earth through water except the family of Noah(8) and the animals with them. Just as it is written in Isaiah 42: 14-15;

> "¹⁴I have held My peace a long time, I have been still and restrained Myself. Now I will cry like a woman in labor, I will pant and gasp at once.
> ¹⁵I will lay waste the mountains and hills, and dry up all their vegetation; I will make the rivers coastlands, and I will dry up the pools."

And after the Lord unleash His fury like a birthing woman, this is what happened on the earth in Isaiah 24:1;

> "¹Behold, the Lord makes the earth empty and makes it waste, distorts its surface and scatters abroad its inhabitants."

These verses give us the before and after picture of how God unleash His fury on mankind and destroy the face of the earth by water (flood). But He give it a new beginning through the family of Noah. A re-birth. Another chance for mankind.

Verse 14 of Isaiah 42 show us God describing Himself like giving birth. But before giving birth, there is an event called "water broke", a sign that the giving birth or laboring is about to begin. The laboring is a nerve-wracking event characterized by violent movements, spasm, cry, panting, and gasping. It is a very energy intensive work for the mother. It is called labor for that reason. A lot of work. But after that is a new beginning.

Perhaps God used this process of giving birth of giving a new beginning to mankind. The earth is like a mother's womb. Noah's ark is like a fetus or an egg that became a baby. The baby is protected by water inside the womb from a violent movement or distortion or changes happening inside and outside the womb.

God distorted the surface of the earth (Isaiah 24:1) during the flood. Perhaps, He reap it a part. From one piece of land (Gen. 1:9-10), it became several continents and islands which we can see now in our modern map that the earth's land masses are like pieces of puzzles. They are distant apart, but their shapes will have resemblance that will fit together to create one piece of land.

During the laboring process, God changed the landscape of the whole earth, distorting the face of the earth, creating mountains and hills (like a garment), and dividing the earth with rivers (Hab. 3: 9) resulting into a large bodies of waters (seas and mighty waters (oceans)) in between land masses. But verse 15 of Isaiah 42, God particularly mentioned that He turned the rivers into isles/islands. We have previously discussed that these rivers originated from the main River that water the garden of Eden then parted into four. These four rivers ended up into the sea at the ends of the earth in the east when it was just one piece of large land. And one of these rivers is the Gihon river which encompasseth the whole land of Cush.

It is these rivers that became islands after the flood where the family of Noah begun to multiply. They are called the islands or isles people of the Gentiles in Genesis 10:5;

"⁵From these the coastland/isles peoples of the Gentiles were separated into their lands, everyone according to his language, according to their families, into their nations."

God scattered the new inhabitants (descendants of Noah) of the earth (Isaiah 24:1) from the islands where the family of Noah begun his new beginning. Perhaps, his ark landed in Mt. Arayat and not Mt. Ararat. And from there, they spread into the islands of the archipelago according to their new family.

But before that, their family migrated to the west until they found a plain in the land of Shinar (Gen.11:2). We might wonder why they are attracted to a plain land. Perhaps they are tired of the mountains, islands, forests, and seas? It became a mundane environment to them that when they saw a new type of landscape, they become attracted to it.

Nevertheless, they love their families so much (like perhaps the

Pilipino extended family tradition?). They do not want to separate from each other that they decided to build a tower that symbolizes their identity so that they will not be scattered abroad in direct disobedience to God's command to them to "go forth and multiply and replenish the earth" (Gen. 9:1).

But God as we know it, scattered them anyway. The scattering is not instant as many of us think, but rather it is a process that took some time. Perhaps in the expanse of 239 years, for that is the days of Peleg in Genesis 10:25;

> "[25]To Eber were born two sons: the name of one was Peleg, for in his days the earth was divided;..."

Notice, "in his days". Not just the time of his birth, but throughout his lifetime. The computation of his days is 239 years from Genesis 11:18-19;

> "[18]Peleg lived thirty years, and begot Reu. [19]After he begot Reu, Peleg lived two hundred and nine years, and begot sons and daughters."

So approximately 239 years took to divide the nations of the earth after the flood beginning from the time God destroyed the tower, for that is the birth or the beginning of "the days" of Peleg.

It is amazing to behold how the seemingly simple verse in the Bible is interrelated to one another. That is why verses are repeated time and time again as it relates to other dots/subjects or meaning of the matrix/puzzle. The dots connect to each other like a matrix. The Bible is so complex (yet so simple) and very mysterious (yet inspiring) that if we understand it, is far more advance than the latest and most complex of a computer program.

So, from the event in the Tower of Babel, the families of Noah begun to separate from each other.

The families of Shem went back to the east. Perhaps, in the islands where they first came from as described in Genesis 10:30-31;

> "[30]And their dwelling place was from Mesha as you go toward Sephar, the mountain of the east. [31]These were the sons of

Shem, according to their families, according to their languages, in their lands, according to their nations."

It is most likely that the families of Japhet (the youngest brother) and some family members of Cush, particularly Canaan, went back to the isles in the east with Shem (the eldest) as described in Genesis 10:5;

"⁵From these the isles/islands/coastland peoples of the Gentiles were separated into their lands, everyone according to his language, according to their families, into their nations."

This verse came just after verses 2 and 4 describes the families of Japheth which may indicate the location of Japheth's family by the time they were separated.

Verse five characterizes the landscape of their place as isles or islands and God named them Gentiles.

Perhaps some members of the tribes of Ham (Cush), particularly Canaan, went back with Shem and Japheth and some remained in their father Cush in the land of Shinar, where Nimrod, the son of Cush, build a kingdom in Babel. Canaan are black people. So is Nimrod. Cush has a son named Havilah also.

This is because Canaan was cursed by Noah to be the servants of Shem and Japheth because his father Ham, saw the nakedness of his father Noah in Genesis 9:25-27;

"²⁵And he said, cursed be Canaan; a servant of servants shall he be unto his brethren.

²⁶And he said, Blessed be the LORD God of Shem; and Canaan shall be his servant.

²⁷God shall enlarge Japheth, and he shall dwell in the tents of Shem; and Canaan shall be his servant."

This curse to Canaan has ancient and prophetic meaning in terms of slavery. Perhaps some of the Canaanites were already their servants as they go back to the east.

I have no knowledge about ancient slavery in Japheth's family, but the history of the Philippines being the ancient land of Shem show that slavery of the black people (the Negritos) already existed. They are called, "alipin sa gigilid". This is similar to the "caste system" of India. Ah, perhaps India is one of the descendants of Japheth.

Shem being the older brother of Japheth (the youngest) is to take good care of his younger brothers. And in verse 27, Noah particularly said;

"²⁷God shall enlarge Japheth, and he shall dwell in the tents of Shem;…"

"Dwell in the tents of Shem", may mean literally and figuratively. Figuratively in a sense that Shem, being the older brother will or should take good care of his younger brother. That is why, whenever Shem go, Japheth will come with him.

Literally, as in literal image of a tent. The top is smaller and wider at the bottom. Like the map of the Philippines, smaller in Batanes and wider in Mindanao and Palawan as the base. And it become more enlarged underneath it with the islands of Indonesia and Malaysia. Or we can say that the territory of Shem is the top of the tent and the territory of Japheth being the larger base of the tent. This is supported by what Noah who said in verse 27, "May God enlarge Japheth".

Japheth is not only to expand or enlarge under the tents of Shem, but also to expand globally, particularly in Asia and perhaps in Latin America.

In Asia, they expanded and perhaps become the modern-day area of Thailand, Myanmar, Vietnam, and other surrounding nations, to China, Russia, and Japan. One of the clues to this connection is the eyes. From the normal eye opening of the Pilipino people, it begun to narrow at the sides in Indonesian people. Then a little bit narrower in Malaysians and become more noticeable in Thailand, Vietnam, Cambodia, Myanmar, and other surrounding nations. Then it further narrows in Russians, Koreans, Japanese, and peak in Chinese people.

Latin America is mixture of Shem and Japheth's family. The distinctive identity of Japheth in Latin America is the building of temples, ziggurats, and pyramids of the Incas up to Mexico. But in Indonesia, the discovery of the Gunung Padang Pyramid will change history as we know it. Estimated to have been constructed in 10,000 B.C., the pyramid is proof that human civilization started far earlier than assumed. We can say that Japheth's descendant is the origin of pyramid, temple, and ziggurat building technology for their pagan worship. Perhaps, it is Japheth's idea to build the tower of Babel because he is the youngest and is afraid to be separated from his family. The huge temples, and ziggurats in Indonesia have great resemblance to that of the Hindu and Buddhist temples as well as that of the Mayans and Incas.

As I was studying these temples all around the world, I was wondering why the Philippines have no such kind of temples built. I actually envied these nations because they have marks of ancient civilization because they have wonders of engineering and architecture visible to this day. I was really beginning to think the Pilipino people are really lazy and poor that we cannot develop such things. We have no tourist attractions of such pagan god worshipping temples or a massive structure such as pyramid.

But as I begin to truly understand where Abraham came from and paste the clues and the puzzle together. I understand why.

With this temple/ziggurat/ pyramid correlation, we can say that the author of building the tower of Babel is from the family of Japheth. It was not Nimrod who build the tower of Babel because the kingdom that he builds in Babel is after the tower was destroyed when their language was confused by God. It is the reason why the place was called Babel. The building of tower was before Nimrod.

The Ur of the Chaldeans where Abraham came from is full of idolatry as mentioned in Joshua 24:2;

> "²And Joshua said to all the people, "Thus says the Lord God of Israel: 'Your fathers, including Terah, the father of Abraham and the father of Nahor, dwelt on the other side of the River in old times; and they served other gods. ³Then I took your father Abraham from the other side of the River,…'"

We know that this River (capital R) is not Euphrates as was footnoted in the Bible translations because it is related to the ends of the earth, which is related to the isles. Present-day Euphrates river is not at the ends of the earth in the east mentioned in Isaiah 41: 8-9. That is another clue to the identity of the Ur of the Chaldeans where Abraham came from;

"⁸...The descendants of Abraham My friend.

⁹You whom I have taken from the ends of the earth,..."

The "ends of the earth" is interchangeably use with the word isles/islands/coastlands.

The other side of the River is where the garden of Eden is prior to the flood and that the four rivers emanating from the main River was turned into islands by God (Isaiah 42:15) after the flood.

So, the Ur of the Chaldeans was an idolatrous place. People serve other gods. And God send them to Babylon as fugitives in Isaiah 43:14;

"¹⁴Thus says the Lord, your Redeemer, the Holy One of Israel: "For your sake I will send to Babylon, and bring them all down as fugitives— The Chaldeans, who rejoice in their ships.""

Why as "fugitives"?

Perhaps God did something to the isles that made them repented and turn back to God. And some of the Chaldeans who do not want to repent of their idolatry and sorcery practices was brought by God to Babylon which is an idolatrous nation also. Perhaps God destroy any idolatrous temple built in the land of the isles because it is His land. He destroyed those idolatrous places of worship by fire, storm, earthquake, volcanic eruptions, tsunami, etc.

Perhaps, Japheth's family also repented later as their temples in Indonesia was eaten up by the jungles and later were rediscovered. Perhaps, other family of Japheth who do not want to repent move away from their place and move to South America (became the Incas) and to Asia (Buddhist temples) to continue their idolatrous practices like the Chaldeans. That is why there are temples that are visible up to this day.

This is perhaps one of the reasons why there is no temples made in the Philippines. This is the territory of Shem and perhaps, the Shemites destroyed or did not allow this paganism to continue in their land. In fact, according to the account of Antonio Pigafetta, the people they found or met in the isles, worship their God by clasping their hands into their foreheads and said, "ABBA Father".

This gesture was recently performed by a tribe in Indonesia as they offer prayers to those who died in the submarine disaster on May, 2021.

Perhaps, the isles including the island territories of Japheth, repented and turn back to God until the time that the agents of Satan deceived them once again into idolatry through Catholicism and Islam.

So, these are the isles that are bounded by the rivers. But the river bounding the southern side is the river Gihon which encompasseth the land of Cush.

The family of Cush, the son of Ham is thought to be the origin of the black people in Africa particularly Ethiopia according to human history. And one of the sons of Cush that was specially mentioned is Nimrod in Genesis 10: 7-8;

"⁷The sons of Cush were Seba, Havilah, Sabtah, Raamah, and Sabtechah; and the sons of Raamah were Sheba and Dedan.
⁸Cush begot Nimrod; he began to be a mighty one on the earth."

Why did the Bible separate Nimrod from his brother's description?

Nimrod became the god of the Babylonians through the making of his wife Semiramis. He was a mighty hunter and regarded as the leader of the Giants. Therefore, we can say that he is also a giant according to Alexander Hislop account in his book, The Two Babylonians pp 63;

"But let the reader only reflect who were the real Giants that rebelled against heaven. They were Nimrod and his party; for the "Giants" were just the "Mighty ones" of whom Nimrod was the leader."

But what is the color of his skin?

Alexander Hislop accounted in page 69 of his book that;

"Whenever the negro aspect of Nimrod was found an obstacle to his worship, this was very easily obviated. According to the Chaldean doctrine of the transmigration of souls, all that was needful was just to teach that Ninus had reappeared in the person of a posthumous son of a fair complexion, supernaturally born by his widowed wife after the father had gone to glory."

This is how the worship of "mother and child" deity becomes into being. The mother being Semiramis and the child being Ninus (reincarnation of Nimrod). He is a negro, but through transfiguration doctrine, he become a fair skinned child at his supernatural reincarnation by his mother/wife Semiramis.

Nimrod is called by many names and one of them is Ninus according to Hislop in page 22;

"This lamented one, exhibited, and adorned as a little child in his mother's arms, seems, in a point of fact, to have been the husband of Semiramis, whose name, Ninus, by which he is commonly known in a classical history, literally signified "The Son". As Semiramis, the wife, was worshipped as Rhea, whose grand distinguishing character was that of the great goddess "Mother", the conjunction with her of her husband, under the name Ninus, or "The Son", was sufficient to originate the peculiar worship of the "Mother and Son", so extensively different among the nations of antiquity, and this, no doubt, is the explanation of the fact which has so much puzzled the inquirers into ancient history, that Ninus is sometimes called the husband, and sometimes the son of Semiramis."

This mother and child tandem is called by many names in different places in page 20;

"In Egypt, the Mother and the Child were worshipped under the names of Isis and Osiris. In India, even to this day, as Isi and Iswara; in Asia, as Cybele and Deoius; in Pagan Rome as Fortuna and Jupiter – puer, or Jupiter, the boy; in Greece, as Ceres, the Great Mother, with the babe at her breast, or as Irene, the goddess of Peace, with the boy Plutus in her arms; and even in Thibet, in China, and Japan, the Jesuit missionaries were astonished to find the counterpart of Madonna and her child as devoutly worshipped as in Papal Rome itself; Shing Moo, the Holy Mother in China, being represented with a child in her arms, and a glory around her, exactly as if a Roman Catholic artist had been employed to set her up."

We should take note that the existence of this mother and child worship was thousands of years before the birth of Christ. But the Babylonish religion of the Vatican, Christianize this pagan worship into "Mary and Jesus" whom Catholics worship as Mary and Sto. Nino (Ninus). And like Nimrod who is black, become white to be worshipped. The counterfeit Christianity represent Jesus and Sto. Nino (Ninus) as either black and white, but mostly white or fair skinned. There is this Black Nazarene paraded every holy week in Catholic celebration and there is this black Sto. Nino, I saw paraded as Sto. Nino de Cebu. This Sto. Nino of various colors and names are the one being displayed, adorned, worshipped during Christmas. All of these are representative of Nimrod and not the real Jesus which is unknown to many.

Rome wants us to believe that the mother and child worship came from Christ of the Bible. But "The Two Babylons" by Alexander Hislop, was first published more than a hundred years ago, proves that the "Mother and Child" worship begun with the ancient pagan Babylonian religion even before the birth of Christ.

Catholicism is one of the major religions Rome have created in order to deceived the whole world into worshipping false gods. Revelations 17:5-6, 9 describes Vatican (Rome) as;

"[5]And on her forehead a name was written:

MYSTERY, BABYLON THE GREAT,
THE MOTHER OF HARLOTS
AND OF THE ABOMINATIONS
OF THE EARTH.

[6]I saw the woman, drunk with the blood of the saints and with the blood of the martyrs of Jesus. And when I saw her, I marveled with great amazement."

How can we be so sure that this Babylon the Great is the Vatican? "[9]Here is the mind which has wisdom: The seven heads are seven mountains on which the woman sits."

The seven hills or mountains by which the Vatican City sits are; Palatine, Capitoline, Esquiline, Aventine, Caelian, Quirinal, and Viminal. Geographically, Rome sits on top of these seven hills. Rome and

Vatican are used interchangeably. And the bastion of power of Rome is the Vatican City. Rome also pertains to papacy.

There is no other woman-church, great city-nation with great power and glory that is situated around seven hills than the Vatican.

This woman (Semiramis, Vatican, church) is perhaps the very reason why Nimrod was distinctively separated from his other brothers in their genealogy. He will be the new beginning of Lucifer's deceptions of humanity from the time of Noah. Lucifer was a great angel of God until the time that he rebelled against his Creator – God and wanted to replace Him and be worshipped by His creation. He later became Satan the Devil – the great deceiver.

No wonder why this woman-church proclaim Lucifer as their creator-god and the father of their counterfeit Christ (anit-Christ) as stated in there chant below;

"Flammas eius lúcifer matutínus invéniat: ille, inquam, lúcifer, qui nescit occásum. Christus Fílius tuus, qui, regréssus ab ínferis, humáno géneri serénus illúxit, et vivit et regnat in sæcula sæculórum."

Translation in Google;

"Let the early morning light find out its flames: he, I say, the morning star, who does not know the setting. Christ your son, who, returning from the underworld, has shone serenely upon the human race, he lives and reigns forever and ever."

This is a proclamation of Lucifer as their counterpart Christ.

To understand the hidden message of this (although it is not really so hidden but only the blind cannot see), one need to know that the Bible is a very mysterious book of instruction that uses codes or even parable to hide the meaning of the word of God to whom it is not intended to understand. So, is Lucifer – Satan – the Devil the great deceiver uses code to hide his deceptions also in a very subtle way?

Names have meaning. Most of the names in the Bible have hidden meaning like Immanuel – "God with us". It is a prophetic name for Yeshua (Jesus Christ). And Yeshua is called by many other names too. He is the Beginning and the End, the Redeemer, to name a few. Yeshua is our Creator because everything was created by Him and through Him and for Him as God the Father commanded Him to do. He created the angels called by other name as "stars" and "Sons of God". Created sons of God because Yeshua is God. They are already sons of God. Unlike human beings which need to be begotten to become sons of God. We shall be "begotten sons of God", Yeshua being the First among many. Yeshua is the Light. He created the stars (angels) which symbolizes light and therefore they are "sons of Light" and "sons of God". Different terminology, different words but have one and the same meaning.

Cherub Lucifer, Michael, and Gabriel are the great archangels of God. The name Lucifer means "Shining star of the dawn," or "Bringer of light," when he was first created by God. He was one of the perfect creations of God – a supreme masterpiece of God's creative power in Ezekiel 28: 15;

"¹⁵You were perfect in your ways from the day you were created, till iniquity was found in you."

Lucifer was the king of Tyre (Tyre is Vatican. Will be discussed in another chapter) mentioned in Ezekiel 28: 12-13;

"¹²..."You were the seal of perfection, full of wisdom and perfect in beauty. ¹³You were in Eden, the garden of God; every precious stone was your covering:..."

God send him to earth as its ruler. He was given a throne on earth that is why he said in Isaiah 14:13-14 (KJV);

"¹³For thou hast said in thine heart, I will ascend into heaven, I will exalt my throne above the stars (angels) of God: I will sit also upon the mount of the congregation, in the sides of the north: ¹⁴I will ascend above the heights of the clouds; I will be like the most High."

Lucifer allowed his thoughts to be occupied with iniquities of greed, vanity, envy, jealousy, lust, and self-centeredness that eventually developed resentment and a rebellious heart to his Creator God. He developed a perverted, distorted, warped, and twisted mind. He can never straighten them out, nor think rationally, honestly, and rightly.

Just as he deceives the world today to be like him. He became the "bringer of darkness" rather than the "bringer of light".

He wanted to replace God. He wanted to be God -to be worshipped and adorned just as he is worshipped and adorned (knowingly and unknowingly) today by the many religions of this world in many forms, colors, and names.

He attacked God in heaven, but he was defeated by the angels of God (the war in heaven) and was cast down back to earth as his prison house in Isaiah 14: 12 (KJV);

> "¹²How art thou fallen from heaven, O Lucifer, <u>son of the morning</u>! how art thou cut down to the ground, which didst weaken the nations!"

And so, darkness was and is on the face of the earth. Lucifer from being on the side of light to become the author of darkness, error, confusion, and evil. He became Satan the Devil who <u>deceives the whole world</u> in Revelation 12; 7-9;

> "⁷And war broke out in heaven: Michael and his angels fought with the dragon; and the dragon and his angels fought, ⁸but they did not prevail, nor was a place found for them in heaven any longer. ⁹So the great dragon was cast out, that serpent of old, called the Devil and Satan, who deceives the whole world; he was cast to the earth, and his angels were cast out with him."

Satan's throne today is in Vatican, that is why his minions is praying to him in that Latin chant of the Vatican. Although many Catholics will have a cognitive dissonance saying that Lucifer in the Latin words is in small letter or used as an adjective in denial that it can mean Satan the Devil to portray that it just mean "early morning light" or "the morning star" or just light (lucent, lucifer, luciferous in C19 "vaccine"). They willfully ignore the fact that those meaning given was personified in the words <u>he</u>, <u>who</u>, and <u>your</u> as underlined and in italic (lucifer in Latin) below;

> "Let the *early morning light* find out its flames:
> <u>he</u>, I say, *the morning star*, <u>who</u> does not know the setting.

Christ your son, who, returning from the underworld, has shone serenely upon the human race, he lives and reigns forever and ever."

It is clear here that this chant proclaimed that Christ is the son of the morning star/light (lucifer). Christ son of Lucifer (Satan). That is why there is a counterfeit Christianity today. We must remember that angels are "stars" too. They are sons of God. God is Light and therefore they are sons of Light also. Lucifer before he rebelled against God, he was one of the supreme angels of God. The "morning star" and "bringer of light" until iniquity was found in him that he became the angel of darkness and the god of this world to this day. Counterfeit of light.

Lucent means light. Luciferous is the "light-bringing, emitting light". And one of the many dangerous components in C19 "vaccine" is the enzyme called luciferase. This is used for bioluminescence by various organisms in nature like firefly. This enzyme is used in the "vaccine" to experiment in genetically modifying (mRNA technology) human beings into a glowing organism under the black light (purplish blue light). The luciferous hydrogel in the vaccinated will glow under this light to identify those who are not vaccinated.

Lucifer's mind became perverted and twisted to be the great deceiver and counterfeiter of God. He counterfeits every God's plan. God send His only begotten Son Jesus Christ, Satan also created his own version of Jesus Christ as his son whom the world worshipped and adorned today. The real Jesus will reign on earth forever and ever, Satan also claimed he will rule the earth forever and ever. God proclaimed His Sabbath day to be Saturday, Satan proclaimed his sabbath on Sunday and Friday in other religion. And to some, whatever day they want sabbath day to be (self-centeredness). It does not matter what God commanded them to do.

God wants people to "go forth and multiply and replenish the earth". Satan killed hundreds of millions through his schemes of wars, pandemics, abortion, and he attacked the family system instituted by God for this purpose. But his time is near, and he is doing a lot of things to deceive mankind to his ways.

God will establish His Kingdom (Millennial Kingdom of God –

the government of God) here on earth under one God and one King of kings (Yeshua). Satan is currently establishing or resetting the world into his bogus New World Order (NWO) ushered in by the "World Economic Forum" (WEF) under Satan's counterfeit "one world government" and "one world religion". The central command of Satan's government is in his throne in the Vatican and his one world religion is Catholicism through ecumenism. For those who know, their banner is "for the common good" (in Laudato si'). When you hear a person or a politician saying this, that means that he/she is one of them.

According to Wikipedia, "Laudato si' is the second encyclical of pope (current 2021). The encyclical has the subtitle "on care for our common home". In it, the pope critiques consumerism and irresponsible development, laments environmental degradation and global warming, and calls all people of the world to take "swift and unified global action."" (exactly what WEF is doing)

This encyclical was signed on May, 2015 calling for the re-education of the world through their "Global Compact on Education" beginning with the global leaders both religious and political. The theme of this conference in Rome is "Reinventing the Global Compact on Education". It was to take place on May, 2020. But it seems that the global leaders are ignoring his call, so he made the plandemic on full swing giving control of the world leaders through drastic commands echoed by UN and WHO. What a best way to unify the world than to create a global crisis (either financial or health).

And according to the Secretary-General of the UN (his name is not worth mentioning in this book), "This is, above all, a human crisis that calls for solidarity." There you go, from their very mouth. Their response to a disease (a virus or whatever) is to call for global unity or solidarity under their control.

Seeing the pattern already? It seems they are very concerned for the greater good and not for the cure of the disease. For sure, every country knows a solution or two in their localize environment and can easily mitigate the situation immediately in a shortest possible time (they want it long term). But no! They are the only one who have the solution – the coming injections (as they planned). All other solutions (both natural and chemical) that has been proven to work for a long time was demonized and declared illegal like drugs. It was almost a crime to share a cure to the public, even medical doctors to their patients. Wonder, why? They (Vatican, UN, WHO, WEF) are the only one who have the solution (unified solution, solidarity). There is no other brain on earth capable of solving the problem than them.

See the mind control, mind manipulation? And majority of the people around the world, loved it. They have been primed for a long time for this particular event (201). The mass media, the social media, the medical industry, the entertainment industry, and the governments are their channels to program and control the mind of the people (to become the sheeple). And the people loved it, not knowing that the second phase of their plan is the imposition of their control through "climate change" where in the surface they care for the welfare of the people and of their "mother earth" but on the back of the pages is their sinister plan to kill as many people(sheeple) they call "useless eaters". Humanity have become a "thing"(transhuman after vaccination) for them at their disposal controlling from what they own ("you own nothing, and you will be happy", from WEF whose name is not worth mentioning in this book), to what they eat (real meat will be illegal, only manufactured meat/food), to what they think, and when it is time for them to go (turn off their life).

And so, the conference was moved to October, 2021 when most of the leaders of the world paid attention to Rome. It is at this very time that most of the leaders of the world have gone missing for a few days. Humored to be sick or dead like the president of the isles (his name is not worth mentioning in this book). And when they reemerged, they are different person that even their loved ones recognize. They become more vibrant, healthy, and younger looking but tyrannical to the core.

Satan (through his plandemic) is currently transforming humanity under his full control. Mind control through his deadly injections that created transhuman he can control through the implants that people willingly accepted without questions. They are called sheeple under their great reset.

This is the great counterfeit of Satan to God's plan in reeducating the people by turning back to Him through the preaching of the Gospel of Yeshua (Jesus Christ) which is the announcement of the coming Kingdom of God and His salvation. His Gospel will be preached around the world, but majority of humanity will choose the oppression of Satan rather than real peace, joy, happiness, and prosperity that the real God will bring upon the earth during the Millennial Kingdom. In fact, many people will even hate Christ when He comes back.

People tend to defend their religions even without knowing what their religion really is. They just want to get along with it. Even if it is too obvious that they are being lied to in front of their face. Or even not being lied but the intention and purpose is so obvious and so direct such as this chant of adoration of the Vatican to their god, Lucifer (Satan) the god and king of this world (for now) and the father of their christ. It is no wonder why Vatican continue to have child sacrifices and the center of sexual immorality such as pedophilia. The people of the world are so blinded that they cannot see. The darkness is in the eyes of the people because they refuse to seek the light. They love to be lied and deceived rather than seek the truth. "Lovers is blind that lovers cannot see". Even when the Light comes to this world, mankind will still hate the Light that He needs to pour out His wrath upon humanity to shake up the nations into submission to God, their Creator. Just as it is written in Isaiah 26:21;

> "²¹ For behold, the Lord comes out of His place to punish the inhabitants of the earth for their iniquity;..."

To those who are interested in digging deeper into this "woman-church" – the "Mystery Babylon the Great", the book of Charles Chiniquy – "50 Years in the Church of Rome", and "The Two Babylons" by Alexander Hislop are a great start to question what this church is all about.

God will be calling the peoples of the isles to be His end-time servants (Isaiah 49: 6) for the preparation of His way, and to serve Him in His coming Kingdom. These servants He will call His people, that in Revelation 18:4 He said;

> "⁴And I heard another voice from heaven saying, "Come out of her, my people, lest you share in her sins, and lest you receive of her plagues."

Revelation is for His end-time servants as stated in Chapter 1:1-2;

> "¹The Revelation of Jesus Christ, which God gave Him to show His servants—things which must shortly take place. And He sent and signified it by His angel to His servant John, ²who bore witness to the word of God, and to the testimony of Jesus Christ, to all things that he saw."

The peoples of the isles (the servants) should pay close attention to the fact that Revelation is the testimony of Jesus Christ for us. This is very important.

Now, let us go back to our discussion about Nimrod. We have seen the proof that Nimrod was a black man (Negro) and we infer that perhaps Cush, his father is also black. But we cannot say that all the line of Cush are blacks because from his son Raamah who begot Sheba and Dedan. Dedan as mentioned in Isaiah 21:13 was associated with the land of Arabia which has a fair skin complexion. Dedan must be where the Arab tribes came from. In fact, Dedan is considered to be one of the capitals of the oldest kingdoms of Arabia today.

But what about Canaan the son of Ham whom Noah cursed to be servants of both Shem and Japheth?

Canaan begot Sidon, his first born and Heth (Gen. 10:15). Sidon is where Jerusalem is located. Just as written in Ezekiel 16:3;

> "³...and say, 'Thus says the Lord God to Jerusalem: "Your birth and your nativity are from the land of Canaan; your father was an Amorite and your mother a Hittite....""

But when God give the land of Canaan as inheritance of Abraham (1 Chron. 16:18, Ps. 105:11), He removed Canaanites from the land in the times of Moses is Deutronomy 7: 1;

"'When the Lord your God brings you into the land which you go to possess, and has cast out many nations before you, the Hittites and the Girgashites and the Amorites and the Canaanites and the Perizzites and the Hivites and the Jebusites, seven nations greater and mightier than you,...'"

Could these seven nations, particularly the Canaanites are black people because some African people are claiming that they are the Israelites people. Their basis on this belief is that black people have a migration pattern from the land of Canaan to Africa. They cannot be Israelite according to the Bible, but the theory of migration from the land of Canaan to Africa might be true because God removed them from the land because it is promised by God to be an inheritance of Abraham which was fulfilled after the death of Moses in the time of Joshua.

Could the slavery of black people in Latin American countries and later in the United States of America be the fulfillment of the curse of Noah to Canaan because of the sin of his father Ham (Gen. 9:25-27)?

Latin America is composed of people from the line of Japheth and some from the line of Shem. Latin America has the oldest and longest of black slavery. While the US have slaves later and was driven mainly by the civil wars in Africa. African people at that time and even today wanted to move away from their miserable places due to continuous violence and civil unrest. Africa, like the isles seems to be cursed land because of our idolatry and evil ways that we were driven into slavery. And so, some entrepreneurial Africans begun to trade their own people as slaves. And because of the dire and dismal situation in Africa, people are willing to be traded to find a better future for themselves and their families. Perhaps paid the traders so that they will be traded as slaves. This is assumption is not far way off from just imagination because we can see it too in our present situation specially the issue of illegal immigrant in the USA today where those who want to cross the border are willing to pay large sum of money to the drug cartel to be transported across the US border. And who knows where else they are being sold after they crossed the border. Similar thing is happening in the war-torn regions of Europe and in the Middle East. Drug cartels have become a billion-dollar industry from their other business – of human trafficking. The good thing about their business model is that their commodity (people) is the one coming to them. And the customer (the deep state government - destination) is supporting them. Commodity and customer paid them both ways.

People were and are willing to be slaves in prosperous countries such as the USA and Europe just to escape the poverty, hopelessness, and violence from their own country. They are willing to pay the drug cartels thousands of dollars and some willingly become sex slaves just to cross the border. But even when they are already inside the US or other target destinations, they are not only slaves to whom they work for, but they are passive income as slaves to drug cartel who brought them inside. This is because their family left in their places of origin are threatened to be harmed by the cartels if they do not continue to pay their taxes or their debt to the cartel. But we should remember that the situation in their places of origin is designed and executed by the gangs of the cartels sponsored by their very own government to oppress their very own people.

So, the curse of Noah to Canaan most have been fulfilled in African people which became servants to Japheth (Latin America) and Shem (USA and the isles).

Back to the identity of the river Gihon which encompasseth the whole land of Cush (Gen.2:13), we can say that the ancient land of Cush is the whole islands of New Guinea with the Northern side being the modern-day territory of Indonesia and the Southern part of the island is Papua New Guinea today. This is because the whole islands inhabited by black people which must have originated from the lines of Ham which is the father of Cush who is black.

When God said in Isaiah 42:15 (KJV), 15 "… I will make the rivers islands,…", He probably made the river Gihon to become the islands of Java (from Javan the son of Japheth), Indonesia to the island of Papua. On the other hand, the river Pison become the islands of Palawan, Luzon, Taiwan, and up to the islands of Japan.

The amazing thing about solving the puzzle of the identity of the rivers Pison and Gihon is the black and white color. White for

Pison from the color of Bdelium which is giant white pearls in Palawan and pearl culture in Japan. Black for the river Gihon represented by the people of Papua – the land of Cush, the son of Ham. Could there be a black pearl in Papua?

The other two rivers, Hiddekel and Perat became the islands of the Philippines particularly beginning at the Archipelago de Sulo and the islands of Sulawesi of Indonesia.

The word Assyria in Genesis 2:14 might be a mistranslation or misrepresentation as with the translation of the river Perat into Euphrates River. This is because Assyria and Euphrates River are not located at "the ends of the earth" in the east and not islands. Besides, these rivers flowed southward instead of eastward.

This is the mystery of the identity of the four rivers mentioned in Genesis 2 which might give us the reason why the isles at the ends of the earth is important to God in this end-time and in the preparation of His coming Kingdom. For this is the place where humanity's rebirth (Gen. 10: 5) after God cut off mankind from the face of the earth through the great flood in the time of Noah (Gen. 6: 11) because of the sinfulness of man in Genesis 6: 5-7;

> "⁵Then the Lord saw that the wickedness of man was great in the earth, and that every intent of the thoughts of his heart was only evil continually. ⁶And the Lord was sorry that He had made man on the earth, and He was grieved in His heart. ⁷So the Lord said, "I will destroy man whom I have created from the face of the earth, both man and beast, creeping thing and birds of the air, for I am sorry that I have made them." ⁸But Noah found grace in the eyes of the Lord."

So, God saved Noah and his family and representative couple of every animal on earth. Noah symbolizes a re-birth of mankind. The regeneration of a new humanity.

The ark commanded by God to be built by Noah symbolizes an egg or a fetus for a new beginning. A re-birth is going to happen.

But giving birth never been easier since God cursed Eve in Genesis 3: 16;

"[16]To the woman He said: "I will greatly multiply your sorrow and your conception; in pain you shall bring forth children;...""

God became like a woman giving birth in this situation. He wanted to destroy the earth because of the sinfulness of man (Gen. 6: 5-8).

But because of Noah who is the only one on earth that believe in God, He is willing to give humanity another chance. But it does not come easy. It will be really like a pregnancy of a woman.

And this is what the Lord said in Isaiah 42: 14-15;

"[14]I have held My peace a long time, I have been still and restrained Myself. Now I will cry like a woman in labor, I will pant and gasp at once.[15]I will lay waste the mountains and hills, and dry up all their vegetation; I will make the rivers coastlands (isles), and I will dry up the pools."

If we internalize what the Lord is saying here, we can say that it is a very violent and painful process. Like a woman giving birth. There is this tearing and reaping apart. Panting and gasping and a water broke.

First, the water broke (the flood – from the fountains of the great deep and from the windows of heaven (Gen.7:11)) signaling that the giving birth is about to happen.

Then, there is tearing and ripping apart. Panting and gasping and a load cry from the great pain of laboring.

But his event is actually happening on the face of the earth during the flood in Genesis 7: 11-12;

"[11]...on that day all the fountains of the great deep were broken up, and the windows of heaven were opened. [12]And the rain was on the earth forty days and forty nights."

Perhaps, when God broke up the fountains of the great deep that the tearing and ripping apart (distortion) of the face of the earth happened that it is to this day's world map. This might be the event that happened in creating the present continents of the earth from a single piece of land surrounded by waters in Genesis 1: 9-10;

"[9]Then God said, "Let the waters under the heavens be gathered together into one place, and let the dry land appear";

and it was so. [10]And God called the <u>dry land</u> Earth, and the gathering together of the waters He called Seas. And God saw that it was good."

- A circular land as described in Isaiah 40:22;

"[22]It is He who sits above <u>the circle</u> of the earth,…"

- To seven continents and multiples of islands, seas, and oceans.

This is the new face of the earth in its rebirth like events as described in Isaiah 24:1;

"[1]Behold, the Lord makes the earth empty and makes it waste, <u>distorts its surface</u> and scatters abroad its inhabitants."

This is clearly what happened during and after the flood and after Noah's family have multiplied on the face of the earth and then scattered abroad later.

But God give emphasis on the four rivers that emanate from the River that water the garden of Eden in Isaiah 42: 15;

"[15] …I will make the rivers isles/islands/coastlands,…"

We already know that the garden is in the east and the main River flowed to the east to water the garden and it splits into four riverheads and flowed to the ends of the earth in the east (into the ocean). These are the only river system mentioned by God in the Bible prior to the flood in the time of Noah.

And God emphasizes that He is the Creator of the ends of the earth in Isaiah 40: 28;

"[28]Have you not known? Have you not heard? The everlasting God, the Lord, the <u>Creator of the ends of the earth</u>,…"

How do we know for sure that the ends of the earth mentioned here is the isles – Philippines?

Because God identifies them with the following clue in the verses of Isaiah 40;

1. The people at the ends of the earth are weak in verse 29;
   "[29] He gives power to the weak, and to those who have no might He increases strength."

We are weak, poor, and needy people, yet many are so proud and arrogant both rich and poor that we become easily deceived and followers of Satan's prison houses. We cannot make our own. We depend on others.

2. Majority of the Pilipino are waiting for the Lord Yeshua's coming in verse 31, even though people belong to many different religions (denominations) today;
    "³¹But those who wait on the Lord shall renew their strength;…"

3. We have the great Philippine eagle in verse 31;
    "³¹…They shall mount up with wings like eagles,…"

The ends of the earth in the west (California, USA) have their own great eagles too. But Americans are not weak people. They are strong wealthy nation, and they are not islands. We are followers of the USA. We do what they do because we are weak.

God emphasizes that He created the "ends of the earth". God turned the four rivers into islands just as the Philippine islands. He created and arranged the islands in a very special manner. It is beyond beautiful to express and behold. It is an abstracted human form of a woman. Perhaps, because she is the one who begot the new generation of mankind in a figurative sense in the times of Noah and in the dawn of the new era of humanity under the coming Kingdom of God.

The Philippines is the only nation in the map of the earth that is composed of many islands, yet beautifully landscaped and arranged. The arrangement of the islands is noticeably amazing to wonder and admire. Not to mention the beautiful flora and fauna and aquatic marine ecology – a beautiful wilderness. That is why God give emphasis that He specially created the "ends of the earth" because its beauty is beyond human words to express. And when we recognize God as the One who created all these things, we should be thankful and should utter praises and glory to our Creator-God for giving us the opportunity to live in His marvelous special creation and possession.

When God mention or emphasizes that He created it, then it must be special to Him. The same thing when He said in Isaiah 43 : 15;

"¹⁵I am the Lord, your Holy One, the <u>Creator of Israel</u>, your King."

It is from these islands that human civilization will flourish once again from the family of Noah as described in Genesis 10: 5 (KJV);

"⁵ By these were the isles of the Gentiles divided in their lands; every one after his tongue, after their families, in their nations."

It is from these islands also that the righteousness and the light of God will begin to shine in all the face of the earth that is in darkness as foretold in Isaiah 60: 1-2;

"¹Arise, shine; for your light has come!

And the glory of the Lord is risen upon you.

²For behold, the darkness shall cover the earth, and deep darkness the people; but the Lord will arise over you, and His glory will be seen upon you.

³The Gentiles shall come to your light, and kings to the brightness of your rising."

Early on, God called the family of Noah – Gentiles. All the people of the earth are Gentiles until He had chosen His people Israel from the line of Shem – Abraham, Isaac, and Jacob who became Israel and the father of the nations of Israel (composed of the twelve tribes of Israel).

The islands of the Philippines perfectly fit into the description of Genesis 10: 5. The Philippines is composed of more than 7,640 islands and hundreds of different languages. Each is distinct to each other. Our history accounted that the island nation is composed of many different kingdoms with their own leaders (kings, Datus, Chieftains, etc.) and have their own distinct people (tribes and colors). And from this tiny island nations came the various people of the world who build their own kingdoms and civilization in many other parts of the world. It is no wonder why the country has all the representation of the skin color of the world. From white people (anak araw) to black people (the Negros and Negritos) and yellow and red skin color in between. And from shorter to taller stature or from the dwarfs to the giants all can be found in the land of the isles.

Later on, the island nations became mostly of Shem's descendants. And Japheth's descendants became the inhabitants of the islands now known as Indonesian and Malaysian archipelago. For Japheth's dwellings is under the tents of Shem (Gen. 9: 27), and his descendants spreads (enlarge) throughout the world. From Indonesia to Malaysia, Thailand, Vietnam, Myanmar, Cambodia, Laos, Taiwan, Korea, China, Japan(Javan), Russia(Gomer and Magog) and some parts of South America (Latin America, e.g. Incas and Aztecs). For some descendants of Shem's also occupied part of South America particularly Brazil and the Amazon. This is because of the mark of Rio, Reu or Riau which is a descendant of Shem. Some of Shem's descendants also migrated to Mexico, the USA (native Americans), to Alaska (natives).

Reu is the son of Peleg, the son of Eber from the line of Shem. Reu is the father of Serug, the father of Nahor, the father of Terah, the father of Abraham (Gen.11: 10-26).

Indonesia maybe mixes of Shem's and Japheth's descendants because of the Reu's mark of Riau in the island of Sumatra and Riau Island in the Riau Archipelago in the northwestern Sarawak. Perhaps, Borneo is the former location of the garden of Eden because it looks like the four arrays of islands (archipelago) emanates from Borneo it seems. But we have no way of knowing for certain because it was distorted by God during the flood. But we can only make assumptions based on the clue that we have so far. Especially when we paste back together the islands of Borneo in front of Hanoi, Vietnam to Hong Kong. Taiwan in front of Qinhuangdao, China and Luzon, Philippines in the Yellow Sea between China and Korea. At this point, Borneo and the Philippines is directly east of Jerusalem when we put back the puzzles together.

Majority of the descendants of Ham remained in the land of Mesopotamia (the Land of Shinar) where they built the Tower of Babel and the beginning of the changes in their languages. They spread to Africa and in the Middle East regions.

The boundaries of such area such as the Mediterranean area, India, Pakistan, Afghanistan, and other nations in that area might be a mixture of the descendants of Ham and Japheth. This topic alone deserves a separate book of discussion.

So, the modern-day island-nation of the Philippines was the beginning of the rebirth of human civilization. It is no wonder why the isles at the ends of the earth is mentioned several times in the Bible as a prominent active trader and a trading hub of several important kingdoms such as Tyre and Sidon (Jer. 25: 22) of the Bible as the source of gold of King David and King Solomon to build the Temple of God in Jerusalem.

While the modern-day isles/islands nation of the Philippines is weak, sinful, and full of evil deeds just like the Chaldeans as described in the Bible, God will raise him up in the end times as the book of Habakkuk 1: 5-7, said;

"⁵Look among the nations and watch—be utterly astounded!

For I will work a work in your days which you would not believe, though it were told you.

⁶For indeed I am raising up the Chaldeans, a bitter and hasty nation which marches through the breadth of the earth, to possess dwelling places that are not theirs.

⁷They are terrible and dreadful; their judgment and their dignity proceed from themselves."

What a fitting description for us Pilipino people. We are everywhere in the face of the earth, even in the small islands of Faroe between Iceland and Scotland and Norway, we are there. Even in the poorest places of Africa, we are there. Indeed, our dwelling places are not ours because most OFW's just work in contracts that needs to be renewed every year or every two years. We enslaved ourselves in almost every corner of the world. Yet we are proud and arrogant people.

We are bitter people. We despise and become jealous to other people's success. We become a traitor to our fellow Pilipino specially abroad that one group of our countrymen are well known for its traitorous acts that are called "dugong aso (dog's blood)". We all know our evil traits of having a "crab mentality" that even in a professional workplace, feels like a silent war zone (cold war). One does not know when one will attack each other because the air is full of animosity. Constant fighting in the workplace is a common thing. There is no harmony. One always wants to prove or make an impression that he/she is better than another by getting closer to their bosses as their personal police called "sipsip (sucker)". Everybody is a critic. But they made themselves like a fool because of their selfish ambition and self-righteousness. Eventually, they will all fall.

We are a hasty nation. We always want to get an instant result. Many of us lacks patience, knowledge, and understanding of how life works. We all want to be instant millionaires so that we can be on vacation mode doing nothing. We want to have instant success that is why we do not develop anything that we can call our own compared to Japanese people. We are very far away in terms of innovation, patience, diligence, and industriousness. That is why we are left behind and no leader after Ferdinand Marcos have ruled the Pilipino people with a rod of iron because we lack and need discipline. That is why his administration have a slogan saying, "Sa ikauunlad ng bayan, disiplina ang kailangan".

We are so hasty that we become lazy people. We think only of short term and does not know how to look beyond the horizon. Do not get me wrong into thinking that am I better than anyone else in terms of the things I mentioned above. These are the things I observed and experienced to myself and from other people. That is why I struggled hard to change these things to be a reality in my life. And the best key to fight these evil things in our life is to humble ourselves and despise and throw away pride and arrogance. Because if we live and face the reality in our lives, there is a bigger chance that we can find a way to better up ourselves in due time. It is not instant. Just like there are Pilipino who have achieved extra ordinary success because they have overcome the evil attitude and characters inherent in our lives. They become successful in life and was able to build a legacy for their name and their family. We need to discipline ourselves or somebody else will discipline us.

Our judgement and dignity proceed from ourselves that we are described as terrible and dreadful people because of our self-righteousness. Indeed, our good judgement and dignity have departed from us.

Let us look at the sexual immorality of the young people and the young adult as an example. It has gone to the roof more than our western counterparts. The young adults and the working class were given the opportunity to have a job in the call center industry that give them a descent source of income. Yet, they turn it into an adulterous and immoral platform more horrendous than prostitution because it is free. Men and women both single and married splurge themselves to their adulterous and promiscuous sexual desire (lust) and have lost their family and dignity and eventuality their health and sanity.

As a result, the call center industry has brought more cases of sexually transmitted diseases (STD) such as HIV more than the prostitution industry. HIV- AIDS cases are at a very alarming rate. And that is not to mention yet the perverted homosexual people who allowed themselves to be instruments of Satan towards the destruction of family system which God have instituted and ordained.

Both young adults and adults of this generation have used technology toward the advancement of their sexual immorality. Instead of using technology to enhance and develop their economic and social well-being, they created a hook-up culture worse than the western sexually immoral culture. And from this hook-up culture, they become smokers in the beginning, then become alcoholics and then become drug addicts. Their self-centered judgement and dignity destroy their lives and devastate the lives of their loved ones and people around them.

O isles, where is your judgement? Where is your dignity? For God have subjected you into a debased mind because of your idolatry and immorality.

On the other hand, those who are wiser have used technology such as google, ecommerce platforms, and YouTube to improve their lives and the lives of others helping one another. Although, it is challenging and sometimes difficult what they are doing, they find their rewards in enjoying the things they love doing (helping others) plus the joy of receiving financial substance because of their painstaking struggle to create value from their own hands using their mental capacity that God have given them. At the end of the day, they are countering the rapid decent of humanity to oblivion by stiving to improve their life's situation and the lives of others on their way up.

Example of this is the YT vlogger Japer Sniper. His name is worth mentioning in this book than any politician of the country. He knows how to think to better up himself and his family. Although he created mistakes in the fast, he strives hard to correct and learn from his mistakes. In his way up, he accidentally pulled up other poor people like him to have a decent income through vlogging hoping that one day, they too will alleviate themselves from poverty. He was able to create communities that look up to him as their leader. He became the role model of the Bucana vloggers in Nasugbu, Batangas. This branch out to the Burias vloggers in Burias Island, Masbate. And now, he is building a community in Piñan, Zambuanga del Norte while building up his agricultural business venture.

His community have shown that there is still hope for us Pilipino people. This community is not only composed of vloggers but also of the subscribers/viewers. They are even more than a family because some subscribers not only just watch, but they support the vloggers financially. Some even finance vloggers to buy land, motorcycle, fishing boats, and even in building houses. Some even finance or sponsor vloggers who are doing charity works.

Imagine, ordinary people helping one another no other politicians have ever done. That is one of our very good spirit – the "Bayanihan" spirit. And if we unite in this spirit and humble ourselves before the God of the Bible, we can tremendously change our current situation and help change the world with our light in the darkness of this hour. And who knows, we shall build our kingdom by the spirit of "bayanihan".

However, there are group of individuals who exhibits the negative aspects of Pilipino culture. Some viewers or subscribers, who are unable to offer any assistance, make comments as though they have a personal connection with the vloggers and the situation (issue). These individuals aim to disrupt and divide the community through their harmful language. The verbal attacks from these keyboard warriors are so cutting that they penetrate the vlogger's soul. Their goal is to assert their power (power trip) and inflict emotional harm on the vloggers, with the ultimate objective of bringing them down. Most Pilipino love to power trip others.

Meanwhile, most of the politicians, the so called "leaders" of democracy have brought more misery to the already miserable people of the isles. They continue to enrich themselves to the extent of the people's well-being without a single remorse of their pride and arrogance. Dreadful and terrible people indeed. The day of reckoning for these people is near. The wrath of God will be upon them all according to what they have done to God's chosen people. Specially to those who intentionally betrayed the isles and sold their souls to the devil for their selfish prestige, power, and financial gain. Those who have served and are serving the deep state of the Vatican through their secret societies shall be persecuted to the full extent of God's Law.

We really need to judge and condemn ourselves so that we can free ourselves from this chain that hold back our potential. Bad habits are hard to break. So is developing a good habit, attitude, and character. But if we recognize it and decide to change our perspective in life, then we can deal with it fair and square.

But most of us will immediately get into a defensive (cognitive dissonance) mode and say, "no, we are good, and industrious people, intelligent, etc., etc." But the result speaks lauder than the words. Evidence defeats conversation all the time. So, we better man up and face our Achilles heel. It is better to change for the better than to remain the same forever. And to those people who have overcome these things already, congratulations and well done. May your light shine on others.

And if you are not yet convinced that we are the people being mentioned in the Bible, how about Jeremiah 4: 22 that said;

"²²"For **My people are foolish**, they have not known Me.

<u>They are silly children</u>, and they have no understanding.

They are wise to do evil, but to do good they have no knowledge.""

Are we not silly people? We laugh at anything and everything even in times of disaster. Big and small things we make fun. Almost everybody are jokers. That is our identity that no other country on earth has.

God is going to raise us up from the misery that we are in. But we need to show to God that we are willing to change. Change our characters, attitudes, and habits in life. Change from being proud and arrogant to a humble servant's heart.

There is a Japanese fisherman of Ayu fish or sweet fish who said, he does not eat Ayu fish that he caught because he threats it as a special offering for his friends and other people whom he knows. Ayu fish is hard to catch in its season. That is why, this fish is an expensive specialty fish in Japan. Cooking this fish needs special technique to experience its best flavor.

This Japanese fisherman have a very humble heart to think that his friends or neighbors is most worthy than himself to eat this very special fish. He is like their servant serving the best for his master that he himself think is not worthy of eating because it is too precious in value (intrinsic or not). And what does he expect in return? Nothing, but the joy of serving them with his work.

It can be challenging to overcome our innate selfishness and adopt a humble, selfless mindset characterized by a genuine concern for others. But if we come to think about it, the world today is full of pride, arrogance, and selfishness. And what have we become today?

The rapid deterioration of the world has made it a very dangerous place to live in, with no indication of improvement on the horizon and a feeling of hopelessness has taken over. Darkness has set in.

But God is going to call the people of the isles to be His servants. And His light will come to us so that we may show the light also to our brothers and sisters around the world – the light of hope in the coming Kingdom of God.

In return, God promised His protection in the times of the

darkest hours and tribulation and against our enemy. He will prosper us and give us peace that we may be ready to restore and revitalize the earth after its destruction from the tribulation period and from the wrath of God. That we maybe His servants in helping Him establish the coming Kingdom of God and serve Him in His government until all the kingdoms on earth are establish under Christ rulership as our King of kings and Lord of lords.

We are the Chaldeans, we are the isles, we are the "ends of the earth" in the east. We are the eagles. We are the gold. We are the rivers. We are the wilderness.

We are Shemites in the land of Ophir, the end-time servants of our Creator God – the Father Almighty and of our Lord Jesus Christ.

The Chaldean Connection

Who are the Chaldeans? Why is it mentioned many times in the Bible? What is its importance?

People who have heard about the Chaldeans or the Ur of the Chaldeans often thought of it as people from Southern Mesopotamia in the ancient times. Some think they are Babylonians because they lived and thrived in Babylon. But they are different race of people who went to Babylon. Babylon at that time is a race hub. People of many races have come and visited Babylon at that time. Perhaps because of what have been written that Mesopotamia is the cradle of civilization. The only reason Chaldean became well known in the Middle East region is that they became many in Babylon and they became great warriors. They are also known as wisemen, magician, astrologers, sorcerers, etc.

Historians called Babylon in modern times as Iraq. Many Iraqis associate or called themselves Chaldeans. But some of them despised being called or associated with Chaldeans because of its bad history. Another reason is that Chaldeans have no ancient historical record that they really are originally coming from Babylon. No written history has mentioned Chaldean in any cuneiform or archeological findings attesting them as originally from Babylon. They reasoned that like many other races who come to Babylon, they have no record of their historical origin. The first mention of the Chaldeans in the historical account was when they are first found in the shore of Southern Mesopotamia. They just pop out from nowhere.

Why?

Because God brought the Chaldeans to Babylon as stated in Isaiah 43:14 (NKJV);

"14 "Thus says the Lord, your Redeemer, the Holy One of Israel: "For your sake I will send to Babylon, and bring them all down as fugitives—The Chaldeans, who rejoice in their ships.""

Notice very carefully here that the Lord send the Chaldeans to Babylon through their ships. They are not originally from the Mesopotamian region. They came from somewhere else through the sea using their ships.

Some people argue that Chaldeans came from Northern Mesopotamia and not from the South because Abraham mentioned to find a wife for his son Isaac (Gen. 24: 10) in his country Nahor. Nahor is in Northern Mesopotamia and so is Haran, the city or town where Abraham and his family stayed for awhile and where his father Terah died.

But how can God say that the Chaldeans "rejoice in their ships" (v. 14) if their origin is in the north? There is no sea in Northern Mesopotamia. It is all arid land, or some portions are part of the fertile crescent. Maybe it should be that Chaldeans "rejoiced in their boats" instead of ships because they might be near the Euphrates or Tigris River. Rivers are mostly shallow body of water and ship is not fitting for the place because of variable depths unless they excavated it like Mississippi River for ships to pass. Besides, the Bible told us in Acts 7: 2 that God called Abram in Mesopotamia before they dwelt in Haran which in Northern Mesopotamia. And from their when Abram was 75 years old that he moves to the land of Canaan that God has promised him (Gen. 12: 1-4).

God clearly said in verse 14 that the Chaldeans rejoiced in their ships. This indicates the Chaldeans live near the sea or coastlands/isles to have ships. We can also infer that they are good mariners because they loved their ships. That is why they are also well known to be very good astronomers because they use celestial bodies (stars) for navigation. They loved what they are doing. They loved the sea and not an arid wilderness.

Therefore, we can say that the account that the Ur of the Chaldeans originated in the marshland at the northern tip of Persian Gulf where the first written historical account or evidence that they were first found might be true. For they can have ships in the Persian Gulf. Plus, Chaldeans are very good navigators for they are well known to be very good astronomers. They can navigate via the sky using the stars as their guide both land and sea. If they are using the Tigris and Euphrates Rivers (assuming the rivers are navigable by big ships) for their ships, they do not need to use stars to navigate the rivers because it is a well-defined route.

But if they are native to the region (area), and their occupation is mariners, therefore they might be using the ships for either trading or fishing. And trading and fishing is a very important part of any human civilization to be left out in any historical account.

There was no historical account of such things that have existed because they are not from that region. They just arrived there suddenly according to historical accounts. Why? Because God brought them to that region through the oceans and mighty seas as stated in Isaiah 43: 16;

"16 "Thus says the Lord, who makes a way in the sea and a path through the mighty waters,..."""

We might think that verse 16 pertains to Israelites crossing the Red Sea from Egypt because verse 17 mentioned about the chariots and horses which might also be right and have dual meaning. But we need to consider that this chapter of Isaiah talked about the Israelites as well as the Chaldeans who love their ships. And when Israelites cross the Red Sea, they do not have ships but hey were chased by Egyptian army who are buried under the sea. Also, verse 17 when applied to the Chaldeans will testify to the size of the ships they have because it can contain army and horses which can also indicate that they are not just navigating within Tigris and Euphrates Rivers.

Note also that verse 16 mentioned two types of bodies of waters where God made a way and a path – the sea and the mighty waters. Mighty waters here pertain to large expanse of body of water or sea which we can equate in our modern times as the ocean. Perhaps the journey started from the isles in the east passing through the now called China Sea, then Andaman Sea, into the mighty waters of Indian Ocean, then to the Arabian Sea and finally into the Persian Gulf.

The path and way in the sea and in the ocean mentioned in verse 16 is clearly not for Israelites but provided by God to the Chaldeans when He brought them to Mesopotamia/Babylon through their ships.

Like Abraham whom God have taken from the Ur of the Chaldeans (Gen. 15: 7), Chaldeans must have come from the same place also because they named after their place of origin.

But where is the Ur of the Chaldeans if they are not originally from northern or southern Mesopotamia. We are sure that they are not originally from Babylon because God brought them to Babylon through the way of the sea and a path in the mighty waters (ocean) (Isa. 43: 16). They are surely were mariners because "they rejoiced in their ships" (v. 14).

Does the Bible give us clue as to the direction or the location of the Ur of the Chaldeans? Where are the sea and ocean whom the ships of the Chaldeans passed by going to Babylon?

Indeed, God give us a clue in Isaiah 41.

Isaiah Chapter 41 opening is about God talking to the coastlands (in NKJV) or Islands or Isles (in KJV) to "listen up!". I will be using NKJV translation with side comments as to other names in KJV translation.

> "¹"Keep silence before Me, O coastlands (isles, islands), and let the people renew their strength! Let them come near, then let them speak; Let us come near together for judgment.
> ²"Who raised up one from the east? Who in righteousness called him to His feet?

Who gave the nations before him, and made him rule over kings? Who gave them as the dust to his sword, as driven stubble to his bow?""

God's voice must have sounded a little angry to the coastland/isles (past and present) trying to remind them that He is the God who created them (created the ends of the earth (Isa. 40: 28) and verse on created the rivers into isles(Isa. 42: 15)) and pointing out the one person, whom He raised up from the east. The isles (coastlands) must have known very well this person to be reminded of such personality because this person once was among them?

But who is this one God is talking about?

There is no other man God called in righteousness and promised the nations before him and made ruler over kings than Abram (who later became Abraham).

First, Abram was called by God in righteousness among evil and idolatrous people of his land in Joshus 24:2-3;

> "² "And Joshua said to all the people, "Thus says the Lord God of Israel: 'Your fathers, including Terah, the father of Abraham and the father of Nahor, dwelt on the other side of the River in old times; and they served other gods. ³Then I took your father Abraham from the other side of the River, led him throughout all the land of Canaan, and multiplied his descendants and gave him Isaac.'""

God "raised up and called" Abraham in righteousness among idolatrous people of the Ur of the Chaldeans. Even his father Terah served other gods.

God took Abraham from the other side of the River. This other side of the River is also the place where the Ur of the Chaldeans is. The River (note capital letter) mentioned here cannot be Euphrates or Tigris or Nile for two reasons;

One, God took Abram from the Ur of the Chaldeans in Genesis 15:7;

> "⁷"Then He said to him, "I am the Lord, who brought you out of

<u>Ur of the Chaldeans</u>, to give you this land (Canaan) to inherit it.'""

This is similar to Joshua 24:3;

"³ "Then <u>I took your father Abraham from the other side of the River</u>, led him throughout all the land of Canaan,...'""

Two, the Ur of the Chaldeans is not originally in Babylon because God brought the Chaldeans from the Ur of the Chaldeans to Babylon by the way of the sea and a path through mighty waters (Oceans). Could this way also he way by which the family of Noah travelled from the east to the west in the land of Shinar which is Mesopotamia?

It might be that this way of the sea and path of mighty water is the former River itself and "the other side of the River" is where the Ur of the Chaldean is, which we have clue that is located in the east where God raised Abraham. Could the name of this River be Pishon, the first river that went out of Eden to water the Garden of Eden planted by God in the east in Genesis 2:8, 10-14?;

"⁸ "And the LORD God planted a garden eastward in Eden; and there he put the man whom he had formed."

"¹⁰And a river went out of Eden to water the garden; and from thence it was parted, and became into four heads. ¹¹The name of the first is Pison: that is it which compasseth the whole land of Havilah, where there is gold; ¹²And the gold of that land is good: there is bdellium and the onyx stone."

We really do not know yet what exactly is the name of the main River mentioned in Joshua 24. For sure God will reveal to us one day. Pison is one of the four branches of the main River, so it could or could not be the name of the main River. The only difference is that it described precious stones that can be found in the land which the river passes through. Nothing was mentioned on the other three except their coded location and its name. Gold, bdellium (pearl), and onyx stone can be all found in the Philippines. But most importantly, only the Philippines have the mother of pearls or bdellium.

We should notice also how the verses of the other three rivers were mistranslated to fit the narrative that the garden of Eden is located in Mesopotamia, the so-called cradle of civilization.

> "[13] "And the name of the second river is Gihon: the same is it that compasseth the whole land of Ethiopia (Cush). [14]And the name of the third river is Hiddekel (Tigris): that is it which goeth toward the east of Assyria (Ashur). And the fourth river is Euphrates."''

The translators willfully translate the original into their humanly knowledge of the facts. The fourth river is not Euphrates but Perat (Phirath). Hiddekel is not Tigris, and it does not run to the east of Assyria but to the east of Ashur. The river Gihon does not circumnavigate around the land of Ethiopia but the land of Cush. Even if we accept that these mistranslations are correct it does not make sense geographically. The rivers flowed to the ends of the earth in the east and into the sea and not in the Middle East.

On the other hand, given that the translation of the names of the rivers and places are correct, could Noah (after the flood) have named the rivers Tigris and Euphrates in the Land of Shinar, known as Mesopotamia, and now known location is in the Middle East particularly Iran and Iraq?

We must consider that Noah boarded the Ark when he was already 600 years old. He must have known and have been to a lot of places and have been and have known the names of the main River and four rivers after the Garden. And after the flood when his family multiplied and journeyed to the land of Shinar as mentioned in Genesis 11: 1 (from east to west), he named the two big rivers that they found there as Tigris and Euphrates from the previous names of the two rivers in the east before the flood.

The four rivers in the east that branched out from the River after watering the garden of Eden no longer exist because God said in Isaiah 42:15;

> "[15] "... and I will make the rivers islands, ...""'

God change the four rivers into isles/islands in the east when He distorted the face of the earth (Isa. 24: 1) during the flood. He changed the earth from one single dry land (Gen. 1: 10) into many dry lands (islands and continents).

We will discuss this further in another chapter. But let us go back to the second reason why the "one" mentioned by God in Isaiah 41:2 is Abram.

Second, God reiterated his covenant with Abraham in Isaiah 41:2 from Genesis 17:4-6;

> "⁴As for Me, behold, My covenant is with you, and you shall be a father of many nations. ⁵No longer shall your name be called Abram, but your name shall be Abraham; for I have made you a father of many nations. ⁶I will make you exceedingly fruitful; and I will make nations of you, and kings shall come from you."

Also in Genesis 12: 2, God said to Abraham;

> "²"I will make you a great nation; I will bless you and make your name great; and you shall be a blessing.""

The fourth to sixth lines (or sentence) of verse 2 of Isaiah 41 reiterates God's protection and guidance to Abraham in defeating his enemies directly or indirectly (his descendants).

One example of this is when Abraham rescue Lot from his captors in Genesis 14 with only 318 trained servants against four kings under the command of Chedorlaomer.

The group of Chedorlaomer defeated the group of five kings of Sodom in verse 8-9;

> "⁸And the king of Sodom, the king of Gomorrah, the king of Admah, the king of Zeboiim, and the king of Bela (that is, Zoar) went out and joined together in battle in the Valley of Siddim ⁹against Chedorlaomer king of Elam, Tidal king of nations, Amraphel king of Shinar, and Arioch king of Ellasar— four kings against five."

When the group of Chedorlaomer defeated Sodom, Lot was captured for he dwells near Sodom when he separated from Abraham.

And when Abraham defeated the group of Chedorlaomer, he was able to rescue Lot and brought back all the goods and the people and give it back to the king of Sodom after he gave tithes of all to Melchizedek King of Salem who blessed him in Genesis 14:19-20;

"¹⁹"…Blessed be Abram of God Most High, possessor of heaven and earth; ²⁰And blessed be God Most High, who has delivered your enemies into your hand.""""

Verse 19 and 20 clearly identified who is the "one" that God have <u>raised from the east</u> whom He delivered his enemies into his hands in the fourth sentence of Isaiah 41:2.

We know that God's promise to Abraham is not only personal but will have an effect from generation to generations of his descendants, from the likes of Joshua to King David until the tribes of Israel was separated and lost.

Now, let us continue Isaiah 41:3-4;

"³"Who pursued them, and passed safely by the way that he had not gone with his feet?""""

Now God is telling the people of the isles that He is the One who saved Israelites fleeing from the Egyptian army chasing them by opening a way in the Red Sea. A way that no man has ever pass before because it is the sea floor of the Red Sea. We know that Israel comes from the lines of Abraham, Isaac and Jacob who later become Israel.

"⁴ "Who has performed and done it, calling the generations from the beginning?

'I, the Lord, am the first; and with the last I am He.""""

God has proclaimed to the people of the isles that He is the God who performed all those things and have chosen the Israelites people to be His servants and have declared their generations beginning from Abraham.

"⁸ "But you, Israel, are My servant, Jacob whom I have chosen, The descendants of <u>Abraham My friend</u>.

⁹You whom <u>I have taken from the ends of the earth</u>,…""""

Now, God is saying in verse 9 that He had taken His friend Abraham <u>from the ends of the earth</u>. The "you" here have dual meaning. First, it may pertain to Abraham as a directional code from where God took Abraham from (similar to "I took you from the Ur of the Chaldeans (Gen. 15: 7)) and the "ends of the earth" is in the east for God raised Abraham in the east in verse 2. The second meaning may pertain to the future taking back of Israelites to their lands from the ends of the earth after the tribulation period.

We now know that God;

- Raised Abraham from the east (Isaiah 41: 20),
- Brought out Abraham from the Ur of the Chaldeans (Genesis 15: 7),
- Took Abraham from the ends of the earth (Isaiah 41: 9),
- Took Abraham from the other side of the River (Joshua 24: 3).

The other side of the River here means the "ends of the earth" because Psalms 72: 8 and Zechariah 9: 10 said,

"[8]"He shall have dominion also from sea to sea, and <u>from the River to the ends of the earth</u>.""

"[10] ... 'He shall speak peace to the nations; His dominion shall be 'from sea to sea, and <u>from the River to the ends of the earth</u>.'"

The River mentioned here is the pre-flood river that water the Garden of Eden in the east towards the ends of the earth in the east when the earth is just one piece of dry land (Genesis 1:9-10). With the above verses, we can say that "the other side of the River" in Joshua 24 means the other end of the River at the "ends of the earth" in the east. This can also mean the directional flow of the River from the west to the east.

Did God take Abraham from three different locations at different moments in time? Or are the places mentioned above where God took Abraham from, are one and the same? Perhaps these are one place hidden as codes and symbols to hide the true location of the Ur of the Chaldeans until His appointed time to reveal His purpose.

Definitely, Isaiah 41 reveal to us that the Ur of the Chaldeans is in the east because God raised Abraham from the east. Abraham is a Chaldean because he came from the Ur of the Chaldeans. Some argue that Abraham is not a Chaldean because the Bible did not directly mention that he is a Chaldean. It is just a philosophical argument. It does not mean that you are not called by the name of the people from which you came from, that you do not belong to that people. Besides, Genesis 11:28 tell us that the Ur of the Chaldeans is the native land of his younger brother Haran. If the younger brother considers the Ur of the Chaldean his native land, how much more the older sibling as stated in Genesis 11:27-28;

> "²⁷ This is the genealogy of Terah: Terah begot Abram, Nahor, and Haran. Haran begot Lot. ²⁸And Haran died before his father Terah in <u>his native land, in Ur of the Chaldeans</u>."

God raised Abraham in righteousness from the beginning in the east, in the land of the Chaldeans (where people worship other gods (Joshua 24: 2), an idolatrous nation) which is at the ends of the earth. These are coded words which means that the Ur of the Chaldeans where Abraham came from is located in the ends of the earth, in the east.

Now, the question is why God is telling this to the people of the isles (coastlands/islands in other translation)?

Because the isles recognize God and feared Him in verse 5;

> "⁵The <u>isles</u> (coastlands) saw it and feared, the <u>ends of the earth</u> were afraid; they drew near and came."

Did the isles know God beforehand, yet chose to serve other gods too, like the people of the Ur of the Chaldeans where Abraham came from? Are they hardheaded and disobedient people too like Israelites that even God is in front (in the presence) of them and directly talking to them through Moses in Mt. Sinai and yet choses to build a golden calf and wordship it? That is how foolish we are as human beings. We look for proof, but even if the proof is in front of us, still we chose not to believe the truth (cognitive dissonance).

But wait! Verse 5 also tells us that the isles is also the ends of the earth where God took Abraham from!

The Bible is full of coded identity (or words) mentioned in two different words, names, or location, yet have one meaning. Examples of these is the name Israel repeated as Jacob in Isaiah 43:1;

> "¹But now, thus says the Lord, who created you, O <u>Jacob</u>, and He who formed you, O <u>Israel</u>: "Fear not, for I have redeemed

you; I have called you by your name; You are Mine.'""

Similarly, in Isaiah 43:22;

"²²"But you have not called upon Me, O <u>Jacob</u>; and you have been weary of Me, O <u>Israel</u>...."

And in Isaiah 46:3;

"³ "Listen to Me, O <u>house of Jacob</u>, and all the remnant of the <u>house of Israel</u>,..."""

Isaiah 48:12;

"¹² "Listen to Me, O <u>Jacob</u>, and <u>Israel</u>, My called:..."""

And in Isaiah 49:6;

"⁶"...To raise up the tribes of <u>Jacob</u>, and to restore the preserved ones of <u>Israel</u>;..."""

We know that Jacob is Israel for God change his name in Genesis 35:10;

"¹⁰And God said to him, "Your name is <u>Jacob</u>; your name shall not be called Jacob anymore, but <u>Israel shall be your name</u>." So He called his name Israel.'""

There are many more of these coded words all throughout the Bible that mentioned two different words but with one symbolic meaning. Psalms and Proverbs are an example.

We can look at also the word Jerusalem and how God called it another name such as in Isaiah 4: 4;

"⁴"When the Lord has washed away the filth of the <u>daughters of Zion</u>, and purged the blood of <u>Jerusalem</u> from her midst, by the spirit of judgment and by the spirit of burning,..."""

The same pattern can also be observed in Isaiah 10: 32;

"³²"...He will shake his fist at the mount of the <u>daughter of Zion</u>, the hill of <u>Jerusalem</u>.'""

There are many instances that the same pattern was repeated several times in the book of Isaiah just as the daughter of Zion which means Jerusalem.

The prophecy of the coming King (the Messiah) was foretold in Zechariah 9: 9 which is known as the Triumphal Entry in the New Testament mentioned in John 12:15;

"⁹"Rejoice greatly, O daughter of Zion! Shout, O daughter of Jerusalem!
Behold, your King is coming to you; He is just and having salvation, lowly and riding on a donkey, a colt, the foal of a donkey.""

Fulfilled by Jesus Christ in John 12: 14-16;

"¹⁴Then Jesus, when He had found a young donkey, sat on it; as it is written: ¹⁵"Fear not, daughter of Zion; behold, your King is coming, sitting on a donkey's colt."
¹⁶His disciples did not understand these things at first; but when Jesus was glorified, then they remembered that these things were written about Him and that they had done these things to Him."

In these verses, Jerusalem was coded as the "daughter of Zion". Yet in Zechariah 9: 9, both "daughter of Zion" and Jerusalem was mentioned.

Verse 15 of John 12 is also future comforting of the Lord to His City - Jerusalem. Something is going to happen in Jerusalem that causes fear. But God give them assurance in that time that their King is coming to save them. The Jews do not need comforting at that time because they are full of pride and arrogance. In John 1:11 said, "He came to His own and His own did not received Him."

God appointed the ends of the earth/isles to remind Jerusalem of His comforting promise that God will save them during this troublesome time (Jacob's Trouble) as mentioned in Isaiah 62:11;

"¹¹Indeed the Lord has proclaimed to the end of the world:
"Say to the daughter of Zion, 'Surely your salvation is coming; behold, His reward is with Him, and His work before Him.' ""

This verse clearly is saying that the Lord Jesus Christ (Yeshua) have special job for the people of the "ends of the earth". That is why He is talking to the people of the isles reminding them that He is God and the Creator of the Israelite people (Isaiah 43:15, 21) through His friend, Abraham;

> "[15]"I am the Lord, your Holy One, <u>the Creator of Israel</u>, your King." [21]"This people I have formed for Myself; <u>they shall declare My praise</u>.""

Similarly, God also reminded the people of the isles that He is the Creator of the ends of the earth in Isaiah 40: 28;

> "[28]"Have you not known? Have you not heard? The everlasting God, the Lord, <u>the Creator of the ends of the earth</u>,…""

Why would God give special mention that He created the ends of the earth like Israel?

This must be the reason why the isles or the coastlands have some kind of special arrangements. It has unique beautiful design among many nations in the map of the earth. It is the only nation on earth that was artistically arranged or constructed.

Using the poetic style of the Bible, mentioning two different symbols or phrases, yet one meaning as shown in the previous verses as an example, we can say that the isles/coastlands mentioned in Isaiah 41:5 and the ends of the earth are one and the same.

Here are other examples how God mentioned the isles and ends of the earth at the same verse or within a chapter;

> "[10]"Sing to the Lord a new song, and His praise from <u>the ends of the earth</u>, You who go down to the sea, and all that is in it, <u>You isles/coastlands</u> and you inhabitants of them!"" - Isaiah 42:10

And if we go a little farther to verse 11, God give us a clue to the color of the skin of the inhabitants of the isles/coastlands/ends of the earth;

> "[11]Let the <u>wilderness</u> and its cities lift up their voice, the villages that <u>Kedar</u> inhabits."

Kedar are brown or dark colored people (Song 1: 5-6) and so are the people of the isles. Kedar symbolizes as a representative of eastern culture in the Middle East. And here is a great revelation of the mystery of the people of the isles and Kedar connection. First, God proclaimed in Isaiah 40: 28 that He created the ends of the earth;

> "²⁸ The everlasting God, <u>the Lord</u>, the <u>Creator of the ends of the earth</u>,…"

And then, He said in Isaiah 50: 2;

> "²…I make the <u>rivers a wilderness</u>;…"

And finally, He said in Isaiah 42: 15;

> "¹⁵…I will make the <u>rivers isles/coastlands</u>,…"

As we know it, the rivers here pertain to the four rivers that came from the main River that water the garden of Eden in the east at the ends of the earth. Eventually, all rivers flow to the sea or ocean (Ecc. 1:7). In this case the sea or ocean in the ends of the earth in the east is now called the Pacific Ocean. And God turned these four rivers into wilderness islands (isles/coastlands- after the flood, Isaiah 24:1) - the Islands Philippines – the land of Ophir.

Here is another verse showing the connection of the isles and of the ends of the earth as written in Isaiah 24: 15-16;

> "¹⁵ Therefore glorify the Lord in the <u>dawning light</u> (east), the name of the Lord God of Israel in <u>the isles/coastlands</u> of the sea. ¹⁶From the <u>ends of the earth</u> we have heard songs: "Glory to the righteous!""

These verses, testify or confirm the location of the isles/coastlands at the ends of the earth in the east (dawning light-sunrise-silangan).

The east location of the isles/coastlands is further magnified by Isaiah 59: 18-19;

> "¹⁸…The <u>coastlands</u> He will fully repay.
> ¹⁹So shall <u>they fear the name of the Lord</u> from the west, and <u>His glory from the rising of the sun</u>; when <u>the enemy comes in like a flood</u>, the Spirit of the Lord will lift up a standard against him."

These verses clearly tell us that the isles/coastlands is in the east because they fear the name of the Lord from the west (from Jerusalem). And the glory of the Lord will come from the rising of the sun (east, silangan). The glory of the Lord will come from the east.

Furthermore, the last two sentences of verse 19 pertains to the attack of the beast to the isles/coastlands after the beast attacked the Holy Land in Daniel 11:16 and 18;

"[16]But he who comes against him shall do according to his own will, and no one shall stand against him. He shall stand in the Glorious Land with destruction in his power.

[18]After this he shall turn his face to the isles/coastlands and shall take many. But a ruler shall bring the reproach against them to an end;..."

That is why the isles shall prepare a great army to defend our kingdom from the enemy before and after this event.

Then after the beast have been defeated on his war with the saints (the righteous Isa. 24: 16) in the isles/coastlands, he shall return to his place and having hated the harlot (the woman, the Mystery Babylon the Great, the Vatican) he shall destroy it. This event is described in Revelation 17:14-18, similar to what has been foretold in Daniel 11 verses;

"[14]These (meaning the beast and the ten horns) will make war with the Lamb, and the Lamb will overcome them, for He is Lord of lords and King of kings; and those who are with Him are called, chosen, and faithful.

[15]Then he said to me, "The waters which you saw, where the harlot sits, are peoples, multitudes, nations, and tongues.[16]And the ten horns which you saw on the beast, these will hate the harlot, make her desolate and naked, eat her flesh and burn her with fire. [17]For God has put it into their hearts to fulfill His purpose, to be of one mind, and to give their kingdom to the beast, until the words of God are fulfilled. [18]And the woman whom you saw is that great city which reigns over the kings of the earth.""

The woman is the Catholic Church and also the great city of Vatican that reigns all the nations on earth today.

Now that we have seen the connection of the ends of the earth with the isles/coastlands in the east, let us look further evidence that can really zero-in the identity of this symbols/codes.

But first, let us review what was revealed to us.

We know that God took Abram/Abraham from the Ur of the Chaldeans (Gen. 15: 7), from the other side of the River (Josh. 24: 3), and from the ends of the earth (Isa. 41: 9). We also know that these symbolic places are one and the same, for how can God took a man in three different places at the same time. And why? But we know that the River runs to the ends of the earth or in other words to the other side of the River which is at the ends of the earth where God raised Abram in the east according to Isaiah 41:2.

We also know that Chaldeans are not originally from anywhere in Mesopotamian region because God brought them as fugitives to Babylon (Isa. 43:14) by means of a way in the sea and a path through the mighty waters (oceans) (Isa. 43:16). Besides, Chaldeans rejoice in their ships (Isa. 43:14) which may also mean that they are seafarers that love their ships.

We should note that the verse mentioned ships and not boats which means large sea vessels perhaps for long travel and cargo shipping which makes sense because Chaldeans are well known to be very good in astronomy for navigation. With this skill set, they will be able to travel both in land and in large bodies of water without a problem because they use the stars in heaven as their navigational guide (ancient GPS).

We also know that the ends of the earth in the east is also the isles, islands or coastlands in the east because of the poetic style of the Book of Isaiah mentioning two different words but have one and the same meaning. For example, Jacob and Israel in Isaiah43:1;

"¹ But now, thus says the Lord, who created you, O Jacob, and He who formed you, O Israel:..."

We know that Jacob is Israel and Israel is Jacob because God change the name of Jacob to Israel. They are one and the same.

Another verse for Jacob and Israel is in Isaiah 44: 21;

"²¹"Remember these, O Jacob, and Israel, for you are My servant; I have formed you, you are My servant; O Israel, you will not be forgotten by Me!'"''

And in Isaiah 48: 1;

"¹"Hear this, O house of <u>Jacob</u>, who are called by the name of <u>Israel</u>,…'"''

In these verses, God is telling us the root name or origin of the name Israel for which He created them for. Israel was created to be His servant. A helper for His supreme purpose for mankind.

As for the ends of the earth and isles/coastlands connection, we can see it in Isaiah 41:5;

"⁵ The <u>isles/coastlands</u> saw it and feared, the <u>ends of the earth</u> were afraid; they drew near and came."

We see in this verse that the "ends of the earth" and the "isles/coastland" are one people who responded positively to God's calling.

It is important to note and to put into consideration and deep meditation as to why God mentioned that He created the "ends of the earth" in Isaiah 40: 28 and mention that He is the Creator of Israel in Isaiah 43: 15. Of course we know that He is the Creator of everything. But why give emphasis to the "ends of the earth" and Israel?

Here are the verses once again:

Isaiah 40: 28 for the "ends of the earth";

"²⁸Have you not known? Have you not heard? The everlasting God, the Lord, <u>the Creator of the ends of the earth</u>,…"

And for Israel, Isaiah 43: 15;

"¹⁵"I am the Lord, your Holy One, the <u>Creator of Israel</u>, your King.'"''

Perhaps God emphasizes these things because He created Israel to be His servant, but they disobey Him. So, God is emphasizing to the "ends of the earth" which is also the isles/coastlands, that He is their Creator and also their God, and that He is calling the isles to be His end time servants in Isaiah 49:6;

"⁶ Indeed He says, 'It is too small a thing that <u>You should be My Servant</u> to raise up the tribes of Jacob, and to restore the preserved ones of Israel; I will also give You as a light to the Gentiles, that

You should be My salvation to the ends of the earth.' "

This is a very complicated verse of Isaiah 49 if we do not understand who is the one talking and to whom the speaker is talking to.

Isaiah 49 is addressed to the people of the isles/coastlands which is also known as the people from afar in verse 1;

"¹"Listen, O isles/coastlands, to Me, and take heed, you peoples from afar!""""

God is talking to the people of the isles through prophet Isaiah. Why is He talking to the people of the isles? Who is the one talking to the isles? Is it the Almighty Father or Yeshua (Jesus Christ)?

Yeshua is the one talking to the people of the isles through the prophet Isaiah. He is talking to the people of the isles in a manner that they will understand it, in the human sense possible. And yet the whole chapter of Isaiah 49 is very mysterious and puzzling to understand. It is multi-faceted in meaning.

But for now, let us try to understand how it concerned the peoples of the isles.

The Lord Yeshua talked to the people of the isles with great authority. He told the people of the isles to listen to Him very carefully, like how He talked to Israel and the isles in another chapter of Isaiah.

Verse one continued with;

"¹…The Lord has called Me from the womb; from the matrix of My mother He has made mention of My name."

What is His name?
Isaiah 7:14 identified His name as Immanuel;

"¹⁴Therefore the Lord Himself will give you a sign: Behold, the virgin shall conceive and bear a Son, and shall call His name Immanuel."

This prophecy during the time of Isaiah was fulfilled in Matthew 1: 21;

"²¹And she will bring forth a Son, and you shall call His name Jesus (Yeshua), for He will save His people from their sins."

Verses 22 and 23 confirmed that this is the prophecy in Isaiah 7:14;

> [22]"So all this was done that it might be fulfilled which was spoken by <u>the Lord through the prophet</u>, saying: [23]"Behold, the virgin shall be with child, and bear a Son, and they shall call His name Immanuel," which is translated, "God with us.""

From the mystery of His conception, the Almighty Father made Him into a Mighty God full of grace and glory in Isaiah 49:2;

> "[2]And He (the Father) has made My mouth like a sharp sword;..."

This is confirmed in revelation 1:16;

> "[16]He had in His right hand seven stars, out of His mouth went a sharp two-edged sword, and His countenance was like the sun shining in its strength."

We know that this is Yeshua (Jesus Christ) when He console John in verse 17 to 18;

> "[17]And when I saw Him, I fell at His feet as dead. But He laid His right hand on me, saying to me, "Do not be afraid; I am the First and the Last. [18]I am He who lives, and was dead, and behold, I am alive forevermore. Amen. And I have the keys of Hades and of Death.""

This is confirmed further by Jesus Himself when He said to the compromising church of Pergamos in Revelation 2:16;

> "[16]Repent, or else I will come to you quickly and will fight against them with the sword of My mouth."

And this is the might and power Yeshua who has the sword in His mouth in Revelation 19: 15 and 21;

> "[15]Now out of His mouth goes a sharp sword, that with it He should strike the nations. And He Himself will rule them with a rod of iron. [21]And the rest were killed with the sword which proceeded from the mouth of Him who sat on the horse."

Now we have proven beyond reasonable doubt that the one speaking through Isaiah 49 is Jesus Christ.

Jesus said to Isaiah in verse 3;

"³And He said to me, 'You are My servant, O Israel, in whom I will be glorified.'"

Isaiah expressed his disappointment with Jesus upon hearing this in verse 4. Yet as a lowly servant, he still submitted to his master. It is like the case of Jonah who was also disappointed to God when he was sent to warn Nineveh and save them. In Jonah's mind, the people of Nineveh are so sinful that they do not deserve forgiveness or salvation. They should die.

Jonah protested to God and went into the east side of the city of Nineveh fully exposed to the sun because he wanted to die. But God give him a plant to shade him and to relieve him from his misery (Jonah 4:6). Jonah was thankful and grateful for the plant. But God killed the plant the following morning and Jonah get angry again. This time for the plant. But God showed His kindness to Jonah in Chapter 4 verse 10 to 11;

"¹⁰But the Lord said, "You have had pity on the plant for which you have not labored, nor made it grow, which came up in a night and perished in a night. ¹¹And should I not pity Nineveh, that great city, in which are more than one hundred and twenty thousand persons who cannot discern between their right hand and their left—and much livestock?""

Perhaps Isaiah was thinking also like Jonah to Israel. Maybe he was thinking and protesting to Jesus as to why He will be glorified through Israel. This sinful and disobedient people who repeatedly disobey and break His laws. They deserve to die.

Perhaps Isaiah was also thinking that, "I worked hard for You and You will not call me Your servant and You will not be glorified in me! What a waste of time."

But as verse 4 tell us that Isaiah still submits to His God. His Master;

"⁴Then I said, 'I have labored in vain, I have spent my strength for nothing and in vain; yet surely my just reward is with the

Lord, and my work with my God.'"

This comes to my mind also concerning the people of the isles. This people are terrible and dreadful people. They are gossipers, traitors to each other and their country, lazy, greedy, materialistic, disobedient to God, idolaters, sorcerers, and every evil we can muster in our mind is in the isles. They do not deserve salvation. They do not deserve protection. They do not deserve prosperity for they are self-righteous people. These applies to those people who are proud and arrogant, both rich and poor.

But to those who are meek and humble, they deserve God's protection and deliverance from their misery. And there are millions of them.

And as we know it, God is calling the peoples of the isles to be His servants. And like the people of Nineveh, they will repent and come to God. God has his plans and "Thy will be done on earth as it is in heaven" (Matthew 6:10).

Now, Yeshua told Isaiah in verse 5 to 6 about who sent Him and what is his mission (the works before Him);

"⁵"And now the Lord says, who formed Me from the womb to be His Servant, to bring Jacob back to Him, so that Israel is gathered to Him (For I shall be glorious in the eyes of the Lord, and My God shall be My strength),…""

God the Almighty Father so loved His chosen people – the Israelites that He send Yeshua to be begotten in flesh to be His Servant in bringing back Israel to Him (Jesus came for the lost sheep (tribes) (Matthew 15:24)) that through them the world might be saved and be glorified in them. Israelites are lost because they continue to disobey God, especially the Sabbath which is the sign between them and God (Exodus 31:13). But Israel needs to be saved because salvation of mankind is contingent upon the salvation of Israel. For Israel is the Branch upon which the Gentiles shall be grafted in and be co-heirs with Christ. This is the mystery of salvation in Ephesians 3: 6 and Romans 11: 13-21. Without the branches, the scions will be meaningless and will surely die. For God will be glorified in Israel (Isaiah 49:3). That is why the light will come to the isles to bring revelation to the Gentiles and the glory of His people Israel (Luke 2:32).

We, the people of the isles/coastlands should put in our hearts and minds that Yeshua is calling us to be His servant for the salvation of Israel so that we, the Gentiles and of the world shall also be saved. We shall be loyal and faithful servants to our Master Yeshua as He is faithful and loyal to His Master and God – the Almighty Father.

We shall be helpers to the Helper and servants to the Servant of God.

Yeshua in verse 6, shares His mission and calling from His God to His servants – the people of the isles;

"'Indeed He says, 'It is too small a thing that You should be My Servant to raise up the tribes of Jacob, and to restore the preserved ones of Israel; I will also give You as a light to the Gentiles, that You should be My salvation to the ends of the earth.' "

The You and Servant here pertains to Jesus Christ as God the Father speaks to Him. But as Jesus Christ speaks to the people of the isles, the You becomes the people of the isles and the Servant becomes the servants. The sequence of this calling is coming from the Father to Jesus Christ, to Isaiah, to Paul, and to the peoples of the isles.

Whatever the mission the Father has given to Yeshua – His Son, He will accomplish it through the help of His servants – the people of the isles. So that Israel might be restored and accomplish the works stored upon them as His Servant and to perform and execute the grand schema of plans of the Father for the whole creation of God. Therefore, it is contingent upon us, the people of the isles to give due respect and admonition to the Israelite people however evil or hardheaded they might be for now, because they are God's chosen people and God has His own way to make them kneel and bow down before their Maker. We must remember that God give us this opportunity to be His servants (to serve our God and Maker) and to be called His people also because of the disobedience of Israel.

God uses people to accomplish His purpose. He uses His Son

and later His sons, prophets, ministers, angels, disciples, and people to execute the works He needed to achieve. He is not a fiat God to make things like magic. He is the God of process. God share the opportunity for His servants to experience the real joy as result of accomplishing great works. He created all things through Jesus Christ. And Christ labored for all the creation that He made. It is not instant. It takes time and energy beyond our imagination. He used the Word to whom all things were created by Him and for Him for the salvation of mankind even though He regrated creating humanity and wants to destroy them (Genesis 6:6-7). Perhaps this is the only way and our last chance. So, we really need to listen up!

Isaiah in verse 7 further described who the Lord is speaking in Chapter 49. The Redeemer of Israel, their Holy One whom people despise and afflicted, and whom the nations abhor (regarded with disgust and hatred);

> "⁷Thus says the Lord, the Redeemer of Israel, their Holy One, to Him whom man despises, to Him whom the nation abhors, to the Servant of rulers:…"

People hate Jesus Christ past, present, and future (until His wrath has come upon them) that they replaced Him with another Jesus (the counterfeit Christianity (Christianized Paganism)) and they will mourn and hate Him when He arrives and reign in the Kingdom of God here on earth.

Even the Jewish people of the present-day Israel is having a law (2023) to be passed banning and making the mention of the name Jesus Christ illegal or a crime. Two Israeli Knesset member have introduced a bill that will ban or criminalize any efforts to tell people about Jesus. What a twisted and perverted mind these people have. They do not know that Jesus Christ is not only their expected Messiah but also their maker – their Redeemer. The breath of life they have came from the very person/God they abhor and despises. Let us see if it will pass.

But Jesus said in continuing verse 7,

"Kings shall see and arise, Princes also shall worship,

Because of the Lord who is faithful, the Holy One of Israel;
And He has chosen You."

In this phrase, Jesus Christ particularly said that He has chosen You – the isles to be His servants/helpers. The You that was mentioned in verse 6 was Jesus Christ as the mission was given to Him by His Father. Then Jesus chose You – the isles to be His servants. The You now in verse 6 has dual meaning and purpose. The You is Jesus Christ and also the isles. The mission and works were given to Jesus Christ to whom He is giving to the peoples of the isles.

But on our own, we cannot do it. So, Jesus assured the isles in verse 8-9;

> "⁸Thus says the Lord: "In an acceptable time I have heard You, and in the day of salvation I have helped You; I will preserve You and give You as a covenant to the people, to restore the earth, to cause them to inherit the desolate heritages; ⁹That You may say to the prisoners, 'Go forth,' to those who are in darkness, 'Show yourselves.'"

These are tremendous works ahead of us. I feel excited for us and at the same time nervous and doubtful for we are so weak and foolish people and as a nation. But Jesus said in verse 12;

> "¹²Surely these shall come <u>from afar</u>; Look! Those from the north and the west, and these from the land of Sinim."

He assures that the work and the people will come from afar. The afar here is another symbol/code for the location of the isles as mentioned in verse 1 of Isaiah 49 (KJV);

> "¹Listen, O <u>isles</u>, to Me, and take heed, you peoples <u>from afar</u>!"

We know that the location of the isles is in the east that is why verse 12 mentioned to "those in the north and the west" and Sinim (which is the south) to look to the east – from afar. Sinim might have other meaning too.

How will the isles do these works? We do not know yet. As the saying said, "we will cross the bridge when we get there". But Jesus will arise over us (Isaiah 60:1) as a light. He will be our guide in times of darkness, and He said in verse 9-11 that He will protect us, feed us and guide us as we perform the works that will be bestowed upon us. But most of all, we shall wait for His Law according to Isaiah 42:4;

> "⁴"…And the isles shall wait for His law.""

And the Lord God Yeshua have called us into righteousness in verse 6 to 9;

> "⁶I, the Lord, have called You in righteousness, and will hold Your hand; I will keep You and give You as a covenant to the people, as a light to the Gentiles,…"

For if the Light comes to us (Isaiah 60:1) and accept Him that we become lights also. And His light will shine upon us that we maybe light also unto the Gentiles just as it is written in Isaiah 42: 7-10;

> "⁷To open blind eyes, to bring out prisoners from the prison, Those who sit in darkness from the prison house."

What is this prison house? These are the deceptions of Satan that entangled humanity into darkness of his counterfeit religions and ideologies that deceives the whole world. And through these evil religions, the nations have fornicated with the woman (the Church) – the Mystery Babylon the Great, the Mother of Harlots and of the Abominations of the Earth (Revelation 17:5), now known as the Vatican (the prison house of Satan).

> "⁸I am the Lord, that is My name; and My glory I will not give to another, nor My praise to carved images.
> ⁹Behold, the former things have come to pass, and new things I declare; before they spring forth I tell you of them.""

Please, people of the isles, when You have read this, when You have heard this, do not harden Your heart. For the Great I AM is calling us into righteousness that our former idolatrous mind and paganic practices may come to pass and new things will be declared upon us. So, that we may free ourselves from the prison houses (religions) of Satan.

For surely, we shall rejoice in the Lord and serve Him with all our might and soul.

"¹⁰Sing to the Lord a new song, and His praise <u>from the ends of the earth</u>, You who go down to the sea, and all that is in it, <u>You isles/coastlands</u> and you inhabitants of them!"

This verse is truly amazing on how God answers prayer. I always read this verse many times just in passing. Until one Sabbath, I have my full attention to this verse. Perhaps because I have seen this praise since I was a kid. And then ask God in prayer, who is this "You" who go down to the sea? At the time, I did not know yet that the "ends of the earth" and the "isles/coastlands" are one and the same place. One is directional, and the other is physical characteristics of the place. And the other, is its people.

Then one day I saw a documentary in YouTube titled, "The Most Dangerous Road to School". That episode featured the Philippines particularly in Zamboanga. The kids are literally climbing the side of the mountain vertically because the school is on top of the mountain from their side. They use the roots of the trees and rocks as they climb. They prefer this method in going to school because this is the shortcut from their place. The other way is far from them, and they do not have enough money to pay for the tricycle going back and forth to school on a daily basis. So, every day, they climb the mountain going to school. The community there was able to establish a rule of passage or some sort of traffic rule that priority should be given to the person going down.

In that documentary, a fisherman was shown descending from on top of the mountain with his fishing net in his back and shoulder. Of course, many fishermen in the Philippines also go down to the sea from the mountain. But not as extreme as shown in this documentary which put greater emphasis on the identity of the "You" who go down to the sea as mentioned in Isaiah 42: 10.

God answers prayers in many amazing ways. But in this verse, God revealed the modern-day identity of the "isles" as the present-day Philippines. All the coded identity were mentioned in just one verse.

But of course, we need more proof, because humans are full of disbelief. Human mind is attuned to believing lies and despises the truth. This we will discuss further in another chapter on the human nature.

Let us go back to verse 11 to 13;

"¹¹Let the <u>wilderness</u> and its cities lift up their voice, the villages that <u>Kedar inhabits</u>. Let the inhabitants of Sela sing, let them shout from the top of the mountains.

¹²Let them give glory to the Lord, and <u>declare His praise in the isles/coastlands</u>.

¹³The Lord shall go forth like a mighty man; He shall stir up His zeal like a man of war. He shall cry out, yes, shout aloud; He shall prevail against His enemies."

Verse 11 gives us clue to the skin color of the people who lived in the mountains of the isles and of the seas which is Kedar. The color of the skin of Kedar people is brown or dark skinned. And as previously discussed, the wilderness here is also the isles when God made the rivers into isles (Isaiah 42:15) and the rivers into wilderness (Isaiah 50:2). The rivers is the common denominator in the identity of these codes.

The people of the isles/coastlands shall declare praise and the glory of the Lord for He shall prevail against His enemies. We may be His servants, but we are also His soldiers. Just as Abraham have prepared his servants and activate them as soldiers in times of war (Genesis 14:14) such as when they rescue Lot from their enemies, so will our God be. In times of peace, we are servants – builders, farmers, makers, merchants, etc. But in times of war, we shall be great warriors of God. We shall also be soldiers of peace and of beauty. For we shall help God in establishing His Kingdom and of peace and prosperity on earth. For we shall help in rebuilding the desolate places after the tribulation period.

The fight is already won. We just need to do the works that will be given to us one day at a time. And in all of this, we shall look up to God and trust Him. For He said in Isaiah 45:22;

"²²"Look to Me, and be saved, all you ends of the earth!

For I am God, and there is no other.""

Now, we certainly know without a doubt who this verse is talking to. Peoples of the isles, we need to reconsider our ways and look up to the real living God of the Bible and let us hear our calling and serve Him only.

Tracing Abraham's Real Origin

It is important to understand the origins of Abraham and his significance in God's plan for humanity. In the Bible, Abraham is described as the father of many nations and God's chosen leader to carry out his plan. His journey and the events that transpired in his life have a significant impact on the history of humanity. Understanding the context and background of Abraham's story can provide valuable insights into the Bible and God's plan for humanity.

Now that we have clearly established that the isles mentioned in the Bible is no other than the present-day Philippines, let us look where Abraham came from and why. This is a very important event in God's plan that will shape the history of humanity.

Let us look at Isaiah 41: 2-4 and compare it to Nehemiah 9: 7-11 in Table 1.

Table 1. Comparison of Isaiah 41: 2-4 and Nehemiah 9: 7-11.

Isaiah 41	Nehemiah 9
²"Who raised up <u>one from the east</u>?	⁷"You are the Lord God, Who chose <u>Abram</u>, and brought him out of <u>Ur of the Chaldeans</u>, and gave him the name Abraham;
Who in <u>righteousness</u> called him to His feet?	⁸You found his heart faithful before You,
Who gave the nations before him, and made him rule over kings?	And made a covenant with him to give the land of the Canaanites, the Hittites, the Amorites, the Perizzites, the Jebusites, and the Girgashites—
Who gave them as the dust to his sword, as driven stubble to his	To give it to his descendants. You have performed Your words,

bow?	for You are righteous. (also verse 22-23)
³Who pursued them, and passed safely	⁹"You saw the affliction of our fathers in Egypt, and heard their cry by the Red Sea.
By the way that he had not gone with his feet?	¹¹And You divided the sea before them, so that they went through the midst of the sea on the dry land; and their persecutors You threw into the deep, as a stone into the mighty waters.
4Who has performed and done it, calling the generations from the beginning? 'I, the Lord, am the first; And with the last I am He.' "	-Emphasis mine- Indeed You are my Lord God Almighty, the Creator of the heavens and the earth, and Israel Your people (Isaiah 43: 15). Amen.

What are the important points in this comparison?
1. Nehemiah 9: 7-11 interprets Isaiah 41: 2-3;
2. God raised Abram from the east whom God took him from the Ur of the Chaldeans;
3. The Ur of the Chaldeans is in the east;
4. Abraham is the beginning of Israel's generation.

Shem is the root of Abraham and the descendants of Shem went back to the isles in the east to Mt. Sephar after the Tower of Babel disaster (Gen. 10: 5 and 30).

This is the genealogy of Shem to Abraham (Gen. 11: 10-20):
Shem – Arphaxad – Salah – Eber – Peleg – Reu – Serug –
Nahor – Terah – Abraham

There was no mention in the Bible where any of the descendants of Shem migrated back to the west or any other place than in the isles in the east.

But there is an indication that the Ur of the Chaldeans is near body of water in Isaiah 43: 14;

"[14]... "For your sake I will send to Babylon, and bring them all down as fugitives—The Chaldeans, who rejoice in their ships.""

It is clear here that the Chaldeans are not native to Babylon. Besides, Chaldeans seems to be sailors or mariners because they "rejoice in their ships". They travel by water and not in the arid desert land of Babylon or Mesopotamian region. That is why, aside from being famous for being astrologers, witchcraft, magic, and other abominable practices, they are also good in astronomy that they use stars in navigation.

And God indicated in verse 16 that He brought the Chaldeans through;

"[16]Thus says the Lord, who <u>makes a way in the sea</u> and <u>a path through the mighty waters,</u>...""

And in Joshua 24: 2-3, God said;

"[2]... "Thus says the Lord God of Israel: 'Your fathers, including Terah, the father of Abraham and the father of Nahor, dwelt on <u>the other side of the River</u> in old times; and they served other gods. [3]Then <u>I took your father Abraham from the other side of the River</u>, led him throughout all the land of Canaan, and multiplied his descendants and gave him Isaac."

Abraham came from the "other side" of the River. What river is this?

In verse 2 it said, "the River in old times". There is no other River mentioned in the Bible in the old times than the river that run from the center of the earth which is Jerusalem to water the garden of Eden in the east ends of the earth.

The present Jerusalem is the center of the earth when it was just one piece of land prior to the flood.

The other side of the River are the four riverheads that God turned into isles in Isaiah 42: 15;

"¹⁵ "I will make the rivers coastlands (isles, islands),…""

This means that the "other side of the River" is now the isles in the east at the ends of the earth – the present-day Philippines.

So, God took Abraham from the Ur of the Chaldeans (the Philippines) and brought him to the center of the earth in Jerusalem which is in the land of Canaan. The portrayal of the Chaldeans as how evil they are in the Bible is very similar to the current state of the unrighteousness among many of the Pilipino people.

Habakkuk 1: 6-7 said;

"⁶For indeed I am raising up the Chaldeans, a bitter and hasty nation which marches through the breadth of the earth, to possess dwelling places that are not theirs.
⁷They are terrible and dreadful; their judgment and their dignity proceed from themselves."

Are we not this people? The Chaldeans in history are long been gone. They did not march throughout the earth. But the Pilipino are almost in every corner of the earth trying to find a living. Many of our women have become a modern-day slave – called domestic helpers, nurses, teachers, and many other professions we can find just to make both ends meet.

And yet many of us who was able to work abroad became so proud and arrogant. Uplifting themselves above others and trying to project their financial edge through jewelries, signature bags, expensive gadgets, etc. Even to the point that they barrow money just to party when they come back home, just to show neighbors and friends their fake prosperity. The one-day millionaire attitude to project that one is better off than the other.

Are we not the one described in verse 7 who are "terrible and dreadful people whose judgement and dignity proceed from ourselves"? We are self-righteous, self-centered, traitors to one another (crab mentality), proud and arrogant (mayabang), practices idolatry, witchcraft (mangbabarang), sorcery and magic (mangagayuma at budol budol), astrologers (manhuhula, paham, pantas), politicians (sinungaling, mangagantso, magnanakaw), and many more practices that are abominable to God.

These we need to change and repent for us to be able to heed and hear God's calling and works ahead of us. I know many will be offended, go into defensive mode, trigger their cognitive dissonance (denial of truth), and even will attack the messenger before they understand the message. But we need to offend first ourselves so that we can judge and condemn ourselves in order for us to humble before God and ask for His forgiveness towards repentance. We need to acknowledge where we have wronged God and ask for His forgiveness. Then we need to fear God and submit to Him so that He will give us strength, knowledge, and understanding of the things He will command us to do in these very challenging times ahead of us. Then we shall judge and condemn this world in love and tell them the wonderful world tomorrow of the coming Kingdom of God before the dawn of darkness fully engulf human civilization.

We need to turn to God rather than to ourselves or our fellow men for us to obey Him and be protected from the darkness and lawlessness of our time.

Notice that the vision of Prophet Habakkuk 2:2-3 is a prophecy for the end time when God answered him saying;

> "²"Write the vision and make it plain on tablets, that he may run who reads it. ³For the vision is yet for an appointed time; but at the end it will speak, and it will not lie."

Today as you read this prophecy of Habakkuk about God's word pertaining to the Chaldeans (the Pilipino people) is fulfilled. The vision speaks now unto us for we are in the end time. It does not lie who we are as a people.

The vision of rising up the Chaldeans is seconded through a parallel in rising up the isles in the end-time (which is now) in Isaiah 60: 1-2;

> "¹ "Arise, shine; for your light has come! And the glory of the Lord is risen upon you.
>
> ²For behold, the darkness shall cover the earth, and deep darkness the people; but the Lord will arise over you, and His glory will be seen upon you.""

Who is the "you" God is talking to in these verses?

Isaiah 60: 8-9 answered;

"⁸"Who are these who <u>fly like a cloud</u>, and <u>like doves</u> to their roosts? (emphasis mine: Is this not an <u>eagle</u>?)

⁹Surely the <u>coastlands</u> (isles, islands) shall wait for Me; and the ships of Tarshish will come first, to bring your sons <u>from afar</u> (east, ends of the earth),…""

See the very important clues? The eagle, the coastlands (isles), and from afar (east). What nation on earth is composed of islands, with a great eagle, and described as a far east nation than the land of Ophir – the modern-day Philippines.

Both the Chaldeans (in Habakkuk 1) and the isles (in Isaiah 60) will be risen up in the end times. Is there any more doubt that they are one and the same based on the <u>characteristics of the people</u> and the <u>geographic indication</u> described in these verses? And both the Ur of the Chaldeans and the isles is in the east at the ends of the earth.

Similarly in Habakkuk 1: 8-9;

"⁸ "Their horses also are swifter than leopards, and more fierce than evening wolves. Their chargers charge ahead; their cavalry comes from <u>afar</u>; They fly as the <u>eagle</u> that hastens to eat.

⁹"They all come for violence; their faces are set like the <u>east</u> wind. They gather captives like sand…""

We see in these verses that Chaldeans description in Habakkuk 1 is coded also like in Isaiah 60 with the words eagle (fly like a cloud), from afar, and east. But Isaiah 60: 9 identified it further as an "isles/coastlands" whom the people is waiting for Him. Could it be that the "isles" and the "east" are the codes or dots that connects the "isles" and the Chaldeans pertaining to the identity of its original location – the isles in the east?

We must remember that God raised up Abraham from the east (Isaiah 41: 2) from the Ur of the Chaldeans and God brought the Chaldeans as fugitives to Babylon. They are fugitives, they must be really dreadful and terrible people indeed as further described in Habakkuk 1: 6-11.

These verses described Chaldeans for what they are famous for when they are in Babylon. They became many generations and famous for being fierce warriors or soldiers at that time. They were involved in the captivity of the Israelite people and brought them to Babylon. God used them to fulfill the prophecy to the disobedient people of Israel that they will be in captivity.

But why did God said in Isaiah 43: 14-15;

"¹⁴Thus says the Lord, your Redeemer, the Holy One of Israel:
"For your sake I will send to Babylon, and bring them all down as fugitives—The Chaldeans, who rejoice in their ships.
¹⁵I am the Lord, your Holy One, the Creator of Israel, your King.""

God said, He sent the Chaldeans for the sake of Israel for He is their Creator, King, God, and Redeemer. The Chaldeans should be working for the welfare of Israel in the past and not to be their captors and enemy, right? Why would God have said that Chaldeans is for the benefits of Israel when in fact they were their enemy who brought them into captivity in Babylon? Could this have a prophetic meaning for the future when the Chaldeans is sent by God once more for the salvation of Israel around the world from their modern-day captivity of Babylon (the Vatican)? The modern-day Chaldeans as the people of the isles will be risen up in this end-time for the sake of Israel. Because the salvation of mankind is contingent upon the salvation of Israel. This, we will discuss in the missions of the people of the isles chapter.

Perhaps, Habakkuk 1 describes the past and future of the Chaldeans based on historical events they were involved in and their characteristics as a people and their place of origin.

The Chaldeans is a code identifier of a nation that God have punished and despised because of their sinfulness in the past and will be risen up in this end-times because they are waiting for the Lord and His Laws. As a locational identifier, we can consider that there are two sets of people that can be identified from the Ur of the Chaldeans. One, are those who remained in the land of the Chaldeans that perhaps repented and turned back to God's faith. And the other are those who are unrepentant, who are the fugitives and were brought to Babylon. Perhaps, they have become part of the Holy Roman Empire past and present.

CHAPTER 4

THE PROPHETIC EVIDENCE

The Philippines in Bible Prophecy

Now that we have traced the identity of the isles from the beginning, we will be able to understand what God have stored for the isles in the very near future.

Amidst our sinfulness, pride, and arrogance, we have further descended into immoral people and into deeper poverty. Our society have lived in darkness almost to the brink of oblivion. Many false teachers and prophets have reigned on our land through various religions. And the people that live in ignorance about the true Living God, followed them blindly. One religion after another. Idolatry upon idolatry. Some who have heard the truth have a hard time turning to God. They rather obey the commandments and traditions of man rather than God. But then, we blame God for the terrible situation we are in because of our disobedience to Him. And those who believe in God, (either the true God or the god of this world) think that God revolves around them as if God is their servant. Calling Him to be of service to them on demand. When they pray as if God is their servant. Commanding Him to their whims and wishes. Demanding answer even what they pray is against God's way. They think God revolves around them. They are the center and God is in the outer circle of their lives. Commanding Him when they need Him.

As a result, humanity have been corrupted to the core. The governments of this world that are supposed to protect and look after the people have become deeply evil and lawless. The rights of the people as fundamentally protected by the constitution have been violated and neglected. The laws are bent according to their will and perceived power. It is no longer about what is right and what is wrong. It becomes relative to what they think is right for the working of their agenda.

Like many governments of this world, ours have also become like a terrorist/communist country to its own people specially during the time of the pandemic hoax. The so-called democracy of freedom suddenly flipped into communism/terrorism mode in just a flick of the finger by the supreme commander in the Vatican. And the world bowed down and obey. Willingly and excitedly lining themselves for a shot of the most awaited witchcraft (pharmakeia) potion to save their lives. Only to find out (to those who are still alive) that it is a very dangerous potion and will make them dependent to it like drugs for the rest of their lives.

People are easily deceived or gullible when they are lied to. But it is hard for them to believe on the truth. People question the truth, but never question the lies and deceptions of Satan even if it is so obvious that it is a lie.

Then we blame God on the consequences of our selfish actions. We go against God's way and government, then we expect to be rewarded with peace, good health, happiness, and prosperity.

We are lazy in many ways specially in seeking God. We look at God as if He owe us something. We forget or do not understand that we are only given this wonderful opportunity to become a member of His family. God does not owe us anything. We owe everything to Him. We are so ungrateful to our Maker.

So, we need to wake up from our slumber and move away from

darkness into light. For God is calling us today in Isaiah 60: 1-2;

"¹Arise, shine; for your light has come! And the glory of the Lord is risen upon you.

²For behold, the darkness shall cover the earth, and deep darkness the people; but the Lord will arise over you, and His glory will be seen upon you."

First and foremost, it is important to recognize that the message conveyed in these verses is not directed towards individuals, but rather towards a nation as a whole. Regardless of one's skin color, religion, social status, or physical characteristics, God is calling all the peoples of the isles to put Him at the center of their lives, and to come together as humble servants united in His glory and righteousness.

Second, we need to know who is the "you" being addressed to, in these verses.

Exactly, "arise" in verse 1 carries the connotation of standing up or waking up from a state of slumber or inactivity. This refers to waking up from a state of sinfulness and unrighteousness and moving from darkness to light. It is like the sunrise in the east after a night, or like a person who is blind, who can finally see the light. This verse is calling on the people to make a conscious effort to move away from their sinful ways and towards righteousness and holiness, and to be a shining example of that righteousness to others.

"For your light has come!"

Who or what is the light that will come?

Let us get directly the answer from our Lord Jesus Christ in John 9: 2-5 as He was talking with His disciples;

"²And His disciples asked Him, saying, "Rabbi, who sinned, this man or his parents, that he was born blind?"

³Jesus answered, "Neither this man nor his parents sinned, but that the works of God should be revealed in him. ⁴I must work the works of Him who sent Me while it is day; the night is coming when no one can work. ⁵As long as I am in the world, I am the light of the world.""

<u>Jesus Christ is the light of this world</u> that we may see the revelation of the "works of God". Just as He spoke to His disciples again in John 8:12, saying;

"12... "<u>I am the light of the world</u>. He who follows Me shall not walk in darkness, but have the light of life.""

We sinned because we disobey the law. We are blinded with unrighteousness because we disregard the law. We live in darkness because there is no light. But now, the light is coming back. For He was in the world to do the works of His Father who sent Him. And when He went back to heaven darkness came and the work stopped.

Jesus is the light of this world. He is coming back to us to help Him continue the works. The light will come that we may see and serve Him.

"And the glory of the Lord is risen upon you."

Who or what is the "glory of the Lord"?

In Ezekiel 43: 2 and 4 said;

"2And behold, <u>the glory of the God</u> of Israel came <u>from the way of the east</u>. His voice was like the sound of many waters; and the earth shone with His glory.

4And the glory of the Lord came into the temple <u>by way of the gate which faces toward the east</u>."

In verse 2, Jesus Christ is referred to as "the glory of the Lord" and described as having a voice like the sound of many waters. This imagery emphasizes the power and majesty of Jesus Christ. The verse is saying that He will rise up in the hearts of the people of the isles, as they turn away from darkness and towards righteousness. This is similar to the image of the rising sun in the east, bringing light to the darkness of the night. This rising of the Lord and His glory within us will also bring light to the world, so that those who are still in darkness may see and be saved, just as the blind man in John 9: 3 who was able to see the light of Jesus Christ and have his sight restored.

Ezekiel 43: 1-5 mentions the direction "east" three times; twice saying "toward the east" (verses 1 and 4) and once "the way of the east" (verse 2). This repetition emphasizes that the source of "the glory of the Lord" (Jesus Christ) is coming from the east and that it will be accompanied by a powerful voice like the sound of many waters. This passage is emphasizing that the coming of the Lord and His glory is imminent and will come from the east.

On the other hand, the "voice of the Lord" in verse 2 can be understood literally as the sound of many waters in various forms, such as the sound of a thundering and roaring sound of a tsunami, but it can also be understood figuratively as the many tongues or languages of the peoples mentioned in Revelation 17: 15. The waters in this verse "are peoples, multitudes, nations, and tongues". These peoples of the isles in the east speak many different languages. And as they are scattered abroad, they learn the languages of many nations and multitudes on earth, which qualifies them to become the voice of God, preaching the gospel of Jesus Christ about the coming Kingdom of God and His righteousness in all the earth. This is in line with Jesus' statement in Matthew 24: 14 that "this gospel of the kingdom will be preached in the whole world as a testimony to all nations, and then the end will come."

By understanding the meaning of the "voice of the Lord" in verse 2, we can be motivated to let the Lord's voice be heard and prophecy to the nations of the whole earth. This is in line with the message in Jeremiah 25: 30-32, which calls on the people to make noise and proclaim the Lord's message to all nations. By understanding our role as the voice of God to the world, we can boldly proclaim His message and bring the light of His glory to all those in darkness, fulfilling our calling to be a light to the nations (Gentiles).

> "[30]"Therefore prophecy against them all these words, and say to them: 'The Lord will roar from on high, and utter His voice from His holy habitation; He will roar mightily against His fold. He will give a shout, as those who tread the grapes, against all the inhabitants of the earth.
>
> [31]A noise will come to the ends of the earth— for the Lord has a controversy with the nations;

He will plead His case with all flesh. He will give those who are wicked to the sword,' says the Lord."

[32]Thus says the Lord of hosts: "Behold, disaster shall go forth from nation to nation, and <u>a great whirlwind shall be raised up from the farthest parts of the earth</u>."

The Gospel of Jesus Christ that should be preached in all the earth is a message of hope and a warning about the coming dreadful day of the Lord.

Now, who is the "you" in Isaiah 60?

As we have previously mentioned, "the glory of the Lord" will come from the east in Ezekiel 43: 2 and 4 to enter the temple in the west (Jerusalem). And in Isaiah 59: 18- 19;

"[18] ...<u>The coastlands(isles)</u> He will fully repay.

[19]So shall they fear the name of the Lord from the west,

And <u>His glory from the rising of the sun</u>;..."

Verse 19 coded the "east" as "from the rising of the sun" where "the glory of the Lord" will come from. And verse 18 mentioned the people of the isles who "fear the name of the Lord in the west" because the isles is in the east.

Furthermore, Jesus said in Isaiah 60: 8-9;

"[8]Who are these who <u>fly like a cloud</u>, and <u>like doves to their roosts</u>?

[9]Surely <u>the coastlands (isles)</u> shall wait for Me; and the ships of Tarshish will come first, to bring your sons <u>from afar</u>,..."

Isaiah 60 is about the role of the isles in relation to Jerusalem and its people. The first nine verses describe how God will use the isles to work on behalf of Jerusalem. The next twelve verses describe how God will use the isles to rebuild and comfort Jerusalem, and how it will be in the future, after the Millennial Kingdom. In verse 22, God states clearly that His words will come to pass. He raises up a humble and unknown servant to deliver His message to the isles, to do the work for Israel, and to the world. This one servant will become a thousand, and the isles will become a whole nation, united, strong, and mighty, abiding in the works of the Lord.

THE PHILIPPINES IN BIBLE PROPHECY

"²²A little one shall become a thousand, and a small one a strong nation."

In Isaiah 60: 8-9, Jesus Christ provides four clues as to the identity and location of the people He is addressing in this chapter, beginning in verse one;

1. "Who fly like a cloud" – we have extensively discussed this to be the Philippine Eagle. In the previous chapter. This is parallel to Habakkuk 1: 8-9 when Jesus Christ told him about the identity of the Chaldeans whom He is raising up also in the end times(Hab. 1: 6; "For indeed I am raising up the Chaldeans);

   "⁸ ...Their cavalry comes from afar; they fly as the eagle that hastens to eat.

   ⁹ ...Their faces are set like the east wind....."

   Notice the connections of the coded words, from afar, eagle, and east. They are all pointing to the isles.

2. "Surely the isles shall wait for Me" – What and who is the isles in the east that is waiting for the coming of our Lord Jesus Christ? Only in the Philippines! (Sounds familiar?).

   The Philippines, which will become the Kingdom of Ophir, is often referred to as the only Christian nation in Asia. However, it is more accurate to say that it is the only Catholic nation in Asia. We believe in a counterfeit Christianity that Satan created to deceive the whole world and therefore the isles worshipped another Jesus (2 Cor. 11: 4). The Jesus in Satan's counterfeit Christianity is actually Nimrod = Ninus (Sto. Nino – mother and child, aka baby Jesus (Nimrod) and Mary (Semiramis)) and called by many other names, color, and faces in different countries and cultures. The Jesus of the Catholic and its many confusing religions is a very different Jesus from what the Bible has proclaimed to be.

   Still, the sign that the isles is waiting for Christ coming back (believed to be the second coming, though it is uncertain how many times Jesus Christ has visited Earth as

He is the creator of it.) is very popular belief in the Philippines. Majority of the isles is still blinded by darkness today just as it is written in Isaiah 44: 17-18 because our country is an idolatrous nation. But the time has come that the light is coming (and has come) to remove the scales in our eyes just like Saul whom Jesus called to become Paul the Apostle to the Gentiles (of the isles in Genesis remember?) in Acts 9:18. So God will remove the scales in our eye when we humble ourselves before the Lord and pray Psalms 119: 17-24 so that we may see His glory and serve Him;

"¹⁷Deal bountifully with Your servant, that I may live and keep Your word.

¹⁸Open my eyes that I may see wondrous things from Your law.

¹⁹I am a stranger on the earth; <u>do not hide Your commandments from me.</u>

²⁰My soul is consumed with longing for Your judgments at all times.

²¹You rebuke the arrogant—the cursed who stray from Your commandments.

²²Remove my scorn and contempt, for I have kept Your testimonies.

²³Though rulers sit and slander me, Your servant meditates on Your statutes.

²⁴Your testimonies are indeed my delight; they are my counselors."

And in 2 Corinthians 4: 6;

"⁶For it is the God who commanded light to shine out of darkness, who has shone in our hearts to give the light of the knowledge of the glory of God in the face of Jesus Christ."

We must remember the words laws, commandments,

statutes, and the testimonies (of Jesus Christ which is Revelation), for this is where Satan deceived the whole world.

3. " To bring your sons from afar" – What does this "from afar" means?

First, let us understand who these "sons" are. The "sons" here are the descendants of Israel as God comforted them during the tribulation period when they are scattered abroad in captivity in Isaiah 43: 5-6;

"⁵Fear not, for I am with you; I will bring your descendants from the east, and gather you from the west;

⁶I will say to the north, 'Give them up!' And to the south, 'Do not keep them back!'

Bring My sons from afar, and My daughters from the ends of the earth—"

Verse six tells us that "afar" is at the "ends of the earth". And we know that the "ends of the earth" is in the east. The "east", "afar", and the "ends of the earth" will be involved in bringing back the people of Israel, just as written in Isaiah 11: 11-12;

"¹¹It shall come to pass in that day that the Lord shall set His hand again the second time to recover the remnant of His people who are left, from Assyria and Egypt, from Pathros and Cush, from Elam and Shinar, from Hamath and the islands of the sea (the isles).

¹²He will set up a banner for the nations, and will assemble the outcasts of Israel, and gather together the dispersed of Judah from the four corners of the earth."

God will set up a sign in the east, from the nations (islands) from afar in Isaiah 5: 26;

"²⁶He will lift up a banner to the nations from afar, And will whistle to them from the end of the earth;..."

Who are the people in the east, from afar, at the ends of the earth who loves to whistle (sipol)?

These are the same people that are in the isles as mentioned in Isaiah 59:1(KJV);

"¹Listen, O <u>isles</u>, unto me; and hearken, ye people, <u>from far</u>; ..."

To which God have commissioned them in verse 6 to;

"⁶And he said, it is a light thing that thou shouldest be my servant to raise up the tribes of Jacob, and to restore the preserved of Israel:"

And again, verse 12 confirmed the location of these people;

"¹²Behold, these shall come <u>from far</u>:..."

To bring the descendants of Israel, just as it is written in Isaiah 60: 4;

"⁴Lift up your eyes all around, and see: they all gather together, they come to you; Your sons shall come <u>from afar</u>, and your daughters shall be nursed at your side."

And in Isaiah 66: 19-20;

"¹⁹I will set a sign among them; and those among them who escape I will send to the nations: to <u>Tarshish</u> and Pul and Lud, who draw the bow, and Tubal and Javan, to the <u>coastlands (isles) afar off</u> who have not heard My fame nor seen My glory. And they shall declare My glory among the Gentiles. ²⁰Then they shall bring all your brethren for an offering to the Lord out of all nations, on horses and in chariots and in litters, on mules and on camels, to My holy mountain Jerusalem," says the Lord, "as the children of Israel bring an offering in a clean vessel into the house of the Lord."

You see, we profess to be believer or follower of Jesus Christ, yet Jesus Christ Himself denied us for we are a nation who have not heard His fame nor have we seen His glory. We are just professing Christianity worshipping another Jesus.

4. "The ships of Tarshish" – Like Sidon, the isles is an ancient trading hub of the world as mentioned in Isaiah 23: 2-3;

> "²Be still, you inhabitants of the coastland (isles), you merchants of Sidon, whom those who cross the sea have filled.
>
> ³…The harvest of the River, is her revenue; and she is a marketplace for the nations."

It makes more sense that the isles is a leading global commerce center in the past because all the nations from the time of Noah came from her (Gen.10:5). The nations know the resources they needed from the isles such as gold, animals, spices, etc. Abraham also came from the isles to Canaan (Isaiah 41: 2-5) and so are the Chaldeans from the isles that came to Babylon through their ships (Isaiah 43:14).

Sidon is a Canaanite city 20 miles north of Tyre. It is also in the northern boundary of Israel. Tyre is the great city (Joshua 19:29) of the kingdom of Tyre under the rulership of King Hiram who is a trader or merchant to King Solomon (1 Kings 5: 1-10) and famous for commerce (Ezekiel 27: 1-36).

The ships of Tarshish is the one carrying the merchandises of the isles to Sidon and Tyre and vice versa. King Hiram and King Solomon have their own fleets of ships for trading as mentioned in 1 Kings 9: 26;

> "²⁶King Solomon also built a fleet of ships at Ezion Geber, which is near Elath on the shore of the Red Sea, in the land of Edom."

Perhaps, the ships of Hiram and Solomon are made in Tarshish, for the isles have abundant trees that can be made into ships or boats at that time.

King Solomon hired the help of Hiram for the acquisition, purchase, and transportation of materials needed to build the Temple and other infrastructure projects of King Solomon as mentioned in 1 Kings 7:13 (KJV);

"¹³And king Solomon sent and fetched Hiram out of Tyre."

And in 1 Kings 9:28 and 1 Kings 10:11;

"²⁸And they went to <u>Ophir</u>, and acquired four hundred and twenty talents of gold from there, and brought it to King Solomon."

"¹¹Also, the ships of Hiram, which brought gold from <u>Ophir</u>, brought great quantities of almug wood and precious stones from <u>Ophir</u>."

Perhaps, the ships of Hiram is also the one used by the Queen of Sheba to carry her and her merchandises to King Solomon during her visit to Jerusalem. For why would verse 11 of 1Kings 10 be inserted after the account of the Queen of Sheba's visit to King Solomon. And the verse also started with the word "also". Meaning in connection to or with. It was mentioned simultaneously based on the account of the queen's merchandise of gold and precious stones that are being carried also by the ships of Hiram to king Solomon from Ophir. And the Queen of Sheba came from the ends of the earth as mentioned in Matthew 12: 42. The ends of the earth as we know it is also the isles.

Tarshish is a city in the isles as mentioned in Isaiah 23: 6-7;

"⁶Cross over to <u>Tarshish</u>; wail, you inhabitants of the <u>coastland</u> (isles)!

⁷Is this your <u>joyous city, whose antiquity is from ancient days, whose feet carried her far off to dwell</u>?"

Notice once again the mention of two different words but could have one meaning in verse 6. Tarshish here could be another name of the isles or it is in the isles. And notice farther in verse 13 when it jump suddenly into a different subject mentioning the word Chaldeans;

"¹³Behold, the land of the Chaldeans, this people which was not;..."

This could mean that the land of the Chaldeans is also the

THE PHILIPPINES IN BIBLE PROPHECY

isles (Tarshish). Which they are not as we have known them previously. Remember that the Chaldeans love their ships (Isaiah 43:14). Here, the connection of Tarshish (which reference also to Ophir, isles, and indirectly to the "ends of the earth") and of the Chaldeans is ship. We should take note also that Chaldeans was mentioned or have existed before Abraham and therefore prior to the reign of King Solomon. And in verse 7 of Isaiah 23 mentioned the two very important points.

One is, "whose antiquity is from ancient of days". This give a strong indication that the city of Tarshish is very old. Perhaps, since the beginning? But Daniel 7:13 said;

"[13]I was watching in the night visions, and behold, One like the Son of Man, coming with the clouds of heaven! He came to the Ancient of Days, and they brought Him near before Him."

Here, Ancient of Days is the name of the Almighty Father. Could the city of Tarshish be the former city of God in the east, at the ends of the earth in the garden of Eden? Could God give us the clue from which these ships might have come from?

In the late 1970's, a group of boats or ships were unearthed in Butuan. It is called the Butuan Boats (also known as balanghai/balangay) which is believed to be from 10th to 13th CE. It is composed of one big mother ship that was excavated recently and have approximately 25 meters length and accompanied by several smaller boats or ships. I called it ships or boats interchangeably because for me 25 meters is already a massive boat for that time. For me boats are small. Like the ordinary fishing boat of a fisherman. For me, anything that carry a lot of passengers and cargoes can be considered as a ship. That can be compared to the seventh fleets of USA today although not as a warship but as a trading vessel.

The discovery of ancient boat or ship remnants in the isles is astounding, as boats and ships were historically used for commerce. If we think about the fake history of the Philippines which portrayed us

342

as if we are ignorant and primitive people when "discovered" by Portuguese and Spanish explorers sent by the Vatican, we will not believe this. But if one believes in the God of the Bible, He give us concrete evidence of these ships that indeed the isles have been in commerce with other nations because of this large fleet of ships/boats. The discovery of the boats of Butuan is a testament of the great possibility that the isles have trading relationship with Jerusalem.

Two is, "Whose feet carried her far off to sojourn?". Sojourn or dwell (in NKJV) means foreigner or strangers to a place which are not theirs. Sounds familiar?

It is description of the Chaldeans in Habakkuk 1:6;

""⁶...Which marches through the breadth of the earth (sojourners), to possess dwelling places that are not theirs (foreigners, strangers)."

Then verse 13 of Isaiah 23 declared like an "aha" moment;

"¹³Behold, the land of the Chaldeans, this people which was not;..."

The isles, where the city of Tarshish, is the land of the Chaldeans or the Ur of the Chaldeans. This is where Abraham came from to sojourn in the land of Canaan. This is where the Chaldeans being fugitives came from to sojourn in the land of Babylon. And this is where the Pilipino people came from to sojourn in almost every place on earth being positioned and will be prepared to preach the gospel of the coming Kingdom of God throughout the world at an appointed time. They are in places that are not theirs. Meaning, not originally from their current dwelling places historically.

So are all the people of the earth of various skin colors, races, and tongues. They all came from one place – the isles of the Gentiles (Gen. 10: 5) and from one family (Noah). We are all brothers and sisters in Christ if we chose to, because we have one Creator and one God and Father of us all. The One who give us opportunity to be part of His family. We are all sojourners and strangers (Psa. 119: 19) in this earth just as it is written in 1 Chronicles 29 :15 (KJV);

"¹⁵For we are strangers before thee, and sojourners, as were all our fathers: our days on the earth are as a shadow, and there is none abiding."

Spiritually and physically, we are all sojourners (strangers) on this earth. That alone is a great reason why we should not fight against each other, but to seek God and all His glory. Being sojourners in this world should be one of the great reasons we should not be greedy and accumulate material things more than what we need at the expense of others. Our priority should be to seek God and His truth and to look up to one another. If we live unselfishly, God's way which is the way of giving and outgoing concern for others instead of Satan's way which is the way of getting and competition, we can turn over these misery and sufferings of humanity that we are in today. These are caused by our sinfulness and the people who are willing to betray their fellow men and sell their souls to Satan for next to nothing.

Now, let us go back to the "ships of Tarshish".

The isles is one of the great merchants of Sidon and Tyre (Isa. 23: 2). The ships of Tarshish carried its merchandises to Tyre, a great city who is well known for its commerce, especially the nobles as mentioned in Isaiah 23: 8;

"⁸… Tyre, the crowning city, whose merchants are princes, whose traders are the honorable of the earth?"

Tarshish or the isles must be very dependent on Tyre for its prosperity because the downfall of Tyre is also the downfall of the isles or Tarshish as it is written in verse 15;

"¹⁵ Now it shall come to pass in that day that Tyre will be forgotten seventy years, according to the days of one king.…"

And in verse 9;

"⁹The Lord of hosts has purposed it, to bring to dishonor the pride of all glory, to bring into contempt all the honorable of the earth."

That is why on the downfall and destruction of Tyre, the ships of Tarshish lamented and mourned as it is written in verse 1 and 14;

"¹ The burden against Tyre. Wail, you ships of Tarshish! For it is laid waste, so that there is no house, no harbor;…"

¹⁴Wail, you ships of Tarshish! For your strength is laid waste."

Perhaps, during the heights of prosperity of Tyre and Tarshish (the isles) is when the nobles of Ophir (Philippines) were portrayed or illustrated in the Boxer Codex. It illustrates the huge gold ornaments and jewelries in the nobles of Ophir. No record in history will approach to surpass the display of wealth in their body as well as their weaponry. The record of the Boxer Codex can be attested by the "Philippine Gold: Treasures of the Forgotten Kingdoms" exhibited on January 3, 2016 in New York and brought back to Ayala Museum.

But God restored Tyre after seventy years of destruction as mentioned in verse 17;

> "¹⁷And it shall be, at the end of seventy years, that the Lord will deal with Tyre. She will return to her hire, and commit fornication with all the kingdoms of the world on the face of the earth."

Chapter 5 will reveal to us the present-day identity of of this revived kingdom of Tyre that fornicates with the kingdoms of this world. The new identity of Tyre will astound us and yet how the Bible described this revived Empire is very clear who it is.

The Poor and Brokenhearted - Isaiah 61 and Luke 4

Yeshua read these particular verses of Isaiah 61: 1-2 in Luke 4: 18-19 in Table 2 and proclaimed in verse 21;

> "²¹…"Today this Scripture is fulfilled in your hearing.""

Because He has proclaimed, preached, and delivered the gospel of the coming Kingdom of God to the world, Yeshua claimed this prophecy that He is the anointed **One** to fulfill the tasks that is written in Isaiah 61. This is confirmed in Luke 4: 1 as the Spirit of the Lord God in Isaiah 61: 1 entered unto Him;

> "¹ Then Jesus, being filled with the Holy Spirit, returned from the Jordan and was led by the Spirit into the wilderness,…"

Table 2. The poor and brokenhearted of Isaiah 61 and Luke 4.

Verse	Isaiah 61 (KJV)	Verse	Luke 4 (KJV)
1	The Spirit of the Lord GOD is upon Me; because the LORD hath anointed Me to preach good tidings unto the meek; He hath sent Me to bind up the brokenhearted, to proclaim liberty to the captives, and the opening of the prison to them that are bound;	18	The Spirit of the Lord is upon Me, because He hath anointed Me to preach the gospel to the poor; He hath sent Me to heal the brokenhearted, to preach deliverance to the captives, and recovering of sight to the blind, to set at liberty them that are bruised (oppressed),
2	To proclaim the acceptable year of the LORD, and the day of vengeance of our God; to comfort all that mourn;	19	To preach the acceptable year of the Lord.

Notice that He left out reading the phrase, "and the day of vengeance of our God; to comfort all that mourn;" because the martyrdom of His servants has not been fully fulfilled in the end times in Revelation 18: 20;

> "20Rejoice over her, O heaven, and you holy apostles and prophets, for God has avenged you on her!"

God has not avenged yet the former apostles and prophets because there are apostles and prophets who will prophecy in this end times in all the world about His gospel of the coming Kingdom of God before He come (Matt. 24: 14). They will deliver and warn the world of the gospel and many will be martyred and many will mourn for in

Revelation 18: 24;

"²⁴And in her (Vatican) was found the blood of prophets and saints, and of all who were slain on the earth."

Notice also that Yeshua give meaning, clarity, and interpretation to the poetic presentation of Isaiah 61: 1 in Luke 4: 18. The phrase "to preach good tidings unto the meek", became "to preach the gospel to the poor". Here, "good tidings" is interpreted by Yeshua to be His "gospel" of the coming Kingdom of God that He preached during His fleshly ministry on earth. He fulfilled it, preaching the gospel to the meek and poor in His time and to the meek and poor of the peoples of the isles (His end-time servants) in this time through His messengers that they may preach it also in all the world. Just as it is said in Luke 6: 20 - 23;

"²⁰Then He lifted up His eyes toward His disciples, and said:

"Blessed are you poor, for yours is the kingdom of God.

²¹Blessed are you who hunger now, for you shall be filled.

Blessed are you who weep now, for you shall laugh.

²²Blessed are you when men hate you, and when they exclude you, and revile you, and cast out your name as evil, for the Son of Man's sake.

²³Rejoice in that day and leap for joy! For indeed your reward is great in heaven, for in like manner their fathers did to the prophets."

The gospel of Yeshua is about the coming Kingdom of God here on earth. This is the message of hope in these coming troublesome times of darkness and lawlessness. For the government of God will be establish by Yeshua on earth. And He will reign with the rod of iron so that people will see and remove the blindness from their eyes. With Christ reign, humanity will be forced to have peace, joy, happiness, and prosperity contrary to today's Satan's reign that is full of wars, violence, deceptions, suffering, fear, and darkness. And yet, humanity love evil rather than good. And will fight God when He come.

Could humanity been programmed by Satan to hate God through their vaccine and metaverse (alternate reality)? Covid injection is composed of nano particles with electronic chips that reach through the neural network of the human brain. It also contains transmitters of internet signals (Internet of Man) that can be controlled by an outside receiver. Human become hackable animals as one of the WEF minions said. It is powered by graphene oxide that harness electricity of the human body. From this, Satan can control human thinking and emotion and can be blinded by their metaverse experiences. And people allowed it to happen to them willingly. They empower Satan to control their lives and they will not be able to think for themselves. They are blinded.

Luke 6 : 20-23 is talking to the meek and the poor. A code name for the peoples of the isles. They will be His people, servant, and nation that will be His helper in accomplishing Isaiah 61 and many other missions for the isles He enumerated in the book of Isaiah. And because of these, they will be hated by all nation as stated in Matthew 20: 9;

"⁹Then they will deliver you up to tribulation and kill you, and you will be hated by all nations for My name's sake."

And in Matthew 10: 22-23 Jesus said to the isles;
"²²And you will be hated by all for My name's sake. But he who endures to the end will be saved. ²³When they persecute you in this city, flee to another. For assuredly, I say to you, you will not have gone through the cities of Israel before the Son of Man comes."

The coming of our Lord Jesus Christ is contingent upon the fulfilment of the gospel preached in all the earth.

And this is His commandment to His servants in verse 27-28;
"²⁷Whatever I tell you in the dark, speak in the light; and what you hear in the ear, preach on the housetops. ²⁸And do not fear those who kill the body but cannot kill the soul. But rather fear Him who is able to destroy both soul and body in hell."

It is disheartening, but many of us will be persecuted and killed (martyred) for the sake of His name and His works. But if this is the only way to pave the way of His coming and to end the reign of Satan here on earth and for the salvation of mankind, who are we to complain. If the Father sacrificed His only Son for the salvation of mankind, how much more can we sacrifice our lives for His glory. For He said in Matthew 16: 24-25;

> "²⁴Then Jesus said to His disciples, "If anyone desires to come after Me, let him deny himself, and take up his cross, and follow Me. ²⁵For whoever desires to save his life will lose it, but whoever loses his life for My sake will find it."

Now, let us examine another phrase in Isaiah 61: 1 as read by Yeshua in Luke 4: 18. The phrase "the opening of the prison to them that are bound" to become, "recovering of sight to the blind, to set at liberty them that are bruised (oppressed)". Who are these prisoners that He will set free and give liberty from their blindness of darkness and oppressions?

> In Isaiah 60: 1-2 God said;
> "¹Arise, shine; for your light has come! And the glory of the Lord is risen upon you.
> ²For behold, the darkness shall cover the earth, and deep darkness the people; but the Lord will arise over you, and His glory will be seen upon you."

In this end times when darkness of lawlessness and unrighteousness will abound, God talk to the isles in Isaiah 60 calling them to rise up in the light of God which is Jesus Christ (Yeshua). And He will arise over us to free us from oppression, prison houses (false religions), and deceptions of Satan that blinded the peoples of the isles.

But now, the isles is blinded by its sins and iniquities fueled by pride and arrogance that it cannot see the light. All that can be seen is darkness. But Christ (the Light in John 9:5) said, He will come to the isles – the blind, the meek, and the poor, so that the works of God might be revealed to them (John 9:3).

And because of the sinfulness of the isles, they become imprisoned or prisoners of Satan in his various and confusing religions, systems, and governments. Vatican – the throne and bastion of Satan have oppressed and imprisoned the isles for a long, long time that they become poor and dependent to the dictate of the Vatican through its tentacles. Although the isles possess the greatest wealth on earth, the Vatican (Satan) used their very wealth to oppress and enslaved them.

This is the reason why we will be brokenhearted because we though with pride and arrogance that our religious beliefs are the truth. Each one believes according to its own thinking and belief system. We love our churches. We love our governments. And we put our trust in them with all our hearts and soul. Only to find out that we have been deceived. We are in bed with our enemy literally.

It hurts to realize that we have been deceived by the one whom we love. But the Lord prophesied that He would come to us, to free us from our sins, prison houses of deceptive religions and from the grip of the Babylonish religion (the Vatican) so that we may serve Him and become His servants. To prepare the way of His coming and the establishment of His Kingdom.

When all of us (the isles) have turned to Him, He will tell (proclaim) us "the acceptable year of the Lord" to begin the works of the Lord.

And while doing the work of preaching the gospel of the coming Kingdom of God in all the earth, many will be martyred for His name's sake. But He will avenge the death of His saints and prophets, both of old and new as written in Isaiah 61: 2;

"2...And the day of vengeance of our God; To comfort all who mourn,..."

And in Revelation 18: 20 and 24;

"20Rejoice over her, O heaven, and you holy apostles and prophets, for God has avenged you on her!"

24And in her (Vatican – the harlot, the woman, City of Babylon) was found the blood of prophets and saints, and of all who were slain on the earth."

God will use the isles to comfort Zion in Isaiah 61: 3;

"3 To console those who mourn in Zion,..."

Israel will become the servant of God once more when He take away their sins. And we shall serve the Servant, for we are the servants of the Servant and we are the helpers of the Helper. For Yeshua is the Helper and Servant of God the Father Almighty. And Israel was supposed to be the servants of Yeshua, but they did not served God and disobeyed Him instead. And so, they will go into tribulation until they repent and turn to God. The isles will become the servant of our Lord Jesus Christ (Yeshua) because of the sinfulness and disobedience of Israel. God will call us His people and nation too like Israel. And we shall serve God in the restoration of His land and His people and the whole earth after the tribulation period. We shall join the Lord as His servants just as it is written in Isaiah 56: 6;

"⁶Also the sons of the foreigner who join themselves to the Lord, to serve Him, and to love the name of the Lord, to be His servants—Everyone who keeps from defiling the Sabbath, and holds fast My covenant -"

We shall usher the Kingdom of God under Christ reign for 1000 years as it is written in Isaiah 61: 4;

"⁴And they shall rebuild the old ruins, they shall raise up the former desolations, and they shall repair the ruined cities, the desolations of many generations."

And in Isaiah 51: 3;

"³For the Lord will comfort Zion, He will comfort all her waste places; He will make her wilderness like Eden, and her desert like the garden of the Lord;..."

For God said in Isaiah 49: 3;

"³...'You are My servant, O Israel, in whom I will be glorified.'"

And in Isaiah 62: 7;

"⁷...And till He makes Jerusalem a praise in the earth."

For God will call the isles His people and His nation in Isaiah 51: 4-5;

"⁴Listen to Me, My people; and give ear to Me, O My nation: For law will proceed from Me, and I will make My justice rest as a light of the peoples.

[5]My righteousness is near, My salvation has gone forth, and <u>My arms will judge the peoples; the coastlands (isles) will wait upon Me, and on My arm they will trust.</u>"

Notice the mention of the isles (coastlands) and light, just as mentioned in Isaiah 60. And the Lord has proclaimed a mission to the isles in Isaiah 62: 11 during Jacob's trouble (Jer. 30: 7);

"[11]Indeed the Lord has proclaimed to the end of the world (the isles): "Say to the daughter of Zion (Jerusalem), 'Surely your salvation is coming; behold, His reward is with Him, and His work before Him.' ""

We shall deliver this message of hope to Jerusalem to comfort them in their times of trouble.

God has appointed works for us – the peoples of the isles. And He has appointed work also for the Israelite people during the Millennial Kingdom of God (1000 years).

We are the blind, the deaf, the poor and the meek, the proud and arrogant, and the idolatrous nation of the Ur of the Chaldeans. But God will make us see and guide us in Isaiah 42: 16-20;

"[16]I will bring the blind by a way they did not know;
I will lead them in paths they have not known.
I will make darkness light before them, (just like in Isaiah 60:1-2) and crooked places straight. These things I will do for them, and not forsake them.
[17]They shall be turned back, they shall be greatly ashamed, who trust in carved images, who say to the molded images, 'You are our gods.'
[18]"Hear, you deaf; and look, you blind, that you may see.
[19]<u>Who is blind but My servant</u>, or <u>deaf as My messenger whom I send</u>? Who is <u>blind</u> as he who is perfect, and <u>blind</u> as <u>the Lord's servant</u>? [20]Seeing many things, but you do not observe; opening the ears, but he does not hear."

This is God's urgent message for us. But as I see the Pilipino people today, it looks like impossible. Like many people of the world, they are so blind and deaf to the truth. And yet, they are so <u>proud and arrogant</u> to continue believing and following the lies and deceptions that Satan fed their minds. Satan being "the prince of the power of the air" have great influence in the minds of the people, just as it is written in Ephesians 2: 1-3;

> "[1]And <u>you He made alive, who were dead in trespasses and sins,</u> [2]in which you once walked according to the course of this world, according to <u>the prince of the power of the air, the spirit who now works in the sons of disobedience,</u> [3]among whom also we all once conducted ourselves in the lusts of our flesh, fulfilling the desires of the flesh and of the mind, and were by nature children of wrath, just as the others."

Human beings love lies rather than the truth. They love their self-centered and self-righteous way of life, even though the results of these actions are nothing but troubles, disasters, and sufferings upon sufferings. And yet, they love to continue to walk in the way of lies leading to death (the way of Satan) rather than the way of truth leading to life (the way of God). It is relatively simple to deceive people with a falsehood, but it can be difficult to correct or undo that deception once it has taken hold. As the saying goes, "it is easier to fool people than to convince them that they have been fooled". This is because Satan deceives the whole world (Rev. 12: 9). He blinded us with darkness.

But God has His own marvelous ways. He has a plan and He will do it. And with God, nothing is impossible (Luke 1: 37).

Like Jonah, he does not want to obey God in delivering the message of salvation to the men of Nineveh because he felt it is useless because the people seem incorrigible and hard headedly sinful. He thinks perhaps that this people do not deserve the salvation of God. Jonah hates the people of Nineveh because of their sinfulness.

But Jesus said in Luke 5: 32;

> "[32]I have not come to call the righteous, but sinners, to repentance."

He was sent by God the Father only to the lost tribes of Israel in Matthew 15: 24;

> "²⁴But He answered and said, "I was not sent except to the lost sheep of the house of Israel.""

He did not even come for His own people the Jews because they have their own time when the scales in their eyes will be removed and see the truth. But the lost tribes of Israel are scattered abroad that need to be reached out and need to hear the gospel so that they may know once more their identity upon repentance and obedience to His commandments.

Even though Israelite people are so sinful to the point that He will subject them to Jocob's trouble until they repent, just as it is written in Deuteronomy 31: 16-18;

> "¹⁶And the Lord said to Moses: "Behold, you will rest with your fathers; and this people will rise and play the harlot with the gods of the foreigners of the land, where they go to be among them, and they will forsake Me and break My covenant which I have made with them. ¹⁷Then My anger shall be aroused against them in that day, and I will forsake them, and I will hide My face from them, and they shall be devoured. And many evils and troubles shall befall them, so that they will say in that day, 'Have not these evils come upon us because our God is not among us?' ¹⁸And I will surely hide My face in that day because of all the evil which they have done, in that they have turned to other gods.""

And yet, God said in Isaiah 49: 3;

> "³...'You are My servant, O Israel, in whom I will be glorified.'"

God has His plans, and surely, He will work His way.

And so, Jonah delivered the message to the men of Nineveh, and they repented and turn to God (Matt. 12: 41). And indeed, nothing is impossible to God (Luke 1: 37). So shall it be to the peoples of the isles as well as the peoples of Israel.

Even though the peoples of the isles in general is proud and arrogant and yet deaf and blind, God's Light will come to us and remove the scales of blindness in our eyes and the plugs in our ears so that we may see and hear the light of truth and see the face of our God one day.

I pray that when we hear and read this message that we should not harden our hearts to God. Least we shall experience great trouble before we turn back to Him. We shall turn to the true God of the Bible like little children and put our trust in Him alone.

And when that time come, we shall change our name to Ophir/Ophirians symbolizing the wealth and treasures of God (Haggai 2:8). And we shall begin to build the Kingdom of Ophir and come out from the shadow and reign of the Vatican (Satan). And we shall pray to God His anointed king to lead us into righteousness and prepare the way of His coming.

Just as God said to us in Isaiah 45: 22;

"²²Look to Me, and be saved, all you ends of the earth! For I am God, and there is no other."

God requires us ALL to turn to Him. Not one, not thousands, not one million, but all of us. United as one people, one kingdom, under one God.

"May the Lord bless us and heal us,
and make His face shine upon us!"
Amen.

CHAPTER 5

THE VATICAN CONNECTION

Tyre – the Great City

Who is Tyre of today? She is a great city. A very wealthy and influential city who fornicates with many nations on earth.

What is fornicates or fornication?

Fornication is essentially having intercourse or sex outside of marriage whether it is pre-marital sex (for those who are not marriage including cohabitation or engage) or adultery (to those who are marriage). It involves servitude to one another on a secret sinful way and symbolic of an idolatrous activity.

On the above verse, the resurrected kingdom of Tyre commits secret sinful relationship with the governments of all the kingdom/nations of the world. Adultery to those who are democratic and monarchical forms of government because they pretend to serve the people or are bound to the people's will (married to the people). Yet they serve their master in Tyre.

On the other hand, pre-marital sex to those who are communist, dictatorship, and tyrannical forms of government because their government is separate from the people's will. Meaning they are not committed to the people but wants to impose their self-will and desires. But those are all just illusions because in actuality they look down the people (their wife) as their subjects or slaves to serve their mistress or master in the great City of Tyre. They do not serve their subject (their wife), but they serve a satanic master (a whore) in the city of Tyre. These relationships have become so obvious in this pandemic and climate change hoax if one will care to think, see, hear, and believe in God of the Bible.

Although she is not directly running the nations of the earth, her minions (deep estate (aka shadow government) and secret societies (which is not) = the Cabal) in the governments of every nation on earth, do the works for her.

The city of Tyre is the harlot or the whore mentioned in Revelation 17 and as mentioned in Isaiah 23: 15-16;

"[15]...At the end of seventy years it will happen to Tyre as in the song of the harlot: [16]"Take a harp, go about the city, you forgotten harlot; make sweet melody, sing many songs, that you may be remembered."

Tyre is the harlot and the woman of Revelation 17: 1-6 as an angel talking to John, saying;

"[1]Then one of the seven angels who had the seven bowls came and talked with me, saying to me, "Come, I will show you the judgment of the great harlot who <u>sits on many waters</u>, [2]with whom the kings of the earth <u>committed fornication</u>, and the <u>inhabitants of the earth were made drunk with</u> the wine of <u>her fornication</u>."

[3]So he carried me away in the Spirit into the <u>wilderness</u>. And I saw a woman sitting on a scarlet beast which was full of names of blasphemy, having seven heads and ten horns. [4]The woman was arrayed in purple and scarlet, and <u>adorned with gold and precious stones and pearls</u>, having in her hand a golden cup full of abominations and the filthiness of her fornication. [5]And on her forehead a name was written:

MYSTERY, BABYLON THE GREAT, THE MOTHER OF HARLOTS AND OF THE ABOMINATIONS OF THE EARTH.

"[6]I saw the woman, drunk with the blood of the saints and with the blood of the martyrs of Jesus. And when I saw her, I marveled with great amazement."

Notice that she is adorned with the wealth of Ophir (wealth of the isles, wealth of the land of Havilah (Gen. 2:12) (gold, precious stones (onyx stones in Ezek. 28: 13), and pearls (bdellium))) in verse 4. She has or is controlling the wealth of Ophir. She is running the economy of the world with the wealth of Ophir. This is signified by the word "pearls" which can only be found in Palawan in the ancient of times.

And take note also that John was in the wilderness when He sow the vision of the woman. As was previously discussed, the wilderness is a code for the isles with their common denominator of "the rivers". In Isaiah 42: 15;

"[15]...I will make the rivers coastlands(isles),..."

And in Isaiah 50: 2;

"[2]...I make the rivers a wilderness;..."

This might mean that the people of the wilderness (aka: isles, ends of the earth, present-day Philippines) will see the true color and identity of the woman in the vision of John in Revelation. We must remember that Revelation is for the end time servants of God. And these servants are the peoples of isles as called by God in Isaiah 42 and 60.

The identity of the woman and the beast is described in Revelation 17: 7;

"[7]But the angel said to me, "Why did you marvel? I will tell you the mystery of the woman and of the beast that carries her, which has the seven heads and the ten horns.""

Table 3 below will show the parable and its interpretations of the "Woman" and the "Beast" of Revelation 17.

The Woman/Harlot and the Beast of Revelation 17

Revelation 18: 4 said; "⁴And I heard another voice from heaven saying, "Come out of her, <u>My people</u>, lest you share in her sins, and lest you receive of her plagues."

Who are these "My people" Jesus Christ is warning to come out of the shadows, influences, prison houses (religions and governmental systems) of deceptions of the Great City of Vatican who deceives the whole world?

Table 3 showed us the Biblical identity of this Great City which is the present-day Vatican. No other city on earth is so great and powerful financially and militarily than the Vatican. Its political tentacles that grip the whole world include UN, WHO, and WEF. Its financial claws include two of the biggest asset managers on earth namely BlackRock and Vanguard, etc. Together, they can control, hostage or destroy any country that will not obey or implement Vatican's agenda in a very sinister way.

We must take note that Revelation (1:1) is given by the Father to His Son Jesus Christ, delivered by His angel to His servant John to deliver it to His "end-time" servants;

"¹ The Revelation of Jesus Christ, which God gave Him to show <u>His servants</u>—things which must shortly take place. And He sent and signified it by His angel to His servant John,…"

Remember that Revelation are prophetic events that will take place before Christ coming to establish the Kingdom of God (the Millennial Kingdom) here on earth and to end the reign of Satan as the god and king (ruler) of this world. God will bring plagues to her and his followers (the whole world's tribulation) except to His "end-time" servants (including the elect and the very elect) whom He is calling to repent and turn to Him and away from Satan's influences and power.

Who are these servants?

Isaiah 49 mentioned three servants. One is Isaiah who is delivering this message or work (Isa. 49:4). The second servant is Israel

Table 3. The Woman/Harlot and the Beast of Revelation 17.

Verse	Parable/Talinghaga	Verse	Interpretation
1	"… "Come, I will show you the judgment of the great harlot who sits on <u>many waters</u>…""	15	"The <u>waters</u> which you saw, where the harlot sits, are peoples, multitudes, nations, and tongues.
3	*The Harlot is the Woman* "So he carried me away in the Spirit into the wilderness. And I saw a <u>woman sitting</u> on a <u>scarlet beast</u> which was full of names of blasphemy, having <u>seven heads</u> and <u>ten horns</u>."	18	"And the woman whom you saw is that great city which reigns over the kings of the earth."
		9	"Here is the mind which has wisdom: The <u>seven heads</u> are <u>seven mountains</u> on which the <u>woman sits</u>."
		10	"There are also <u>seven kings</u>…." (meaning: seven kingdoms or empire)
		12	"The <u>ten horns</u> which you saw are <u>ten kings</u> who have received no kingdom as yet, but they receive authority for one hour as kings with <u>the beast</u>."
		8	"<u>The beast</u> that you saw was, and is not, and will ascend out of the bottomless pit and

			go to perdition. And those who dwell on the earth will marvel, whose names are not written in the Book of Life from the foundation of the world, when they see <u>the beast</u> that was, and is not, and yet is."
		11	" And <u>the beast</u> that was, and is not, is himself also the eighth, and is of the seven, and is going to perdition."
2	"…with whom the <u>kings of the earth committed fornication</u>, and the <u>inhabitants</u> of the earth were <u>made drunk</u> with the <u>wine of her fornication</u>.""	18:3	""For all the nations have drunk of the wine of the wrath of <u>her fornication</u>, the <u>kings of the earth</u> have <u>committed fornication</u> with her, and the <u>merchants</u> of the earth have become rich through the abundance of her luxury.""
		18:23	"For your <u>merchants</u> were the <u>great men</u> of the earth, for by your sorcery <u>all the nations were deceived</u>."

6	"I saw the woman, drunk with the <u>blood of the saints</u> and with the <u>blood of the martyrs</u> of Jesus."	18:24	""And in her was found the <u>blood of prophets</u> and <u>saints</u>, and of all who were <u>slain</u> on the earth.""
		18:5	"For her sins have reached to heaven, and God has remembered her iniquities."
5	And on her forehead a name was written: MYSTERY, BABYLON THE GREAT, THE MOTHER OF HARLOTS AND OF THE ABOMINATIONS OF THE EARTH.		--The harlot, the woman, Babylon the Great is also the Great City of Vatican in Rome who reigns in all the kings of the earth. –
16	And the ten horns which you saw on the beast, these will hate the harlot, make her desolate and naked, eat her flesh and burn her with fire.	18:8	"Therefore her plagues will come in one day—death and mourning and famine. And she will be utterly burned with fire, for strong is the Lord God who judges her."

whom God said in Isaiah 49: 3;

"3...'You are My servant, O Israel, in whom I will be glorified.'"

But Israel, God's chosen people and His servant is lost because of their disobedience to Him. And they will undergo the tribulation period because they are under the influence of Satan as they continue to disobey God until they bow down and kneel before the Lord their Maker. And when they are down and have repented of their sins, they need to be risen up and be restored (Jer. 30). Because at the end of the day as it is written in Romans 11: 26-27;

> "²⁶And so all Israel will be saved, as it is written: "The Deliverer will come out of Zion, and He will turn away ungodliness from Jacob;
>
> ²⁷For this is My covenant with them, when I take away their sins.""

And so, a third servant of Isaiah 49: 1(KJV) is called by God to be His servant in accomplishing this work;

> "¹Listen, O <u>isles</u>, unto me; and hearken, ye people, <u>from far;</u>"

And Yeshua said to the people of the isles from afar in verse 6-7;

> "⁶Indeed He says, 'It is too small a thing that <u>You</u> should be <u>My Servant</u> to raise up the tribes of Jacob, and to restore the preserved ones of Israel; I will also give <u>You</u> as a light to the Gentiles, that <u>You</u> should be My salvation to the ends of the earth.' "
>
> ⁷Thus says the Lord, the Redeemer of Israel, their Holy One, to Him whom man despises, to Him whom the nation abhors, to the Servant of rulers: "Kings shall see and arise, Princes also shall worship, because of the Lord who is faithful, the Holy One of Israel; and He has chosen <u>You</u>."

The "You" here is the isles as signified by verse 12;

> "¹² Surely these shall come from afar;…"

We should remember that all the Gentile peoples of the earth came from the isles in Genesis 10: 5 and is located at the east ends of the earth. From afar.

Just as Israel was God's chosen people to be His servant, so is the "isles" have been chosen by God to be His servant in this end times. And He will call us His people (Rev. 18: 4) also just as it is written in 1 Peter 2: 9-10;

> "⁹But <u>you are a chosen generation, a royal priesthood, a holy nation, His own special people</u>, that <u>you may proclaim the praises of Him who called you out of darkness into His marvelous light;</u>

[10]who once were not a people but are now the people of God, who had not obtained mercy but now have obtained mercy."

For the peoples of the "ends of the earth", the "isles", "the queen of the south" have repented and rise up into judgement and condemnation of this evil and adulterous generations (Matt. 12: 39) just like the people of Nineveh who have repented at the preaching of Jonah in Matthew 12: 41-42;

"[41]The men of Nineveh will rise up in the judgment with this generation and condemn it, because they repented at the preaching of Jonah; and indeed a greater than Jonah is here. [42]The queen of the South will rise up in the judgment with this generation and condemn it, for she came from the ends of the earth to hear the wisdom of Solomon; and indeed a greater than Solomon is here."

For indeed, in Isaiah 24: 14-16;

"[14]They shall lift up their voice, they shall sing; For the majesty of the Lord they shall cry aloud from the sea.
[15]Therefore glorify the Lord in the dawning light (sunrise, east), the name of the Lord God of Israel in the coastlands (isles) of the sea.
[16]From the ends of the earth we have heard songs: "Glory to the righteous!""

We shall be helpers to the Helper, servants to the Servant of God and shine the Light (Yeshua) of righteousness to the ends of the earth and to all the Gentile nations on earth.

Blessed be the name of our Lord God Almighty Father! Blessed be the name of our Lord Yeshua! And blessed be the peoples of the isles whom God have called to be His servants to perform the works He had appointed! Amen.

The Fall of the Great City of Babylon

The world will mourn on the fall of the Great City of Babylon otherwise known as the Vatican City today, for in Revelation 18: 3 said;

"³For all the nations have drunk of the wine of the wrath of her fornication, the kings of the earth have committed fornication with her, and the merchants of the earth have become rich through the abundance of her luxury."

The Pandemic and Climate Change Hoax give us the concrete evidence that Vatican is the one controlling the world's affairs. Pandemic is a pretext to the Climate Change, all for their mantra of lies "for the common good" in the encyclical of the evil man in his Laudato Si in 2015 who claimed he is the holy father (but he is the black pope and a Jesuit of the highest order). But behind this is the satanic plan to implement the New World Order (NWO) or the Great Reset as a counterfeit to God's coming Kingdom. In the NWO, the world is going to worship Satan knowingly and unknowingly as the city continue to conduct the ritual of child sacrifices and as his minions continue to drink the blood of children (adrenochrome) with impunity. The Vatican implement their agenda through their Jesuits minions who hold high positions in governments of all nations on earth through the mandates of UN, WHO, IMF, WEF, and many others. The economy of the world is controlled by Vatican's two biggest hedge funds that controls tens of trillion upon trillions of dollars. From this, they control the economy of the world from energy, health, financial industries and almost every head of states of the world that implement their plan. And the people are excited and happy to drink the wine (deceptions such as the deadly injections) of her fornication. The pandemic hoax has executed the greatest transfer of wealth from the ordinary people of the world to the giant industries of the Vatican doubling and tripling their wealth in just one year while the people descended into poverty and oblivion.

But Revelation 18: 5, 8-11 said;

"⁵For her sins have reached to heaven, and God has remembered her iniquities.

⁸Therefore her plagues will come in one day—death and mourning and famine. And she will be utterly burned with fire, for strong is the Lord God who judges her.

[9]"The kings of the earth who committed fornication and lived luxuriously with her will weep and lament for her, when they see the smoke of her burning, [10]standing at a distance for fear of her torment, saying, 'Alas, alas, that great city Babylon, that mighty city! For in one hour your judgment has come.'

[11]"And the merchants of the earth will weep and mourn over her, for no one buys their merchandise anymore:..."

This is a repeat of what happened to the City of Tyre and a prophecy of the future events in Ezekiel 26, 27, and 28. And also in Isaiah 23. The City of Tyre was and is the City of Vatican whose popery is the prince of Tyre who proclaimed they are god (holy father – a blasphemy) but they are man (Eze. 28: 2). The king of Tyre (Vatican in Isa. 23: 17) is Lucifer (who became Satan - the Devil) who was the seal of perfection of the creation of God and an anointed cherub (angel) who covers (Eze. 28:12-16) until iniquity was found in him. Tarshish and the isles were among the merchants of Tyre in old times (as previously discussed). But the punishment of this great city in the end times continue in Revelation 18: 21- 24;

"[21]Then a mighty angel took up a stone like a great millstone and threw it into the sea, saying, "Thus with violence the great city Babylon shall be thrown down, and shall not be found anymore. [22]The sound of harpists, musicians, flutists, and trumpeters shall not be heard in you anymore. No craftsman of any craft shall be found in you anymore, and the sound of a millstone shall not be heard in you anymore. [23]The light of a lamp shall not shine in you anymore, and the voice of bridegroom and bride shall not be heard in you anymore. For your merchants were the great men of the earth, for by your sorcery all the nations were deceived. [24]And in her was found the blood of prophets and saints, and of all who were slain on the earth."

The Vatican have and will murder and kill prophets and saints in the past and in the coming end times. These are the people who proclaim the gospel throughout the world and they who carry the testimony of Jesus Christ. And through her medical industry, she murdered millions upon millions of innocent people in her well-orchestrated pandemics on a regular basis (hoaxes such as yellow fever, Spanish flu, swine flu, covid 19, etc.). All in the name of population reduction (depopulation agenda) to defile God's command to go forth and multiply and fill and replenish the earth (like in the Tower of Babel).

God provides everything mankind needs because that is His purpose. But Satan control everything, every supply of food, energy, health, education, money, climate, and religions to deceive the whole world. And people allow themselves to be deceived right in their very eyes because they forgot or will not want the true Living God in their lives.

The city of Tyre that is well known for its commerce around the world during the time of King Solomon, have become the harlot, the woman and the city of Babylon which in our current time is the Vatican City in Rome.

There is no other city/kingdom on earth that controls the whole world through her great wealth, influence, and power, than Vatican. She controls, the European Union through Germany, Britain, USA, China, and almost all the countries in the world through her political, military, and economic tentacles. She controls the worlds global banking system, medical, educational, energy, food production industries, and many other systems and industries around the world. She can change regime to her liking using her deep states and intelligence agencies in the US and in all nations on earth.

Satan is the king and god of this world. He reigns the people of the world from his throne in Vatican where children are sacrificed to him by her priests and prophets. He is the enemy of God. He was defeated and will be defeated by Jesus Christ, and he knows that his time is near. And the real King is coming and will role the earth with the rod of iron because people are so blinded that they love Satan (the creation) rather than their Maker. Mankind is so foolish that he cannot muster himself to the point that God told him to learn from the ants in Prov. 6: 6-11;

"⁶Go to the ant, you sluggard! Consider her ways and be wise,

[7]which, having no captain, overseer or ruler, [8]provides her supplies in the summer, and gathers her food in the harvest.
[9]How long will you slumber, O sluggard? <u>When will you rise from your sleep?</u>
[10]A little sleep, a little slumber, a little folding of the hands to sleep—[11]So shall your poverty come on you like a prowler, and your need like an armed man."

Now we know who and where is the "ships of Tarshish" as mentioned in Isaiah 60: 9, its relation to Tyre – the ancient Vatican (not by location but by identity), and its location in the isles – from afar. They shall bring Israelites (sons), the silver, and the gold to Jerusalem after the tribulation period.

In summary, Isaiah 60 is about Jesus Christ (Yeshua) coming to the isles in the east and protecting them from darkness (lawlessness and tribulation period). For they are the end time servants of God to restore the preserve ones of Israel, to restore the desolate places, to help in rebuilding the Temple and the city of Jerusalem, and reestablishment of the nations of Israel.

CHAPTER 6

YESHUA – THE CREATOR

Yeshua the Creator of Heavens and the Earth

God the Father Almighty created all things through Yeshua. And He commanded and all things were created in Revelation 4: 11;

"[11] You are worthy, O Lord, to receive glory and honor and power; for You created all things, and by Your will they exist and were created."

And in John 1: 1;

"[1] In the beginning was the Word, and the Word was with God, and the Word was God."

Since Yeshua (Jesus Christ) is the Beginning (Rev. 22: 13), we can translate this verse into;

"Yeshua was the Word, and Yeshua was with God, and Yeshua was God."

Similarly, Genesis 1: 1 can be;

"God created the Beginning, the heavens, and the earth."

This is the order of creation.

But the following verses of John 1 will confirm that the Word is really Yeshua (Jesus Christ).

"²He was in the beginning with God. ³All things were made through Him, and without Him nothing was made that was made. ⁴In Him was life, and the life was the light of men. ⁵And the light shines in the darkness, and the darkness did not comprehend it. ¹⁰He was in the world, and the world was made through Him, and the world did not know Him. ¹⁴And the Word became flesh and dwelt among us, and we beheld His glory, the glory as of the only begotten of the Father, full of grace and truth."

It is very clear from these verse that the Word is no other than Jesus Christ.

And in Ephesians 3: 8-9, Paul said;

"⁸To me, who am less than the least of all the saints, this grace was given, that I should preach among the Gentiles the unsearchable riches of Christ, ⁹and to make all see what is the fellowship of the mystery, which from the beginning of the ages has been hidden in God who created all things through Jesus Christ;..."

And in Hebrew 1:1-2;

"¹God, who at various times and in various ways spoke in time past to the fathers by the prophets, ²has in these last days spoken to us by His Son, whom He has appointed heir of all things, through whom also He made the worlds; (notice plural)."

The worlds here being plural may mean the first earth and the second earth (Rev. 21: 1, 2 Pet. 3: 5-7) or it can be that there are many earths like planets in the universe as astronomers estimated that there are approximately 13 trillion earth-like planet on the visible dimension of the universe. Or perhaps there are other dry lands (earth) in and above the waters below the firmament (Heaven). We just don't know.

And God the Father glorified His Son Jesus Christ and testified that He is the Creator of the heavens and the earth in Hebrew 1: 8-12;

"[8]But to the Son He says:

"Your throne, O God, is forever and ever;

A scepter of righteousness is the scepter of Your kingdom.

[9]You have loved righteousness and hated lawlessness;

Therefore God, Your God, has anointed You

With the oil of gladness more than Your companions."

[10]And: "You, Lord, in the beginning laid the foundation of the earth, and the heavens are the work of Your hands.

[11]They will perish, but You remain; And they will all grow old like a garment; [12]like a cloak You will fold them up, and they will be changed. But You are the same, and Your years will not fail."

God the Father called and proclaimed His Son as – Lord and God. Yeshua (Jesus Christ) is the Lord and God of the Old and New Testament. He never changes (Heb. 13: 8). He is the Lord in Isaiah 44: 24 who said;

"[24]Thus says the Lord, your (Israel) Redeemer, and He who formed you from the womb: "I am the Lord, who makes all things, who stretches out the heavens all alone, who spreads abroad the earth by Myself;...""

The Redeemer of Judah and the King of Israel is Yeshua as mentioned in Isaiah 44: 6-7 and confirmed in Revelation 21: 6 and 22: 13;

Isaiah 44: 6-7;

"[6]Thus says the Lord, the King of Israel, and his Redeemer, the Lord of hosts: 'I am the First and I am the Last; besides Me there is no God.

[7]And who can proclaim as I do? Then let him declare it and set it in order for Me, since I appointed the ancient people. And the things that are coming and shall come, let them show these to them."

Revelation 21: 6, 22: 13;

"[6]And He (Jesus) said to me, "It is done! I am the Alpha and the Omega, the Beginning and the End....

[13]I am the Alpha and the Omega, the Beginning and the End, the First and the Last."

And He said in Isaiah 45: 18;

"¹⁸For thus says the Lord, who created the heavens, who is God, who formed the earth and made it, who has established it, who did not create it in vain, who formed it to be inhabited: "I am the Lord, and there is no other....""

And He said to Jacob in Isaiah 48: 12-13, 16;

"¹²Listen to Me, O Jacob, and Israel, My called: I am He, I am the First, I am also the Last.

¹³Indeed <u>My hand has laid the foundation of the earth</u>, and <u>My right hand has stretched out the heavens</u>; when I call to them, they stand up together.

¹⁶"Come near to Me, hear this: I have not spoken in secret from the beginning; from the time that it was, I was there. And now the Lord God and His Spirit Have sent Me.""

Perhaps Jesus Christ is saying to the Israelites of today specially the Jewish people (the House of Judah), "Hey, this is Me. The Messiah whom you have been waiting for. I have come to my own (Jewish Israelites in John 1:11) but you did not received Me. But I will save you in your time of trouble (Jacob's Trouble) in His time.

And Yeshua said to Job in Chapter 38: 1 and 4;

"¹Then the LORD answered Job out of the whirlwind and said:...⁴Where were you when I laid the foundations of the earth?...""

And the Lord said in Isaiah 45: 11-12;

"¹¹Thus says the Lord, The Holy One of Israel, and his Maker: "Ask Me of things to come concerning My sons; and concerning <u>the work of My hands</u>, you command Me.¹²<u>I have made the earth</u>, and <u>created man on it</u>. I—<u>My hands</u>—<u>stretched out the heavens</u>, and all their host I have commanded."

God the Father created us all through Jesus Christ. He is our Maker and He said in Isaiah 51: 13;

"¹³And you forget <u>the Lord your Maker</u>, who stretched out the heavens and laid the foundations of the earth;..."

He warns those who continually despise Him in Isaiah 45: 9;
"⁹ "Woe to him who strives with his Maker! Let the potsherd strive with the potsherds of the earth!
Shall the clay say to him who forms it, 'What are you making?'
Or shall your handiwork say, 'He has no hands'?""

Listen carefully people from afar and the Jewish people, Jesus Christ (Yeshua) is our Maker and soon to be the King (Messiah) of this world. But many of us mocks and insult the One who created us and give us life. Some who believe in Him and profess to follow Him worship another Jesus (that is why God did not allow the Jewish people to believe in this counterfeit Jesus) because we are blinded by Satan who is the present-day god of this world. And people fear Satan rather than God. Instead, Jesus said in Matthew 10: 28;

> "²⁸And do not fear those who kill the body but cannot kill the soul. But rather fear Him who is able to destroy both soul and body in hell."

Yeshua Comes from the East

Jesus Christ – the Son of Man will come from the east as He stated in Matthew 24 : 27;

> "²⁷For as the lightning comes from the east and flashes to the west, so also will the coming of the Son of Man be."

And again Jesus said to His disciples in Luke 17: 24;

> ²⁴For as the lightning that flashes out of one part under heaven shines to the other part under heaven, so also the Son of Man will be in His day."

But where is the east? Do we have a clue?
In verse 28 of Matthew 24, Jesus said;

> "²⁸For wherever the carcass is, there the eagles will be gathered together."

Who is this carcass? And who are these eagles that will be gathered together? And why use the symbol of eagle?

When the disciples heard Jesus comparing Himself or His coming like a lightning from the east to the west and from "one part under heaven shines (east) to the other part under heaven (west)", they wanted to make sure that they understand Him because He is talking metaphorically as mentioned in Luke 17: 37;

"³⁷And they answered and said to Him, "Where, Lord?"

So He said to them, "Wherever the body is, there the eagles will be gathered together.""

The "carcass" mentioned in Matthew 24: 28 became "the body" in Luke 17: 37 which means "the body of the Lord" Yeshua – the Son of Man who will come from the east to the west like a lightning.

Why carcass?

Because it symbolizes His body when He was slain on the cross for our sins. When He died on the cross, His body was like a carcass of an animal full of wounds, lacerations, blood, body fluids oozing out, and beyond recognition and a picture of too much pain and suffering just as it is written in Isaiah 53: 5;

"⁵But He was wounded for our transgressions, He was bruised for our iniquities; The chastisement for our peace was upon Him, and by His stripes we are healed."

The eagles here are associated with the members of the Church of God – the Woman with regards to the direction of their travel (eagle = east) and their destination as mentioned in Revelation 12: 14;

"¹⁴But the woman was given two wings of a great eagle, that she might fly into the wilderness to her place, where she is nourished for a time and times and half a time, from the presence of the serpent."

The eagle is also a locational symbol where the wilderness is and as a place of safety for the Woman – Church from the presence of the serpent (Satan). But where is this wilderness?

Let us examine Psalms 72: 8-10;

"⁸ He (Yeshua) shall have dominion also from sea to sea, and from the River to the ends of the earth.

⁹Those who dwell in the <u>wilderness</u> will bow before Him, and His enemies will lick the dust.

¹⁰The kings of <u>Tarshish</u> and of <u>the isles</u> will bring presents; The kings of <u>Sheba</u> and Seba Will offer gifts."

Take note how the underlined words are related to each other and how it will help us locate the wilderness of Revelation 12: 14.

As previously discussed, the "ends of the earth", "the "isles", Tarshish, and Sheba are located in the east. The River in verse 8 is the river that water the garden of Eden in the east which become four riverheads.

Where did this River started in the west? Ezekiel 29: 9, gives us a clue that it is near Egypt;

"⁹And the land of Egypt shall become desolate and waste; then they will know that I am the Lord, because he said, 'The River is mine, and I have made it.'"

Moreover, 2 Chronicles 9: 26 give us a solid proof that the River begins in Jerusalem where the center of King Solomon's kingdom is;

"²⁶So <u>he reigned over all the kings from the River</u> to the land of the Philistines, as far as the border of Egypt."

So will the dominion of Jesus Christ be, from sea to sea and from the River to the ends of the earth (Psa. 72: 8). Could the River be another code name for Jerusalem like in the vision of Ezekiel 47: 1-12 where the water that flowed into the river started from the temple as described in verse 1;

"¹"... and there was water, flowing from under the threshold of the temple toward the east, for the front of the temple faced east; ..."

The water was shallow in the beginning. Just in the ankles (verse 3) when they measured a thousand cubits from the east gate of the temple. The river become deeper and deeper as they measured three thousand cubits as described in verse 5;

"⁵Again he measured one thousand, and it was a river that I could not cross; for the water was too deep, water in which one must swim, <u>a river that could not be crossed</u>."

"A river that could not be crossed" meaning it is very far, very wide, and very long that it overflowed to the eastern sea in verse 8;

> "⁸Then he said to me: "This water flows toward the eastern region, goes down into the valley, and enters the sea. When it reaches the sea, its waters are healed.""

And notice in verse 9 that the River became rivers (plural);

> "⁹And it shall be that every living thing that moves, wherever the <u>rivers</u> go, will live. There will be a very great multitude of fish, because these waters go there; for they will be healed, and everything will live wherever the <u>river</u> goes."

And then, in verse 10, it became about the fishermen and the Great Sea;

> "¹⁰It shall be that <u>fishermen</u> will stand by it from En Gedi to En Eglaim; they will be places for spreading their nets. Their fish will be of the same kinds as the fish of the Great Sea, exceedingly many."

Who are these fishermen and what is this Great Sea?

The Great Sea here could not be the Dead Sea (verse 11 – given over to salt) east of Jerusalem because it can be crossed over and is not too deep (unless it become full of water). The Great Sea here could be the Pacific Ocean as it is called today, for it is in the eastern side of the Temple. And like the River that water the garden of Eden in Genesis, it become four riverheads (rivers) and enters the sea (overflow verse 8) and into the Great Sea (the Pacific Ocean) in the east at the ends of the earth. And as we know it from previous chapter, "the ends of the earth" is also the "isles" in the east – the Philippines where fishermen abound as we can see in the many young fishermen vloggers today.

So, the healing water that flowed in the River begins in the front of the Temple that faced east, branched into rivers and ended up in the Great Sea.

Although this is a vision of the future as given to Ezekiel, the significance of the River and rivers is very similar and parallel to the river that water the garden of Eden prior to the flood. It both ended up in the east end of the earth because it come from the center of the earth in the west, in Jerusalem. That is why verse 8 of Psalms 72 stated that Christ will also reign from the River to the ends of the earth. A very important relationship of the west and the east.

Now, where is this wilderness that the eagles will bring the Woman- Church?

In Isaiah 50: 2 clearly said that He changed the rivers at the ends of the earth into wilderness;

"^{2} I make the rivers a wilderness; ..."

And in Isaiah 42: 15 He said;

"^{15}I will make the rivers coastlands (isles),..."

It is very clear here that the wilderness is at the end of the River in the east where it splits into four riverheads where God turned it into wilderness and islands (during the flood). It is also where Tarshish is located for the River overflow through in Isaiah 23: 10;

"^{10}Overflow through your land like the River, O daughter of Tarshish;..."

And Tarshish is also the isles in verse 6;

"^{6}Cross over to Tarshish; wail, you inhabitants of the coastland (isles)!'"

Take note that there are dwellers or inhabitants in the wilderness (Psalms 72: 9) just like there are inhabitants in Tarshish and of the isles and of the ends of the earth where Sheba is located (Matt. 12: 42). This is contrary to what some of the remnants of the Church of God claimed that the wilderness (the place of safety) is located somewhere in the deserted place in Jordan called Petra. An idolatrous place.

Would God bring His people to be protected in an idolatrous place? I don't think so. Besides the desert wilderness in Jordan have no inhabitants. It just become alive because of tourism.

The carcass – Jesus Christ will be in the east where the eagles will gather the Woman-Church in the wilderness (isles).

The only great eagle (Rev. 12: 14) in the east is the Philippine Eagle. It is the most magnificent and largest eagle in the world. It has almost come to extinction. But God revive the eagles so that we will know that He is God and the symbolic meaning it will play in the end time.

The Philippines (the land of Ophir, Sheba, Tarshish, and Havilah) is the modern day meaning of the symbols/codes, the isles (coastlands), the ends of the earth, eagles, east, and sometimes wilderness as it relates to the previous symbols.

Prior to the flood, the modern-day Philippines was at the ends of the earth directly east of Jerusalem when the earth is just one piece of dry land (Gen. 1: 10) and the four rivers from the garden of Eden overflow the land and into the sea. When it was a circle (Isa. 40: 22) and like a clay under the seal as God ask Job in Job 38: 4, 14;

"⁴"Where were you when I laid the foundations of the earth? Tell Me, if you have understanding."

¹⁴It is turned <u>as clay to the seal</u>; and they stand <u>as a garment</u>."

When a seal is stamped into the clay, it is trimmed in a circular manner that the result is called bulla. It is a clay seal impression used to seal documents or items like the seal of King Hezekiah of Judah and the seal of Isaiah (in the cover of the hardcover) discovered in archeological excavation in Jerusalem.

The Bible mentioned that God planted a garden east of Eden in Genesis and a river flowed towards the east to water the garden. And from there it splits into four riverheads (Gen. 2: 10) and the rivers emptied into the ends of the earth as mentioned in Psalms 72; 8 that the river flowed into the ends of the earth;

"⁸And from the River to the ends of the earth."

The ends of the earth is bounded by land (to the west) and by sea (to the east) (Gen. 1: 9-10). The waters of the rivers flowed to the sea at the ends of the earth in the east into the Great Sea (Pacific Ocean) (Eze. 47: 10).

And during the flood, God reap and torn apart the earth and He made the rivers into islands (Isa. 42: 15). Just as Jesus said in Isaiah 44: 24 that He spread out the earth by Himself to our current map today.

Psalms 72: 8- 10 give us the connection of the "ends of the earth" and of the "isles" to the "wilderness" which will be the place of safety for the woman. The verses also tell us that the "wilderness" is located at the "ends of the earth" which is also the isles (islands) in the east.

Isaiah 60: 1-2 and 8 to 9 confirms that the isles is the place of safety because the Lord will come to the isles;

"¹Arise, shine; for your light has come! And the glory of the Lord is risen upon you.

²For behold, the darkness shall cover the earth, and deep darkness the people; but the Lord will arise over you, and His glory will be seen upon you."

We will be the light unto our fellow Gentiles because He will arise over us and His glory will be seen in us. And in verse 8 to 9 tell us who is the "you" in the above verse;

"⁸"Who are these who fly like a cloud, and like doves to their roosts? ⁹Surely the coastlands (isles) shall wait for Me; and the ships of Tarshish will come first, to bring your sons from afar (east), their silver and their gold with them, to the name of the Lord your God (the Father), and to the Holy One of Israel (Jesus Christ), because He has glorified you.""

Verse 8 describes the Philippine Eagle who fly like a cloud because it is big when flying in the sky and yet as gentle as a dove when it lands to its nest (roost). It can also mean the Pilipino people who fly back and forth to their roosts (homes). Roosts is plural because those who are scattered abroad have at least two homes. One in the Philippines and one in the home country where they are working (OFW's). These are also the people described in Habakkuk 1: 6 as;

"⁶...Which marches through the breadth of the earth, to possess dwelling places that are not theirs."

And like the eagle in verse 8 that;

"⁸...They fly as the eagle that hastens to eat."

Verse 9 of Isaiah 60 confirmed that it is the isles. This is a very clear connection of the isles and the eagle. They are one and the same. It also mentioned the ships of Tarshish, silver, and gold. Similarly, Psalms 72: 9-10, mentioned also the King of Tarshish and the Kings of Sheba and Seba. These are the kings of some of the islands in the isles.

The light mentioned in Isaiah 60: 1, "For your light has come!"

is Jesus Christ as He claimed in John 9: 5;

> "⁵"...As long as I am in the world, <u>I am the light of the world</u>.""

Yeshua will come to the isles to be with His servants. Just as He said again in Isaiah 51: 4-5, saying;

> "⁴"Listen to Me, <u>My people</u>; and give ear to Me, O <u>My nation</u>:
> For <u>law will proceed from Me</u>, and I will make My justice rest
> As a <u>light of the peoples</u>.
> ⁵My righteousness is near, My salvation has gone forth,
> And My arms will judge the peoples;
> <u>The coastlands/isles will wait upon Me</u>,
> And on My arm they will trust.""

Verse 5 clearly said that Jesus Christ is coming to the isles as He said, "*The coastlands/isles will wait upon Me*". He will come to the peoples of the isles who are waiting for His law and His salvation.

But when is He coming?

When the servants have fulfilled the works appointed to them in Matthew 24: 14;

> "¹⁴And this gospel of the kingdom will be preached in all the world as a witness to all the nations, and then <u>the end will come</u>."

The "end" here is Jesus Christ as He claimed He is in Revelation 22: 13;

> "¹³"...I am the Alpha and the Omega, the Beginning and the <u>End</u>, the First and the Last.""

And in Isaiah 59:18 -19 confirms the protection that God will provide to the isles (wilderness) against His enemy, the serpent;

> "¹⁸ ...The <u>coastlands (isles)</u> He will fully repay.
> ¹⁹So shall they fear the name of the Lord from the west, and <u>His glory</u> from the <u>rising of the sun</u>; when <u>the enemy comes in like a flood, the Spirit of the Lord will lift up a standard against him</u>."

The connecting words or common denominator between the isles and the wilderness is that they are both attacked by the enemy, "<u>like a flood</u>". This attack of the serpent (the enemy of God) is also mentioned in Revelation 12: 15-17;

> "¹⁵So the serpent spewed water out of his mouth like a flood after the woman, that he might cause her to be carried away by the flood. ¹⁶But the earth helped the woman, and the earth opened its mouth and swallowed up the flood which the dragon had spewed out of his mouth. ¹⁷And the dragon was enraged with the woman, and he went to make war with the rest of her offspring, who keep the commandments of God and have the testimony of Jesus Christ."

We can say that the isles and the wilderness is one and the same because they are both attacked by the enemy in like manner – like a flood. The isles is attacked because of the righteous people of God that are there. While the wilderness is attacked because of the "woman" the Church of God (the Bride of Jesus Christ).

"Like a flood" means a lot of people and war machineries are involved in a sudden attack. Perhaps like "blitzkrieg"? It is defined as an intense military campaign intended to bring about a swift victory.

This attack to the isles/wilderness will be done by the revived Holy Roman Empire, currently called European Union. It will be composed of ten nations (ten horns in Revelation 17) under the German leadership (the King of the North) which is under the command of the Vatican (the Great Harlot, the woman the church of Satan as opposed to the woman – the Church of God).

It is described in Daniel 11: 16 and 18;

> "¹⁶...He (the King of the North) shall stand in the Glorious Land with destruction in his power.
>
> ¹⁸After this he shall turn his face to the coastlands (isles) and shall take many. But a ruler shall bring the reproach against them to an end; and with the reproach removed, he shall turn back on him."

After their defeat, the king of the North (composed of ten kings of the European Union) turns back to Jerusalem in Daniel 11: 31;

> "³¹And forces shall be mustered by him, and they shall defile the sanctuary fortress; then they shall take away the daily

sacrifices, and place there the abomination of desolation."

And in Daniel 12: 11;

"[11]And from the time that the daily sacrifice is taken away, and the abomination of desolation is set up, there shall be one thousand two hundred and ninety days."

This is the beginning of the great tribulation period mentioned by Jesus Christ in Matthew 24: 15 and 21;

"[15]"Therefore when you see the 'abomination of desolation,' spoken of by Daniel the prophet, standing in the holy place" (whoever reads, let him understand), [21]For then there will be great tribulation, such as has not been since the beginning of the world until this time, no, nor ever shall be.'"

This is also the sign for the rest of the offspring of the woman (the Church of God) and those who keep the commandments of God and have the testimony of Jesus Christ (Rev. 12:17) to flea to the wilderness in Matthew 12: 20;

"[20]And pray that your flight may not be in winter or on the Sabbath."

Winter or "dark winter" when the enemy is actively hunting the offspring and Sabbath when the wilderness/isles is close, and no flight can come in.

Now, let us look closer to the sequence of events from the time the woman fled to the wilderness for safety to the time the serpent was defeated and turned back to hunt the rest of the offspring of the woman who did not flea to the wilderness yet.

As we read Revelation 12: 13-17, we should pay careful attention to verse 15. This is the connection of the isles and the wilderness in Isaiah 59: 19. The common enemy of the woman and God is the dragon or the "serpent of old" which is Satan the Devil that is going to attack "like a flood".

Revelation 12: 13;

"[13]Now when the dragon saw that he had been cast to the earth, he persecuted the woman who gave birth to the male Child."

The male Child here is obviously Jesus Christ. And the word woman is symbolically pertaining to the Church of God spiritually.

Please note that when Biblical prophecy in Revelation mention the "woman", it means church. The Church of God as mentioned in Revelation 12 and the church of Satan (the Vatican) as mentioned in Revelation 17.

Revelation 12: 14;

"¹⁴But the woman was given two wings of a great eagle, that she might fly into the wilderness to her place, where she is nourished for a time and times and half a time, from the presence of the serpent."

The eagle here is a locational clue of the wilderness and at the same time an indication that they need to travel by air (to fly literally – perhaps by airplane) to her designated place in the wilderness where she is going to be protected for three and a half years (time and times and half a time). Three times and a half (3.5 years).

This is confirmed in Revelation 12: 6;

"⁶Then the woman fled into the wilderness, where she has a place prepared by God, that they (the isles) should feed her there one thousand two hundred and sixty days."

If we multiply 3.5 years to 365 days a year, the result is 1257.5 days which can be rounded off to 1260 days. It can be almost the same if we use the Hebrew calendar.

Let us continue to verse 15 of Revelation 12;

"¹⁵So the serpent spewed water out of his mouth like a flood after the woman, that he might cause her to be carried away by the flood."

The parallel of this verse is in Isaiah 59: 19;

"¹⁹...When the enemy comes in like a flood,..."

And in Daniel 11:18;

"¹⁸After this he shall turn his face to the coastlands (isles), and shall take many."

Notice that both Daniel 11:18 and Isaiah 59:19 is talking about an attack to the isles while Revelation 12: 15 is an attack to the woman in the wilderness. But Psalms 72: 8-10 decoded that the "ends of the earth" (in the east), the isles, and the wilderness are in the same location in the east (Isa. 59: 18-19). On the other hand, verse 9 of Psalms 72 said, "Those who <u>dwell</u> in the <u>wilderness</u> will <u>bow before Him</u>…" Comparing this to Isaiah 60: 9;

> "⁹Surely <u>the coastlands</u> (isles) <u>shall wait for Me</u>; and the ships of Tarshish will come first, to bring your sons from afar, their silver and their gold with them, to the name of the Lord your God, and to the Holy One of Israel, because He has glorified you."

This verse is translated by the New Living Translation as;

> "⁹They are ships from the <u>ends of the earth</u>, from lands <u>that trust in Me</u>, led by the great ships of Tarshish. They are bringing the people of Israel home from <u>far away</u>, carrying their silver and gold. <u>They will honor the LORD your God, the Holy One of Israel</u>, for He has filled you with splendor."

And in King James Version;

> "⁹Surely the <u>isles</u> shall wait for Me, and the ships of Tarshish first, to bring thy sons <u>from far</u>, their silver and their gold with them, unto the name of the LORD thy God, and to the Holy One of Israel, because He hath glorified thee."

The wilderness, the ends of the earth, and the isles is inhabited by people who will believe and worship the God of the Bible. They will keep the commandments of God and will have the testimony of Jesus Christ (Revelation 19:10).

Here is the response to the attack by the dragon (Satan, the Devil, the serpent of old in Rev. 12: 9) through the revived Holy Roman Empire (the 10 nation European Union) to the woman in the wilderness in verse 16 of Revelation 12;

> "¹⁶But <u>the earth</u> helped the woman, and the earth opened its mouth and swallowed up the flood which the dragon had spewed out of his mouth."

And here is a parallel response in Isaiah 59: 19;

> "¹⁹ "…<u>The Spirit of the Lord</u> will lift up a standard against him.""

And in Daniel 11: 18;

"¹⁸…But <u>a ruler</u> shall bring the reproach against them to an end;…"

Could the ruler here the ruler mentioned in Revelation 1: 5 as Jesus Christ?

"⁵…and from <u>Jesus Christ</u>, the faithful witness, the firstborn from the dead, and <u>the ruler</u> over the kings of the earth."

The response to the attack is coded in three different ways: the earth helped, the Spirit of the Lord, and a ruler. These are three different points of view of the response to the attack, yet the sequence of events and the place of attack is all the same in Isaiah, Daniel, and Revelation. But it is very clear that the serpent, Satan, and the Dragon uses an army (similar to Daniel 11:7) like a flood and he was defeated as it is written in Revelation 17: 12-14;

"¹²"The <u>ten horns</u> which you saw are <u>ten kings</u> who have received no kingdom as yet, but they receive authority for one hour as kings with <u>the beast</u>. ¹³These are of one mind, and they will give their power and authority to the beast. ¹⁴<u>These will make war with the Lamb, and the Lamb</u> will overcome them, for He is Lord of lords and King of kings; and <u>those who are with Him are called, chosen, and faithful</u>.""

Notice carefully that the ten horns (nations/kingdom) have not been in power yet (as of 2023). Therefore, the war that these ten kingdoms going to wedge against the Lamb have not yet happened.

And in Revelation 12: 17;

"¹⁷And the dragon was enraged with the woman, and he went to make war with the rest of <u>her offspring</u>, who keep the <u>commandments of God and have the testimony of Jesus Christ</u>."

So, after his defeat, he went back to his place and at the same time persecute the rest of the people who are Christ believer. He also went back to Jerusalem and sit up the abomination of desolation in the Temple.

Perhaps the offspring mentioned in verse 17 are Pilipino people and other members of the Church of God that are fulfilling the work of preaching the gospel around the world and those who have believed in the preaching but have not yet gone to the wilderness just as described in Daniel 11: 32-35;

> "³²Those who do wickedly against the covenant he shall corrupt with flattery; but <u>the people who know their God</u> shall be strong, and carry out great exploits. ³³And those of <u>the people who understand shall instruct many</u>; yet for many days <u>they shall fall by sword and flame, by captivity and plundering</u>. ³⁴Now when they fall, they shall be aided with a little help; but <u>many shall join with them by intrigue</u>. ³⁵And some of <u>those of understanding shall fall, to refine</u> them, <u>purify</u> them, and <u>make them white</u>, until <u>the time of the end</u>; because it is still for the appointed time."

Now take note that the dragon, the serpent, and Satan the Devil are one and the same as mentioned in Revelation 12: 9;

> "⁹So the great dragon was cast out, that serpent of old, called the Devil and Satan, who deceives the whole world; he was cast to the earth, and his angels were cast out with him."

In summary, these are the sequence of events;

1. The Beast called the revived Holy Roman Empire – the modern-day European Union that will be composed of ten nations (ten horns Rev 17: 12), under the King of the North (Germany) – "shall stand in the Glorious Land (Jerusalem, Israel) with destruction in his power" (Dan. 11:16, 41);

2. After this, the Beast will make war with the Lamb (Rev 17:14) by attacking the isles in Daniel 11: 18;

   > "¹⁸After this he shall turn his face to the coastlands (isles), and shall take many."

   > "¹⁴ "These will make war with the Lamb, and the Lamb will overcome them, for He is Lord of lords and King of kings; and those who are with Him are called, chosen, and faithful.""

3. The Beast will be defeated by "a ruler" who "lift up a standard" against them. Then;

   a. They go back to its place (Dan. 11:18-19),

   b. Persecute the rest of the offspring of the woman (Dan. 11: 32-35),

   c.   Destroy the Vatican City (Rev. 17:16).

4.   Defile the Temple in Jerusalem by placing the abomination of desolation and stopping the daily sacrifices in Daniel 11: 31;

> "³¹And forces shall be mustered by him, and they shall defile the sanctuary fortress; then they shall take away the daily sacrifices, and place there the abomination of desolation."

5.   The king of the North (of the Beast) will declare himself as god in Daniel 11: 36 and 37;

> "³⁶"…he shall exalt and magnify himself above every god,…³⁷"…nor regard any god; for he shall exalt himself above them all.""

6.   Tribulation period begin in Matthew 24: 15 and 21;

> "¹⁵"Therefore when you see the 'abomination of desolation,' spoken of by Daniel the prophet, standing in the holy place,…"
>
> ²¹For then there will be great tribulation, such as has not been since the beginning of the world until this time, no, nor ever shall be."

7.   Jesus Christ ushered in the Kingdom of God and role humanity with the rod of iron;

> "²⁹ Immediately after the tribulation of those days the sun will be darkened, and the moon will not give its light; the stars will fall from heaven, and the powers of the heavens will be shaken. ³⁰Then the sign of the Son of Man will appear in heaven, and then all the tribes of the earth will mourn, and they will see the Son of Man coming on the clouds of heaven with power and great glory."
>
> And in verse 27;
>
> "²⁷For as the lightning comes from the east and flashes to the west, so also will the coming of the Son of Man be."
>
> And He will role humanity with a rod of iron as it is written in Revelation 12: 5;
>
> "⁵She bore a male Child who was to rule all nations with a rod of iron. And her Child was caught up to God

and His throne."

Now let us look at this "rod of iron". What is it and what is it like, so that we may understand and fear the name of the Lord. Because so many professing Christian Evangelicals undermine what is the significance of this word. Many ministers say that it is just a shepherd's staff or rod guiding the flocks in a very relaxing, enjoyable, and fun way. They falsely interpret it as not to be compared to that <u>rod of discipline</u> instituted by God to correct and guide children in Proverbs 13: 24;

"²⁴He who spares his rod hates his son, but he who loves him disciplines him promptly."

This is in view of their belief that God should not be feared for He is merciful and loving and gracious God as if He cannot break a plate. They pictured Him like effeminate being, so gentle and so forgiving that He will not lay a hand to those who disobey Him. They do not want people to think that God cannot beat His children to correct and discipline them, if necessary, like most parents around the world should do. They do not want us to fear Him, contrary to what God requires of His people in Ecclesiastes 12: 13 saying;

"¹³Let us hear the conclusion of the whole matter: <u>Fear God, and keep his commandments</u>: for <u>this is the whole duty of man</u>."

And yet these people voided God's commandments. They say it was done away. Nailed in the cross. And they follow the commandments and traditions of another Jesus and of men.

They do not fear God, forgetting that God destroyed the first earth and all the inhabitants with it (2 Peter 3: 5). It was repeated by God to the inhabitants of the second earth (which is also the first) from the time of the male and female He created to the time of Noah and destroy the inhabitants of the earth. And again, another example is Sodom and Gomorrah where He torch the inhabitants of that land to ashes. Then God will subject hardheaded humanity in a Great Tribulation full of sufferings and pain that has not been done or experienced since the beginning of time. And by the end of the Millennial Kingdom after the judgement day He will destroy the heavens and the earth once more and replace it with a new one. It will no longer be destroyed by water but by fire. And yet mankind does not understand the fear of the Lord for they are blinded by iniquities.

The Philippines and the world are visited by terrible disaster year after year. And yet, instead of turning to the real living God, they turn to their idols (fake gods) again and again. They never learn. And so, the time is coming that a terrible, terrible day will come upon the world. These events are so terrible that it can almost put the earth into extinction. If it is not greater than a rod of iron, I do not know what.

But in the beginning of His reign on earth, mankind will hate Him. Even mourn when He arrives (Matt. 24: 30). Instead of being happy that God will rule over us instead of Satan, who causes so much pain, harm, and deception in the world, people ignore and dismiss God.

They love the way of Satan. They love the lawlessness and violence and sufferings. They love disobedience that they not want God in their lives even in the beginning of the Millennial Kingdom. But this world is God's creation. It is His and He can do whatever He wants according to His plans and purpose for creating humanity. He will enforce His will upon humanity with a rod of iron. Those who will disobey Him will have no rain and will suffer pestilences and troubles until they repent and turn to God. God will reign on earth with a fist of iron until He establish His Kingdom upon humanity. He will force mankind to have real peace, joy, happiness, and prosperity in the absence of Satan so that all humanity may have the chance to become children of God.

God's Kingdom is not about fake freedom that humanity is crying all the time. In God, the real freedom is in the obedience of His Law. Without the Law, there is no freedom. Without obedience, there is no freedom. Disobedience is no longer an option during the Kingdom of God.

The rod of iron is real as a hard punishment to those who do not obey God. It is not just a pat on the shoulder or just a time out like for a kid. It is a real beating like a God-fearing father who beat their children diligently to discipline them into obedience and respect for the authority in the family.

Just pause for a moment and meditate what Revelation 19: 15-

16 will tell you;

> "[15]From His mouth came a sharp sword to strike down the nations. He will rule them with an iron rod. He will release the fierce wrath of God, the Almighty, like juice flowing from a winepress. [16]On his robe at his thigh was written this title: King of all kings and Lord of all lords."

And think about the 200 million army in Revelation 9: 16 in the battle in Armageddon;

> "[16]I heard the size of their army, which was 200 million mounted troops."

And how they will die because they are fighting the Lord in Revelation 14: 20;

> "[20]And the winepress was trampled outside the city, and <u>blood</u> came out of the winepress, <u>up to the horses' bridles, for one thousand six hundred furlongs</u>."

The rod of iron rulership of Jesus Christ is not a walk in the park. It is a terrible wrath of God that cannot be compared to a tyrannical or dictatorship government. God can do more beyond our imagination because He is the author of everything. That is why we need to tremble before Him and in His every word more than we fear those earthly tyrannical rulers that are just human. He is the King of all kings and Lord of all lord. He is not an ordinary president or minister. He is our Majesty. He created the heavens and the earth. He is our Creator. We are at His disposal. It is only during the times of great suffering and hardship, such as natural disasters (calamities) or illnesses (pestilences), that many people turn to God for help and guidance.

Let that sink into your soul before you undermine the power and the wrath of God.

God will redeem His Glorious Land – Israel from the east. The Redeemer shall come from the east in Isaiah 59: 20;

> "[20]"The Redeemer will come to Zion,..."

For He came from the east, from the isles, from the wilderness, from the ends of the earth to establish the Kingdom of God. He will end the reign of Satan on earth. He will begin revealing the truth to mankind. He will be the Light of this world that everyone may see His glory and give everyone the opportunity to become children in God's family to those who are willing to believe and obey.

"³⁵Let the sinners be consumed out of the earth, and let the wicked be no more. Bless thou the LORD, O my soul. Praise ye the LORD."

(Psa. 104: 35 KJV).

Amen. Even so, come quickly, Lord Jesus!

The Mystery of the First Heavens and the First Earth

Genesis 1 verse 1 states that God created the heavens and the earth. But then in verse 2, the earth became "without form and void" and was upon the face of the deep (submerged under water);

"¹In the beginning <u>God created the heavens and the earth</u>.

²The <u>earth was without form, and void</u>; and darkness was on the face of the deep. And the Spirit of God was hovering over the face of the waters."

What happened between this verses?

We know in the Bible that when God created something, it is good and beautiful and bright in Ecclesiastes 3:11;

"¹¹He has made everything beautiful in its time."

When God created the heavens and the earth, He put everything in place. He created the earth to be inhabited and not to be empty and chaotic in Isaiah 45:18;

"¹⁸For thus says the Lord, Who created the heavens, Who is God, Who formed the earth and made it, Who has established it, Who <u>did not create it in vain</u>, Who <u>formed it to be inhabited</u>: "I am the Lord, and there is no other."

So, what happened in verse 2? When God created the earth perfect and beautiful, why did it become formless, empty, and submerge under water full of darkness instead of light? Where did the inhabitants go?

We can infer that something terrible happened between verse 1 (the creation) and 2 (perished). As we have discussed before, Satan, formerly Lucifer (Bringer of light) rebelled against God – his Creator. He was the seal of perfection of God's creation in Ezekiel 28: 12-15;

> "[12]...You were the seal of perfection, full of wisdom and perfect in beauty. [13]You were in Eden, the garden of God; Every precious stone was your covering: the sardius, topaz, and diamond, beryl, onyx, and jasper, sapphire, turquoise, and emerald with gold. The workmanship of your timbrels and pipes was prepared for you on the day you were created.
> [14]"You were the anointed cherub who covers; I established you; you were on the holy mountain of God; you walked back and forth in the midst of fiery stones.
> [15]You were perfect in your ways from the day you were created, till *iniquity* was found in you."

His iniquities include exalting himself before God in Isaiah 14: 12-15;

> "[12]"How you are fallen from heaven, O Lucifer, son of the morning! How you are cut down to the ground, you who weakened the nations! [13]For you have said in your heart: 'I will ascend into heaven, I will exalt my throne above the stars of God; I will also sit on the mount of the congregation on the farthest sides of the north; [14]I will ascend above the heights of the clouds, I will be like the Most High.' [15]Yet you shall be brought down to Sheol, to the lowest depths of the Pit."

And in his rebellion, he attacked God in heaven in Revelation 12: 3- 4, 7-9;

> "[3]And another sign appeared in heaven: behold, a great, fiery red dragon having seven heads and ten horns, and seven diadems on his heads. [4]His tail drew a third of the stars of heaven and threw them to the earth...."
> "[7]And war broke out in heaven: Michael and his angels fought with the dragon; and the dragon and his angels fought, [8]but

they did not prevail, nor was a place found for them in heaven any longer. ⁹So the great dragon was cast out, that serpent of old, called the Devil and Satan, who deceives the whole world; he was cast to the earth, and his angels were cast out with him."

And because of this war in heaven that the first earth was destroyed and its inhabitants that are followers of Lucifer. Total destruction of the surface of the earth through flood, submerged under water and the heavenly bodies were subjected in futility.

Satan wants to dethrone God (his Creator) and he wants to be worshipped and adorned. By whom, we may ask? Perhaps God have already created human beings also during the existence of the first earth by which Satan and his angels are to be ministers to the people of the ancient times in Hebrew 1: 13-14;

"¹³But to which of the <u>angels</u> has He ever said: "Sit at My right hand, till I make Your enemies Your footstool"?

¹⁴Are they not all <u>ministering spirits</u> sent forth <u>to minister for those who will inherit salvation?</u>"

Peter fill and confirm this gap in his second Epistle chapter 3 verse 5 to 7;

"⁵For this they <u>willfully forget</u>: that by the word of God the heavens were of old, and <u>the earth standing out of water and in the water</u>, ⁶by which <u>the world that **then existed perished**</u>, being *flooded with water*. ⁷But the <u>heavens</u> and the <u>earth</u> which are **now** <u>preserved by the same word</u>, are *reserved for fire* until <u>the day of judgment and perdition</u> of ungodly men."

These verses confirms that there was these first heavens and earth that perished (without form and void). And this was confirmed and seconded by Revelation 21: 1;

"¹Now I saw a new heaven and a new earth, for the first heaven and the first earth had passed away. Also, there was no more sea."

But the next verses (verse 2 and 3) lay the mystery of the first heavens and the first earth. Verse 2-3 states that;

"²Then I, John, saw the holy city, New Jerusalem, coming

down out of heaven from God, prepared as a bride adorned for her husband. ³And I heard a loud voice from heaven saying, "Behold, the tabernacle of God is with men, and He will dwell with them, and they shall be His people. God Himself will be with them and be their God."

Many Bible scholars and ministers interpret these verses 1 and 2 as continuous and literal. Meaning that the first earth being mentioned in verse 1 is the earth that we are currently living in today and is going to be destroyed and replaced with a new heaven and a new earth where the New Jerusalem will come down from God in heaven.

Notice that verse one mentioned heaven and not heavens as compared to verse one of Genesis 1 – during the time of creation (recreation).

The heaven mentioned in Revelation 21: 1 pertains not only to the atmospheric portion of the earth, but the whole firmament (Gen. 1:8) above that includes the universe or outer space and heavenly bodies.

Heaven is the firmament (Gen. 1: 8) and underneath the heaven are the heavens (several layers) that encompassed the whole earth.

If the views of various religious leaders and experts on the Bible are accurate, this conflicts with what Peter stated in verses 5-7. In these verses, Peter clearly stated that there was a previous world (earth) that was destroyed by a flood. As previously discussed, this flood is not the Great Flood in the time of Noah, because it did not completely destroy the earth, but rather killed all living things on the surface of the earth.

In verse 7, Peter clearly said that the heavens and the earth that now exist, was restored, or recreated by the same word as to the way the first earth was created.

The word here may have dual meaning. One, the same Word pertaining to the same Creator of the heavens and the earth which is Jesus Christ (John 1: 1-10) by the will of the Father as mentioned in Revelation 4: 11;

"¹¹You are worthy, O Lord, to receive glory and honor and power; for You created all things, and by Your will they exist

394

and were created."

God the Father created all things through Jesus Christ in John
1: 2-3;

"²He was in the beginning with God. ³All things were made
through Him, and without Him nothing was made that was made."

And in Colossians 1: 16-17;

"¹⁶For by Him all things were created that are in heaven and that
are on earth, visible and invisible, whether thrones or dominions or
principalities or powers. All things were created through Him and
for Him. ¹⁷And He is before all things, and in Him all things
consist."

God the Father is the Supreme Designer of the universe and
Jesus Christ is the engineer, physicist, biologist, scientist, artist, and all
the "tist" we can ever imagine involving the creative power of God.
But most of all, He is the humble, faithful, and loyal Servant to His
Father. Nothing He do or say that did not come from the Father just
as it is written in John 12: 49;

"⁴⁹For I have not spoken on My own authority; but the Father
who sent Me gave Me a command, what I should say and what
I should speak."

And in John 7: 16-18;

"¹⁶ Jesus answered them and said, "My doctrine is not Mine,
but His who sent Me. ¹⁷If anyone wills to do His will, he shall
know concerning the doctrine, whether it is from God or
whether I speak on My own authority. ¹⁸He who speaks from
himself seeks his own glory; but He who seeks the glory of the
One who sent Him is true, and no unrighteousness is in Him.""

And in John 8: 28;

"²⁸Then Jesus said to them, "When you lift up the Son of Man,
then you will know that I am He, and that I do nothing of
Myself; but as My Father taught Me, I speak these things.""
And He do nothing of Himself in John 5: 19-20;

"[19]Then Jesus answered and said to them, "Most assuredly, I say to you, <u>the Son can do nothing of Himself</u>, but <u>what He sees the Father do</u>; for <u>whatever He does</u>, <u>the Son also does in like manner</u>. [20]For the Father loves the Son, and shows Him all things that He Himself does; and He will show Him greater works than these, that you may marvel.""

Jesus Christ is our model on how to become sons of God. He is the Word.

The second meaning of the "word" as mentioned by Peter in his second Epistle may pertain to the words (the methodology) of Genesis 1: 3-31 as Jesus Christ recreated the heavens and the earth as the former was destroyed by the rebellion of Lucifer (Satan, the Devil) and become without form and void full of darkness and submerged under water for a time, we do not know.

If these are the meanings of the "word" that Peter said, then the former or the first earth have humans in it also just as it is said in Isaiah 45: 18;

"[18]For thus says the Lord, Who created the heavens, Who is God, Who formed the earth and made it, Who has established it, Who did not create it in vain, Who formed it to be inhabited: "I am the Lord, and there is no other.""

And perhaps the inhabitants of the first earth are the very reason why God sent Lucifer and a third of the angels in heaven. They are to be ministers to mankind living on the first earth under the leadership of Lucifer.

He was supposed to be the "Bringer of Light (Jesus Christ)" to lead the ancient mankind on how to obey the government of God and how to become sons of God. Perhaps, Lucifer being a genius angel was able to implement the government of God in the former earth. And the people of the earth worship, obey, and adore the True Living God.

This is perhaps one of the main reasons why iniquity was found in Lucifer (Ezek. 28: 15). He became envious and jealous to God, and He wanted to become god. To be worshipped and adorned by the people of the earth. So, instead of leading the people to righteousness, he deceives the whole world (Rev. 12: 9) into worshipping him knowingly and unknowingly just as he is doing to the whole world today. As it is written in Ecclesiastes 1: 9-10;

> "⁹That which has been is what will be, that which is done is what will be done, and there is nothing new under the sun.
> ¹⁰Is there anything of which it may be said, "See, this is new"?"

It has already been in ancient times before us.

Everything that is happening today and that is going to happen in the very near future have happened before in the ancient times. Could these ancient times the times of the first earth?

Lucifer lead the people of the earth and his angels away from God instead of towards God. He led the people and the angels to rebellion against God (their Creator) and to worship him (the creature) and influence them with his evil mind.

So, God destroyed mankind on the face of the first earth for it has become evil in His eyes. Just like what He did to mankind on earth during the time of Noah. But instead of wiping out the whole humanity once more, Noah found favor in God in Genesis 6: 5-8 that He saved humanity from total destruction;

> "⁵Then the Lord saw that the wickedness of man was great in the earth, and that every intent of the thoughts of his heart was only evil continually. ⁶And the Lord was sorry that He had made man on the earth, and He was grieved in His heart. ⁷So the Lord said, "I will destroy man whom I have created from the face of the earth, both man and beast, creeping thing and birds of the air, for I am sorry that I have made them." ⁸But Noah found grace in the eyes of the Lord."

So, do you think God is always a loving God, graceful, and an effeminate figure that cannot and will not break glass because He loves us even if we continue to disobey Him and do evil things? Think again!

God sends calamity, sicknesses and diseases, and evil governments not because He wants it. But because of our evil disobedient hearts that bring these things upon ourselves.

Just think about us in the Philippines when year after year we are visited with many major catastrophic events. And just right after the disaster happen, people thanked and praised Satan by parading their evil idols of saints of many kinds and colors. So, what do you think the Father will do? Bring it back again, because we never learned. Because we are blinded by the darkness of Satan in our lives.

Think of the things He had done and about to do to humanity because of our sinfulness. God is going to warn humanity of the great trouble that is coming because of our disobedience. It is so terrible that He said in Matthew 24: 21-22;

> "²¹For then there will be great tribulation, such as has not been since the beginning of the world until this time, no, nor ever shall be. ²²And unless those days were shortened, no flesh would be saved; ..."

This time, God does not intend to destroy humanity because He already have given salvation to mankind through Jesus Christ at an appointed time. He defeated Satan already. But humanity is going into self-destruction because of their evil hearts and mind. Not only mankind became capable of destroying (extinct) itself but also the whole earth in a push of a button. So, God will bring humanity into Great Tribulation so that mankind will know that He is God and bring humanity to its senses and rule them with the rod of iron.

Notice that the flood in the time of Noah happened in chapter 7 of Genesis. It is like a Sabbath for them inside the ark while the world is being subjected into flood. And after the flood, the earth is like in a Sabbath from mankind's evil ways. But Satan and his demons are still bound in the earth, so humanity became of evil nature once again.

Similarly, the isles will become like an ark in the coming troublesome times. They will become like a Noah type, warning the whole earth about the coming great flood (troubles and tribulations) and preaching about the hope of salvation and protection in the ark (isles with the Light).

The people of the isles will find favor in the eyes of the Lord that He will come to us as our guiding light. He will protect us and prepare us for the works that we need to do before and during the Sabbath. But this coming Sabbath (The Millennial Kingdom of God), the Creator of humanity will reign the whole earth with the rod of iron in the absence of Satan and his demons. They will be bound for a thousand years (Rev. 20: 2).

Many ministers of the professing Christianity preach in their congregation that they should not fear God for He is a loving God and Father. It is impossible for Him to harm humanity. So, it is okey to believe that God have done away His very own laws and commandments. And that people are not accountable to it once one accepted Jesus Christ as their personal Lord and Savior. As they say, once save, they will be forever save. For this, they willfully forget that the very Jesus whom they profess to believe and follow said in John 14: 15;

"¹⁵"If you <u>love Me</u>, keep My commandments….""

And John expounded what Jesus said in 1 John 5: 1-4, saying;
"¹Whoever believes that <u>Jesus is the Christ is born of God</u> (come from and begotten by the Father), and everyone who <u>loves Him</u> (Jesus Christ) who begot also <u>loves him</u> (begotten sons/children of God) who is begotten of Him (Jesus Christ). ²By this <u>we know that we love the children of God, when we love God and keep His commandments</u>. ³For <u>this is the love of God, that we keep His commandments</u>. And <u>His commandments are not burdensome</u>."

We can only say that we are a genuine follower of the real Jesus Christ if we love Him and keep/obey His commandments. And this love manifests in us by loving the begotten children of God. We do not mock and despise them who is sent to you for correction so that you too may become begotten children of God. For such, we are commanded by Jesus Christ in John 13: 34-35, saying;
"³⁴A new commandment I give to you, <u>that you love one another</u>; <u>as I have loved you</u>, that you also <u>love one another</u>. ³⁵By this all will know that you are My disciples, if you have

love for one another.""""

It is clear in the above verses that loving Jesus Christ and loving fellow believers is contingent upon the keeping/obeying His commandments. And that is the summary of the Ten Commandments – loving God first and foremost (1-4) and then loving our fellow men (5-10). So, the doctrine that God's law and commandments have been nailed in the cross is not only a deception but unbiblical based on the verses we read above and from what God have appointed mankind to be his duty in Ecclesiastes 12: 13;

"¹³Let us hear the conclusion of the whole matter: <u>Fear God</u>, and <u>keep his commandments</u>: for this is the whole <u>duty of man</u>."

Humankind does not want to fear God and obey His commandments, so they make up their own justice system that only apply to the poor. And laws that they can bend according to their own needs, will, and interpretations. In human made justice system, the law is for sale. Those who have money will be above the law. And the people love it.

Humanity prepares to fear Satan rather than God. So much so that even when Jesus Christ is already on earth that they will hate God and fight with Him. And so, our tribulation and destruction is upon the face of the earth.

This book is like the Little Book mentioned in Revelation 10: 9-10. It is sweet to swallow but hard to stomach (bitter in the stomach). It is good and sweet to know that God has chosen us as an end time servants, and He will be our light and guide and our protection in times of trouble. It is sweet to know that we shall have favor in the eyes of God. He will call us His people and His nation. And yet, this book will be bitter to digest in our stomach because this will deeply offend us from our evil ways, beliefs, and expectations. We will be brokenhearted because our religions (prison houses) whom we loved have betrayed us into another god.

Many will be offended in the end times (Matt. 24:10). It is bitter in our stomach knowing that what we have been taught in the past are all lies and deceptions. Specially knowing the fact that we have been worshipping (knowingly and unknowingly) Satan all along as people celebrate the traditions and commandments of men – the pagan traditions. It is hard for us to accept that we have been deceived because we are full of pride and arrogance that we are self-conceited to pretend that what we hear and see according to what we believe is right (self-righteous - relativism). It is easy for us to believe in lies than to make us believe that we have been lied to. Just like a popular proverb (adage) that said, "It's easier to fool people than to convince them that they have been fooled."

In God, relativism is the teaching of Satan. Things does not depend on what we think is right, but it is dependent on the standards and the Laws of God. It is hard and bitter to know that our expectation of going on eternal vacation grande in heaven when we accept Jesus Christ as Lord and savior is not going to happen. It is hard to accept that the expectation of some going to paradise enjoying life with 70 virgins (forever?) is not going to happen. It is hard to accept that people going to Valhalla enjoying your selfish self in inner peace is not going to happen. It is hard to stomach knowing that everything is not about ourselves but about our outgoing concerns for others and for the glory of God. To the point that we need to sacrifice ourselves for the salvation of others and for the glory of God.

For others, it is very offensive to be called a servant because most people want to be kings and queens. To be served and not to serve.

It is hard to stomach that we are created to work and not to be on vacation mode all the time. But if the Father and the Son continue to work until now in John 5: 17, "[17]But Jesus answered them, "My Father has been working until now, and I have been working."". How can we think that we should not work and just do nothing? We are just His creation and His servants.

On the other hand, it is sweet to know that Satan's time is almost over. It is good to know that the light is coming to the world full of darkness beginning from the isles and its peoples. And for those who have a servant's heart, it is good to know that now, we can serve the greatest Master of our lifetime. To serve our God who give us life and give us favor to see and enjoy His creation on earth. It is great to know also that our Master is willing and giving us the opportunity to be adopted into His Family and He will call us His children also. What can be better off to live under our Master's protection and provision and share in His abundance in peace.

But I digress, so let us go back to Revelation 21: 1 and let us examine it closer if it contradicts 2 Peter 3: 5-6 or confirms it.

As we have discussed previously, what Peter meant by "the same word" in verse 7 pertains to the same Creator (Jesus Christ – the Word) and the same process of creating the world the first time just as it is said in Ecclesiastes 1: 9-10;

"⁹That which has been is what will be, that which is done is what will be done, and there is nothing new under the sun.
¹⁰Is there anything of which it may be said, "See, this is new"? It has already been in ancient times before us."

If that is so, then definitely, the first earth has human inhabitants in it too. And that is why, verse 1 of Revelation 21 said or added (because of the word "also");

"¹ ...Also there was no more sea."

The "sea" in this verse pertains to people, multitudes, nations, and tongues as mentioned in Revelation 17: 15;

"¹⁵Then he said to me, "The waters which you saw, where the harlot sits, are peoples, multitudes, nations, and tongues.""

In the New Living Translation;

"¹⁵Then the angel said to me, "The waters where the prostitute is ruling represent masses of people of every nation and language.""

But you will say, that verse did not mentioned sea, but waters.

But did not God call the waters seas during the creation in Genesis 1: 9-10?

"⁹Then God said, "Let the <u>waters</u> under the heavens be gathered together into one place, and let the <u>dry land</u> appear"; and it was so. ¹⁰And God called the <u>dry land Earth</u>, and the <u>gathering together of the waters</u> He called <u>Seas</u>. And God saw that it was good."

And so, the "sea" mentioned in Revelation 21: 1 is a code for water which means people, multitudes, nations, and tongues that also existed in the first earth that then perished. This might be the reason why there is an expression of "sea of people".

This tells us that Revelation 21: 1-2 does not contradict 2 Peter 3: 5-7 but rather compliment and confirm each other in a highly coded way.

Revelation 21 verse 1 and 2 is not continuous event if the "sea" in verse 1 is indeed "peoples of all nations and languages" because the people are gone with the first earth. And then in like manner, Jesus Christ recreated the heavens and the earth in Genesis 1: 3-31 by which 2 Peter testified in verses 6-7;

> "⁶by which the world that <u>then existed perished (first earth)</u>, being flooded with water. ⁷But the <u>heavens and the earth</u> which are <u>now</u> (recreated earth) preserved by the same word, are <u>reserved for fire</u> until <u>the day of judgment</u> and perdition of ungodly men."

In New Living Translation;

> "⁶Then He used the water to destroy the ancient world with a mighty flood. ⁷And by the same word, the present heavens and earth have been stored up for fire. They are being kept for the day of judgment, when ungodly people will be destroyed."

Notice that God did not totally destroy the first heavens and earth (the creation), but eradicated mankind and all living things on the face of the earth just like in the times of Noah. But unlike in the times of Noah, the inhabitants of the first earth totally perished because the whole earth was submerged under water for a long time until its recreation. And because of Lucifer and mankind rebellion, God subjected the creation into futility just as it is written in Romans 8: 19- 22;

> "¹⁹For the earnest expectation of the creation eagerly waits for the revealing of the sons of God. ²⁰For the creation <u>was subjected to futility, not willingly</u>, but because of Him who subjected it in hope; ²¹because <u>the creation itself also will be delivered from the bondage of corruption into the glorious liberty of the children of God</u>. ²²For we know that the whole creation groans and labors

with birth pangs together <u>until now</u>."

God recreated the first earth and put man on it once more for the purpose of recreating Himself through mankind that they may become children of God. But from the time of Noah until now, humanity have become pure evil once again. And the world is full of darkness, of lawlessness, and unrighteousness.

So, God will subject humanity into tribulation period to wake up mankind who are godless and to establish His Kingdom after that and to rule the world with the rod of iron until they repent and obey Him. But after the Millennial Kingdom Satan will be released once more for a short period of time Revelation 20: 3, 7-8;

"³The angel threw him into the bottomless pit, which he then shut and locked so <u>Satan could not deceive the nations anymore until the thousand years were finished</u>. Afterward he must be released for a little while.

⁷Now when the thousand years have expired, Satan will be released from his prison ⁸and will go out to deceive the nations which are in the four corners of the earth,…"

After this, is the Judgement Day of the ungodly man who chose to obey and follow Satan instead of God. They already have known God during the Millennial Kingdom and yet chose Satan before God. And so, they will be subjected into the second death in a burning hell fire and perhaps together with the destruction of the whole earth through fire just as Peter said.

The "new heaven" and the "new earth" in verse 1 of Revelation 21 pertains to the total new creation of heaven and earth. This is the new earth where God will dwell. This is the second earth for God said in Isaiah 32: 4;

"⁴All the host of heaven shall be dissolved, and the heavens shall be rolled up like a scroll;

All their host shall fall down as the leaf falls from the vine, and as fruit falling from a fig tree."

And Jesus said in Matthew 5: 18;

"¹⁸For assuredly, I say to you, till heaven and earth pass away, one jot or one tittle will by no means pass from the law till all is fulfilled."

And so, when everything is fulfilled, that God will dwell in the new heaven and the new earth for the filthiness of the former have vanished and the new one become worthy to be the habitation of the Almighty Father God. With these understanding we can now understand Revelation 21: 1-7 as a continuous event and not contradictory to Peter. For as it is written;

"¹Now I saw a new heaven and a new earth, for the first heaven and the first earth had passed away. Also there was no more sea. ²Then I, John, saw the holy city, New Jerusalem, coming down out of heaven from God, prepared as a bride adorned for her husband. ³And I heard a loud voice from heaven saying, "<u>Behold, the tabernacle of God is with men, and He will dwell with them, and they shall be His people</u>. God Himself will be with them and be their God. ⁴And God will wipe away every tear from their eyes; there shall be no more death, nor sorrow, nor crying. There shall be no more pain, for the former things have passed away."

⁵Then He who sat on the throne said, "Behold, I make all things new." And He said to me, "Write, for these words are true and faithful."

⁶And He said to me, "It is done! I am the Alpha and the Omega, the Beginning and the End. I will give of the fountain of the water of life freely to him who thirsts. ⁷He who overcomes shall inherit all things, and I will be his God and he shall be My son."

To recap, like Genesis 1: 1 and 2, there is also a gap between verse 1 and 2 of Revelation 21 (the first book and the last book of the Bible respectively). 2 Peter 3 : 5-7 fill both these gaps. These gives us a better understanding of the events that occur before and after the creation and recreation in Genesis 1. Take note that Genesis 1 described both the creation process and also the recreation process or shall we say revival or resurrection of the heaven and the earth according to Peter.

Figuratively speaking, the second earth is also the first. In a literal sense, the first earth was not totally destroyed by God. It perished under water for a time we do not know. The second earth is like a revival (of the land) of the first earth. Born again, bringing it back to the surface of the water (like baptism with water), for it is above the water and in the water in 2 Peter 3: 5-6;

> "⁵For this they willfully forget: that by the word of God the heavens were of old, and <u>the earth standing out of water</u> and <u>in the water</u>, ⁶by which the world that then existed perished, being flooded with water."

And when God lift up the first earth above the surface of the water to revive it or recreate it (born again), He commanded the earth to produce vegetation coming from the seeds it had before it perished in Genesis 1: 9-11;

> "⁹Then God said, "Let the waters under the heavens be gathered together into one place, and let the <u>dry land appear</u>"; and it was so. ¹⁰And God called the dry land Earth, and the gathering together of the waters He called Seas. And God saw that it was good. ¹¹Then God said, "Let the earth bring forth grass, the herb that yields seed, and the fruit tree that yields fruit according to its kind, <u>whose seed is in itself, on the earth</u>"; and it was so."

As was said before, these words are dual in nature. Both creation and recreation or revival of the first earth. But notice carefully in verse 11 that gives us a clue that in a revival point of view of the first earth, the vegetation comes out of earth in itself, "<u>whose seed is in itself, on earth</u>". This indicates the great possibility that seeds of plants were produced and are buried in the soil of the first earth. They pre-existed on earth if we consider that when God created things it started from a mature plant with the functionality and capability of reproducing. Like human beings which started from a fully mature individual and not started from a baby. For who will take good care of the young but the adult.

Besides, Psalms 104: 30 told us that God renewed the face of the earth;

"³⁰You <u>send forth Your Spirit</u>, they are created; and <u>You renew the face of the earth</u>."

This is parallel to Genesis 1: 2;
"²...And <u>the Spirit of God was hovering over the face of the waters</u>."

The "You" here is the "Lord" Jesus Christ who created the heavens and the earth according to the Father in Hebrew 1: 10;
"¹⁰... "You, Lord, in the beginning laid the foundation of the earth, and the heavens are the work of Your hands...""""

God the Father is speaking here with the angels and Jesus Christ testifying that Christ is the one who created the heavens and the earth. That is why the "Lord" being mentioned in Psalms 104 is the Lord Jesus Christ who in verse 2;
"²...Who stretch out the heavens like a curtain."

And in verse 5;
"⁵You who laid the foundations of the earth, so that it should not be moved forever,..."

God the Father as Wisdom said in Proverbs 8: 27- 31 when He witness Jesus Christ sits the heavens and the earth;
"²⁷When He prepared the heavens, I was there, when He drew a circle on the face of the deep, ²⁸when He established the clouds above, when He strengthened the fountains of the deep, ²⁹when He assigned to the sea its limit, so that the waters would not transgress His command, (Look up Psalms 104: 9) when He marked out the foundations of the earth, ³⁰Then I was beside Him as a master craftsman; and I was daily His delight, rejoicing always before Him, ³¹rejoicing in His <u>inhabited world</u>, and my delight was with the sons of men." (The first earth was inhabited with the sons of men).

For who is with the Word in John 1: 1 than the Father. The wisdom is the personification of the Father in Proverbs 8.

Jesus Christ renewed the face of the first earth giving way to the second earth which is also the first.

The death and revival of the first earth can be compared to the death and resurrection of Jesus Christ (born again). He died in flesh because of the sins of the world and was resurrected as a Spirit being full of grace and glory. So will the earth be when it will be totally destroyed (death) by the end of the Judgement Day and be replaced (resurrected) by a new heaven and a new earth where God the Father Almighty will dwell with men – His people (Rev. 21: 3-4).

So, from the revival point of view, the gap between Revelation 21 and Genesis 1 verse 1 and 2 and is the recreation of the heavens and the earth including the first humans (Gen. 1: 27-28) on the second earth (or revived earth (it is the second, but it is also the first)) which will last up to the end of the Millennial Kingdom of God here on earth. By the end of the Millennial Kingdom is the Judgement Day – the day of the second death for those who once again believe Satan and denied God in their lives. Then the earth will be destroyed through fire and be replaced by new heaven and new earth where the New Jerusalem will come down from heaven as the habitation of God.

The earth under the government of God and under the Kingship of Jesus Christ during the Millennial Kingdom will be a wonderful world tomorrow unlike anything ever seen on earth. During this 1000-year reign of Jesus Christ, people will be given a chance know the truth, obey God, and experience real peace, joy, happiness, and prosperity. And a real euphoria to those who listen and obey Him until the final purification of humans at the end of the Millennial Kingdom when Satan is released for a short time. And those who did not remain faithful to God will die the second death. An eternal death. Vanished forever.

So, with the final purification of humans on earth, Revelation 21: 1- 4 becomes a creation perspective of the new heaven and the new earth for the first earth (which is also the second) is totally destroyed through fire and replaced with a new one that it becomes worthy to receive the New Jerusalem where God dwells here on earth;

"¹Now I saw a new heaven and a new earth, for the first heaven and the first earth had passed away. Also there was no more sea.

²Then I, John, saw the holy city, New Jerusalem, coming down out of heaven from God, prepared as a bride adorned for her husband. ³And I heard a loud voice from heaven saying, "Behold, the tabernacle of God is with men, and He will dwell with them, and they shall be His people. God Himself will be with them and be their God. ⁴And God will wipe away every tear from their eyes; there shall be no more death, nor sorrow, nor crying. There shall be no more pain, for the former things have passed away."

God will make all things new after the Judgement Day as it is written in Revelation 21: 5;

"⁵Then He who sat on the throne said, "Behold, I make all things new." And He said to me, "Write, for these words are true and faithful.""

Perhaps this is the main reason Christ will reign on earth with the rod of iron for the establishment of the Millennial Kingdom for the calling of the children of God and in preparation for His bride the "New Jerusalem" which will come out from heaven and for the purification of the earth to be worthy to receive the Father to dwell on earth with His people. After that we do not know what is going to happen. Maybe being the children of God, we can perform the works that God the Father and God the Son have been doing since the beginning of time and the government of God will continue to expand. For as it is said in Isaiah 9:7;

"⁷Of the increase of His government and peace there will be no end, upon the throne of David and over His kingdom, to order it and establish it with judgment and justice from that time forward, even forever. The zeal of the Lord of hosts will perform this."

Christ is calling the people of the isles (Isa. 49: 6) to be His servants to prepare for His coming Kingdom and to serve Him also during the Millennial Kingdom. What an honor for us, the isles to have purpose and meaning for our lives as a part of God's masterplan for the salvation of mankind. It will not be easy. But if we think about that our Creator sacrificed Himself for the salvation of mankind, how much more can we sacrifice ourselves for the sake of our fellow men. Our brothers and sisters in fact.

The New Jerusalem after the Judgement Day will be pure in the brightness of His righteousness and glory that there is no need for the sun and moon to illuminate on it as it is written in Revelation 21: 23;

"²³The city had no need of the sun or of the moon to shine in it, for the glory of God illuminated it. The Lamb is its light."

But before this, the second earth, knowing that it will be sinful once again that Peter said in verse 7 that it is;

"⁷But the heavens and the earth which are now preserved by the same word, are reserved for fire until the day of judgment and perdition of ungodly men."

The Judgment Day of God (Zep. 1) for the ungodly men maybe similar to the Day of the Lord where in 2 Peter 3: 10-13 said;

"¹⁰But the day of the Lord will come as a thief in the night, in which the heavens will pass away with a great noise, and the elements will melt with fervent heat; both the earth and the works that are in it will be burned up. ¹¹Therefore, since all these things will be dissolved, what manner of persons ought you to be in holy conduct and godliness, ¹²looking for and hastening the coming of the day of God, because of which the heavens will be dissolved, being on fire, and the elements will melt with fervent heat? ¹³Nevertheless we, according to His promise, look for new heavens and a new earth in which righteousness dwells."

This verse tells us that he second earth which Peter claimed we are now, will undergo a tremendous and terrible disturbances as in the unleashing of the sixth seal in Revelation 6: 12- 14, 17;

"¹²I looked when He opened the sixth seal, and behold, there was a great earthquake; and the sun became black as sackcloth of hair, and the moon became like blood. ¹³And the stars of heaven fell to the earth, as a fig tree drops its late figs when it is shaken by a mighty wind. ¹⁴Then the sky receded as a scroll when it is rolled up, and every mountain and island was moved out of its place. ¹⁷For the great day of His wrath has come, and who is able to stand?"

And God give further details of <u>the Great Day of the Lord</u> in Zephaniah. You need to read the whole book of Zephaniah to understand the Great Day of the Lord and what will happen after. But I will quote some verses here to give emphasis to the veracity of the word of God in the Day of the Lord.

Here are some verses in Zephaniah Chapter 1 concerning the Great Day of the Lord:

Verses 2 to 3;

"²"I will utterly consume everything from the face of the land," says the Lord; ³"I will consume man and beast; I will consume the birds of the heavens, the fish of the sea, and the stumbling blocks along with the wicked. I will cut off man from the face of the land," says the Lord."

And in verse 7 and 14-18;

"⁷Be silent in the presence of the Lord God; for <u>the day of the Lord</u> is at hand, for the Lord has prepared a sacrifice; He has invited His guests.

¹⁴<u>The great day of the Lord</u> is near; It is near and hastens quickly. The noise of <u>the day of the Lord</u> is bitter; There the mighty men shall cry out.

¹⁵<u>That day is a day of wrath</u>, a day of trouble and distress, a day of devastation and desolation, a day of darkness and gloominess, a day of clouds and thick darkness, ¹⁶A day of trumpet and alarm against the fortified cities and against the high towers.

¹⁷"I will bring distress upon men, and they shall walk like blind men, because they have sinned against the Lord; their blood shall be poured out like dust, and their flesh like refuse."

¹⁸Neither their silver nor their gold shall be able to deliver them in the day of <u>the Lord's wrath</u>; but the whole land shall be devoured by the fire of His jealousy, for He will make speedy riddance of all those who dwell in the land."

God stated His intent on His day in Zephaniah 3: 8;

"⁸"Therefore wait for Me," says the Lord, "Until the day I rise up for plunder; My determination is to gather the nations to My assembly of kingdoms, <u>to pour on them My indignation</u>, <u>all My fierce anger;</u> <u>all the earth shall be devoured with the fire of My jealousy.</u>"

If these words of our Creator God will not make us tremble and fear before Him, I do not know what will. And if you think that it is just a joke from our Creator and will continue with our pride and arrogance, just think about it for a second.

We should fear our heavenly Father more than we fear our humanly or earthly father. Our God can inflict pain, sufferings, and destruction upon humanity or individual because of our disregard, hardheadedness, and disobedience to Him. If God allow, Satan can destroy our physical body too like in Jobs time. But God can destroy both our body and soul.

In the tribulation period, billions will die and suffer great pains and sorrows that has never been experienced since the beginning of time (Matt. 24: 21) until people recognize God.

But after all these things, the Wonderful World Tomorrow of the Millennial Kingdom under Jesus Christ reign for 1,000 years will begin. And in that time, God said in Zephaniah 3: 9;

> "⁹"For then I will <u>restore</u> to the peoples a pure language, that they all may call on the name of the Lord, to serve Him with one accord.""

This is the pure language (Gen. 11: 1) of Noah since they were in the isles (Gen. 10: 5) after the flood until God confused their language (Gen. 11: 7) because of their disobedience to God.

And to the isles (Isa. 49: 1), be steadfast in our trials and tribulations. Repent, humble yourselves, and trust in the Lord. For we are not made by God to have an eternal vacation in heaven, but we are made to serve Him and the rest of humanity towards His purpose. For if God the Father and His Son continuously work for the benefits of His creations until now, how much more the servants whom He called for this service in the end times.

As a humble, faithful, and loyal servants, we should not look after rewards of any form, but rather, we should be inspired for the true peace, joy, happiness, and prosperity of having given the opportunity to serve our beloved Master and our fellow men. Imagine a world without the deceptions of Satan. Imagine a world with people looking after each other and not taking advantage of one another. What a wonderful world it will be. That alone is a great reward in itself. But we should be glad that God give us meaning and purpose for our lives to help in the preparation of His coming, establishment of His Kingdom, and serving Him during and after the Kingdom. Is it not a great reward in itself to serve our Master God?

We have great works ahead of us. But we need to workout first our salvation to repent of our transgressions, to humble ourselves before the Lord, and to obey His commandments, and the way of God, for us to become worthy to be called His servants. Lowly, loyal, humble, and faithful servants, willing to be deployed anywhere at any time in a moment's notice, each according to its calling.

After the Millennial Kingdom is the Great White Throne Judgement – the final cleansing of humanity on earth worthy to receive our Heavenly Father of supreme purity and holiness to dwell on the New Heaven and the New Earth.

This is the mystery of Revelation 21 verses 1 and 2. After the White Throne Judgement preceded Revelation 21: 2-5;

"²Then I, John, saw the holy city, New Jerusalem, coming down out of heaven from God, prepared as a bride adorned for her husband. ³And I heard a loud voice from heaven saying, "Behold, the tabernacle of God is with men, and He will dwell with them, and they shall be His people. God Himself will be with them and be their God. ⁴And God will wipe away every tear from their eyes; there shall be no more death, nor sorrow, nor crying. There shall be no more pain, for the former things have passed away."

⁵Then He who sat on the throne said, "Behold, I make all things new." And He said to me, "Write, for these words are true and faithful.""

May the Lord bless us and heal us and make His face shine upon us.

Amen.

CONCLUSION AND DOXOLOGY

Isles! Let us do this for all mankind and for the glory of our God the Almighty Father and of our Lord Jesus Christ our King and the Father of us all. If you hear His voice, do not harden your heart. Seek Him with all your heart, with all your might and with all your soul. Let us fear Him and humble ourselves before the Lord so that we may glorify Him.

"Arise and shine for your light has come! And the glory of the Lord is risen upon you."

Let the Light of our Lord shine in us so that we become light also unto the world.

Let us begin the work for His glory. From the inside-out.

The world has descended into darkness. There is no peace, lawlessness abounds, and everything are sure troubles ahead.

ONLY by turning to GOD who created us can give us peace and rest from this evil world.

May God Cause His Face to Shine Upon Us
(Psalms 67)

¹God be merciful to us and bless us,
And cause His face to shine upon us, Selah
²That Your way may be known on earth,
Your salvation among all nations.

³Let the peoples praise You, O God;
Let all the peoples praise You.
⁴Oh, let the nations be glad and sing for joy!
For You shall judge the people righteously,
And govern the nations on earth. Selah

⁵Let the peoples praise You, O God;
Let all the peoples praise You.
⁶Then the earth shall yield her increase;
God, our own God, shall bless us.
⁷God shall bless us,
And all <u>the ends of the earth</u> shall fear Him.

THIS IS NOT A DRILL.

ABOUT THE AUTHOR

A servant of God and a Truth seeker.

Delivering His message for His people.

www.ingramcontent.com/pod-product-compliance
Lightning Source LLC
Chambersburg PA
CBHW030350130626
46549CB00004B/1437